ED AND DOROTHY
ROCKY MOUNTAIN ROMANCE

Ed and Dorothy: Rocky Mountain Romance

Book design by: Family Lines Publishing, Alberta.
Written and edited by: Lea Storry of Family Lines, Alberta
Ourfamilylines.ca
Print ISBN: 978-0-9917075-2-2

Disclaimer

This book is a memoir.
It's written to tell Ed and Dorothy's story through their connections with the Calgary Highlanders, the Second World War and Banff National Park. However, this book does not contain a comprehensive history of the Highlanders, the war or the park. Some events have been condensed and some dialogue has been recreated.

DEDICATION

I bet Mum and Dad would be surprised when presented with this book, their book. I can see Dad responding with that wide grin, a twinkle in his eye and a slight shake of his head in disbelief. He was always so humble. Mum would stare in amazement at the cover, holding the book tightly with both hands, and exclaim, "Wow, look at that Ed, a book about us!"

My two brothers, Terry and Brian, as well as me and my daughter Ingrid, felt strongly that a book should be written about Ed and Dorothy. Mum and Dad's journey includes a "war bride story," a "park warden history story," and a "Banff story." However, most of all it is a story of love and lives spent giving and caring – both to people and nature. Mum and Dad experienced many difficulties and challenges, and some tragedies, but throughout laughter and music prevailed.

When I view Banff National Park today, with the masses of visitors milling about in their endless quest for a parking spot, I am so grateful for having experienced the park, and the town, during a much more peaceful era. At Castle Junction, along what is now the Bow Valley Parkway, once stood the stately Mount Eisenhower Lodge with Mum's colourful array of flowers on display beneath the front veranda. Surrounding the lodge were the Mount Eisenhower district signpost, the flag pole proudly flying the Canadian Red Ensign, the woodpile, the saddle shed, the horses assigned from the Ya Ha Tinda Ranch grazing in the corral, and other accoutrements of a district warden station. It was a time when the folks working in the warden service and their families were a very tight-knit, supportive community, when horses were supreme and wardens enjoyed the independence of being responsible for everything that happened in "their district." Now instead of a bustling warden station, there's a large paved parking lot serving as the trailhead for Tower and Rockbound lakes.

When I visit Castle Junction today, memories come flooding back. I enjoy having a look around in the nearby forest and along the gently trickling Silverton Creek, where the three brothers and friends played so often as kids. We are grateful to Mum and Dad for the unique opportunity to live in the heart of Banff National Park and to experience and enjoy the mountains and the wilderness. We were at the centre of the action in the district, as Mum and Dad were dealing with everything from answering silly questions from tourists, to fighting fires and high mountain rescues.

When Mum passed away in 2018, the headline in the Rocky Mountain Outlook newspaper was "Banff Park Royalty Passes at 98." Mum and Dad loved the community of Banff and had so many friends. The "End of the Rainbow" home was always open and often filled with music and song. People loved to stop in and visit, share a story, have a good laugh, and enjoy Mum's signature "rocky roads" treat. After Dad passed away, Mum was at the heart of the community, involved in so many activities and making a huge volunteer commitment.

Mum and Dad, this book is dedicated to you, as one way of saying thanks on behalf of family and friends for all your love and support, for touching so many hearts and for all the opportunities that you gave us.

You were a perfect example of how to live a wonderful life.

Mike
Oct. 2, 2019

Dorothy's Poem
by Karen Messenger

From across the sea, Dorothy did come,
To start a new life after the war was won.
She married Ed, who fought in the war,
Now she was ready for adventure … and so much more!

A rancher of gophers, Ed claimed to be,
"That sure sounds grand!" thought Dorothy.
Turns out ranching gophers isn't all it's cracked up to be,
Then Ed got a job with the feds, thankfully.

Park warden was the gig - Ed was so proud,
When they arrived at Bow Summit, he proclaimed his joy out loud.
Dorothy, however, was taken by some fear,
"Where's the rest of the cabin? Is this all that is here?!"

For the first week, she needed accompaniment to the loo,
In her head, the words of Ed's father: "Behind each tree is a grizzly bear out to get you!"
Perseverance, determination – she was so brave and strong,
Dorothy took the reins to her new life and faced it head on.

Three boys, hearty mountain men, she raised in the woods,
Baking bread, chopping wood, riding horses - she learned all that she could.
She embraced the warden life with style and grace,
With a song in her heart and a smile on her face.

Her words of wisdom are simply divine:
"Think positive and everything will turn out just fine."
She's our inspiration, our role model, and our dear friend,
Dorothy, we thank you and our love for you will never end.

Happy trails to you, until we meet again,
You fill us with sunshine and help us smile through the rain.
Thank you Dorothy, we sing out loud,
We hope that our own lives can make you proud.

Table of Contents

Facing page: Map of Banff National Park warden districts circa 1955.
Photo: Whyte Museum of the Canadian Rockies

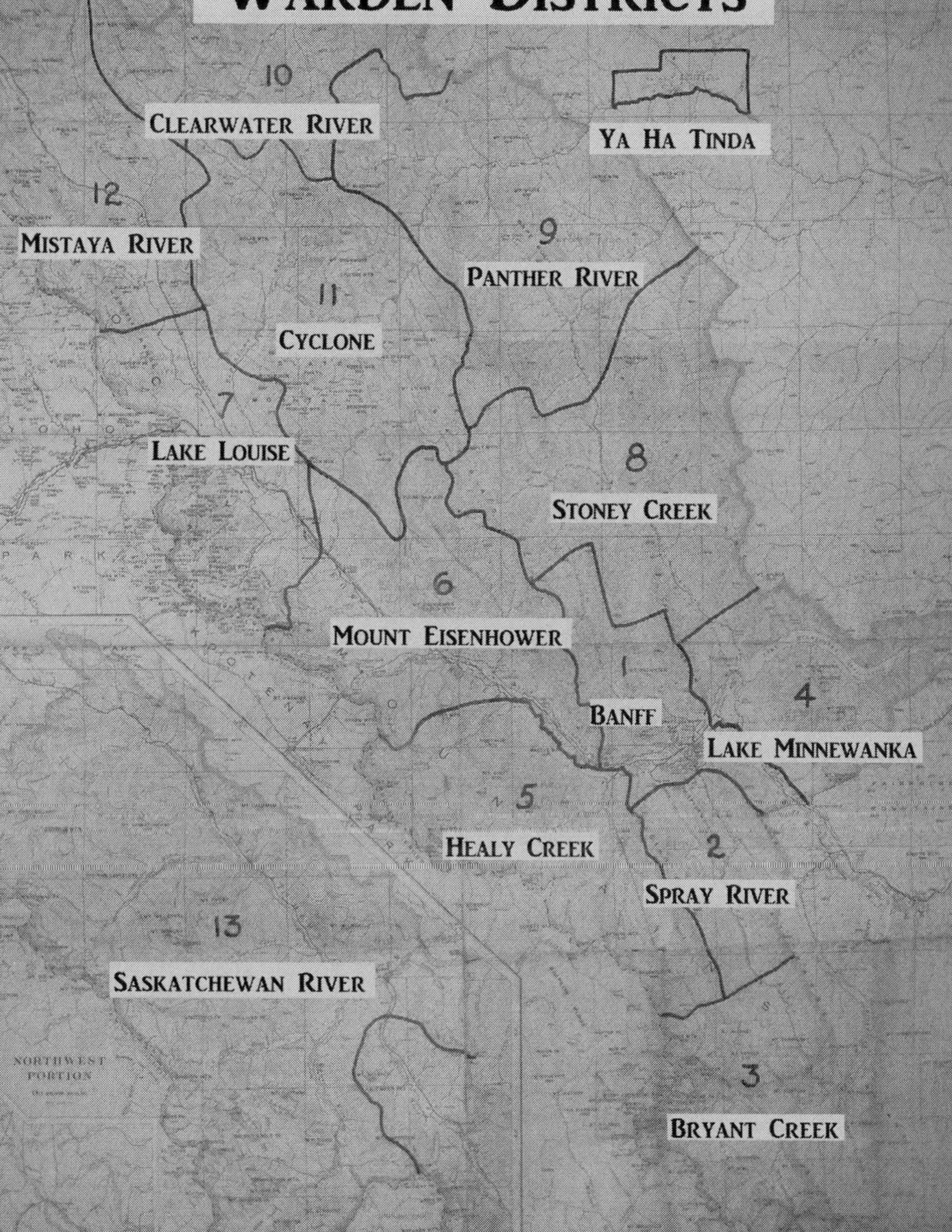

Banff National Park
WARDEN DISTRICTS
10
CLEARWATER RIVER
YA HA TINDA
12
MISTAYA RIVER
9
PANTHER RIVER
11
CYCLONE
7
LAKE LOUISE
8
STONEY CREEK
6
MOUNT EISENHOWER
1
BANFF
4
LAKE MINNEWANKA
5
HEALY CREEK
2
SPRAY RIVER
13
SASKATCHEWAN RIVER
3
BRYANT CREEK
BANFF PARK

FOREWORD

A mostly forgotten piece of Canadian history unfolds in the pages of this book. The Canadian National Park Warden Service does not exist in this day and age as it did in the days of Ed and Dorothy Carleton. Today's park wardens specialize in law enforcement and other park staff are responsible for resource management and visitor safety, including rescue and avalanche forecasting. Up until the early 2000s, the warden service was a multi-functional outfit encompassing all of these duties. Wardens had to be proficient in a multitude of tasks such as horsemanship, winter travel on skis, climbing skills as well as management of fisheries, wildlife and vegetation. This wide-ranging approach has been replaced with total specialization.

When Ed Carleton became a Banff park warden in 1948, wardens were assigned a district and were responsible for the protection of vast tracts of land. Some districts were headquartered along the roads and highways, while others were in remote areas accessible only by horseback. Junior wardens were usually assigned to the most remote districts and had to put in many years to work their way closer to civilization. Warden cabins were primitive structures with wood heat, no running water or electricity. School-age children had to be homeschooled.

Ed was assigned to Bow Summit, a district of perpetual winter on a high point of today's Icefields Parkway that runs between Lake Louise and Jasper. It was a narrow gravel road in those days and mostly closed during the long winters. Dorothy experienced some culture shock when she arrived at her new "home."

I had the privilege of working with Ed for the first 10 years of my career. He was a mentor to all of us less-experienced wardens and was kind and patient with us. During that time, I became close friends with both Ed and Dorothy. After Ed died in the early nineties, I stayed in touch with Dorothy and marvelled at her joyous and compassionate approach to life. In her later years, she became a living legend throughout the Bow Valley and inspired me to write a song for her: *Warden Bride.* My band, The Wardens, recorded the song on our second album, *Bear 66.*

From city girl to mountain legend Dorothy did thrive
With confidence, her skills they grew with each passing year
Came to love this wilderness, this wilderness frontier

Dorothy was a representative for war brides and the culture shock many of them endured in their relocation to Canada. The vast landscapes and wilderness were in stark contrast to the cities of England in their homeland. Dorothy, as the lyrics above say, came to love the backcountry that welcomed her, Ed and their three boys. So throw a log on the fire, pour yourself a hot rum and immerse yourself in the pages of this remarkable tale of Dorothy and Ed.

Scott Ward, former Banff National Park warden and musician with The Wardens

INTRODUCTION

Grey, sharp peaks poke into the blue sky. I've never seen mountains like this before… and so many. Driving from Calgary to Banff, Alberta, I'm thinking the whole time, "How the heck do we get inside those mountains?" I'm a 27-year-old war bride from England and we don't have peaks this big and mighty. They stretch out in front of me and I'm in awe. I feel so small compared to them and little do I realize then, the Rockies will play a huge role in my life. In fact, they'll help build who I am today.

I've lived in Canada for over 70 years now. I'm 98 years-old. It's thanks to my husband Ed that I ended up in the wilderness of the Rockies. Our love may have started in the hustle and bustle of an English city but it is in the isolation of the backcountry that our life truly took root and flourished. I've almost gone full circle as I'm back in the city. I've just moved from Banff into Calgary and I'm settling into another phase. It's Mother's Day 2018 and my family surrounds me. My three sons, their wives and some of my grandchildren and great-grandchildren are here. I sing snatches of songs to them amongst their chatting and laughter, signs of a joyful and contented group.

Well, that's enough of being serious for now. I really do like to laugh and you need a sense of humour to raise a family in the backcountry. It's hard to be stoic about a porcupine eating your toilet seat. Anyway, I'll be telling you my stories and hope you'll chuckle along with me. I can't promise my tales won't be tinged with a bit of romanticism because the Banff I knew, the remote and secluded one, is likely not the one you know today. Here we go.

When you're smilin', when you're smilin'
The whole world smiles with you
When you're laughin', oh when you're laughin'
The sun comes shinin' through

Dorothy (Fowler) Carleton

Chapter One

Edmond Clarence Carleton

Banff, Alberta, Canada is a town in the middle of a national park. People from all over the world come here to see the Rocky Mountains, the wildlife and the sparkling waterways. They fall in love with the steep slant of Mount Rundle, the sharp angles of elk antlers and the grey-green eddies of the Bow River. This book is a love story about this land and its connection with a special couple and their family.

Let us introduce you to Ed and Dorothy Carleton. They lived on Rainbow Avenue for many years and before that, in the Banff backcountry. There's more before that and that's why we're telling their story.

To family and friends, Ed Carleton is like Lake Louise on a calm summer's day: still, deep and brilliant. His wife Dorothy is like the Bow River in Banff: always moving, bubbling over rocks and singing its water song. Ed is the quiet outdoorsman and artist. He's tall and strong like a tree in the mountain forest he loves, although he grew up on the prairie in Didsbury, Alberta, Canada.

Not much is known about Ed's childhood. He didn't talk about it a lot. Of course, we know the standard facts like family and schooling, but otherwise, he never regaled anyone with stories about growing up in Didsbury. He was born in the northern Ontario mining town of Schumacher, now part of Timmins, Ontario, on Dec. 16, 1917. Edmond Clarence Carleton was the third of nine children born to David Oliver (who went by Ollie) Carleton and Hazel (who was known as Millie), whose maiden name was Brown. Most likely Ed was named after Ollie's brother Ed. The older Ed lived in Detroit and visited the family a few times, though the two Eds didn't meet until the younger one was 21.

In 1920, when Ed is three, the family moves to Didsbury, a farming town just under an hour's drive north of Calgary. Ollie's a blacksmith and works at the D. M. Sinclair Blacksmith shop in town. It's backbreaking, hot work but he has to provide for his wife and nine kids (Frank, Herb, Edmond, Russell, Lorna, Baillie, Joan, Audrey and Garry). Audrey, one of the youngest of the Carleton children, says her father is always bending over the scorching coals in all sorts of weather. He does extra work for farmers so he can treat the children to meat, cream and butter — still relative luxuries in those days. The long days are hard on Ollie and his wife, but they have no choice but to be strong.

Times are not easy and are getting tougher in the Dirty Thirties. Drought, hail, wind and grasshoppers destroy farmers' crops and lead to an economic depression. Money is scarce and it's challenging for Ollie and Millie, who are raising such a large family. Adding to the Carletons' financial burdens are two relatives: Ollie's brother Charlie[1] and his wife Louise, who stay with them on and off. Charlie is a Boer War[2]

1. Millie had a twin brother named Charlie Brown who died in the First World War.
2. The Boer War is also known as The South African War, 1899-1902.

Ed's parents, Ollie and Millie Carleton, at their Didsbury family home circa 1935 to 1940. They owned the house.
Photo: Audrey (Carleton) MacKay

veteran and no one seems to know anything about Louise except that she can't speak English when she comes to live with the Carletons. She also likes to smoke a pipe while sitting on a stool by the fire.

One way Ollie and Millie keep everyone fed is by food grown in the family garden. Like most people, especially in prairie towns, they tend a vegetable patch. They grow their own potatoes and other vegetables. Young Ed likes working the soil and he's good at it, too. The family has a few animals and Ollie wins some cash prizes by raising award-winning livestock. He wins several awards for roosters and horses at various Didsbury agricultural fairs over the years.

Millie's a pleasant lady who likes to play cards. In fact, she wins a few whist and bridge games in her later years. In her earlier years, she must have been frequently pregnant – there's more than 20 years difference between her oldest child (Frank) and her youngest (Garry). So we know not all the siblings grew up with each other in the house.

In June 1935, the eldest, Frank, witnesses a horrific accident and sees a man crushed by a train. The man, Gus Risvold, a "transient," is looking for work in Didsbury. Gus had been searching for a farm job and when he doesn't find one, is heading anywhere but Didsbury. At the town's train station, he runs to catch a freight train that's pulling out. He tries to grab the boxcar handrail but doesn't get a good grip. He falls between the station platform and cars. Frank has to give a testimony at the inquest into Gus' death.

The Carletons make sure their children attend church. Ed is in TUXIS (similar to Boy Scouts), a program for Protestant boys. From the time Ed can read, he's a speaker at many young people's services. When he's 16, he's praised for delivering a capable message from the disciples of old to those today. Even as a youth, Ed is unflappable. He takes things as they come. Nothing worries him.

Ed, centre, as Tarzan during Didsbury high school days.
Photo: Carleton Family

Family photos of Ed show him with a huge smile but the images aren't accompanied by many details. In the black-and-white pictures, you can't see Ed's blue eyes. You can see he really enjoys having fun and has a great sense of humour. Why else would he be playing Tarzan?

One of Ed's best friends in his teen years is Earl Cummins. Earl is half-Dutch on his mother's side and Irish on his father's side. Earl lived in Northern Ireland as a child for a few years after his father died. When Earl comes back to town, he regales Ed with tales from the old country.

Another one of Ed's chums is George A. Morasch[3] who grows up on his family's farm a few kilometres east of Didsbury. His parents help to keep Ed's dad in business, as he shoes the horse that pulls the Moraschs' buggy. When the family goes into town, George sees Ollie working by the blazing forge.

George was born in 1923 and despite being five years younger than Ed, the lanky Carleton kid is always nice to him. George doesn't recall their first meeting but it's probably at school. They both like to play hardball and softball together with the other boys.

Another outdoor activity they do together is hunt gophers. It's a way to make some cash, too. For every gopher tail they turn into the municipal clerk, they get a cent. George thinks he can double his money by cutting a long gopher tail in two. The clerk catches on and puts an end to that.

---

3. George is one of the youngest of 14 although some of his older siblings had died from the Spanish flu in 1917 and 1918. "My mum was always pregnant," says George. (Interview with George A. Morasch, Jun. 11, 2018.)

With their pennies, the boys buy candy treats that they won't get otherwise. George says everyone is poor, including the Didsbury townsfolk. However, townspeople consider themselves high society by comparison and call the farm boys things like "stubble jumpers," "rabbit eaters" or "gopher chasers." [4]

Ed on Didsbury Rock.
Photo: Carleton Family

Besides collecting gopher tails for pennies, Ed works after school to add to the family coffers. He's an usher at the cinema and shows people to their seats. Other duties are knowing the start and end times of the movies and keeping the patrons in line. He sees films for free and maybe this explains that Tarzan photo.

Ed graduates from Grade 12 at Didsbury High School in 1936 and his grades are published in the town newspaper, the *Didsbury Pioneer.* Although he isn't outstanding academically, he does fine. His highest score is 75 per cent in history and the lowest is 38 per cent in trigonometry. He must have figured out math somehow because he goes on to train as a surveyor for the Alberta provincial government.

As soon as he's done his schooling, he goes right to work. He does some jobs around Nanton, about an hour's drive south of Calgary. While he's working, the clouds of war are gathering over Europe.

On Sept. 1, 1939, Hitler invades Poland. A couple of days later, Sept. 3, 1939, Britain and France declare war on Germany and it's the start of the Second World War.

Canada officially joins the fight a week later, declaring war on Sept. 10.

Second World War

Now you might have thought that the First World War (1914–1918) would still be somewhat fresh in Canada's collective memory. Ottawa is almost $2 billion in debt and the nation lost many loved ones: approximately 61,000 Canadians died in the Great War.

Nevertheless, Ed, along with other young men, is glad when the Second World War breaks out. The Depression has left its mark on him. He says the war presents opportunities for him and he'll be sure of regular meals. He'll even be paid: $1.30 a day.

So … he leaves for Calgary to volunteer for service.

---

4. Before marrying, Ed told Dorothy that he owned a gopher ranch. That got her attention. She thought that meant he was wealthy. Boy, was she wrong. But in a good way.

Chapter Two

Calgary Highlanders

Hitchhiking to Enlist

Ed hitchhikes to Calgary to enlist with the Calgary Highlanders. The unit started as the 103rd Regiment (Calgary Rifles) in 1910. During the First World War, men from the Calgary unit joined other battalions, such as the 10th Infantry Battalion,[5] Canadian Expeditionary Force, to fight in the Great War. "The Fighting 10th" mobilized in Quebec on Sept. 22, 1914, as part of the First Canadian Division. These men saw action in the second and third battles of Ypres, as well as Vimy Ridge, Hill 70 and Passchendaele. The soldiers earned many honours and decorations and were the pride of Calgary.

In 1920, it was redesignated the Calgary Regiment. The following year, the Calgary Regiment was redesignated as the 1st Bn. (10th Bn. C.E.F.) Calgary Highlanders, Calgary Regiment. In 1924, the regiment was split into the Calgary Regiment (The King's Own Calgary Regiment) and the Calgary Highlanders, a Highland (kilted) unit. The Highlanders were a militia regiment and made up of non-professional soldiers. With conflict in Europe looming in 1939, the Highlanders receive a telegram on Sept. 1 from the federal defence department with the word "Mobilize." The Highlanders are officially ready to be called for duty.

Ed is one of the 30 men a day who arrive in Calgary ready to serve. The Highlanders are headquartered at Mewata Armoury[6] in the city's downtown. With its red brick, turrets and narrow windows, it looks like a fortress from medieval times. To get to this imposing recruitment office, Ed walks through a city brimming with life: streets full of vehicles and trolleys and sidewalks bustling with people going here and there. Ed has thought of what he's about to sign up for, but as a young man of 21, he views it mainly as an adventure.

At Mewata, Ed fills in forms, is interviewed, given a medical examination and finally, sworn in. His "Date of Attestation" (start) is Sept. 23, 1939. He doesn't have any kind of military knowledge before he volunteers. He has no idea about the differences between military ranks, nor has he any insight into the minutiae of army life. The physical aspects of training will come naturally to him though. He loves sports and as a tall (5'10"), lean man, he is fit. Ed's mentally sharp, too. He always has a good outlook on life, and he is ready to put his life on the line to fight for King and country. Without this choice, Dorothy wouldn't have met her husband.

---

5. "The Fighting 10th" was the pride of Calgary and mobilized in the city on Sept. 22, 1914. These men saw action in such battles as the second and third battles of Ypres, Vimy Ridge, Hill 70 and Passchendaele.

6. Mewata is Cree for *O Be Joyful.* The armoury is still in use today. (2020)

Trained into a Soldier

Ed's official photo after enlisting with the Calgary Highlanders, Sept. 23, 1939
Photo: Carleton Family

Mewata Armoury is too small to house the growing numbers of Calgary Highlanders in September 1939. The regiment moves to Sarcee Camp, a site that had been leased to the Department of National Defence by the Tsuut'ina Nation. The camp had been used for First World War training and now the land is back in military service. Recruits live in tents, which is certainly toughening them up for times ahead. Camping in autumn in Alberta can be cold and wet and the men don't have access to hot water for the basics like shaving. Sarcee Camp is not a comfortable place to be. The men are getting sick, too. Mumps make the rounds and the recruits are confined to barracks.

Ed isn't at Sarcee long. Thankfully, before the Elbow River freezes, the Highlanders return to Mewata after wooden huts were built on the armoury grounds. If you know anything about Calgary, it's probably that the winters can be brutally cold. The little sheds that house the soldiers aren't fully insulated and as the cool weather creeps in, the lads wake up to frost on their beds. Sure hope Ed has warm socks. But he won't complain if he's cold. He'll keep his chin up and keep going no matter what.

Around 833 men have enlisted in the Highlanders by the beginning of October 1939. They're learning how to be infantry soldiers by participating in foot drills (marching and organizing into formation when ordered), rifle practice and following officer commands.

Ed is in C Company and the men start forming close friendships. They bond over the weather, the drills and the fact that the Highlanders are ill-equipped. There are uniform shortages during training: too many men wanting to serve and not enough kit. Recruits are sporting a combination of different looks, from khaki trousers, to kilts, to cowboy hats. A woman visiting the camp asks one of the men if his kilt is a handicap.

"Only when I'm climbing trees," he responds.

The Calgary Highlanders are supposed to be following highland traditions and one of those customs is wearing a kilt. However, Ottawa deems kilts too old-fashioned for combat and no Highland regiment in Canada will be wearing the traditional Scottish garment into war, except for pipers and drummers. What the recruits need right now is warm clothing, plain and simple. Some women in Calgary take up the plight of the shivering soldiers and knit mittens and sweaters for them. As for uniforms, it won't be well until into the new year that Ed and his mates receive anything official that's fit for winter.

Meanwhile, Ed carries on with his military education. Saturdays at Mewata are reserved for barracks cleaning. The company with the tidiest bunks and best-scrubbed floors are given a pennant. C Company wins many of them.

Despite the lack of proper attire and equipment, training continues and that means more marching, drills and classroom instruction. Sharpening other skills such as fitness and map reading are also on the agenda. There is a special gas chamber for training at Mewata and it is hardcore. The men run through tear gas, sometimes using a mask, and sometimes without a mask. Mix watering eyes with being tired to the bone and add a dollop of homesickness and you get a recipe for camaraderie. It takes deep root, as the men get used to army routines and strict rules together.

Learning regimental songs, such as *Black and Tan Gun*, is also a must for a Highlander soldier. It's a tradition to belt out the Irish folksong about a courageous fighter. Glenwhorple is another anthem that tells the story of the Calgary Highlanders on board Noah's Ark. The song is sung while marching.[7]

Chorus

Heuch! Glenwhorple Hielan' men!
Great strong whusky-suppin' Hielan' men,
Hard- workin', hairy-leggit Hielan' men,
Slainte mhor Glenwhorple.

Ed's younger brother Russell is singing the same songs as he's a Highlander in C Company, too. Russ signed up on Sept. 12, 1939, before Ed. The news made the *Didsbury Pioneer* on Sept. 21.

Having his younger brother join the army first influenced Ed. He is a helper though, too. It's in his blood (pun intended) as he's part of Didsbury's Voluntary Blood Transfusion Service. In February of the same year he enlists, he goes to Calgary to give blood to an unknown man at the Holy Cross Hospital.

Three other Carleton brothers are serving in the Second World War in different capacities. The oldest, Frank, was a boxer until he developed asthma. He's exempt from service (medically unfit) but has joined the Royal Canadian Ordnance Corps, an administrative branch of the army. He's sent to Eastern Canada.

Herb is the fourth brother to enlist. He signs up with the 31st Alberta Reconnaissance Battalion. in August 1942. The fifth brother to enlist is Baillie. He's a small man and the army doesn't have boots that fit him. He ends up stuffing newspapers

7. It's also sang with foot stomping to set the tempo.

Brothers in Arms, left to right: Russ, Ed and Herb in 1939.
Photo: Carleton Family

in the toes. He serves from Mar. 13, 1943, until Jul. 31, 1946, in Canada, the U.K. and Continental Europe.

Whenever Ed and Russ visit Didsbury while on leave, it makes the town paper. Under the headline Local General and among neighbours' trips to Calgary and calls for buying fall and winter underwear from Scott's, there are the Carleton boys' names. One visit, Feb. 22, 1940, overlaps with their father's journey to a Banff carnival (also reported in the paper). Let's hope Ollie isn't away when his boys are home for a break from army life.

The Highlanders receive high praise in February for the regiment's high standards from Brigadier C. E. Connolly, D. S. O., the new District Officer Commanding. The men are also acknowledged for their soldierly bearing. Ed feels great pride in what he's doing, especially when he's on parade in the city streets. Many Calgarians support the Highlanders and watch the men march past them in wind, rain or snow. The lads are often invited into people's homes during holiday times.

While stationed at Mewata, boxing becomes part of Ed's routine. His eldest brother Frank was a boxer and now Ed is jabbing and punching his way around the ring. It's a very physical workout and he likes it although he won't be picking any fights. Nevertheless, he won't hesitate to put up his dukes if challenged. There's a saying around the camp, "He who hesitates is bossed."

That's not going to be Ed.

To forge stronger bonds and keep the men fit, the army has the Highlanders playing hockey, volleyball and basketball. When the weather is nice, there are cross-country running races complete with men in full kit and carrying rifles. Tugs-o-war, sack races and other events are held on sports days and pit company against company. Team spirits are ignited and will only burn brighter as the Highlanders head to Manitoba.

Camaraderie and Contemplation at Camp Shilo

In the spring of 1940, on May 25, the Calgary Highlanders head east for Camp Shilo in Manitoba. The First Battalion says goodbye to Calgary by laying their stand of Colours (flags historically used in battle, now a symbol of devotion to duty) downtown in the Cathedral Church of the Redeemer. The military flags will wait there for the men until the end of the war. Thousands of Albertans pack the streets to bid farewell to the soldiers as they march to the train station.

Camp Shilo is almost a straight shot east, about 1,150 km (715 mi) away from Calgary. At many of the small train stations dotting the way to Manitoba, people gather to wave to the soldiers as they pass by. When the train stops in Medicine Hat, Alberta, the Highlanders disembark and parade through downtown, led by their band and the Medicine Hat City Band. The lads from the 'Hat get a chance to hug their mothers and say hello to friends. 'Hat resident Private Thomas Gordon "Red" Anderson reassures his mum that he'll be home soon.

Back on the train, Red hands a friend a bottle of rye. A mutual friend had handed the whisky to him so he could give it to their mate. The rye is opened and handed around but soon tossed out the window after an officer warns them that anyone caught with alcohol will be court-martialed. Poor Red was next in line for a drink.[8]

Red's father works on the railway and he gets word to his son to watch for him. He'll be in one of the cars at the siding (a low-speed track section) in Walsh, near the Alberta-Saskatchewan border. When the train passes through the hamlet, father and son have a fleeting reunion. They stick out their hands and touch fingers.

This is Ed's first time going east since he moved to Alberta from northern Ontario with his family. He was a toddler then and doesn't remember a thing about the journey. He'll never forget the excitement of his trip today. The recruits are energized and smiling, happy to be moving on to a new training base.

Camp Shilo is also a move closer to Europe where a month earlier, the Phoney War had ended. There's been action on the continent. The Phoney War (September 1939 to April 1940) is called so because there was little of anything happening until April 9, 1940. That's when Germany invaded Denmark and Norway. Then, at the beginning of May, German troops overran Holland, Belgium, Luxemburg and France. The Second World War is heating up.

While the Axis Powers are showing their strength, Ed's regiment is in Shilo training as part of the 6th Infantry Brigade, 2nd Canadian Division. The Highlanders' first battle in Manitoba is the sun. It's hot and the lads get terribly sunburned when they take off their shirts. It isn't their fault though, their uniforms still aren't sorted. Some men are wearing winter wool uniforms, while others are issued shorts and pith helmets

8. Private Papers of T G Anderson.

Private Ed Carleton on duty at Camp Shilo, spring 1940.
Photo: Carleton Family

as if they're in the tropics. There's also some bloodshed due to mosquitoes. The Highlanders' fight with the sun and insects inspire a poem. Eleanor Kenny has everyone in stitches with her rhymes.

With your stunning summer drills
We know the girls get lots of thrills
With your red knees – redder still;
kissed by mosquitoes on the hill.
(from *The Glen*, a Highlanders newsletter)

From relentless sun, things move to rain – and everything turns to muck and mire. Corporal Henry Woodford writes a poem about the relentless downpours pounding the Highlanders' cone-shaped canvas tents. The floors became lakes as the tents flood. The soldiers can't keep up with the bailing.

Their prayer, if any, might have been,
"Please stop the blessed rain" –
But being soldiers, you may guess
Their words were few and plain.
So to this end, these lines I bring,
Unhappy still to say –
The bally rain's still pelting down,
King Water still holds sway.
It Rained at Shilo
(from *The Glen*, Jun. 30, 1940)

Ed's mattress turns dank and mouldy. The pally ass (mattress) is made out of straw that each man had to stuff on his arrival at Shilo. Ed is mighty sick of the mildewed hay and the constant patter of raindrops above his head. He's not alone. Besides the Highlanders, the South Saskatchewan Regiment and the Queen's Own Cameron Highlanders are included in the 6th Infantry Brigade. There's camaraderie in the tents, but also a spark of competition among the regiments. In the middle of the night, someone decides to paint the Camerons' mascot, a goat, with the letters SSR in green paint. The next morning, the Camerons are in an uproar and pretty testy with the South Saskatchewan Regiment.

One way to level the field is by winning at sports. Ed likes getting out and playing baseball, softball and football. He's also allowed to take leave and free to roam for as long as ordered. At least he can have a cold beer or two off-site — and one Winnipeg brewery hopes he'll choose its ale. Shea's Select Beer is marketing itself as "The drink for a Calgary Highlander."

Booze makes for some shenanigans and hijinks from the lads. Highlander Bert Pittaway's friend steals a car and drives with a few other guys into nearby Brandon to attend a dance. After some fun, the vehicle is driven into the lake. Bert watches the car bubble out of sight. None of the men think anyone will find the car deep underwater. But the police do. Bert and his buddies have to pay for the vehicle and one of the men goes to jail.

***

Marches, lectures, weapons and other military training are, of course, part of Ed's daily life, as are blisters. His world is changing every day, as he grows from a small-town prairie boy to a strong and able soldier ready for war. Training is tough mentally, too and there are tragedies that strike the camp. Men wound themselves to get out of service or kill themselves. One man accidentally drowns in a river. As well, battalion numbers are pared down when men desert and boys who lied about their age are returned to their parents.

While Ed isn't in close contact with his family, he sends the occasional letter home. He has a surprise for his young sister Audrey: a blue silk handkerchief. It's dear to her heart, especially since Ed had the hankie embroidered with a Calgary Highlander in full dress uniform and the words *To Audrey, from Ed.* On another corner, it says 1st Bn Calgary Highlanders C.A.S.F. (Canadian Active Service Force) above the Calgary Highlanders badge. Audrey frames the handkerchief and says it'll always be hanging on her wall.

It's good that Ed has his brother Russ around for support. However, Ed craves the quiet of the Alberta foothills during the trying times at Shilo. The months are dragging on and on. The lads are bored, bored, bored. They've had enough of training and are ready to take on Hitler. In June, a note from famous U.S. dancer, singer and actress Eleanor Powell brings a moment of levity. She's replying to a letter she received from a Highlander admiring her talents and asking for an autographed picture. She says the note made her day because she read it while she was in the hospital recovering from major surgery.

Tell all the Highlanders for me, that I'm flattered and grateful for their praises, now I've got to hurry and get well quick so that I can have a better picture than ever waiting for you when you get back.

Eleanor Powell (from *The Glen*)

Get back? The Highlanders are still stuck in Canada. This isn't the time to be twiddling their thumbs in Manitoba, it is time for action. But in all actuality, they aren't ready. The Highlanders lack equipment as well as tactical and military training. Ammunition shortages mean they haven't had much practice firing the Bren light machine-guns (automatic weapon used by the Canadian infantry). Nor are they educated in other weaponry beyond the basics.

Weekly gas drills begin in June after anti-gas respirators are handed out. Ottawa has earmarked Jul. 1, Dominion Day, as the time to send the Highlanders to England. The date passes and the Highlanders remain in Shilo.

On Tuesday, Aug. 11, 1940, something is definitely supposed to happen. Ed and his battalion are told to get ready to go. Nevertheless, they don't go anywhere but it's clear they soon will be. It has been suggested they change their Canadian bucks for pounds sterling. That can only mean one thing: England. However, the lads are disappointed again when they stay put in Manitoba.

Ten days after the first order was cancelled, Ed is aboard one of two trains and travelling to the east coast on Aug. 21, 1940. On the train, he watches the flat prairie rise into the stony hills of the Canadian Shield. Ed sees lone trees grow into green forests and then give way to concrete and steel as the cars pass through southern Ontario. In Quebec, he spots red-roofed houses and barns from his seat. In several of the cities and small towns during the journey, the trains stop and the men conduct exercise marches. In Truro, Nova Scotia, all the lads are given a chocolate bar by the United Travellers' Association.

Three days after the train left Shilo, Ed's in the port city of Halifax, Nova Scotia on Aug. 23. Many of the men who are shipping out from this large ice-free harbour will never return. At the end of the war, which is a long way off for Ed that August of 1940, Halifax will be filled with war brides and children. If Ed had had a crystal ball, he could have seen Dorothy and his baby son arriving at Pier 21 in six years' time. Alas, Ed has years of hard work and heartache ahead of him.

This is the first time Ed has seen any type of ocean besides an ocean of wheat. Halifax harbour is not a summer picnic spot. No, it is a valuable Allied staging area and Ed finds the military port ramping up its war efforts. Port operations are around-the-clock, ships arrive and depart at all hours and there are constant delays from security alerts, weather, watercraft colliding, vessel rescues and munitions ships that have to be guided safely through the jam-packed waters.[9]

Ed's regiment's train has stopped near the *SS Pasteur*,[10] a turbine steamship known for its speed. While in Halifax, Ed doesn't get a chance to see the city or walk up Citadel Hill to the fort: a centuries-old piece of Canadian military history. The view from the top of the hill is incredible and you can see the whole harbour and straight out to sea on a clear day. On the other side of the Atlantic is war ... and Dorothy.

Ed's orders keep him close to the regiment. As well, he doesn't want to stray too far from his brother and mates. At any rate, on Aug. 27 he's on the *Pasteur*, a former French luxury liner complete with a pool. Joining him are Russ, their fellow Highlanders and advance parties from the Camerons, South Saskatchewan Regiment and 6th Canadian Regiment Infantry Brigade Headquarters. They're all on their way to Gourouck, Scotland, a seaside town about 45 km (28 mi) from Glasgow.

There's a stowaway aboard the *Pasteur,* hidden in a big percussion drum. Heather, a black Aberdeen terrier, is Pipe Major Neil Sutherland's dog and the Highlanders' mascot. She's not supposed to be along for the ocean voyage. It's against military rules and U.K. quarantine laws.

The *Pasteur* is part of a convoy being escorted by two destroyers. Once out on the open water, the pack of six troop ships pushes ahead. Ed finds his sea legs quickly but some of the other prairie boys are sick. So, they decide to make it into a contest: the first guy who misses a meal has to buy a round for the boys at his table. Tables on the *Pasteur* seat 40 to 60 men. That's a lot of dough to throw down the toilet (in more ways than one).

It has been smooth sailing so far. The ocean is like glass. Occasionally, thick fog blankets the ship, but the wind and waves have been behaving. Nevertheless, Private Norman "Moose" Bannon is not feeling well yet there's no way he is coughing up English pounds in exchange for being ill. His way around the bet is to eat and then visit the bathroom directly around the corner from the mess. This is where he pukes his guts out unbeknownst to the other men.

---

9. The Halifax Explosion, during the First World War, Dec. 6, 1917, was caused when the French munitions ship *Mont-Blanc* and the Norwegian vessel *Imo* collided. The incident was the largest human made explosion prior to the atomic bomb.

10. The *SS Pasteur* has its own interesting history. The ship is French but in Allied waters when France surrenders to Germany in June 1940.

As the *Pasteur* sails closer to the U.K., it hits a whale. The marine mammal is struck so hard some think the ship hit a mine. Sergeants William (Bill) Lyster and Bert Pittaway go check it out. They see the poor whale is hooked right on the bow.

This is Bert's second time making the crossing. He made the trip going the other way when his family came to Canada from England in 1927. He was 10 years old then. He'll soon see the English coastline again.

A day out from Scotland, an enemy submarine is spotted in the dark waters. It blasts a torpedo right across the bow of the *Pasteur*. Those who see it think they're under attack and brace for a hit.

However, the sub sinks back into the depths and the Highlanders never see it again.

Because of the threat of submarines, the lads have to wear lifebelts at all times while aboard the ship. They're not allowed to smoke on deck but they can have a beer in the canteen or wet their whistle with champagne, gin or whisky. Most of the men behave.

The master of the ship, British Capt. E. M. Fall, is impressed by the Highlanders. In a message, he tells his passengers that they are crusaders not only protecting Europe but the whole world from Hitler. The captain says the Canadians will never be forgotten.

WELCOME TO ENGLAND

The 6th Infantry Brigade, 2nd Canadian Division arrives off the coast of Scotland early on the morning of Sept. 4, 1940. The *SS Pasteur* is escorted by British destroyers through the Firth of Clyde to Gourock, at the mouth of the River Clyde. On the *Pasteur's* railing, soldiers line up and peer through the fog to catch a glimpse of the sights awaiting them. Ed doesn't see anything except for a tender, a boat used to ferry people off ships, on its way to pick up the Highlanders. When the tender reaches the larger craft, the men scoot down a rope ladder and onto the boat. Before Ed gets on it, he says goodbye to some of the sailors he has gotten to know. They shake hands knowing they will probably never see each other again.

Ed, in his cool and calm way, boards the tender. There are a couple of butterflies in his stomach but whatever is to come, will come. The boat makes its way to shore and deposits him and the Highlanders on the wharf, where soldiers are standing guard. Incoming and outgoing troops are old hat to them. Nevertheless, the Scottish townspeople not in uniform are happy to see the Canadians. They wave Union Jacks and cheer for the lads.

Moose Bannon is ecstatic to get off the ocean. He leans down, kisses the ground and says, "Thank God!"

The Highlanders are then put on trains destined to Guillemont barracks (also known as Guillemon barracks) in Cove, a tiny village about 54 km (33 mi) southwest of London. Ed's surprised at how small the trains are in Scotland. The engines on these trains don't have to haul passengers over mountain peaks. They are also not built for ferrying many people at the same time. Seating is limited and Ed takes his turn standing the 717 km (447 mi) south. It's stuffy and hot in the car filled with men, well, some are mere boys. Ed moves closer to an open window for a breath of air.

He watches the Scottish countryside roll by. It is not pretty at first. The train is passing near Glasgow, a major seaport and working-class city on the River Clyde. Factories with smoke billowing out of stacks, and stockyards with high mounds of black and grey and brown materials make everything look dirty. Adding to the unkempt sights, are large silver balloons that look to be rising out of the banks of the Clyde. They're barrage balloons, tethered to wire cables to block airspace from attacking German aircraft — or to "tangle up Jerry," as some would say.

After a while, the scenery changes and Ed sees the softer side of Scotland. He sees green fields, sheep grazing, vegetable gardens, golden grain being harvested and quaint villages and towns. There are no names for any of these places. They've been blanked out just like the road signs. It's better not to tell the enemy where he's going.

Every now and again, Ed catches a flash of barbed wire or soldiers off in the distance. It's a reminder that he's not on an adventure. This is a country at war. With twilight looming, the blinds are pulled over the carriage windows. It's blackout time and not a pinprick of light can escape. The men get a short break from the bleakness in York, England and Ed is given some food by a kind person there. He says thanks and also accepts the hot mug of tea he's handed. Then the train moves on.

There's barely any space to lie down and sleep so Ed leans against the back of a seat. He falls forward a couple of times and jerks himself awake. He's glad when the train finally comes to a full stop. Night has turned into a sunny morning and he steps onto the platform near Cove. There are some familiar faces at the train station: an advance party of Highlanders who had come over about two months earlier. They greet their comrades with smiles and jokes. An Imperial regiment band plays in the background as the Highlanders get ready to march to the barracks. Ed has been travelling by train or boat for 16 days straight and the rest of his journey is going to be on foot. He has an almost 5 km (3 mi) walk ahead of him. The regiment arrives amid the wail of air raid sirens. It's their introduction to the Battle of Britain.

England is already very familiar with The Blitz – a German bombing campaign targeting British soil. Since the summer (Jul. 10, 1940), the German and British air forces have been fighting in the skies over the U.K. The Highlanders are experiencing a terrible but nonetheless, exciting welcome to England.

There are several phases of the Battle of Britain that started with the Germans attacking coastal targets and British shipping operating in the English Channel. The Luftwaffe (German air force) hit civilians, too. During the air raids, the Highlanders have to wait it out. They either stand or spend time in their barracks. On one occasion, a bomb lands on the cookhouse and the lads cheer. The food had been dreadful.

On Sept. 15,[11] almost two weeks after Ed arrived in the U.K., London is bombed in broad daylight by the Luftwaffe. The Royal Air Force (which also includes Canadians and other Allied pilots), meets the enemy head-on and defeats the Germans.

While war is being waged in the air, Ed is on the ground. It has been just over a year since Canada has declared war. The men must be thinking they'd soon be part

11. September 15 is Battle of Britain Day in the U.K.

of pushing back the Axis powers but instead, the Highlanders have three more years of training to go. For many of the lads who had enlisted right at the start of the war, they're ready to fight. Some of them are fed up with being tantalizingly close and yet so far away from the front. However, there are rumours swirling that the Germans will soon be attacking the English coast and perhaps the Highlanders will get in on that action. Problem is, they don't have any ammunition.

Lieutenant-Colonel Fred Scott, Commanding Officer of The Calgary Highlanders, gathers his men and tells them if "Jerry" shows up, they will be attacked with bayonets. Scott is well-liked by most of the Highlanders. Bill Lyster says he rules with an iron fist but has a heart of gold.

The Highlanders are switched from the 6th to the 5th Infantry Brigade joining the Black Watch (Royal Highland Regiment) of Canada, the Fusiliers Mont-Royal (FMR), le Regiment de Maisonneuve, and le Regiment de la Chaudière. Training continues with the Highlanders honing skills on small arms (Thompson .45 calibre sub-machine gun and the Bren gun), anti-tank instruction and as always, marching and lectures. For practicing mounting mortars, sewer pipes and a tripod are the stand-ins for the real thing.

The men do have some downtime as the threat of England being taken by the Germans lessens (though the Luftwaffe continues nighttime bombing into May 1941) and leaves are granted at the end of September. Some soldiers visit Windsor Castle for Sunday church services and see royalty on the grounds. They spot Princess Elizabeth, King George VI and his wife, Queen Elizabeth. When the Queen spots a Calgary Highlander, she muses about her visit to the city in 1939.

The Canadians make themselves at home in the villages around Guillemont barracks. They socialize with the locals, who hand them eggs, tea and sweets. Folks often invite the lads to attend dances and parties. It would be a nice holiday if the Highlanders weren't getting ready to go into battle.

Damp and Dreary Talavera Barracks

It's Dec. 16, 1940 when the Calgary Highlanders move to Talavera barracks, near Aldershot, about 16 km (10 mi) away from Guillemont barracks. Talavera is a pair of three-storey brick buildings constructed around 1856. Bill Lyster's room has a hole in it that he thinks was blasted out by one of the Duke of Wellington's troops in the middle of the nineteenth century. Nevertheless, the British army charges the damages to Canada. Every month.

Even without the hole, Talavera is cold. A small bucket of coal that usually would take a couple of hours to burn through, is supposed to last the whole day. The damp and dreary English weather doesn't stop Ed from sleeping. He can sleep anywhere at any time. All the men need their rest as training heightens. They'll soon be introduced to the Battle Drill but be kept out of the real action.

12. Dorothy's cousin, Denis Payne, remembers the Canadian soldiers stationed at Bordon Camp, near Bordon, East Hampshire. Denis says the Canadians are so much a part of his life. "Bordon Camp is a large camp formed before the war and is taken over by the Canadians for the duration of the Second World War. The Canadian are in so many ways a 'part of the scenery' and joined in so much of the life of the area."

On Christmas Day, the Highlanders are served a festive feast. The honourary Calgary Highlander colonel and former Canadian prime minister (1930 to 1935) R. B. Bennett has donated money for turkey to be on the table at the regimental Christmas dinner. The Canadian Red Cross also donates to the Highlanders' festive meal. The officers wait on the men, a Christmas tradition.

Many Canadian soldiers give back to the communities they're living and training in and throw Christmas parties for the local children. Little Anne Terry receives a handcrafted wooden blue doll cradle from a soldier.

Presents[12] for the Highlanders from organizations back in Alberta include cigarettes and newspapers. It's Ed and Russ' first time away from their family for Christmas and they miss them terribly. However, with Christmas and New Year's over, it's back to war for the brothers and their fellow soldiers.

The Highlanders make several moves while in England, completing various exercises as well as providing coastal defence. They have stints in places including Port Slade, Shoreham, Eastbourne, Bexhill-on-Sea, Bognor Regis with stays in Aldershot in between. The monotony is starting to wear on the lads.

A lad from C Company pens a poem, *That Frosty Friday Morn*, while the Highlanders are guarding the British coast near Dover. He gives it to Ed, who agrees with the words: the men are tired of army routines. They're longing for home.[13]

That Frosty Friday Morn

On a frosty Friday morning, when this bloody war is o'er,
When the last air raid has sounded from the siren's banshee roar;
When they've taken down the blackouts, and lit the old street lights,
When a man can see for certain, who he's taking home at night,
When there ain't no army rations, and they issue T-bone steaks,
When the Company Sergeant-Majors are all stricken with the snakes;
When the bloomin' noisy sergeants lose their lusty vocal power,
And the water's sometimes warm, when you go to take a shower.
That will be the day my lads: you'll be glad that you are born,
And they tell me that it's coming: some frosty Friday morn.

We'll toss away our battledress, and heavy army shoes,
We'll watch the cooks all dining on their own mysterious stews,
We won't be there on Church parades. No guards and no fatigues,
No blistering route marches or imaginary Blitzkriegs.
We'll hang our rusty rifles upon the Q.M.'s wall,
We'll give him back the four by two, he issued us last fall;
And when our web equipment, some farmer's mule adorns,
We'll all be very happy, on that frosty Friday morn.

---

13. Q.M. means Quartermaster. Four by two is ammunition and NAAFI likely stands for the Navy, Army and Air Force Institutes, an organization that runs canteens and other services for service personnel and their families.

We'll strangle all the buglers, if they dare to blow a note,
And we'll pour a barrel of cold, weak tea, down the blasted NAAFI's throat.
We'll tear up all the orders, burn rifle Lesson twenty-four;
And we'll make the Provost Sergeant mop the guardroom floor.
We'll go back where there ain't no fish and chips,
Where the girls have been around,
Where a five spot, - still a five spot,
And not a blinkin', bleedin' pound.
We know sometimes it's coming, as we sit here all forlorn,
So we'll carry on as usual, - till that frosty Friday morn.

C Company

Life in England is turning dull, and Calgary Highlander George Morasch says the bland food doesn't help. Mutton is always on the menu and although the cooks try to prepare it in various ways, it is still mutton. Fish and chips are getting stale on the taste buds probably because it's the common fare for the men who are courting English girls. Red Anderson says he'll never be able to eat herring in tomato sauce again because he's eating so much of it in England. There's another dish he wishes to forget, too.

Every now and then for our main meal, the cooks would serve us 'horse cock!' [sausage] Looked very much like the real thing and as for taste, I wouldn't know, not having tasted the original. Come in from a 25-mile hike, ask the cooks what we are having for supper and if they yelled 'horse cock,' I lost my appetite right then. (Imagine that).

Courtesy of the *Private Papers of T. G. Anderson*, Esplanade Arts Heritage Centre, City of Medicine Hat

To wash down all the unsavoury meals and endless training, C Company has a special drink that lifts its spirits. The Delayed Action Liquid Grenade is made with double rum, ginger wine to taste and then a splash of soda. [R]epeat and wait precariously for action – it won't be delayed long… The time fuse is generally set for half an hour… (From *The Glen*)

Another type of spirit is invoked on Sundays. The soldiers, religious or not, have to go to church and services are held anywhere convenient, like a farmer's field. Ed is Anglican, which just so happens to be the royal family's denomination.

Grooming is serious business. George says the Highlanders have to shave every day or else lose a day's pay. Who wants to work a day for nothing? Ed's always fastidious about shaving and doesn't have to worry. His brother Russ, on the other hand, is a little more lax when it comes to tending his whiskers.

Back home in Calgary, in February 1941, the Mewata Armoury's new recreation building is destroyed by fire. The men had helped fund the $15,000 construction project out of their pay – 5 cents a day. It's a loss for the Highlanders and the city.

The troops have been subjected to the Blitzkrieg and no doubt the endless wailing of the air raid sirens, but they have yet to see any fighting – only drills and exercises using imagined attacks. Anti-invasion preparations are popular and in March, Ed and his mates take part in Exercise Dog. It's a large movement scheme (full-scale rehearsal of military manoeuvres) aimed at training the men to mobilize as well as familiarizing them with the South Downs area, a region that could be targeted by Germany.

Ed , right, and Moe Powers in St. Leonard's-in-the-fields Church, Perth, Scotland, 1943. Ed wrote on the back of the photo, "We'd had a few drinks." Photo: Carleton Family

The exercise does not go well. There's confusion, traffic jams and bottlenecks. More has to be done to get the troops to where they need to be.

King George VI and Queen Elizabeth visit the Highlanders in spring. The royals are impressed by the soldiers, as are people around England. The *Calgary Herald* receives letters praising the men for their respect and "great responsibility." Albertans should be proud.

Operation Benito is another large-scale movement test for Highlanders and other units in April 1941. They march for four days and then attack the "enemy." The Highlanders complete their task and the higher-ups are glad of the quick improvement.

Other schemes follow for the Highlanders and the exercises often include hours of marching. However, it doesn't seem to tire the lads out too much because they still have the energy to swing the local women around on the dance floor.

On Jul. 1, 1941, Ed and C Company are in Bexhill-on-Sea, East Sussex, on the south coast of England, where the Highlanders celebrate Dominion Day. That month, the men pick up defensive positions and continue their training. Besides firing practice and communications testing, some of the Highlanders help farmers in the fields. There's also a Brigade Sports Day on Jul. 17. Ed doesn't win anything but he claps the winner on the back in a show of good sportsmanship. Ed isn't a sore loser.

There's a dance to lift spirits on the evening of Jul. 19. Dorothy would have danced the night away if she had been there (and probably not with Ed as he had two left feet then). She's in Reading but it's around this time that her story intersects with Ed's, so it's a good time to tell you about her beginnings.

CHAPTER THREE

DOROTHY EILEEN (NEE SWEETZER) FOWLER

Dorothy is a constantly moving mountain creek while Ed is a calm mountain lake. She's always on the go and a lot of it has to do with the way she's raised. Perhaps right off the bat because she's adopted shortly after being born.

Dorothy doesn't know who her biological parents are although she has the name of her biological mother. *Eleanor Annie Sweetzer* was written on a baptism certificate for the rite performed four months after Dorothy was born. Eleanor's address was the exact same as Dorothy's adoptive parents: 55 Grange Avenue. However, no one has ever told Dorothy about the circumstances. There was no name given for the biological father. The one story Dorothy has heard about Eleanor was that she moved to Staten Island, New York, U. S. But that's all Dorothy has ever known about her.

Dorothy was born Dorothy Sweetzer in London, England on Sept. 5, 1919, within earshot of the famous Bow Bells.[14] These bells hang in St Mary-le-Bow, in the East End, and even though Dorothy could call herself a Cockney because of that, she considers herself a Reading gal.

Dorothy's parents George and Alice Fowler in the U.K., 1950.
Photo: Carleton Family

14. You can claim to be Cockney if you are born in earshot of the Bow Bells.

Dorothy became Dorothy Fowler when George and Alice (Edwards) Fowler adopted her as their second and youngest child. She couldn't have picked better parents herself. Her mum's parents are Bob and Alice Edwards. (Yes, there are two Alices. Keep up.) Dorothy's sister, Marjorie, is six years older than her (born in 1912) and her parents' biological child. They live at 55 Grange Avenue in Reading, 37 mi (60 km) west of London, in a row house, (a house joined to other houses by common walls). Their home is close to the River Thames. This particular section of the famous river was once described as "dirty" in 1889 by Jerome K. Jerome, an English writer and humourist. (His name is certainly humorous.)

Another famous author is connected to Reading in a much nicer way. Jane Austen went to school in the city. While the writer and Dorothy do share a bit of sense and sensibility, Dorothy has more in common with Reading's *Sumer is Icumen In* – the oldest song in history. Not because she's old but because she loves to sing. *Sumer is Icumen In* translates to Summer Has Come In and is also known as the Reading Rota. It dates from 1240 and is found at the Reading Abbey. (The abbey is also where King Henry, 1100 to 1135, is buried. Henry is famous for being the son of William the Conqueror and for dying after eating lamprey eels.)

Now, where are we? Oh yes, songs. Dorothy loves singing. It runs in the family. Alice leads the church choir and George sings tenor. The family also has a piano at home and Marjorie and Dorothy play it while their mum and grandmum sing. Dorothy especially likes Ave Maria. (Whenever she hears it, it brings tears to her eyes thinking about her family.) Oh, the music they make together – so full of joy.

At school, the students sing every day before going into their classrooms. You never have to coax Dorothy to sing. She'll sing anywhere – anytime. The children assemble in the hall and ring out *God Save the King* (George V) and *There'll Always be an England.*

There'll always be an England
While there's a country lane,
Wherever there's a cottage small
Beside a field of grain.
There'll always be an England
While there's a busy street,
Wherever there's a turning wheel,
A million marching feet.

Learning and Lifelong Friends at Alfred Sutton Central School

Formal education starts for Dorothy at five years old. She likes going to class because she gets to see her friends and of course, sing. Her school is Alfred Sutton Central School[15] on Wokingham Road – a short "wok" from her home. The school was opened in 1902 and first known as Wokingham Road School. The name changed almost 20 years later because a wealthy family (the Suttons who owned Sutton Seeds) gave money to the institution.

15. In 2016, Alfred Sutton School was renovated, expanded and remains a working school.

Alfred Sutton students have sharp uniforms. Dorothy feels dressed up and proper when she puts her uniform on. Girls wear white shirts and skirts with three box pleats at the front and three box pleats at the back. The boys all wear grey flannel shorts – no matter what the weather. Dorothy bets their knees get cold in the chilly English winter.

School discipline is strict. Dorothy doesn't dare do anything to get in trouble. She's lucky though because she likes learning. Her favourite subjects are music and PT (physical education). Ms. Luxton is her music teacher and choir work is an important part of Dorothy's week. Ms. Lewis teaches PT and gets her students outside to play field hockey and tennis. Dorothy is fond of Ms. Lewis and says she's a great gal and teaches her to be physically active at any age.

After school, Dorothy and her friends walk to the nearby park for activities. The boys play cricket and the girls play tennis or rounders (a bat-and-ball game similar to baseball). It's so much fun. Dorothy never learns to swim because she doesn't like the water much. Too wet.

School is where Dorothy meets two lifelong friends. Phyllis Tucker and Cicely North (Cicely lives on Wokingham Road). Dorothy is a good student and a good girl. Her parents never have to discipline her for being naughty because they are so kind and generous that she never wants to be bad. She always makes sure she treats her mum and dad with the same respect they give her.

The Fowler Family at 55 Grange Avenue

Dorothy's family rent their little two-story house on 55 Grange Avenue. There's a gas stove and gas lights downstairs but not upstairs. When Dorothy climbs the stairs to bed, she takes a candle. As well, there's no running hot water, only a cold-water tap. Bath night is quite the occasion because they have to heat the water in pots first.

Dorothy makes thousands of memories at 55 Grange that she keeps in her heart. In the living room, there's a piano that her family gathers around. When not striking the keys or singing, Dorothy plays cards with her sister Marjorie. After a meal, Dorothy and her dad can be found in the kitchen doing the dishes. George washes them and Dorothy dries. In the scullery, there are big copper boilers hanging on the wall that her mum uses for laundry and the family uses for bathing.

The scullery is also where they keep the tinned food. It's tough to keep the tiny room cool, especially in the hot weather. English weather isn't always cold and dreary. When the sun is shining and Alice is in the kitchen, they're feeling the heat.

Dorothy's mother is a very good cook and prepares delicious bread pudding, suet pudding and apple dumplings. It makes Dorothy's mouth water just thinking about all the food. Shepard's Pie and stews are also tantalizingly wonderful. Dorothy always wants more. She also really likes fish and chips but you buy those at a stand as a treat. Dorothy says there's nothing like fresh fish and hot salty chips wrapped up in newspaper and all for you.

At home, the big dinner is at lunch. They eat without George because he's at work. Alice re-heats the meal for him when he comes home at night. George uses a bicycle to get to and from his job. The Fowlers don't have a vehicle. They aren't poor but they aren't well off. George is a wages clerk at Huntley & Palmers, a huge biscuit (Brit-speak for cookies) factory. Dorothy's hooked on Digestives thanks to her dad. Every Friday, he brings home all the "rejects" – the broken and other non-sellable biscuits, for her and Marjorie. Dorothy says it's the best treat. The sisters empty the bags out on the table and go through them, picking out the ones they like. Dorothy also likes the football-shaped cookies with different creams in them. Nevertheless, she'll always like the Digestives.[16] They'll always be her favourite.

George works hard, very, very hard. He makes up the wages of hundreds of people by hand. Dorothy never visits her dad at his office. Her mum never sends her there on an errand or anything. No, Dorothy is busy with school and friends and Alice is also doing what she can to bring in some money.

Dorothy's mother takes in laundry and sewing. She's a talented dressmaker. Marjorie does some of the housework while their mum is stitching frocks or mending shirts. It isn't all work and no play for the Fowlers. On Sundays, it's a tradition to go for long walks. Alice puts the roast in the oven and then the whole family strolls around the city. Dorothy thinks this is why she never sits still. It has been ingrained in her to walk or cycle or hike – to be on the go. One Christmas, she receives a doll. She doesn't play with it a lot because she's an outdoors person. Even as a small girl, she prefers the fresh air to being inside.

Because Britain is an island, Dorothy is never too far away from the sea. The family goes on day outings to the coast. They take a picnic basket down to the beach on nice days and spread a blanket on the sand. Dorothy paddles her feet in the ocean and splashes around in the saltwater. She hunts for shells and lost treasures. These moments are the gold.

One longer trip is when they visit an aunt on her family's farm. Dorothy's around 14 and rural life is different from her city life. This is why it makes such an impact on her. Dorothy, her mum, dad and Marjorie go to Hollywater, Borden, about 60 km (33 mi) south of Reading to visit the Payne family (maternal relatives). The Fowlers hop on the bus with all their luggage and head for the countryside. The farm, called Hollywater Farm, has been leased from about 1922 and has pigs, chickens and cows. (There are possibly other animals there too but those are the ones Dorothy remembers.)

Her cousin, Denis Payne,[17] is 12 years younger and too little to play with Dorothy. Dorothy looks up to his mother, she's a real lady. Irene[18] has elegant button-up shoes that require a buttonhook to, well, button everything up. (Dorothy has never seen anything like it before.) The whole family is pleasant and it's a nice change of pace to be out of busy Reading.

---

16. You can still buy Huntley & Palmers in the U.K. but the company has changed hands a few times. The snacks are now made in Suffolk. (The factory in Reading closed in 1976.) The almost two hundred-year-old biscuit brand is still cranking out Jaffa cakes and Pub Mix Crackers but Dorothy has to ask: where are her favourites? Those mealy, crumbly Digestive biscuits? They aren't in the online catalogue.
17. Denis Payne lives in Wales now. (2019) He and Dorothy corresponded from time to time. He visited Dorothy and Ed in Banff once.
18. Irene (Brooker) Payne is known as Rene.

Oh, how quiet and lovely it is in the country. The stars are brighter than in the city and there are too many to count. Instead, Dorothy counts the eggs she collects, one of her chores while staying in Hollywater. She takes the eggs, still warm, from the golden hay while avoiding the sharp yellow chicken beaks. Another task is feeding the pigs. She hears them grunting to each other while rooting around for the tastiest morsels. Making butter is fun and there's nothing better than fresh butter on freshly baked bread. Her trip gives her so many stories to tell her friends at home. She bets the closest they've ever come to animals are dogs and cats. Just about everyone in Dorothy's neighbourhood has a dog. The Fowlers have both a dog and a cat. Dorothy's mates will never believe she had this much entertainment in such a rural setting.

Reading in the 1930s

As in Canada, there's a Great Depression (also known as the Great Slump) in the U.K. in the 1930s. Thankfully, Dorothy's father has his job at Huntley & Palmers and her mother has her part-time laundry and sewing gigs. Dorothy never goes without a meal or a necessity like shoes but there are no extras or luxuries.

The First World War had left its mark on Britain and the economy is struggling under the weight of debt. Then the U.S. stock market crashed in 1929, taking with it international trade. In Reading, the agricultural and commercial sectors employ a high percentage of the population. In contrast to the drought happening in the Canadian west, some parts of Reading and surrounding area are dealing with flooding as well as livestock being hit with foot and mouth disease. People are struggling.

Marjorie, being six years older than Dorothy, is working as a nurse and Dorothy feels it's her turn to give something back to her family. She quits school and gets a job. She's only 14 years old when she enters the workforce. It isn't against the norm in 1933. In fact, one-third of British women over 15 work outside the home.

By the time Dorothy leaves for the work world, she's completed Standard 8, similar to Grade 8 in Canada. She's also leaving with a handy skill: Pitman shorthand.[19] Pitman shorthand is a method of rapid writing used to take notes, dictation and meeting minutes. The shorthand symbols kind of look like a bunch of squiggly lines but if you know the phonetic system, it's a great secretarial skill to have because you can jot things down quickly. Because Dorothy knows shorthand, she can earn a living.

Earning a Living at 14 years old – Thornycroft Engineering

Dorothy earns 10 shillings (about 50 pence) per week at her first job with Thorneycroft Engineering.[20] She's in "office support" at the company that builds marine engines for ships. Thornycroft's origins began with a steam lorry designed by John I Thornycroft in 1862. When a wrench is thrown in the works (the company faced tougher vehicle legislation), Thornycroft motored into the ship engine business.

19. Shorthand started in 63BC and now, thanks to modern electronic devices, it's losing its appeal.

20. Thornycroft has since been absorbed by other firms but you can still get spare Thornycroft parts off the internet.

At Thornycroft, her boss' name is Mr. Gregg. Dorothy doesn't dare call him by his first name. This does not happen in polite 1930s British society. Work calls for proper behaviour and etiquette, which means saying please and thank you (hopefully manners that will never go away) as well as being dressed properly for the job. No flannel pyjamas at Dorothy's job.

Her task is taking notes (using shorthand) that Mr. Gregg, or another superior, dictate to her. Then she types up the messages on her Underwood typewriter and when that is finished, she'll collect the signatures she needs. Would you believe Dorothy is the only girl in the office pool? The other typists are all men.

Dorothy cycles to and from work on a bicycle her parents gave her. On her fourteenth birthday, she came downstairs and found this beautiful bike in the living room. It's for her! Her parents bought her the second-hand bike and it's something. That bike gets Dorothy everywhere she wants to go, which isn't that far but then, she doesn't have grand dreams of travelling overseas. Her sights at 14 are set a little closer to home.

Even though her job is bringing in money, it isn't enough. Ten shillings a week is amongst the lowest pay going. Fortunately, Dorothy's dad spots an ad for a position with the English Forestry Association and encourages her to apply.

Mr. Green and the English Forestry Association

For two years, Dorothy is employed at Thornycroft. It isn't terrible work but she works hard and the pay doesn't reflect that. Bottom line – it isn't great for her bottom line. The position with the English Forestry Association (EFA) pays thrice the salary as Thornycroft – 30 shillings a week. She applies for the job and she gets it.

The job, more typing work, is near Caversham Heights, a suburb of Reading, and a long bike ride away (just over 6 km or 4 mi). At one point in her journey, Dorothy has to get off her bicycle and walk up a steep hill. It takes her about half an hour to get to the EFA office. She doesn't mind the cycling commute. When the weather is fine – her ride is great. When the fog and drizzle comes, good old English weather, her ride is good. Either way, she's outside and doing something she loves.

At the EFA, Dorothy's part of coordinating Britain's reforesting program. The U.K. is losing its trees. In 1900, only five per cent of woodland covered the island. (Many people needing land to build on and only so much space, etc.) The First World War increased the demand on the natural resource and the government knew it had to do something. In 1919, it formed the Forestry Association and started cultivating trees. Dorothy's part of the process of planting at Mapledurham Estate.

Mapledurham Estate[21] (Mapledurham means "the maple tree enclosure"), was originally two manor houses in the 11th century in the village of Mapledurham. Later, one house, Mapledurham House, was built, Elizabethan style, on the property.

21. Since 1960, Mapledurham Estate has been a private home and offers tours, wedding venues and event space. You can have freshly baked scones in the manor's tearoom made with the flour straight from the mill. You might have seen Mapledurham Estate and not even known it. Television shows like *Midsomer Murders, Miss Marple* and *Escape to the Country* have been filmed on the property.

Construction was completed in 1612 and this is the grand maison that Dorothy sees. The grounds are magnificent and right on the banks of the Thames. In fact, the last operational watermill on the river still grounds flour here.

Dorothy is a shorthand typist for 30 shillings per week. Once again, she's the only woman, well girl, there. (She's around 18.) The rest of the crew are guys and that's OK with Dorothy. She says they're fine fellows and her boss, Mr. Green, becomes a close friend of hers. At the EFA, Dorothy has a good salary, good work and she says it's a good place to be. She even saves up enough money to buy a brand new bicycle.

Dorothy buys a Hercules[22] bicycle to use as her main mode of transportation. The Hercules Cycle and Motor Company Limited[23] was founded in 1910 in Birmingham, U. K. by the Crane brothers, Harry and Edmund. The bicycles are named Hercules for their sturdy and reliable design. Dorothy's Hercules is a strong steed and he goes with her everywhere. She's proud of her new bike.

Movement is Life – the Women's League of Health and Beauty

At Dorothy's forestry job, she has all male co-workers. She balances everything out when she joins the Women's League of Health and Beauty.[24] It sounds fabulous, doesn't it? An Englishwoman, Mary Bagot Stack, founded the mass fitness movement in the 1930s. After her death in 1935, her daughter, Ann Prunella Stack, continues promoting exercises for women all over the U.K. and around the world. The league's motto, *Movement is Life*, is something Dorothy has taken to heart – literally and figuratively.

The league is affordable, too at sixpence a class. All the women wear a uniform of a white sleeveless blouse and black shorts (really short shorts). Dorothy's mother sews her outfits. (Alice makes all her daughter's clothing, as she's an excellent dressmaker.)

Dorothy enjoys the league's activities from gym sessions to indoor exercises, outdoor exercises and dancing. They do some workouts in Palmer Park, a green space in Reading, and give public performances of their fitness routines. They do most of their training in bare feet – no matter what the weather. Brrrr. Dorothy's toes certainly get cold on more than one occasion while holding a pose on the wet ground on a crisp autumn afternoon. She doesn't complain because she truly likes the workouts and they motivate many women, no matter their circumstances, to get moving.

Dorothy often goes to the Women's League with her friends Margaret and Cicely. Getting there is a feat in itself – it's a 45-minute walk both ways. The pals meet at a church hall, do their training and then start their walk home. Along the way, they pick up a snack to eat. That snack is often fish and chips. Is there anything better? Not according to Dorothy.

22. The bicycle would be a valuable antique now.

23. In the 1950s, Hercules was taken over by Raleigh.

24. In 1999, the Women's League of Health and Beauty becomes Fitness League. A few years later, it changes its name to Flexercise.

The Second World War is Here

At age 19, Dorothy has been in the workforce for five years. She has a close-knit family and gains a brother-in-law when Marjorie marries Melbourne George Tingay in the spring of 1939. Marjorie's husband comes from a wealthy family. He has a car! When he comes to visit the Fowlers, he's the only one with a vehicle parked on Grange Avenue. Everyone else has to walk or cycle.

Dorothy loves her home and life. She has friends who like to walk with her and most importantly, sing with her. She's healthy and happy. What more can she ask for? Her cozy and secure world changes on the morning of Sept. 3, 1939. Two days before her 20th birthday.

There has already been an undercurrent of tension in Britain for several months as England watches what's happening with Germany. The U.K. government has started building trenches and handing out gas masks around the country. In fact, trenches were dug in Palmer Park last year in "case of an emergency." This is the park where Dorothy performs with the Women's League of Health and Beauty and so far, the only emergency has been a leg cramp and a stubbed toe.

When the news comes that Germany invaded Poland on Sept. 1, 1939, a nationwide blackout in the U.K. is proclaimed. It's lights out for England. The government is afraid Hitler is going to bomb the U.K. at night. No one can let a ray of light escape from their windows. Even vehicles have slotted covers fitted over their headlights. The night in the city is as pitch-black as the countryside.

The radio is on at Dorothy's home on Sunday, Sept. 3, 1939, at 11:15 a.m. when she hears the announcement that Britain and France are at war with Germany. Prime minister Neville Chamberlain's words are eloquent yet firm:

We and France are today, in fulfilment of our obligations, going to the aid of Poland, who is so bravely resisting this wicked and unprovoked attack on her people. We have a clear conscience. We have done all that any country could do to establish peace. The situation in which no word given by Germany's ruler could be trusted and no people or country could feel themselves safe has become intolerable.
And now that we have resolved to finish it,
I know that you will all play your part with calmness and courage.

A strange and funny feeling comes over Dorothy. Britain is going to war? What does that mean for her, for her family, for her country? Chamberlain's last words echo across the nation.

Now, may God bless you all. And may He defend the right.
For it is evil things that we shall be fighting against – brute force, bad faith, injustice, oppression and persecution – and against them, I am certain, that the right will prevail.

Dorothy is young but not immature. She knows there are going to be tough years and many sacrifices ahead. She knows about it because of her father. George Fowler was in the artillery, right in the trenches, in the First World War. The worst place to be. Artillery, heavy guns and field guns, won battles. Soldiers dug deeper trenches to try and withstand the blasts from enemy shelling. Guns like the Heavy Field Howitzer and Heavy Siege Gun (Big Bertha) brought fear and caused the greatest loss of life.

The women of the Women's League of Health and Beauty, Reading, U.K., 1937.
Dorothy is fifth in line on the left.
Photo: Carleton Family

George never talked about his service but he had come home wounded. He was injured when a bullet went through his arm. It wasn't too serious and he still has the use of the limb. He received two medals for his service. While George was fighting, Alice carried on with her sewing.

George won't be a soldier again. He's around 50-years-old and not in physical fighting shape. There are much younger and healthier men who will pick up arms. Meanwhile, sirens warning of non-existent air raids ring in London that same Sunday and Britain starts moving ahead with war contingencies and strategies.

London closes its cinemas and theatres and even shuts the Zoological Gardens. The giant pandas are sent to the Whipsnade Zoo, over an hour's drive northwest of the city, and the venomous animals are killed – they could be a threat if the zoo is bombed and the snakes and scorpions start crawling into Londoners' homes.

That Sunday evening, King George V1 takes to the airwaves.

In this grave hour, perhaps the most fateful in our history, for the second time in the lives of most of us we are at war. Over and over again we have tried to find a peaceful way out of the differences between ourselves and those who are now our enemies. But it has been in vain. The task will be hard. There may be dark days ahead and war is no longer confined to the battlefield.

The next day, Monday, Sept. 4, Hitler doesn't march into Reading or London. So…life continues on – albeit under different conditions. Various precautionary defence measures are rolled out (blackouts, air raid sirens, picking up gas masks, etc.). The iron railings around 55 Grange Avenue, as well as around the city, are ripped out as metal is needed for the war effort. Nevertheless, Dorothy continues to bike to Mapledurham and plant trees. It's business as usual in an unusual time.

George continues working at Huntley & Palmers. The factory is churning out what's called *emergency bread* – bread baked and then sealed in tins that supposedly lasts for 10 years. (During the First World War, the company made biscuits for the army and as the factory made its own tins, it also made cases for artillery shells.)

That October, the British government starts the *Dig for Victory!* campaign. Before the Second World War, over 80 per cent of Britain's food comes from Canada and the U.S. (55 million tons of food a year is imported). The U.K. needs to ensure its people don't starve when the island is cut off from exports. The government calls for any piece of land that can grow vegetables and fruits to be turned into an allotment. Formal gardens, lawns and sports fields are turned into garden plots. The Fowlers have a patch of soil about a mile away from their house that they've already been tending.

Dorothy often helps her dad push his wheelbarrow to the allotment, which is in an open area. The family grows everything from cabbage, to Brussel sprouts. George loads up the wheelbarrow with his harvest and the pair walks home. No one steals anything out of the garden because everyone has their own. It's commonplace.

Alice doesn't make her own bread. She buys cottage loaves, a traditional type of English bread made up of two round loaves on top of one another, from a bread cart that's drawn by a workhorse. Dorothy's mum loves the horses and feeds them carrots. It's neat to see the big horse with all his big white teeth oh so gently take the treat from

Alice's small hand. Those strong teeth made short work of the carrot. At Easter, the cart brings hot cross buns. Dorothy's roll doesn't make it into the house. She sits in the front door and gobbles it up as quickly as the horse chomps its carrot.

Some people keep rabbits for food but not the Fowlers. They never miss a meal during the war. They definitely miss their goodies though when they start disappearing. Chocolate and other sweets disappear from shops first. Just after the outbreak of war, in October 1939, the family is given a ration book with coupons in it. Rationing makes sure that everyone gets an equal amount of food no matter what their circumstances. The Fowlers use coupons for almost everything. They could use two coupons for a pound of butter or tea. Fish isn't rationed and is plentiful. (Good thing Dorothy likes to eat fish.)

Rationing is a case of making the best of what you have when you have it. People queue for hours and cookery books are issued with recipes based on the ingredients available. Most of the food is stodge – heavy, filling and high in carbohydrates, and nothing is wasted. Expectant mums and children are given nutrient boosts with orange juice and cod liver oil. Nobody can be fussy or finicky. You eat what you have. It isn't just sugar, meat and butter that are rationed but also petrol and clothing for which families have coupons.

The war takes Dorothy's youth. She has already been working in the adult world but now she also has their problems. War is something that no one escapes. It captures everyone: young, old, rich and poor. Dorothy knows it's time to help her country. She looks into joining the Women's Land Army (WLA) as it seems a good fit. The WLA work in the agricultural jobs the men have left when enlisting. The WLA is also known as Land Girls and Dorothy might enjoy planting and harvesting or milking cows or being a rat catcher! Actually, scratch that. She does NOT like rats. During the Second World War, there are an estimated 50 million rats running around Britain. The pests eat valuable crops and seeds so the WLA form anti-vermin squads.[25] It has been said that two land girls killed 12,000 rats in one year.

Despite asking the EFA to release her to the WLA, Dorothy's told no. The EFA need her as much as the WLA. Growing trees is a reserved occupation. Full stop.

Dorothy wants to branch out from the EFA and since her boss won't release her, she decides to join her father. They both become volunteers in the Air Raid Wardens' Service.

"Put Out That light"

The First World War brought aircraft warfare to the front lines. There's speculation that this "new" threat would one day rain bombs on Britain. Thus, the Air Raid Wardens' Service was formed in 1937. The number in the ARP (Air Raid Precautions) jumps to 1.5 million after the outbreak of the Second World War. George is one of these volunteers. (There are many First World War veterans involved with the ARP.) He's a fire watcher and basically looks for fires and puts them out if he can. If he can't, he alerts the authorities.

25. Perhaps if Dorothy had been on an anti-vermin squad, it might have prepared her better for fighting the mice in her cabin in Banff.

Dorothy, far right standing, at a Civil Defence Service meeting.
Photo: Carleton Family

While nothing much is going on conflict-wise in 1939, the ARP volunteers are laughed at for doing nothing but drawing curtains. Then on Sept. 7, 1940, and in daylight, London comes under attack in a wave of around 300 German bombers. That night, the Germans return. It's the beginning of the Blitz: daily and nightly attacks. That's when Dorothy decides to help defend her country.

Dorothy volunteers for the ARP (which changes its name to the Civil Defence Service in 1941) as an air raid warden. Air raid wardens are trained at a Reading school. They're taught how to fire a Lee-Enfield rifle and how to throw a hand grenade. (Throw it far away from you!) Part of Dorothy's job is to patrol the streets and make sure everyone has their blackout curtains drawn before sunset. The drapes are special curtains made so there are no lights for Mr. Hitler to see.

"Pull your curtains!" air wardens tell people. "Put out that light."

The streets are dark and Dorothy carries a torch (flashlight) that's half covered to guide her from home to home. The government doesn't want light shining out of anything – torch, building or vehicle, to guide the German bombers in England.

It's through her volunteer work that Dorothy makes a close friend, Olive Beasly. They meet when Olive joins the Civil Defence Service in 1942. The women train together in Caversham. One exercise has them hanging out of an upper floor window by their fingertips and then dropping to the ground, luckily onto a bed of straw. They also have to crawl through smoke-filled rooms. The friends are in incredible shape after their CD instructions.

The air warden's job isn't easy and at times, it's frightening. Often, Dorothy and Olive are teamed up with another woman, Ada Mears. (One in six air raid warden positions is held by a woman.) On night duty, they sleep on bunk beds in the basement of Dorothy's former school, Alfred Sutton. (Alfred Sutton is the CD headquarters.) If there's a Red Alert, they're out patrolling the streets until the all clear sounds.

Whenever the air raid sirens go off, people stop what they're doing and find a shelter. The shelters in Reading are either reinforced brick buildings or large fortified sheds.

There's a brick raid shelter right on Grange Avenue. Olive's family have something similar in their neighbourhood.

While others are hurrying to shelters and safety, Dorothy has to go outside, in the black, amidst the hum of German airplanes, with anti-aircraft lights flashing hysterically, and be a beacon of hope. That's ironic as she has to ensure no light streams from anywhere and that people are in the shelters. Oh, and wait to see if any bombs are falling on Reading. That part makes her heart pound.

The air raid sirens go off at any time: night and day. Dorothy says she's scared when the alert sounds. She has to patrol her area, heading out with a flashlight to make sure all the house lights are out until the all clear is called. Then she can go home. She learns quickly the difference between German and Allied airplanes. The German planes have a distinct hum, almost a *woo woo woo* sound. British aircraft roar.

Dorothy volunteers as an air raid warden while being employed at EFA. If the air sirens sound in the middle of the night, she goes on patrol. It doesn't matter if she gets to bed until 4 a.m., she still has to get up in the morning and go to work. She has had some sleepless nights and on top of it all, she has to bike to her job. Cycling to Mapledurham is taxing although she never misses a day. She's tired all right but when you're in your early twenties, you don't seem to need a lot of z's. You can recharge in an hour and be on your way. Olive has a job, too.[26] She's working as a secretary in a factory that repairs Spitfire aircraft (British single-seat fighter aircraft).

Along with their jobs and air warden work, the twosome also tap dance and perform together. Olive introduces Dorothy to a great tap teacher, Eleanor Austin, in Reading. The friends have to walk to Eleanor's studio where they learn rhythm, balance, flow, tone, accent, syncopation and choreography. After getting their act together, Dorothy and Olive do some shows at a convalescent home for injured forces personnel as well as a concert at the Palace Theatre[27] in Reading. The dancing pair raise a little money for the war effort this way.

Dorothy and Olive like singing and dancing. Dorothy isn't shy and neither is Olive and the friends are having the best time. They have a nice band playing for them and Dorothy loves being in front of an audience. She has an enormous amount of confidence stemming from her positive outlook on life. She likes being on stage and doing the things she wants to do.

Dorothy receives a letter from a senior member of the civil defence. The note praises her and Olive for their "clever and charming performance" at one of their shows.

I asked a lot when I asked you to open the show, yet I felt sure that yours is just the bright and happy number to start the evening well. You did your job nobly and I hope you will get some new routines ready to submit to as for our next show.

Yours sincerely, (Possibly?) Charles I. Hibbert [28]

---

26. Olive says she doesn't think any kids these days could go without sleep the way she and Dorothy did. Olive (Beasly) Openshaw, 2018.
27. The Palace Theatre is demolished in 1961.
28. The date and location of the show are unknown as well as the letter writer's name. Olive didn't know this note existed until a scanned copy was e-mailed to her in 2018. She says it's great to get appreciation 75 years later!

The shows, the dancing as well as the physical activity and fearlessness in the face of danger, shapes Dorothy for the future. As a warden's wife in the backcountry, there'll be no time for loafing around or hemming and hawing. There are always things that need to be done and done quickly.

Dances and a Bit of Romance

The Canadians started arriving in Britain on Dec. 23, 1939, with 7,500 soldiers setting foot on the island. Ed comes to the U.K. in 1940. Dorothy won't meet him right away. First, she falls in love with a soldier, an Englishman, from a Manchester Regiment.[29]

She meets the soldier at a dance and he's the first man she falls in love with. The Olympia Ballroom[30] on London Street in Reading holds dances just about every night. Dorothy puts on a nice dress and some lipstick and starts walking with a friend to the dancehall around 9 p.m. Dorothy doesn't have long at the event because she has to catch the bus to be home at 11 p.m. If she misses the bus, it is a long walk.

The dances are energetic and full of fun. Dorothy likes fast dances, not the slow, waltzing ones. She likes to kick up her heels and spin around to the band. Yes, a real live band is performing. The girls stand on one side of the room and the guys on the other. Dorothy says there's nothing like the thrill of watching a man cross the floor to get a dance partner. Who is he going to ask?

Dorothy calls the dances "sixpenny dances" because that's how much they're charged to get in. The money goes towards hall maintenance and paying the band. There's nothing to eat or drink at the event. There might be a water fountain to sip from if you work up a sweat doing the Jive, Jitterbug or Lindy Hop.[31]

Besides the Olympia, there are dances at the local church hall. Dances are an escape for the boys from their daily military grind. There are very few Englishmen at the dances because they are off fighting so meeting the Manchester man is a rare opportunity. There are lots of people at the dances. They are there on leave and at the ballroom for some female company.

At the end of Dorothy's dance nights, she runs to catch the bus. Walking through the door at home, her father is always waiting for her. Never her mother. They both trust her but always ask where she's going. Attending dances is fine with Dorothy's parents although she never lets on she has a boyfriend. She thinks the news might upset them and she doesn't want to do that. She ends up parting with her Manchester man anyway. He'll forever be in her past as her present fills with other opportunities, family and new loves.

---

29. Dorothy is famous for openly telling stories about her life with Ed, her family and being a warden's wife. Nevertheless, some things she keeps close to her heart.

30. The Olympia Ballroom is built in the 1700s and used as an asylum as well as a concert hall where the Rolling Stones and Rod Stewart performed. Today, it's a hotel and conference centre. (2020)

31. The Americans make those styles popular when they entered the war.

Chapter Four

Exercising War

Bullets! Bullets! Bullets! – The Battle Drill

British Lieutenant-General H.R.L. Alexander designed the battle drill and it trains the men physically, tactically and psychologically for combat. The aim is to teach the men to get DOWN immediately while being shot at, CRAWL to cover, OBSERVE the enemy's position and then FIRE back. Soldiers who are steeped in battle drill tactics supposedly develop team skills that'll guide them through anything they encounter in battle.

Calgary Highlander Lt-Col. Fred Scott has seen the battle drill in action, thanks to a demonstration by the British 47th Division. He thinks the tactic will be useful to his battalion. He also thinks it's a way to beat their boredom and so begins instructing his men in the discipline. In the fall of 1941, he starts a school in Burnt Wood, near Bexhill.

Ed is put through his paces during the exercises, which include obstacle courses, long marches and sometimes someone yelling "Bullets! Bullets! Bullets!" at him (instead of live fire). Highlander Bert Pittaway can't see the sense in practicing the military tactic. He can see the sense of visiting his girlfriend while in the middle of a lengthy training march up and over the English downs (grass hills). It's a great time to visit Pam, the English girl he has been courting. He's almost at her doorstep so why not see if she's home?

He leaves his equipment with a buddy and grabs a motorcycle when the battalion stops close to Southwood, where Pam lives. Bert gives her a quick hello and then speeds back to where the troops are supposed to be waiting. They are not there.

He scrambles to find their location after several inquiries into where they went. He joins up with his unit and no one notices that he has even been gone. He's lucky. If they had noticed, Bert says he would have been shot.

The battle drill trains the men to see themselves as professional hunters – killers who stalk their prey with technical and natural knowledge and instinct. However, some soldiers think the drill is a sure-fire way to ensure they'll die in combat. Others think it toughens them up.[32] Either way, when it comes time to be called to the front, the top British brass have misgivings about how prepared the Calgary Highlanders are for war. Officials think Ed and his mates haven't been fully trained as they've been focusing on the battle drill.

Action in the Pacific but None in England

The Calgary Highlanders maintain their training around Britain in 1941 and by the end of the year, Canadian infantry units are running their men through the battle drill. The Canadian army hasn't been actively engaged in the war but that's about to change. However, worlds away from Ed.

32. Now there's a consensus among military historians that the battle drill was not effective in Second World War battles.

The Axis powers have been flexing their muscles. In June, Hitler launched Operation Barbarossa: the invasion of Russia. Japan, an Axis power that has been given greater East Asia, was also flexing its muscle and becoming increasingly worrisome for the Allies. In October of 1941, two Canadian battalions were sent from Canada to Hong Kong to help defend the British Crown Colony in case of a Japanese attack. The Canadians landed in November and they don't have to wait long for something to happen.

On Dec. 7, Japanese forces attack Pearl Harbor, Hawaii and the United States enters the Second World War the next day. Dec. 8 is the same day Hong Kong comes under fire. On Dec. 11, D Company of the Winnipeg Grenadiers trade shots with Japan. The Canadians are the first Canadian Army unit to engage in combat in the war.

On Christmas Day, the Allied forces in Hong Kong surrender. Two hundred and ninety Canadians are killed and 493 wounded.[33] Hundreds more Canadians, along with other Allied soldiers, are sent to PoW (Prisoner of War) camps where conditions are often inhumane.

Meanwhile, in the new year, 1942, it's not out with the old. Ed and the Highlanders are still being prepared for an invasion battle of Britain. There is a change when, in February, Lieutenant-Colonel Fred Scott is sent home to Canada and posted to a battle drill school. Major Donald MacLauchlan, a polarizing man, is now in charge of the Highlanders as acting commander (CO).

Attack on Reading

The war arrives at Dorothy's door on Feb. 10, 1942. A German plane flies over Reading, her beloved city, and drops four 500 kg bombs on it. Forty-one people die that day and 150 are injured, including Dorothy's grandfather.

The bombs go off in the city centre at 4.35 p.m. The first bomb explodes on Simmonds Brewery, leaving a 7.6 m (25 ft.) crater. The second bomb hits the offices of the Reading Labour Party in Minster Street and then explodes in Welsteeds Department store across the road. The third bomb takes out the People's Pantry, an emergency feeding centre, where families are gathered. The fourth bomb detonates outside the town hall, Reading's control centre for civil defence. Then, the Germans fire into the streets with machine guns.

There's no warning. None at all. The air raid sirens go off around the same time as the attack. Dorothy's maternal grandfather, Bob Edwards, is downtown when the bombings start. The chaos is unprecedented. Dust is so thick it's hard to see the dying and injured. Afterwards, rubble falls into the streets and many people are panicking, afraid the Germans are going to return. Bob can't hear the wailing of the alerts or the cries for help, he's deaf and mute. He's a kind and generous man so he assists in any way he can although he is hurt, too. Bob comes home with shards of glass lodged in

---

33. There are plaques in Hong Kong commemorating the Canadians and one in particular: Company Sergeant-Major John Robert Osborn. On Dec. 19, 1941, he used his body to cover a grenade that would have probably killed his fellow soldiers.

his head. He had been standing near a window during the attack and is fortunate pieces of glass didn't strike his eyes. Dorothy's grandfather is taken to the hospital to be treated.

Michael Bond, the author of the Paddington Bear stories, grew up in Reading. The day of the bombing, he's working as an engineer for BBC installing a radio transmitter in an office on the top floor of a building. Someone looks out the window and says they see a Dornier aircraft, a Luftwaffe bomber, coming – fast. There's no chance to react. The plane drops a bomb and it hits the ground floor of the seven-story building where Michael is working. The bottom two floors collapse into the basement while Michael and others are on the top floor. Thankfully, the staircase is still standing, albeit it's very rickety. It's a shaky walk down to the street. Michael says he is lucky to be alive. He witnesses horrors as he climbs over all the debris to get to flat ground. Michael passes a girl who has had her legs blown off. He also sees a hand coming up out of the rubble clenching – false teeth. The man, almost buried alive, is trying to save his dentures.

All of Reading is in shock. "Why us?" the townspeople ask. Turns out, the Nazis thought they were targeting a railway. They missed.

Busy Beavers

There's quite a contingent of handsome servicemen in the U. K. including two brothers from Didsbury, Alberta: Ed and his brother Russ. Spring 1942 turns the Calgary Highlanders into busy beavers. Literally. A series of exercises named *Beaver* sees the men marching long distances with little sleep. These schemes are more offensive force than defensive as well as an introduction to tank and infantry coordination.

Another scheme is *Tiger* where tactical training and endurance are pushed to the limit in May. Some men marched for 11 days, 18 hours a day, for a total of around 403 km (250 mi). Ed has to walk a little over half that distance and spends a few nights dozing under hedgerows. The lads attack "enemy" tanks, gather "prisoners" and hold off an armoured division for eight hours during the exercise. After the scheme is over, Ed marches the 284 km (177 mi) back to camp. (He's allowed to do it in stages.) There's free beer in the canteen when he makes it "home."

***

Canadians are supposed to see action in Operation Rutter, a short-term seizure of Dieppe, scheduled for Jul. 5. Members of 2nd Canadian Infantry Division are training for the operation on the Isle of Wight, including a number of Calgary Highlanders. The raid schedule is ultimately scrapped due to bad weather.

Ed, who wasn't selected for Rutter, participates in Jumbo, a field firing exercise, on Jul. 8. He's using live ammunition in the mortar he's firing. A mortar is an artillery weapon and the Canadian army commonly uses 3-inch mortar bombs, shells that are dropped into a tube of mortar (paste) and then shot out. The weapon is portable and Ed learns how to carry it. There is one thing he can't get use to – the smell. There's an odour to the smoke wafting around after the bomb is discharged. It's a sharp yet sweet smell and not at all pleasant.

Russ has found someone to be sweet on. He meets Dorothy's friend Phyllis Tucker when he's in Reading on leave. Phyllis is with the Women's Auxiliary Air Force (WAAF).

Russ and Phyllis and a kitten.
Photo: Carleton Family

WAAF's posts include everything from being a kitchen orderly, a driver, a mechanic, an engineer, an electrician or a fitter for airplanes. (WAAF's help with the code-cracking at Bletchley Park.) Phyllis is stationed at bomber command and meets Russ when they strike up a conversation at Forbury Gardens, a public park. One thing leads to another.

It's the same with official army business. Acting CO Donald MacLauchlan is promoted to lieutenant-colonel on July 21 by Lieutenant-General H. D. G. Crerar. It took longer than usual for MacLauchlan's move to be approved because some military leaders don't approve of him. They, including senior British Army office Bernard Law Montgomery (Monty), don't think he knows what he is doing. Monty says MacLauchlan is "Completely out of his depth as a battalion commander."

Dieppe Raid

In the middle of the summer of 1942, the Calgary Highlanders don't expect to be going anywhere exciting soon. Earlier in the spring, General Bernard Montgomery, the British Allied commander, had thought the 5th Brigade, the one that included the Highlanders, wasn't up to fighting strength. The Highlanders are left out of training for Dieppe.

Ed and his mates are stationed at Halnaker Camp in West Sussex county in August. The men are scrambling up cliffs and navigating the land, among other things. Ed, along with Bert Pittaway, Bill Lyster, Moose Bannon, Red Anderson and George Whitehead, belong to Mortar Platoon 3. Mortar Platoon 3 has proven itself to become very proficient at firing mortars. Red is the best at it. Bill says it's like his buddy has four hands he's so quick.

Ed and the platoon are separated from the battalion and loaned to the Royal Canadian Artillery (RCA) on Aug. 10. They move to a place George calls Pepperidge. Here, they do mortar drill after drill after drill. One day, they're taken to a field where their platoon sergeant, F. J. (Jack) Reynolds, says they'll be competing against the Black Watch and Maisonneuve.

The men do the exercises and supposedly "win" the championship for 2nd Division. Their prize is that they're going to be sent to the coast to put on a demonstration for the king. It's an honour for sure but Ed and the lads would rather be fighting for real.

On Aug. 18, Lieut. Jack Reynolds orders his men to put on their best battle dress. Then, they get into a truck to be transported to perform for the king. Arriving in the port city of Southampton, the Highlanders see the harbour is full of landing craft. Ed wonders what this all means. A Highlander who has been training with a battalion in the 6th Brigade, Private Scott Rhodes, spots his mates.

"You're going to Dieppe," he says.

"What the hell are you talking about?"

***

The order comes on Aug. 18, 1942, for Ed and his platoon to march aboard Tank Landing Craft (TLC) 6 at Southampton. On the boat already are three Churchill tanks (British heavy infantry tanks) named Bob, Bill and Bert, a bulldozer belonging to the B Squadron of the 14th Army Tank Regiment (The Calgary Regiment (Tank)) and other Canadian and Allied servicemen.

Once the men sail past the Ilse of Wight, Lieut. Jack Reynolds gathers the Highlanders around him.

"Fellas, we are on our way to Dieppe. We are going into action. I know that I feel good about it because you are the best-trained mortar men in the army."

Ed and his mates are charging to France.

Mortar Platoon 3 is up against a solid and fierce German force. While the Nazi regime is still trying to make headway in Russia, the Germans have been occupying France and most of the continent (Fortress Europe) for at least two years. They aren't stopping there and are intent on moving into Britain. The Allies need to drive the Germans out of Fortress Europe and push them back to Germany… except there's no way the Allies can launch a full-scale assault on mainland Europe just yet. They need to gather experience and intelligence first as well as test its amphibious assaults against the Axis powers. This is where the port town of Dieppe[34] comes in.

The Canadians don't know it but they are about to get the brunt of the German wrath in Operation Jubilee. Jubilee is Operation Rutter remounted and the Canadian Army's first engagement in the European theatre of the Second World War…and it includes Ed. It's all thanks to some Canadian politicians and generals who thought it was about time our soldiers saw action. The troops, too, are frustrated by the lack of battle.

34. Clementine Churchill, Winston Churchill's wife, spent time as a teenager in Dieppe, France.

Approximately 5,000 of the 6,100 soldiers ready to face battle at Dieppe are Canadian with hundreds of Canadian airmen and sailors supporting the raid. The other fighters include British Commandos, (around 1,000), American Rangers (around 50) and a handful of French Nationals.

British Lord Louis Mountbatten and naval Captain John Hughes-Hallet come up with the plan that's led by Canadian Major-General John Hamilton "Ham" Roberts.[35] Before the doomed raid, he utters the words, "Don't worry men, it'll be a piece of cake." That is far, far from reality.

There are problems with preparations for Operation Jubilee such as lack of updated information but the planners think the element of surprise will offset any obstacles.

The 21 Calgary Highlander men are indeed surprised to be heading to France. During the hours-long convoy, escape kits with waterproof maps and French francs, escape money, are handed out. Men write letters and give them to Sgt. Bert or Sgt. Bill to send home if they don't make it back to England. Bill doesn't know how he'll get the mail and himself off the landing barge but he keeps his thoughts to himself.

Ed isn't writing. He's taking the voyage one moment at a time. He does try to sleep and leans against the cold steel tank. There aren't even any lifebuoys or life jackets on board to soften the sharp metal edges of the war machine. Red Anderson is using a sack of potatoes as a pillow. Around midnight, they're both jerked awake by a loud racket and bright white light. It's the Allied convoy exchanging fire with a German convoy. There's no surprising the Nazis now.

At this point, Ed's trepidatious but eager to put all his training to good use. He doesn't know what awaits him on the stony beaches of Dieppe.

At 4:30 a.m., Aug. 19, British airplanes are roaring towards France and dropping their bombs on Dieppe. There are tracers (ammunition that lights up) flying everywhere. Ed has never seen fireworks like this before. At first light, 237 Allied ships and landing craft are greeted by the pebbled beaches of Dieppe, a shoreline that's walled in by high, chalky-white cliffs. On these bluffs, are heavily fortified German defences: concrete bunkers housing anti-aircraft guns and machine guns. The beaches and the town are also protected by batteries of guns, barbed wire, mines and Hitler's ferocious men.

The Dieppe Raid is on. The Calgary Highlanders orders are to follow the infantry, set up their mortars on Red Beach (a code name[36]) and then start firing. But they are in the midst of the melee while still on the water. The ocean is boiling and the beach is churning. Ed and the Highlanders are stranded in the landing craft while Allied aircraft streak overhead and German anti-aircraft fire respond on land. Tanks rolling off landing crafts sink into the water while the tanks that make it to land fire away. There's incessant machine-gun firing from all sides. Violent explosions go off

---

35. According to David O'Keefe in his Aug. 17, 2017 *Maclean's* article *Vindicating 'Ham' Roberts*, Roberts is a scapegoat for the doomed raid. He's enthusiastic and focused and will do anything to get the job done.

36. Beaches were code named Yellow, Blue, Red, White, Green and Orange.

every second. Noise and smoke and bullets and blood surround the Highlanders. Men, Canadian men, are dying everywhere. It's a massacre.

Ed watches as Bob, the first tank to rattle off his landing craft, is shelled right away and the turret is ripped right off. Second tank Bill goes next but his tracks are thrown off by the shale on the beach. Third tank Bert makes it to shore and almost up to the beach but can't get up a small hill. A bulldozer gets off the boat and Sgt. Bill calls to the men to load their rifles. George Whitehead has a revolver and he trades it with Bill for a rifle.

George flips the safety on and squeezes the trigger to test it. A bullet whizzes by Bill, narrowly missing him. The peculiar thing about war is that some things that shouldn't be funny, are funny. Three months earlier, Bill made George clean the cracks of a floor with a knife and toothbrush as punishment for an infraction. George had told Bill then that he was going to get him if it was the last thing he did.

He didn't mean he was going to shoot Bill in the midst of fighting the enemy. Moose also has a unique experience when he's helping the galley crew peel potatoes. A shell hits the bag and it explodes, sending pieces of spud everywhere. It looks like brains.

Ed peers through the hazy smoke screen. He sees soldiers crumple on to the beach after being shot by the heavy German guns and machine guns. The Canadians have nothing to protect them while the Nazis are hidden under thick concrete bunkers. They keep pounding away at the sea.

The Highlanders can't get to their target and Lieut. Jack Reynolds tells his men they won't be going to the stony shore. They'll fight from the landing crafts when they can and rescue those who can't. Ed and some other men take up their guns and Red grabs the fire hose because the landing craft is on fire. The engine room was hit by a shell. Nothing is coming out of the spout. Instead, the water is hissing hysterically out of the holes that have just been shot through it.

Bert, Bill and Red are taught on the spot how to use the Ack Ack (a quick firing anti-aircraft gun also known as a pom pom gun). Bert is scared out of his wits until he starts firing. Bill sits down on a lumpy tarp and then peers under it. He's sitting on dead bodies.

George doesn't care if he dies. He cares about being wounded. He moves to an Ack Ack gun and when he looks down the sight, it has a hole shot through it. George notices the previous operator of the gun is dead beside it, his brains in his tin hat.

Ed doesn't have a single second to think about death. His training kicks in and he is all about instinct. He and the Highlanders pump the beach with shells. They take aim at Dieppe's grand Metropole Hotel and then the casino. In the midst of the storm, a man jumps into the sea from his blazing landing craft and calmly swims over to the Highlanders. His name is Lieutenant Commander Cook and he hadn't shaved that morning. He finds the time to finish his morning constitution and get rid of his red stubble once aboard the Highlander's TLC.

Meanwhile, the Highlanders pitch in and help the wounded who are coming from all sides. The landing craft goes back and forth picking up wounded and prisoners and dropping them off at the hospital ship. It's during their third and final run that Bert and Bill take down a Messerschmitt, a Luftwaffe fighter.

The enemy is coming straight for them. The plane seemed to have come out of nowhere. Despite the fear that's making everything either slow down or speed up, they get the Messerschmitt in their sights. Then they let him have it. The fighter with its belly full of shells goes down in flames, smoke and cheers. The Highlanders have shot down a German fighter plane. Nevertheless, the chaos on the water continues.

The order to withdraw is given late that morning instead of early afternoon as planned. It has been 10 hours of hell. The Highlanders never made it to shore.

The news of the failed raid is sent to England by a carrier pigeon:

Very heavy casualties in men and ships. Did everything possible to get men off but in order to get any home had to come to sad decision to abandon remainder?
This is a joint decision by Force Commanders. Obviously lacked surprise.
General Roberts

Entire battalions are lost at Dieppe and many men are wounded. Around 4,963 Canadians fought and 2,210 return to England, including Ed and his men. A Calgary Highlander did die in the battle. Captain Theodor Marie Insinger was aboard the destroyer H.M.S. *Calpe* when he was killed by a shell strike. He's one of 913 Canadians who lost their lives in the fray.

In the boat on the way to England, there are so many wounded that there aren't enough stretchers. When someone is pronounced dead, he's flipped overboard and another man takes his stretcher. Ed can't bear to watch the bodies being thrown into the ocean. A few hours ago, that was a living and breathing person.

Back in England, the Highlanders who had been left behind, including Russ, had watched the sky fill with planes and anti-aircraft fire. They knew something huge was in the air. When they discover that Mortar Platoon 3, one of their own, had been involved in Dieppe, they're astounded. The men are sent to Portsmouth to aid the wounded and guard the prisoners.

When Ed walks off the landing craft, he's given a shot of hot rum. Before he and the other men from Mortar Platoon 3 can rest after all they've been through, they need blankets. The quartermaster won't give them any because he thinks they're trying to scam him. That is until Bert cuffs him. Then the Highlanders get what they need including new teeth for another soldier.

Those who had been left out of Dieppe see the carnage the raid wrought and some of them are glad to have missed the brutal fight. Others want to hear all about what it's like to see action. Ed's upfront about the battle with his mates and someone pens a poem about the raid a couple of days later. It's published in *The Glen*, the Highlander newsletter, on Aug. 21, 1942. Canadians at Dieppe by F. W. M. describes men full of courage and men who deserve to have their names remembered by history.

All were fearless fighters,
All did do their best,
None flinched amongst them –
They were worthy of the test.
Canadians at Dieppe by F. W. M.

Red remembers a frightening day of tumult and turmoil.

I said, "If this is war you can send me home tomorrow!"
On the way back to England, we had 6 dead and 25 wounded on our craft.
Our captain of the boat said he had been on 20 raids to France but this one is by far the worst one.
I believed him.

Courtesy of the *Private Papers of T G Anderson*, Esplanade Arts & Heritage Centre, City of Medicine Hat

Corporal Amos Wilkens is another one of the Highlanders at Dieppe who knows what the men went through.

I, well, we never landed - we are manning anti-aircraft guns.
But on the approach to the beach, there is a piece of shrapnel that took the top of a man's head off, a piece of his skull as big around as that glass.
If I live to be 200, I'll always be able to see that laying there on the bottom of that landing craft.
Two of our sergeants shot down a German plane. But we are right there and we are in and out of the beach several times packing up the wounded. It is, I guess, scary, but I was fortunate in a way. I was a corporal at the time and I've always thought that, to have responsibility in a case like that, is not a bad thing, because it takes you out of yourself. You have other people and other things to think about.

Courtesy of *The Memory Project*, Historica Canada

The day after returning from the bloody shores of Dieppe, sergeants Bert and Bill are drinking away their "sorrows" in a pub in Chichester when a bunch of American soldiers walk in. Bert asks what the boys are doing in England.

"We've come over to win the war for you," says a U. S. soldier.

That is not the right thing to say to two men who were just in Dieppe. Bert hits the guy right through a French door. The Highlander chaps are in the mood for a fight they can win and let's just say, the pub isn't the same after the brawl.

Later, the friends start feeling guilty and think they'll be bumped down to privates if the pub owner complains about the altercation. So, Bert and Bill go and talk to him. The pub owner tells them he has never seen a fight like that before and not to worry about the damage.

Bert and Bill are two of the Highlanders at Dieppe who garner the regiment's first battle honour in the war: a mention in dispatches. Bert thinks Lieut. Jack Reynolds should have received recognition too for saving the lives of his men. He blames this oversight on Lt.-Col. Donald MacLauchlan, the Highlander's commander, whom Lieut. Jack Reynolds does not respect.

Despite the heavy losses to Canada (German losses paled in comparison), the experience of Dieppe is valuable to the Allies. The leaders realize it's going to take more than tanks and surprise to defeat the Nazis.

Ed knows he flinched more than once during the raid as soldiers were blown up around him. But rather than relive the memories, he tucks them away. He rarely talks about the raid. No one who wasn't there can imagine what he went through. He'll stay silent for the rest of his life about Dieppe. His experiences there are best left in the past.

CHAPTER FIVE

LOOKING TOWARDS THE FUTURE

ED MEETS DOROTHY

Dieppe ripped the Canadian army to shreds and it needs rebuilding. With actual combat experience behind them, military leaders introduce new ideas, new manoeuvres and new artillery to Ed and his Calgary Highlanders in England.

There is something to celebrate in the middle of the war -- Russ and Phyllis are getting married. They tie the knot on Oct. 25, 1942, in England. As Dorothy is Phyllis' best friend, she's a bridesmaid at their wedding. Ed, being Russ' brother, is his best man. The rest is history! Well, there is more.

"That's one good looking man," says Dorothy to herself when first meeting Ed. His wide smile tugs at her heart and it doesn't hurt that he's a very handsome Irish Canadian with his dark hair and blue eyes. Being easy on the eyes is his "in" with Dorothy because he certainly doesn't impress her with his dancing at the wedding. She says English guys are really good dancers but Ed can't dance at all. He kind of shuffles along until Dorothy teaches him some steps.

Ed and Dorothy start courting. Whenever Ed and Russ have leave, they take the train to Reading. Ed treats Dorothy to the cinema to see a picture playing at Odeon Cinema, one of six in Reading. Sometimes they go for a walk or just talk to each other. He tells Dorothy about his family in Didsbury and about his five brothers and three sisters. Another thing that's attractive to Dorothy about Ed is his mother's care packages. Millie sends him parcels with chocolate bars in it. Dorothy really likes chocolate bars and Ed gives his to her. The candy's made sweeter because of the rationing in the U.K. – you can't buy it in the shops. Dorothy says Ed himself is a sweet guy.

Ed and Dorothy also spend many hours with Russ and Phyllis at her parent's house on Battle Street in Reading. The Tuckers buy or barter food from the black market to feed the couples. They are fond of Dorothy and her Canadian boyfriend. George and Alice, Dorothy's mum and dad, are also impressed with Ed. They like his pleasant nature and smile. At this point, Dorothy isn't thinking about a future with him. She has her own life: a job, her air warden work, singing, dancing, friends and the League of Health and Beauty. Ed has his life that centres on being a soldier – a Canadian soldier at that.

What is Canada to Dorothy? A cold country with bears. Why would she leave her family and friends to go there? It's going to be a couple more years until she starts thinking of Canada as a place for her. Reading is her home sweet home.

Meanwhile, in Canada, Ed's friend Earl Cummins joins the Royal Canadian Air Force. Another buddy, George Morasch, becomes a Calgary Highlander on Nov. 12, 1942. He is Ed's younger friend from Didsbury and the two will cement their friendship as soldiers.

Top left, left to right: Ed's brother Baillie, mother Millie, father Ollie and younger siblings Garry, Audrey and Joan.
Top right: Russ and Phyllis at their wedding.
Bottom, back row, left to right: Ed's brothers Baillie, Frank and brother-in-law Johnny Malaka.
Front row, left to right: Ed's siblings Audrey, Joan and Lorna (Carleton) Malaka.
Photos: Carleton Family

George enlists at age 19 and does his basic training in Camrose, Alberta. He's transferred back to Currie Barracks in Calgary and within several days, told he's shipping out. A train carries him across the country to Halifax where he's put aboard the troopship Queen Elizabeth and what he calls "the fastest transport ship at the time." There are 20,000 troops and staff on the ship…and only lifeboats for 8,000. The Battle of the Atlantic is in full swing and U-boats (German submarines) are a constant threat. The ship uses evasive measures to avoid them – changing course every seven minutes as that's how long it takes a U-boat to detect and zero in on a ship. George disembarks in Glasgow, Scotland and is sent via train to Aldershot. There, he's posted to the Calgary Highlanders D Company as a Bren gunner private.

A new year, 1943, brings the same old thing to the Highlanders – drills, education, exercises, practice, instruction – you can call it a variety of words but they all mean the equivalent of…training. How frustrating for the lads.

R. B. Bennett, honourary Calgary Highlander colonel, pays the soldiers a visit on Feb. 12 in Bognor Regis. Ten days before, Nazi forces had collapsed during the long and drawn out Battle of Stalingrad. It's Germany's first major defeat. Later that spring, Italy and Germany are defeated by the Allies in North Africa and in July 1943, Italian's fascist dictator, Benito Mussolini, is arrested by his own government, partly due to the Allied invasion of Sicily. This is all setting the stage for Italy's surrender.

A Visit from Ike

British Prime Minister Winston Churchill has been credited for calling Italy "Europe's soft underbelly."[37] Attacking France directly was out of the question, it was a German stronghold, but Italy, Italy could be the way into Fortress Europe. After repeated Allied bombings and shortages of food among other troubles, Italy is in turmoil in more ways than one. July 1943 saw the Allies, including Canadian troops, take Sicily and Benito Mussolini was deposed.

The Calgary Highlanders are stationed on the west coast of Scotland undergoing commando training in October. They're climbing cliffs, running obstacle courses, climbing mountains and, of course, marching. They have to hike to Calgary, Scotland, a hamlet on the Ilse of Mull, and about a 20 km (12.4 mi) trek. The lads who are from Calgary, Canada aren't too pleased about the long trek to the Scottish namesake.

Ed and George are from Didsbury. Bet they're glad they don't have to walk all the way to Didsbury, U.K. (it's near Manchester) from Scotland. That's a 548 km (341 mi) hike! The one good thing about Scotland is the bottled whiskey is bigger, cheaper and goes down smoothly after a long day of marching. The men are enjoying their time amongst the strong brogues and ancient castles although Ed is a long way from Dorothy.

In the meantime, the Allies are pushing further into Italy. They hold southern Italy and the Germans are holding fast to northern Germany. The Gully, Ortona, Gustav Line and the Hitler Line are synonymous with intense and violent fighting where Canadians are involved.

---

37. Italy was Canada's longest Second World War army campaign.

Ed is stuck training on the foggy U.K. shores while the war goes on all around him: Europe, Russia, Africa, the Atlantic and the Pacific. In the spring of 1944, the Highlanders are sent to the coast where they look across the English Channel and see occupied France.

On a chilly night patrolling the shoreline, George Morasch's teeth are chattering something awful. A sergeant asks him to take a sip of rum to warm up. George says no thank you several times until the sergeant pleads with him to have a drink just for him. George finally has a gulp and his teeth stop clacking and his body stops shaking.

On Apr. 2, 1944, the Highlanders are woken from sleep by rain that soaks their bedding. There are blankets drying all over the place in the morning. A diary on this day gives some insight into the dealings of Lt.-Col. Donald MacLauchlan, the Highlander's commander. To some, including fellow officers, MacLauchlan is not a good leader: high-strung and aloof. Whatever the men think of him, that April day he's studying assault crossings with company commanders. The diary author writes:

Many good arguments arose and the morning is very instructive. The troops spent a rest day today. The writer goes on to say that the ADJT (Adjutant – a military appointment given to an officer who assists the commanding officer with unit administration) has a meeting with Rear Div. HQ [Rear division Headquarters] and comes back with "a number of good points with him."

It is pointed out to him that although it is desirable to get the training down as realistically as possible, due to the limitations of grounds and roads, it is not always possible.
However, we should not lose our perspective in such matters or confuse the speed of movement on these exercises with that of actual ops [operations]. It is also pointed out that all administrative problems would be corrected on this exercise – the last of its kind.

The platoons relax by playing softball while the pipers return to the Highlanders. The musicians have been gone for two weeks. Someone else who had gone on leave is Russ. Always a bit of a rabble-rouser, he goes a little longer than allowed and is written up.

L/Cpl Carleton returned from leave today – one day late. It appears that while on leave, his wife presented him with a baby girl, but took a turn for the worst. However, all are doing well now with the exception of L/Cpl (Rusty) Carleton, who is not doing so well waiting to "explain" to Lt. Col. D. G. MacLauchlan. WWII Diary (P) Apr. 2, 1944

The baby is Maureen, born at the end of March. Russ, who is nicknamed Rusty and Rusky, has another name now: dad.

***

Ed and Dorothy see each other whenever Ed has leave. The couple goes for fish and chips or walks around Reading. Eventually, Ed has to return to the Calgary Highlanders. Each goodbye is tough. Ed doesn't know when he'll see Dorothy again and Dorothy doesn't know if she'll ever see Ed again. He's a soldier and at any moment, he could be ordered to the battlefield.

A visit from U. S. General Dwight "Ike" Eisenhower on May 29, 1944 perks up the bored Highlanders. Eisenhower is the Supreme Allied Commander of the Allied Expeditionary Force (appointed on December 1943) and impresses many of the Highlanders.

Ike is in Shorncliffe, an English Channel port town, for a ceremonial inspection.

Afterwards, he chats with the Highlanders, assuring them that they will indeed be used to help bring the Axis powers down. Ike is a powerful and charismatic man and gestures for the soldiers to gather around him. They relax and break ranks and listen as he tells them about the rough times ahead. He also has good things to say about the regiment and Canada. A couple of days later, May 31, 1944, the Canadians (except for the 1st Canadian Armoured Brigade) are put on leave. D-Day is coming.

JUNE 6, 1944 - D-DAY

A couple of months after Russ became a father, Allied Forces land on the beaches of Normandy, France. The Calgary Highlanders aren't involved at the start of the liberation of Western Europe on Jun. 6, 1944 however, other Canadian, British and American forces (14,000 of the 150,000 Allied troops are Canadian) are assaulting the heavily fortified coast. Five beaches are designated landing spots in Operation Overlord, another name for D-Day, and the Canadians storm Juno Beach by land, sea and air. The Allies are about to break through Hitler's Atlantic Wall (the fortified French side of the English Channel).

Hough Nordlund from Prince Albert, Sask., a lieutenant with the Royal Canadian Naval Volunteer Reserve, says landing on the beach is nothing short of terrifying. Lights flashing on the shore are supposed to lead the men to the beach but they cannot see because of thick smoke. The noise is just as thick and you can't distinguish one sound from another. Even if a soldier sinks into the water, he'll still be able to hear the heavy mixture of shooting, bombing and clangs of bullets off the LC-3 (landing craft), a small personnel-carrying barge. The men must move forward in the din despite their mates dying in front of them.

That day, the skies over Reading, are darkened by thousands of Allied aircraft, all in a V-formation and all flying in the same direction. The air is filled with what sounds like the hum of a million wasps. It must hurt to hear for the many people who have loved ones heading into the battle. Ed is going to face the front, too.

The Allies get a foothold in France on D-Day, forcing the Axis powers to take a step back. The Canadians have made it further than any of their Allies. D-Day is a small victory yet it has not been easy. One of the British main objectives is Caen, a city at the junction of several important roads, railways and waterways. They need to break the Norman capital in order to get to Paris but they hadn't made their target. The German's entrench themselves there and on Jun. 7, counterattack.

Stationed in Folkestone, the Highlanders have seen convoys in the channel on their way to France as well as Axis shells from long-range guns that had fallen in the area. From the French shores, doodlebugs (doodlebugs are also called buzz-bombs. They are bombs with wings that made a buzzing noise) whir on their way to England. The bombs are set for certain targets and when they reach their locations, their engines turn off. Those on the ground have 15 seconds to find cover. Ed's heartbeat speeds up a little when he hears a doodlebug cackling above the Highlanders' camp. Some action spills over into Folkestone. A buzz-bomb is shot down by Spitfires and ends up in town – landing with a huge boom. Allied convoys on the water are often attacked and some ships have a fiery end.

All this sets up the Highlanders to believe they're heading to battle for real. There's a heightened sense of anticipation. The soldiers are ready. During the wait for battle, the Highlanders are marching, learning street-fighting techniques and how to clear houses.

At the end of June, Caen remains in German hands but Cherbourg, one of the U.S. Army's first major targets, has been liberated. The French city was a significant base for German forces and now it's in the Allied's hands. They can advance south and have port access. General Montgomery moves his headquarters to northern France.

While fight wages into the beginning of July, on Dominion Day, the Highlanders are playing softball in England. That afternoon, the men get their marshalling orders. They are moving to the coast tomorrow and about to get their chance to prove their mettle.

The next morning it's cool and grey in Folkestone. Some of the men have a hard time getting out of bed. Not Ed. He likes to rise early. He has had a good breakfast and then is marched to trains with the rest of the lads and their baseball bats and mitts. They're on their way to Newick Chaley.

At the train station, British officers meet the Highlanders and the men are taken to the marshalling camp. They have an excellent supper and Ed's spirit is high as he heads to bed, ready to take on what tomorrow brings.

Not even the downpour on the morning of Jul. 3 can dampen the Highlanders' enthusiasm when they wake up. It's raining so hard they can't do any training. Not that Ed is disappointed about that. The lads are handed "Mae West" life jackets (the inflated front vests make people appear buxom) and vomit bags. The canteen has beer and so the men are occupied for the time being. Some of the soldiers play an afternoon baseball game when the rain lets up.

The rain is back on Jul. 4. The Highlanders are issued embarkation cards with ship numbers and handed 200 French francs. Tommy-cookers (a portable stove), 24-hour rations, emergency rations and water sterilization pills are also given to the Highlanders. Somehow, Ed manages to stuff the extra gear into his small pack. He carries it on board the boat he has been assigned and claims his hammock.

The *Henry Austin*, a U.S. cargo ship, the *S.S. Isle of Guernsey*, a twin-screw, oil-burning steamship, and a New Zealand freighter *Marwarri* are among the vessels heading to France. As well, the Black Watch and the Régiment de Maisonneuve are coming along with the Highlanders as part of the 5th Canadian Infantry Brigade. The ships loaded with troops and vehicles sail into the Thames Estuary. However, there has been a change of plans. They're not leaving until tomorrow. It's back to camp for Ed.

The next morning, tea and cakes are served at the docks before Ed and the other men board the ships. It's not until that Jul. 5 evening, that Ed, Russ (both C Company) and George Morasch (D Company) start moving towards France. It's finally the Calgary Highlanders turn to fight. They're putting their years of training to the ultimate test.

The Highlanders are on their way into the fray. Dorothy never gets the chance to give Ed a hug and a kiss goodbye. She never gets the chance to hold him tightly. He never gets the chance to tell her not to worry. Dorothy paces when she's stressed and so she walks back and forth in the living room of 55 Grange Avenue, wringing her hands the whole time Ed is gone. Ed, on the other hand, takes things as he goes along. He has a job to do and the Highlanders have been training for this for four years. Nevertheless, Dorothy's whole world is being swallowed by a black hole when Ed leaves England.

When the convoy nears the French shore in the morning of Jul. 6, the soldiers transfer to smaller landing crafts that take them ashore near Courseulles. Ed takes in the peaceful scene – calm water, a nice beach ahead and no enemy to be seen. In the harbour, there is a sea of vessels: landing crafts, destroyers, cruisers and many other ships and boats.

The Highlanders are transferred to land and march into France. It's a hot afternoon and Ed is sweating through his uniform. He's cooled off by the rain that falls in the evening. The next day, Jul. 7, there's more waiting. Then, in the evening, Allied airplanes start pounding away at Caen. Ed sees the planes overhead and hears the whooshing, whines and rat-ta-ta-tat of artillery coming from the city. The Canadians face German Panzer (armoured) troops including the elite 12th SS Panzer Division. The division is made up of fanatical *Hitler Jugend*, Hitler Youth, and the teenagers are steeped in Nazi ideals.

On Jul. 9, Lt-Co MacLauchlan attends a talk with "Monty" at the 2nd Canadian Division headquarters. During the meeting, a report arrives saying Caen has fallen. Victory is fleeting when another report arrives soon after. Caen has not fallen but is expected to later in the day. Indeed, the northern part of the city is occupied by the 3rd Canadian Division and the 3rd British Division by evening.

The Highlanders are still waiting for their turn to fight. They are biding their time near Banville, near Juno Beach, and have dug slit trenches (narrow trenches) for cover from the Nazi planes. It's quiet and George Morasch and some other soldiers stroll around the area. On one excursion, he sees a beautiful purple glove on the ground. He picks it up and there are a man's fingernails inside.

The Highlanders are on the move again. They're put into vehicles and in the evening, driven to Cussy, a hamlet on the northwest outskirts of Caen. Cussy is near Abbaye d'Ardenne,[38] a centuries-old monastery that has just been liberated by the Regina Rifles.

Ed and his mates aren't on a jaunt through the lovely French countryside. It's dark but even if they could see around them, they are looking at devastation. The area has been shelled heavily by Canadian troops and the Germans. As the Highlander's convoy approaches Cussy on Jul. 11, the Germans start firing at them. Ed sighs in

---

38. The Normandy countryside is thought to be where approximately 156 Canadian prisoners of war were supposedly executed by the 12th SS Panzer Division (the Hitler Youth) in the summer of 1944. Abbaye d'Ardenne is one location where 18 Canadians were killed.

relief when he realizes the shells are landing well past where he's supposed to sleep.

The lads have already experienced some sleepless nights and long days due to bombings and the sights and sounds of combat. Now they're introduced to the smell of war. George walks into a church and suspended across the rafters, are dead German soldiers. He's told they were spies.

"The smell is something awful," says George, "it is horrendous."

German planes fly over the Abbaye and the Highlanders respond with their Ack Ack guns. Pipe Major Neil Sutherland digs a trench so deep the men joke that they'll have to lower a rope to pull him out. Ed, Russ and some of their mates scout the area. The Germans have left some of their equipment behind along with paperwork. Some lucky Highlanders find German cigars and some bottles of French wine. Amid the laughter and the cheers, an order goes out that'll send the Highlanders to the front tomorrow.

The Germans have been shelling the Highlanders every day and not hit one man. That changes on the afternoon of Jul. 12. The Highlanders have their first causalities in the war when three men are killed and two are wounded. Padre Percy holds a service for the soldiers at the Abbaye d'Ardenne.Crosses are made to mark their graves. Ed and the rest of the Highlanders are raring to get to the front line and settle the score but the 5th Canadian Infantry Brigade will be staying put. The Germans return though, flying over Ed's head. The Highlanders spray the Nazi planes with fire.

There's no doubt who the lads are up against: tough and war experienced German defences. Red Anderson knows these soldiers aren't going to give an inch without a very tough fight.

Every time we were going into battle, they would tell us what we would be doing and what German Division we would be fighting. You didn't mind fighting but when we were up against the 12th S.S. Division, the shit hit the fan. They were 18 and 19-year old kids that would die for Hitler. I wasn't fussy on dying for Winston Churchill.

When we captured some of them, they would say "Hitler is our God." (Big deal).

Courtesy of the *Private Papers of T G Anderson*, Esplanade Arts & Heritage Centre, City of Medicine Hat

The following day, a combined British and Canadian force is halted just outside of Caen by extremely violent hand-to-hand fighting. Locals flee the area and two French civilians have wandered into the Highlanders' area. They're being interviewed by military police who will decide what to do with them.

Tension is mounting in the Highlander camp. Some of it's washed away with a bath. Water is drawn from a well near a destroyed house and baths are set up by the 2nd Mobile Bath Unit. Another treat offered is a bottle of beer for everyone. Officers get a bottle of scotch. Everyone gets their mail when it arrives and Ed is hoping for a letter from Dorothy. There it is. He reads it several times over, chuckling at her quips and wishing she wouldn't worry so much about him.

Once asleep, Ed doesn't have much time to dream about his sweetheart. The Highlanders are ordered to get out of bed at 4:30 a.m. Heavy gunfire shouts out on France's *fête nationale*, Bastille Day, Jul. 14. The Germans drop in on the Highlanders with coloured smoke and shells for breakfast. Six Focke-Wulf fighter planes are dealt with by one solo Spitfire.

It shoots one German plane down, another one crashes and the rest speed off into the horizon.

The rest of the day is uneventful. Lt.-Col. MacLauchlan attends a service for France's national holiday. A local French woman has made her daughter's hair ribbon into presents for the officers. She has cut up the bow and hands the pieces of blue, red and white, the colours of France, to the men.

Over the next couple of days, there's more shelling. At night, flares light up the darkness. It's one time Ed can't sleep and he looks like the rest of his mates: black circles under his eyes and red in them. If there is a time to go to the paymaster for francs, it's now amid the blasts from the enemy. "Roly" Higgins can't keep his books straight when he has to keep jumping into a slit trench. To ease the nerves, Pipe Major Sutherland plays for an hour.

It's Monday on Jul. 17 and that means washing day. Ed scrubs his clothing and then hangs his undergarments and other items under the branches of trees or bushes. It's important the laundry not be seen from the air by the enemy. The weather has been a mixed bag recently: warm, then cool, then rain. The lads are a bit rank and a sponge bath ensures they won't be smelled in the air either.

Some men scout for GAFs (German Air Force, Luftwaffe) who might have dropped into the area. But no enemy is uncovered. Other Luftwaffe appear in the evening and two planes are shot down. The bombings by the Germans are increasingly hitting close to the Highlanders.

Jul. 18 is the launch of Operation Atlantic, a Canadian offensive during the Battle of Normandy in conjunction with Operation Goodwood, a British offensive. The goal is capturing the eastern, southwestern and southeastern area of Caen. The Highlanders have their orders: march into the city and be ready for the order to join the offensive.

As Ed waits for battle, the Allies and Axis fight viciously along the River Orne and through villages such as Touffréville and Troarn. The German resistance is strong and the 88-mm guns of the Nazi Tiger and Panther tanks annihilate 16 British tanks in only a few minutes.

The Highlanders aren't immune from the combat surrounding them. They're hit by German mortar. Fourteen Highlanders are wounded. Two are dead: Pte. Marshall Watts and Pte. G. W. Reddington. Regardless of the tragedy, Lt.-Col. MacLauchlan says the men must eat. Ed's meal is served on time for once.

The following day, the Allied forces strike back and finally, on Jul 19, Caen[39] is liberated. With the city firmly in Allied hands, the Highlanders march through rubble that was once historical buildings and sites.

"While going through the city, the devastation is horrendous," says George. "Dead animals lay in the street. The smell is beyond [anything you can imagine], how could you ever stand such a smell?"

The city is still being targeted by the Nazis and shells whiz by and explode in the distance. The men are on their way to Fauberge de Vaucelles and then Fleury-sur-Orne.

39. Today, there's a memorial garden overlooking the southern part of Caen.

This is George's first time in combat and the Highlanders' first time fighting as a unit. It's Ed's second time facing the Germans. He knows what is coming. Ed isn't terribly religious but he has respect for the church. He received a Bible when he was nine years old and he still has it. He says some prayers while thinking a great deal about his family and Dorothy.

At Fleury-sur-Orne, the Highlanders are to storm Hill 67, a ridge connected to Verrières Ridge, and take it at all costs. Hill 67 (also called Point 67) rises out of the countryside. Before the war, the rolling countryside and quaint villages were perfect for tourists wanting a quintessential French holiday. Today, Hill 67 and surrounding ridges offer perfect viewpoints for the much-feared SS Panzer divisions – they can see everything. The Nazis are determined to push the Allies back to the ocean and out of France. They are prepared to not give up an inch of Hill 67.

The Highlanders have a long and hot wait in the summer heat before they are given the order to move forward. The Highlander pipers accompany the troops for the first and last time. The men start wading through golden grain fields hiding the enemy.

George says the grain is waist-high, even up to their chests in some spots. It makes a great cover for the Germans, who start shooting at the Highlanders. The lads duck and take cover as quickly as possible. George gets down while bullets are zooming near his feet. He's fortunate the bullets hit the ground and not him.

The Canadians are struggling to get through the field.

"It is horrible," says George.

They finally reach the hill and make it to the crest. Here, they dig their slit trenches as quickly as they can, trying to get out of the way of the Germans' shelling.

"You could see there are fewer Calgary Highlanders," says George. "They must have been killed or wounded going through the grain field."

A fellow Bren gunner, Bob Harbut, calls to George, asking him to come into his slit trench.

"Come, George — come as quickly as possible," Bob says. "Come to me and we'll be together."

George runs to the trench and dives in. The Highlanders duck their heads while the heavy, heavy shelling continues around them. When George peeks over the trench, the hole he just vacated is now a large crater. It had been hit. He's glad Bob had called out to him.

George had seen Ed before they entered the grain field.[40] He had jumped a caragana hedge to get to his childhood friend. They had wished each other good luck and locked their index fingers together for a moment. There are so many courageous Highlanders lads, far away from home and loved ones, who are putting their lives on the line. Thank you, boys.

---

40. George Morasch still tears up 70 years later when he talks about meeting Ed. He says Ed was such a prominent, well-respected, honourable man that there is no doubt he could have become an officer if he hadn't been wounded. Interview with George A Morasch (2019)

Wounded

We'll meet again
So will you please say "Hello"
To the folks that I know
Tell them I won't be long
We'll Meet Again by Vera Lynn

The Calgary Highlanders reach the top of Hill 67 as the Germans rush down it on Jul. 19, 1944. However, one of the Germans' military tactics is a counter defence – which means destroying what they've just given up. Here they come at Ed – with tanks, machine guns and bombs. It's a fight for life.

Ed and C Company are positioned on the southwest corner of the hill. The Highlanders can't see much from their post, but the Germans have a commanding view of everything.

The enemy, including the 1st SS Panzer Division, is pounding the Highlanders.

C Company and Ed firmly hold their position against great odds, as do the other Highlander companies, all the while being under intense fighting. Fortunately, the German numbers are low and they don't have the strength to take back the hill. Unfortunately, six Highlanders are dead and 92 wounded. Many are from C Company.

Morale is high amid the wet, dirty and exhausted men. Ed gets some shut-eye here and there. It's tough to sleep when the Germans are banging on your door. The lads joke that today has given MacLauchlan a few more grey hairs. Pipe Major Sutherland's pipes are gone. They were blown up when the ammunition truck he was riding in exploded from enemy fire. No matter what though, the "green horners" proved they have what it takes to be soldiers and have proven their worth.

Ed and his mates are tired but feeling good when dawn breaks on Jul. 20. The Germans haven't quite given up and are being a nuisance. However, the Highlanders are ready for another day of battle.

Snipers have the Highlanders in their sights. The Highlanders are holding Hill 67 and it's the end of Operation Goodwood in the southwest of Caen. It is also the end of Ed being a soldier. Sometime on that rainy mid-July day, he's shot in the head by a marksman. Ed's losing litres of blood and is taken from the battlefield and transported to a British field hospital in Bayeux. He's leaving alive though, unlike many of his buddies. The bitter fighting has ripped apart his friends – mates he had known for a long time. George remains on the battlefield, holding tight until the order to move forward is called.

"In the morning they took a roll call of D Company," says George, "All that is left and alive is one officer, one corporal and 11 men. I am one of the men."

He can't help but think about the rest of the surviving boys.

"Did the Germans nearly annihilate the Calgary Highlanders when the regiment captured Hill 67?"

Above: A photo from an unidentified newspaper showing Ed (standing left) with fellow soldiers and a mortar gun.
Below: Camp Shilo.
Photos: Carleton Family

Unknown man and Ed (right) during respite after his injury received on Hill 67. Photo: Carleton Family

Twenty-one Highlanders are killed, 10 die of wounds and 97 are wounded in three days of fighting for Hill 67 and the village of Etavaux. Ed discovers that Russ has also been injured on the same day. He was struck in the back of the head by shrapnel.

George isn't among the wounded, but he can't stop coughing and is loaded into a Jeep (the ambulance was blown up) and sent to the hospital. Alongside him is a church minister.

"What brave men they [ministers] are. Their concern for all the men involved. They are not armed, they only carried a Bible," George says.

In the Jeep, George passes the grain fields where he had fought so hard to stay alive. Like Ed, he's also taken to a British field hospital in Bayeux, where he is treated amongst fellow soldiers and Axis PoWs.

Across the world in Didsbury, the Carletons wait for their boys to return home. Mother Millie is constantly in tears. The youngest girl in the family, Audrey, sees her mother always crying. Millie and Ollie talk about the war openly and Audrey, around 10 years old, hears the tales of evil doings by the Axis powers. When she and her older sister Joan receive dolls as presents, they don't cuddle the playthings. They take them out into the backyard and smash their heads in. Why? Because the dolls have been made in Japan and that's a bad place.

Life goes on for Dorothy in Reading while she waits for Ed to return to her. She keeps abreast of the news through the wireless, newspapers and newsreels. However, she doesn't get the whole story. It's not known which news coverage is censored (the

U.K. government says censorship is voluntary) and there's a lot of government propaganda floating around. Dorothy has no choice but to "keep calm and carry on"[41] – a slogan on a British government poster. Then, Dorothy's world crashes around her. Ed is wounded.

It's Jul. 25, 1944,[42] when a telegram states that Ed has officially been reported wounded in action on Jul. 21. The nature and extent of his injuries aren't known. He's in hospital and when further information comes about, the family will be contacted.

This is the second telegram the Carletons have received in two days. The first was for Russ. Audrey runs to their father's blacksmith shop both times to tell him the terrible news. It's a sad time for anyone with family serving. Anyone with someone involved in the war is always on pins and needles because they don't know what's happening. They also have to wait days, weeks and months for news.

In England, Dorothy is beside herself with worry. She doesn't know if Ed's going to live or die. She thinks about the man she loves, a genuinely caring man who has shared his heart, time and chocolate bars with her. She's numb for days and everything is a blur.

Telegrams are usually followed with a letter from the military and sometimes a personal letter from an officer or a chaplain. On Aug. 28, 1944, H/Major W. H. Morgan, District Chaplin M.D. 13, Calgary, Alberta, with the Department of National Defence, writes Ollie and Millie.

> *We wish to express to you our most sincere sympathy as we know he* [Ed] *is so far away from you, it will cause you much worry and anxiety. I can assure you, however, that every possible care and attention will be given to him, and, that as soon as it is possible, you will be hearing direct from overseas.*

Ed has been flown to England, where a steel plate is put in the right side of his head to replace his missing skull bone. He's recovering in Aldershot, not too far from Reading. Dorothy takes the train to visit him. Ed doesn't know his brother is in the same hospital. Unlike Ed, Russ gets a plastic plate for his head wound instead of metal.

For two weeks, the brothers don't know they're only floors apart because there are so many soldiers being treated. A nurse finally puts two and two together and unites the lads. Meanwhile, George stays at the Bayeux field hospital for 23 days. He never returns to the front lines. The army discovers he has had two years of typing at school and so he's given a desk job. He keeps his Calgary Highlanders badges and uniform and spends the rest of the Second World War as a Highlander attached to the North Shore (New Brunswick) Regiment in Holland.

The Normandy campaign ends on Aug. 22, 1944. Canada suffers 18,700 casualties with more than 5,000 soldiers killed. Normandy is considered a monumental victory, especially for Canadians.[43] Ed, Russ and George survived it. Many others didn't.

---

41. Today, "Keep calm and carry on" is a popular internet meme.
42. Verrières Ridge: the bloodiest day also took place on Jul. 25, 1944. The Black Watch (Royal Highland Regiment) of Canada was led up an open ridge when it came under enemy fire. Only 15 of the approximately 300 men survived.
43. Some historians think the Canadians weren't ready for the battle while others say what Canada accomplished was exceptional.

Chapter Six

Mr. and Mrs. Ed Carleton

Liberation and a Wedding

In the late summer of 1944, the Calgary Highlanders are still in Normandy, sans Ed, Russ and George Morasch. After breaking through Hill 67, the Highlanders are fighting their way through the countryside and small towns such as May-sur-Orne, Bretteville and Clair Tizon as part of Operation Spring (Jul. 25, 1944 to Jul. 27, 1944). Spring, combined with the American attack Operation Cobra, is designed to move the Allies into Falaise and push German forces further from Normandy.

Tuesday, Jul. 24 is Go Day – or Go Night for the attack on May-sur-Orne. The Highlanders face assaults from land and air, and are further challenged because the Queen's Own Cameron Highlanders of Canada failed a mission to secure the start-line. It seems like the enemy has no shortage of fresh soldiers. (In fact, the Axis has cut tunnels into the limestone, creating a safe way to get reinforcements to the fight.) There are also German army snipers targeting Allied stretcher-bearers and Red Cross sites. The Germans are also gunning down their own soldiers who are being taken prisoner by the Highlanders. It is nasty and there's nowhere to hide.

C and A companies manage to make it to May-sur-Orne but they're driven back. The Highlanders fail to reach their objective and many are killed, wounded and missing but they call the battle a win. The Canadians had helped delay the Germans from heading towards the American offensive, and they've kept the Allies moving forward in France.

It's during Operation Spring that 5th Brigade commander Brigadier William Jemmett Megill is seeing the war's effect on the Highlanders' commander. He says Lt.-Col. MacLauchlan is nervous and his own men make different plans behind his back. Megill claims MacLauchlan doesn't have the inner strength to get through a war. He has the knowledge, he has the training but he doesn't inspire confidence in his men.

MacLauchlan was George Morasch's commanding officer before the Didsbury man was wounded. George says as a soldier, he knows Megill is doubtful about MacLauchlan. However, George respects Lt.-Col. MacLauchlan. It's under his command that the Highlanders are making an arduous night march under orders to seize Clair Tizon on Aug. 12, 1944.

The area is supposedly being supported on the right side by another brigade. The Highlanders are under heavy shell and mortar fire but press on. They aren't using the main road and have no idea where the Germans are positioned. In the morning, the Highlanders discover that not only are they on their own, but they're advancing into enemy territory. They collect prisoners who smell like they haven't had a bath in weeks and look like they haven't had a solid meal in that time, too. The Highlanders also capture a crossing and form a bridgehead over the River Laize and hold it.

The Highlanders are distinguishing themselves and taking up the lead while pursuing the retreating Germans.[44] They're among the first Allies to enter the medieval city of Rouen, France to a hearty welcome of wine, fruit and roses. Highlander Lt.-Col. Ross Ellis compares it to a very merry Stampede Parade.

Meanwhile, Paris is liberated, the Japanese army is facing losses in the Pacific and Russia is gaining momentum. It's September 1944 when the Highlander lads head to the port city of Dieppe[45] as liberators. George Whitehead is one of the first to parade through the streets. He had been with Ed during the 1942 raid. George goes back to the beach where his mortar platoon had tried to land and where hundreds of Canadians had been killed. He's astounded to find that the Germans could see every square inch of the stony coast. The Canadians never had a chance.

"It was sheer suicide to go in there," says George.

The Highlanders parade through Dunkirk, France, too. Amid the cheers, there's no doubt the men are tired and weary of battle. They've lost friends and family and many will never be the same again.

Ed is recovering from his injury in England. Dorothy is glad when he returns to her and holds her in his arms. He's back from the front, wounded but alive. Ed is missing his mates. He's been with them for four years and it's obvious he's not going back to the Highlanders. They miss him, too. Ed is a friend to many and well-respected. Dorothy visits Ed and tries to keep his spirits up with her songs and smiles.

Ed is now 27 and doesn't know what the future holds except for one thing: Dorothy. He asks her father, George, for her hand in marriage (as per tradition) and when he gets the all-clear, pops the question to 25-year-old Dorothy. Well, Dorothy somehow knows a proposal was coming. The couple has talked about moving to Canada and Dorothy knows Ed owns a gopher ranch back home. She doesn't really understand what that is but anyone who owns a ranch must be rich. Surely, the ranch is a large property on some nice countryside with horses and other animals. It's probably going to be a busy life but that doesn't scare her. She loves being active and being outdoors.

"Yes," says Dorothy to Ed's offer of marriage.

Little does she know what she's in for. Getting married in the middle of the Second World War, well, there aren't many luxuries. The wedding won't be a grand affair with thousands of dollars spent on outfits and food and wine and beer and the "perfect" venue. They only need a marriage licence and rings.

Approximately 48,000 women (British, European and other nationalities) marry Canadian servicemen during the Second World War. Dorothy and Ed's date is set for spring. They'll be wed on Mar. 3, 1945. England's feeling the pinch of wartime.

---

44. Lt.-Col. MacLauchlan earns a Distinguished Service Order for his outstanding leadership and personal courage when making advancements at Clair Tizon (Aug. 11, 1944, to Aug. 13, 1944). Gen. Megill says the honour bestowed upon MacLauchlan is warranted. *"I felt like he had thoroughly deserved it because he stuck through a job that made a great drain on someone with his particular makeup. It was hard. He didn't have the mental ability to shrug off the difficulties. In action, it was always a strain."* Interview with Gen. Megill, Kingston, May 23, 1992.
45. The war diary says the Canadians have a real score to settle with Dieppe.

Dorothy can't walk into a boutique and order a beautiful gown. Nor can she plan a big feast topped off with celebratory sweets. One thing she can be sure of is that Ed will be there. Other brides aren't so lucky. Those women who have fiancés still in active service, can't count on their men being at the end of the aisle. Sometimes the soldiers are called away for duty or aren't given leave and thus can't attend their own weddings.

There isn't a day when Ed doesn't think about his mates who remain on the front. The Allies (mainly U. S. and the Brits) launch Operation Market-Garden, the largest airborne operation in history, on Sept. 17. The areas of concentration are chiefly the Dutch cities of Eindhoven, Arnhem and Nijmegen. Market-Garden's main mission fails when the Allies can't secure a key bridge in the Netherlands, Arnhem, stalling their entry into Germany.

That fall of 1944, the Highlanders, along with the Black Watch and the Régiment de Maisonneuve, are part of the Battle of the Scheldt, the border area between northern Belgium and the southwestern Netherlands. The Allies need to knock the Germans out of their way to secure a critical port. The Nazis are not ceding and the Allies are face-to-face with serious resistance.

The Highlanders are an integral part of the Scheldt battle, a series of military operations and what has been called Canada's toughest Second World War campaign. On Sept. 18, the Highlanders are in Antwerp, Belgium. Antwerp is a port city, about 100 km (62 mi) inland on the Scheldt River, and of critical importance for the Allies, who need a safe shipping route to keep driving eastward. The Scheldt River flows past the port and empties into the North Sea, the entryway to Antwerp and where the Germans are staked out. To get access to the port, ships pass by the Scheldt estuary and through a canal, locks and then into the city. The Allies are holding Antwerp but the Germans aren't letting them rest and are constantly trying to blow up the locks.

At first, life is not too bad for the Highlanders in Antwerp. The men have access to "liquid refreshment" and entertainment. Nevertheless, war work remains and the Highlanders are tasked with securing a vital point for the Allies: Albert Canal. The waterway is near the town of Wyneghem and that's where the Highlanders find themselves next.

The canal is a watery border separating the Allies from the Germans. A damaged lock gate is picked as the spot for the Allies to advance and attack. The Highlanders have to secure the bridgehead so engineers can start building a bridge and get troops across.

Sergeant G.R. "Ken" Crockett[46] from Ed's company comes up with a plan to get to the enemy bank. Under the cover of darkness, he and eight volunteers cross the canal via a pipe. They make easy targets for the enemy as they go hand-over-hand while dangling over the water. On the other side, they silence a German sentry with a knife. This all makes way for the Highlanders to secure the bridgehead and the engineers to build the bridge, all under heavy enemy fire. The Germans have to take a step back and the Highlanders press on.

46. Sergeant G.R. "Ken" Crockett receives a Distinguished Conduct Medal for his actions.

***

The waterways into Antwerp pass through the Netherlands and include the Scheldt River as well as the banks of the South Beveland isthmus and peninsula and the island of Walcheren. This territory is controlled by Wehrmacht soldiers. The muddy and flooded terrain, the well-fortified German positions and miserable cold weather make fighting some of the worst in the war. The Canadians are fighting not only battle-hardened SS and Wehrmacht units but some of the most challenging geography on the Western Front.[47]

In early October, the Highlanders go from Belgium into an already liberated area of the Netherlands. Nevertheless, as they march closer to Hoogerheide and closer to the opening of the channel, the more enemy bullets start whizzing by. The Highlanders are under attack by elite paratroopers. The Highlanders push past them into the South Beveland peninsula.

The Highlanders are shouldering the worst of the fighting in the area but it's the Black Watch that'll suffer the most. On Oct. 13, the Black Watch is decimated while advancing over beet fields with no cover. There are 145 casualties, including 56 dead and 27 men taken prisoner. One company of 90 men had four survivors. The day becomes known as Black Friday.

Finally, South Beveland is rid of Germans but there is one area, the most important area, where they remain entrenched: Walcheren Island. The island is the entryway to Antwerp and its causeway, a strategic point. The causeway is a mile-long (1.6 km) land bridge with no cover, stretching from South Beveland to Walcheren Island. On Oct. 31, 1944, the 5th Canadian Infantry Brigade is ordered to take the eastern side. The Germans have been on the island for a few years now and have fortified their positions. They're not about to leave anytime soon and have been told not to surrender an inch of ground.

The Black Watch goes first. The Germans don't flinch and the Black Watch falls apart. It's time for the Highlanders. The lads are about to walk straight down the causeway and onto the island. Without any cover except for night, nor any means of protection except for some artillery support.

About 100 Highlanders in B Company head out. It's just before midnight on Halloween. Then, the Germans unleash the demons. The Highlanders start going down. There's confusion as the earth shakes and mud flies from the shelling. It's an inferno and the lads fall back. Later, D Company tries its luck advancing in the early light. They make it, allowing other companies to cross the causeway. The Germans are not letting up though and are hammering the soldiers. In the midst of heavy fighting, Sergeant Emile Laloge of D Company makes it to company headquarters and back to his platoon after arranging for artillery support. Not only that, but he picks up grenades lobbed at his men and tosses them into the sea. He then repairs a Bren gun dropped by a fallen soldier and starts firing it at the Germans.

---

47. As J.L. Granatstein says in the article *Five battles that shaped Canada*, the Canadian army went from being "untrained, ill-equipped and ill-led," to being "the best little army in the world."

The Highlanders are forced off the island. They suffer 65 casualties, of which 18 are killed. Two soldiers are missing in action (and presumed to have been killed by a 220-millimetre shell strike), and 45 are wounded. Major Ross Ellis (Acting Battalion Commander) says the Highlanders were cannon fodder. The Battle of the Walcheren Causeway is known in Highlander history for the bravery and sacrifice of its men. For his heroic efforts, Sergeant Emile Laloge earns the Distinguished Conduct Medal.

The Battle of the Scheldt ends on Nov. 9, 1944, and a Canadian merchant ship, *Fort Cataraqui*, leads a convoy into Antwerp. The Allies are looking ahead to victory while Axis forces scramble to find a way around defeat.

In England, happier memories are being made. Wedding planning is underway despite lean times. Because of rationing, there are long lineups for items such as liver and kidney and heart. Needless to say, fine materials aren't easily come by. Dorothy's sister Marjorie is up for the challenge and starts gathering coupons to trade for wedding gown material. The Fowler family barters with neighbours and trades cheese coupons for taffeta. Alice gets to work on her daughter's dress: a long-sleeve white gown with a high V-neckline. Dorothy makes her own veil and headdress. There. She's sorted. Now all she needs is the groom for the Mar. 3 nuptials.

The ceremony is at a local church, the Park Congregational Church on the corner of Palmer Park Avenue and Wokingham Road. It's spring in Reading and Dorothy's bouquet is filled with tulips while Marjorie, her bridesmaid, carries daffodils. Little nephew Roger, the ring bearer, has a carnation pinned to his suspenders. Dorothy's father gives her away to Ed, who looks dashing in his uniform, complete with plaid trousers and a big smile. Because of his head injury, his hair is clipped close on one side. His new look doesn't put off Dorothy and she beams at the man soon to be her husband. Standing beside Ed is his best man: his brother Russ.

Russ' wife and daughter don't attend the wedding. Maureen is 11 months old so it's too difficult for Phyllis to travel with the baby. Herb is the only other Carleton sibling to be at Ed's big day. Unfortunately, petrol rationing keeps the guest list to a minimum. Local friends like Olive Openshaw, who is seven months pregnant, and Margaret Voake, who is pregnant too, watch as Dorothy and Ed exchange gold rings and vows: promises to spend their lives together. Photos are snapped outside among the fresh blossoms of March. Spring is a time for growth and the couple is ready for their life together.

The reception is at the church hall and the celebrations spill into 55 Grange Avenue, making the home truly a place of wonderful memories. It's a lively party. How can it not be with Dorothy at the helm? There isn't a huge spread, but there are some refreshments thanks to friends and family who saved up their food coupons to help with the meal. As always, there's dancing and singing. The piano is put into use as popular wartime songs such as *Don't Sit Under the Apple Tree* and *When the Lights Go on Again* are belted out.

When the lights go on again all over the world
And the ships will sail again all over the world
Then we'll have time for things like wedding rings and free hearts will sing
When the lights go on again all over the world

Ed and Dorothy Carleton on their wedding day, Mar. 3, 1945, at Park Congressional Church in Reading, U.K.
Photo: Carleton Family

Left to right: Russ as best man, Dorothy's nephew Roger Tingay, Ed, Dorothy, Dorothy's father George and her sister Marjorie (Fowler) Tingay outside of the Park Congregational Church in Reading, U.K. on Mar. 3, 1945.
Photo: Carleton Family

The lights will go on in just over a month. Apr. 23, 1945 is the end of the blackout in the U. K. Meanwhile, Mr. and Mrs. Carleton are young and in love. The Carletons take a short honeymoon to the coast. They visit Hayling Island, in the south near Portsmouth. The island was part of the training grounds for a D-Day rehearsal but for the newlyweds, it's a place where they can be alone. They can't afford a nice hotel, but a "self-catering" holiday at a place where they cook their own meals, fits the bill. Strolling along the coast, the salty air and waves are refreshing after months of being in the city. The couple is enjoying their seaside jaunt before making decisions about the rest of their lives. They've just made one of the biggest commitments to each other and life is propelling them forward. Even so, Ed doesn't have a clue about what the couple is going to do next.

Apart Again

Dorothy's work as an Air Raid Warden is winding down in March of 1945. The Germans are still firing flying bombs (V1) and rockets (V2) at England from June 1944 to March 1945 but the targets are mainly large cities like London. However, on Mar. 19, a long-range rocket explodes over a small village about a 20-minute drive away from Reading. It leaves 12 people injured, damages homes, farms and two pubs. That's the last the Reading area sees of the hostilities. In late March, the Germans halt the air raids.

The Calgary Highlanders remain in Europe and in the middle of April 1945, they're part of the battle for Groningen, Netherlands and its liberation.

In Groningen,[48] George Whitehead thinks he has a shot at a medal when he stumbles upon six German soldiers sitting around a table in a home. He yells at his buddy to get over there because he's found some prisoners. His friend shouts back to hell with them, he's found eggs! However, he arrives and discovers one of the "Jerries" is an admiral.

Once the prisoners are out of the house and onto the street, other German soldiers start revealing themselves. For his troubles, George doesn't get a medal but he does pluck the admiral's watch from his wrist and 40,000 guilders (Dutch currency) from his pockets.

Then I went around and lifted their sleeves and everybody that had a wristwatch, I took them.

Interview with George Whitehead Mar. 20, 1992

Next, George and the Highlanders are off to Germany. On Apr. 26, they're directed to capture Gruppenbühren and Bulterei. They try to attack under the cover of smoke but it's blown away by a change in the wind. The lads are in full view and the enemy opens fire. The Highlanders keep going despite their falling friends and capture German guns and prisoners. Causalities for the Highlanders include six dead. This is the last battle where a Highlander is killed in action.

At the end of April, Adolf Hitler kills himself. It'll take a couple of weeks for the Second World War to wind down in Europe, and Germany surrenders on May 7, 1945. The Highlanders are in Nordenham, Germany when VE-Day (Victory in Europe) is announced on May 8. In Reading, Ed and Dorothy jump up and down for joy and join the partying in the streets.

On Sept. 2, 1945, the war is officially over when Japan formally surrenders. People around the globe breathe a sigh of relief. There are more celebrations in the streets and parties held in homes. Many a beer is had and many a Canadian soldier is kissed by those they liberated. Families and friends remember those they've lost.

Welcome Home

Ed's overseas service is terminated in September 1945 and he's discharged from the army near the end of October. His pay for his services: $1,399.99.

Soldiers are returning to their loved ones all over the world, launching the start of the baby boom (1946 to about 1965). Ed and Dorothy are a bit ahead of the curve – their son Mike is born in December 1945 (a respectable nine months after the wedding). Ed isn't at the hospital to meet his son. In August, he and Russ returned home to Canada.

Since Dorothy was pregnant then, she wasn't able to make the voyage. She'll join Ed in the following months. It's the only option for the new family. The U.K. is rebuilding its nation and economy and has a large war debt. Canada, on the other hand, has become a significant military power and economic player. New industries popped up during the war, such as motor vehicle manufacturing, and the country's agricultural and natural resources sector expanded too. Canada is where the jobs are going to be.

Ollie and Millie are happy to have all their five boys back, safe and sound. The boys, most definitely now men, see how much the worry and strain of war have aged their parents. More wrinkles and white hair. The siblings the men had last seen as children have

48. The Battle of Groningen is known as one of the largest divisional level urban battles (street fighting) fought by the Canadian Army.

grown up. Garry, the youngest of the nine children, had been a baby when Ed left. Now the baby is seven years old.

Didsbury looks much the same except there's something missing. Men who would be walking around the Alberta town are gone. Ed's mates Earl Cummins and George Morasch survived the war but so many others didn't. Ed passes the houses of friends who will never come home. He walks past his school, where students had planned for their futures, futures that are now in ruins. Ed thinks about what could have been had there not been a war. Being a practical man, he doesn't dwell in the past for too long. Besides, his future as a family man is hardly one to scoff at. Many of his pals will never get the chance to become fathers or old men.

In England, on the outskirts of London, the Calgary Highlanders are waiting to come home to Canada. How quickly a soldier, sailor or airperson returns to civilian life is determined by a Department of Veterans Affairs point system. There are points for the length of service, location — and if you're married, you get a 20 per cent bonus. At the top of the list are Pacific War service people. Once you're home, you get 30 days leave and then you're discharged from the military and become a veteran. (Unless you choose voluntary redeployment to the Pacific war theatre or occupied Europe.) Veterans, through the Veterans Charter, get some benefits too, such as a hundred bucks for street clothes. There's also financial aid for university, vocational training or money to buy land.

Train stations and ports across Canada are crowded with people reuniting with loved ones. Committees are struck to welcome the men and women home and on train platforms everywhere there's cheering and bands and in some cases, free cigarettes and ice cream. Some volunteers even help with marital woes, as is the case in Toronto. Volunteers with the Toronto Volunteer Reception Committee drive a soldier home and convince his wife to stick with him instead of kicking him to the curb.

Calgary has been seeing service personnel returning home since June. The city throws a welcome ceremony for its own Calgary Highlanders on the afternoon of Nov. 25, 1945. Radio station CFAC[49] broadcasts the cheers of the homecoming festivities. Announcers Don Oaks[50] and Jack Stewart, known as the voice of wartime big-band broadcasts from the Palliser Hotel, are the commentators for the event. The Highlanders will come into the city in a special troop train and then march to Mewata Armoury.

Waiting at the Canadian Pacific Railway station on 9th Avenue[51] are Ed and other Highlanders who have already returned home. A bus filled with wounded Highlanders from the Colonel Belcher Hospital is there too, along with thousands of people. Don and Jack note the hum of excitement as the train chugs closer.

As the whistling train pulls up to the platform, the announcers see happy faces leaning out the carriage windows and many arms waving at familiar faces. It's a hero's

---

49. It's now SN960 The Fan, a sports station. (2020)

50. There are two spellings of Oaks/Oakes on the History of Canadian Broadcasting's CFAC-AM page.

51. The train station is near today's Fairmont Palliser Hotel.

welcome as 476 Calgary Highlanders are greeted by Albertans. The Highlanders don't wait for any order to get off the train and pour out of the cars "like water out of a glass" with their full kit. There are cheers and shouts and smiles for these boys, say the announcers.

The mayor of Calgary, Andrew Davison,[52] addresses the Highlanders. He keeps his message short, as he believes the men shouldn't be wearied with long speeches.

We have gloried in your accomplishments and are justly proud of your record.
We welcome you home in all sincerity. We thank you for a difficult job splendidly done.

The soldiers who have just returned start their march to Mewata Armoury. Stewart says it's a great day in the history of Calgary. There's a large crowd of 13,000 to 20,000 people gathered to greet the Highlanders on the clear, blue-sky day. There are what Stewart calls "bobby socksy" teens, young children waving the Red Ensign and the Union Jack amid men and women of all ages shoulder-to-shoulder on rooftops, balconies, hanging out of windows and covering the streets of downtown. The Highlanders are marching with the Highlander pipes and drums leading them. Ed and the other men who have been home for a while are following. Ed is wearing his uniform, while others are in civilian clothing. The bus of wounded is at the rear.

Commentator Jack Stewart talks about how some of these soldiers have been gone for five years and two months, a long time to be away from loved ones. Thirteen men have served as Highlanders continuously from Shilo to now. Stewart says 403 Highlanders were killed in action and over 1,000 were wounded.

These men are stalwart looking, says Stewart. They're seasoned veterans. There are short men and tall men, thin men and heavyset men — but they are all outstanding men.

The shouts and clapping in appreciation of the Highlanders are so loud that you can barely hear Stewart over the din. He says confetti and strips of coloured paper float "gently down" on the men.

At Mewata, the 1st Battalion, Calgary Highlanders is dismissed and released from duty. They are no longer active soldiers. Ed eats doughnuts and drinks coffee with his mates, catching up during this reunion of sorts. He hears both sad and happy news and makes promises to visit his friends soon. He waves them off as they're taken home in "Welcome Home Cars." Calgarians have volunteered their vehicles and drive the men home. The next month, the Highlanders are disbanded (stop operating as a single unit) on Dec. 15, 1945, a day before Ed turns 28 and two weeks before his son is born.

Dorothy and Ed have been writing to each other almost daily and together, they pick a name for their baby. They both like Michael. Mike for short. In England a few days after Christmas, Dorothy is rushed to the Berkshire Independent Hospital. Labour has started. She has no trouble giving birth, a testament to the League of Health and Beauty's fitness regime. George and Alice are a great help when she brings Mike home to 55 Grange Avenue. Dorothy is proud of her English roots and glad her son is born in Reading. He's an Englishman even though he'll be living in Canada soon.

---

52. Calgary's 24th mayor: 1930-1945.

Dorothy and her son Mike.
Photo: Carleton Family

The plan is that Ed will send for Dorothy and Mike once he's settled in Alberta. Dorothy is uncertain about what "settled" means. A job? Their own home? Nevertheless, the couple has already spent time apart and this is no different. Except that Ed's new job hopefully won't be one where someone is shooting at him every day.

Post-war Britain is struggling economically and rationing continues. (Rationing officially ends in the U.K. in 1954.) Packages from Canada arrive for Dorothy, Mike and the Fowlers with tinned meat, cakes and other goodies. While England tries to find its footing in a new world, Dorothy likes her new role as a mum. She's a natural and sings songs to her little son, takes him for long walks in the pram and brings him to friends' homes. It's a nice life, but it's a life without Ed. He's working on bringing her to Canada as one of the 48,000 war brides.

Leap of Faith

Change is the one thing that's constant in life. Alberta has seen a lot of it and it's not stopping as veterans return home.[53] Oil is spewing out of the ground in Turner Valley — and soon, Leduc. The province is transforming from agriculture to industry. The soldiers landing back in the province have put their lives on hold for many years. Some of them were just out of school when they became soldiers. Now they have decisions to make about their post-war lives.

53. Some service personnel return to things being much the same such as some ethnic groups and Indigenous people, who are faced with racism once again.

The five Carleton brothers who went off to war move back in with their parents. Audrey says when the boys come home to Didsbury, it's very hectic as the family adjusts to one another again. Russ soon finds an apartment above the town's theatre while Ed remains with Millie and Ollie. All five men need work.

Ed's looking for a job one day in February 1946 when he spots a familiar face – a face he had last seen in an enemy-filled grain field in Normandy. George Morasch made it home. He returned to North America via the same ship he went to war on: the *Queen Elizabeth* troopship. He sailed from Southampton, U.K., to New York. On the voyage, giant waves dwarfed the vessel and they found one person was missing during roll call, likely swept into the Atlantic.

There wasn't much for George to do aboard the troopship except reflect. He says he has mixed feelings about returning home. He's happy he's alive but he's sad for the friends he left behind. He considered these men his brothers and now they're dead and buried on foreign soil.

Approximately 1,080,000 Canadian men and women served in uniform from 1939 to 1945. Out of those, 44,000 are killed and 55,000 wounded. George is elated to see Ed and they chat about their next moves. Ed tells George he's a husband and a dad and his wife and son will soon be travelling from Reading to Didsbury. George is happy for his friend. Ed's smile lights up the street. He can't wait to show his family their new home.

On the other side of the world, Dorothy knows she and Mike are leaving Reading at some point. She loves Ed but her heart aches as she thinks about having to leave her parents, sister, nephews, friends and the only place she has ever called home. She's heard stories of Canada from Ed and Russ and seen a photo of Mounties (Royal Canadian Mounted Police) in their red serge dress uniforms. But she's also seen pictures of bears and wolves — and the thing that scares her most: piles of snow. She shivers when she thinks about how cold it must get in Canada. She could barely stand the cold grass on her bare feet a few short years ago!

Spouses and children of Canadian soldiers are granted immediate citizenship and free trans-Atlantic passage if they apply through the Canadian Wives' Bureau, a department the Canadian government set up in July 1944. Dorothy contacts the bureau's offices on Regent Street in London. She isn't sent a date for departure – just a cookbook of Canadian cooking and some literature on her new country that explains some different-from-England habits.

Do not be surprised to see marmalade being eaten with bacon.
It is one of those odd combinations of foods, which tastes so much better than they sound.

-Canadian Cookbook for British Brides

Canadians are very democratic and take a dim view of people who try to impress them.
They are, generally speaking, energetic and fun-loving. They'll join you happily in a good-natured "grouse" but it might be just as well to remember that they don't like criticism based solely on the fact that some customs may be different from those of other countries.

-Department of National Defence

On Apr. 2, 1946, Dorothy receives a letter from the Civilian Repatriation Section Canadian Wives' Bureau at Sackville House, 40 Piccadilly, London.

Dear Madam,

Arrangements are now being made for your passage to Canada in the immediate future, which would involve you being ready to travel at twenty-four hours' notice from 11 April 46.

Dorothy and baby Mike are going to Canada.

By now, Dorothy knows Ed doesn't own a gopher ranch. In fact, he doesn't have any sort of long-term employment. She's hopeful he'll have some kind of work by the time she crosses the ocean … and who knows when that'll be. The letter says Dorothy is to wait for another letter telling her to take a train to London. Meanwhile, there are immediate instructions for Dorothy to follow. She needs to get her marriage certificate, as well as her birth certificate and Mike's. And she needs to start packing. She's also given information about financial matters like life insurance policies, war savings certificates and bank savings. She's not allowed to bring more than 15 pounds, or $66 (Canadian equivalent)[54] aboard the ship. She doubts she has much more anyway. Women who exceed the allowed amount have to hand it over to an immigration inspector. The bureau adds some details about what Dorothy should expect when travelling from Halifax, Nova Scotia to Didsbury on the train. However, she still has to cross the ocean before she gets to Canada. Here's what she reads about the sea journey:

A) That you are travelling on board a ship operating as a transport and that you will find few, if any, of the ordinary peacetime amenities.

B) That it may be necessary for you to berth in accommodation in company with other female passengers of perhaps 20 or 150 in number.

C) That the supply of fresh water is limited and is only available during certain hours each day, salt water is used for washing.

D) That children's nurseries and nurse-maids are not available on Transports and the care of the children must, therefore, be the responsibility of their mothers.

E) That the Class of accommodation you will be berthed in will NOT be governed by the rank or appointment of your husband in the services.

It's going to be third-class all the way, baby.

Dorothy has to sign the form that's included at the bottom of the message, tear it off and return it to the office. It's proof that she knows what she's getting into.

There aren't any clothing coupons included for "Canadian clothing" because of the shortage in the U.K. (Clothing was rationed in England because raw materials and labour were needed for the military.) It's up to Dorothy to make sure she and Mike dress appropriately (warmly) for April in Canada. In all of her 26 years, Dorothy has never been out of England. Ever. She has never seen snow. Of course, she's experienced lots of rain and fog but never that cold, white stuff. Dorothy has always dressed in skirts and dresses, so that's all she'll bring with her. That should be sufficient for spring in Canada.[55]

---

54. Almost $27 CAD in 2020.

55. Now with her many years in Alberta, Dorothy knows that it snows any and every season, even summer.

There is so much to do, and yet any day the call to leave for London could come. Dorothy sets about packing her life into boxes. She has a baggage limit and is allowed to bring only 500 lbs. She can't go over the weight. Allowed to go with her are personal things like photographs, as well as household items like linen. Among those things, she brings along her badges from the Air Raid Warden service, a couple of jewellery boxes and a small box with 20 or so fine embroidered handkerchiefs (that will never be used). The Canadians won't accept furniture or large musical instruments, so her beloved piano stays at 55 Grange.

In between packing, Dorothy spends time with family and friends. She has a farewell drink with Olive Openshaw and her husband Danny. Mike, at four months old, comes along to the pub, the Jack of Both Sides Public House. The adults toast Dorothy's next step with a Bristol Cream sherry, a favourite drink, and promise to stay in touch.

On Apr. 8, the wait is over. A letter from the Canadian Wives' Bureau arrives at 55 Grange. Dorothy's mother Alice has been dreading it. She does not want her daughter and grandson to leave. Not only is she attached to baby Mike but they're moving thousands of kilometres away. Dorothy's friend from the EFA, Fred Green, also doesn't want to see her go. But go Dorothy must. The letter gives her the details.

Dear Madam, We take pleasure in advising you that arrangements
have now been completed for your passage to Canada.
You will leave your present address on SUNDAY, April 14, 1946, for LONDON.

Attached to the letter are train and baggage instructions, as well as baggage labels among other things. Dorothy is also told to get a doctor's certificate declaring her and Mike to be healthy and not carrying any infectious diseases. With their good health verified, it's time to say goodbye. Alas, no one is allowed to go with Dorothy to London while she waits for transport to Canada. It's a "security risk," the Canadians say. Farewells are held at 55 Grange and the Reading train station. There are tears and hugs, many more hugs, and promises to write often. Despite the sadness, Alice and George know this is the right path for their daughter. George especially thinks of this as a great adventure for Dorothy. She has always done things her own way and this is nothing new.

At exactly 2:02 p.m., the train pulls away from Reading Station. Dorothy is off to London with Mike, fortified by her family's love and the songs she grew up with. One of the songs her father taught her years ago is *It's A Long way to Tipperary*. She sings it now to remind herself of home along the journey to Ed.

Up to mighty London came an Irishman one day,
As the streets are paved with gold, sure ev'ryone was gay;
Singing songs of Piccadilly, Strand and Leicester Square,
Till Paddy got excited, then he shouted to them there:
It's a long way to Tipperary it's a long way to go
It's a long way to Tipperary to the sweetest gal I know
Farewell to Piccadilly so long Leister Square
It's a long way to Tipperary but my heart lies there

ONE-WAY TRIP

The whistle of a train is usually a happy sound, signalling a trip and exciting times ahead. For Dorothy on Apr. 14, 1946, the whistle signals leaving her family behind and a long journey ahead. Getting to London takes just over an hour and a half. When Dorothy and baby Mike arrive amid the hustle and bustle of Paddington Station, the first thing they do is find a Canadian officer. Dorothy's letter had instructed her to report to a man wearing a white armlet with a maple leaf and the letters Cdn. M.C.[56] written on it. She finds the officer and reports to him.

The Canadian Repatriation officer gives Dorothy her passport, an ocean passage ticket and other necessary documents. The man then takes their hand luggage and sends Dorothy and Mike to a hostel.

As per the Apr. 8 letter, the hostel is where Dorothy and Mike will stay until they get the nod to go to the port city of Liverpool. At the London lodgings, mum and son are welcomed by Canadian Nursing Sisters. These women cared for wounded soldiers during wartime and will now take care of the war brides and their children before heading to sea with them. Red Cross workers are there too. Dorothy is social and likes meeting new people, so she chats with some of the other women leaving for Canada. A couple of the London ladies tell her that they had attended a school for war brides but even then, they don't have a clue about their new homes. They talk to one another and tell each other that at least they'll be with their husbands and their children will have fathers.

The war brides are given all their meals at the hostel. They don't need to buy anything, although mothers whose babies need a particular brand of formula are advised to bring enough milk to last 21 days. Dorothy and her friends chat about what else they're taking with them. One woman is shipping her big English pram, which she also packed full of stuff. The war brides are from all walks of life and will be going all over Canada. Dorothy probably won't see them again once they land in North America.

Dorothy and Mike spend one night in London before getting their sailing orders. They take a train heading for Liverpool and from there, the path turns to water. They're put aboard the turbine twin screw (a screw is a marine propeller) hospital ship, the *HMHS Letitia*. The *Letitia* is one of several specially-commissioned "war bride ships," including the *Queen Mary* and *Aquitania*. Some of the vessels are imposing, with four funnels (smokestacks/steam vents), like *Aquitania*. Others have only two, like *Queen Mary*. The *Letitia* has just one.

The *Letitia*, originally a British ocean liner, was requisitioned for service at the start of the Second World War. The armed merchant cruiser mostly patrolled the Atlantic from October 1939 until it ran aground in Halifax, Nova Scotia in 1941. It was then used as a troopship until it was damaged in 1943. After being repaired in the

56. Have not been able to uncover what M.C. stands for. Perhaps for Movement Control Staff.

The *HMHS Letitia*, the ship that sails Dorothy, Mike and many others to Canada. Photo: Carleton Family

U.S., the *Letitia* was turned over to the Canadian government and made into a hospital ship. This is Dorothy and Mike's ship.

No one is in Liverpool to wave Dorothy and Mike off. Dorothy carries her baby up the gangway to the deck of the ship. Besides war brides, there are the Canadian Nursing Sisters, Red Cross workers as well as servicemen onboard. The *Letitia* is travelling in a convoy since underwater mines and other unexploded munitions remain in the cold waters of the Atlantic.

Dorothy isn't frightened of the leftover bombs or being on the deep, wide ocean — but she is definitely feeling something once the vessel sets sail: seasickness. Being ill on the ship just makes things uncomfortable but more importantly, Dorothy is disappointed she can't eat. After years of rationing and doing without sweets and other goodies, Dorothy can only feast her eyes on what's being offered in the galley. There's so much beautiful food: white bread, bananas, whipping cream and pasties. And she can't taste a morsel of it.

Dorothy in Reading, U.K.
Photo: Carleton Family

Many of the women feel like her. Dorothy counts herself a tiny bit lucky during the two-week crossing. Mike is a four-month-old baby and so he sleeps much of the time. He seems to like being rocked by the choppy seas while the side-to-side motion turns Dorothy's stomach. Some mothers have toddlers who are running around or else crying their eyes out all day and night. Dorothy's glad Mike slumbers in a carrycot on their top bunk.

Lower bunk beds are reserved for pregnant women, so Dorothy climbs up and down a ladder with her "bundle of joy" every time she gets out or into bed. Mike never falls off the bunk, even when the ship pitches this way and that. He sleeps through most of his journey to meet his dad.

The women who don't feel green often get stuck with the ill women's children. The perk of being a healthy war bride, though, is enjoying the tasty food. As well, depending on which season you're sailing in, you get to watch icebergs drift by. April to May is considered iceberg season. The Titanic sank when it hit one of the giant pieces of floating ice. It went down off the east coast of Canada on Apr. 15, 1912.

Dorothy is so sick she can barely get out of bed. When she has ventured outside, she thinks the waves will sink her ship before an iceberg. The waves are so high that they spill through the ship's portholes and drench the unfortunate women sitting below. Dorothy's had enough of all the saltwater. It's also used for washing and has chapped her hands, making them rough and dry. She sings songs of home to perk herself up.

Prime Minister William Lyon Mackenzie King[57] calls the women who left their homes to become Canadians, a splendid addition to the country.

The war bride ships bring many loved ones together, but also separate daughters from parents they might never see again. Jeannie Booth and her two small children leave Scotland for Halifax a couple of weeks after Dorothy and Mike leave England.

---

57. Prime Minister William Lyon Mackenzie King made the announcement aboard the *Queen Mary* on Aug. 31, 1946 while sailing with war brides. According to Kay Ruddick, an escort officer on the ship, Mackenzie King was asked to give a speech. A life-long bachelor, he said, *"I'm a fine one to make a speech to brides, I've never had one myself."*

Jeannie and her kids board *Aquitania* and settle in for the long ocean voyage. The young mother doesn't join the other women gathered on the ship's deck, craning their necks for a last glimpse of home.

Once I got on the boat, I never looked back. I remember everybody else watching as long as they could see the British Isles. They just sat and watched until they couldn't see anymore. Not me.

My eldest daughter and I were sick on the boat. It was terrible.

We hit rough weather and icebergs and ended up having to go a different way.

We were a day late docking in Halifax because of the icebergs. I was so glad to get off the boat.

Jeannie Booth

On a foggy, grey day, the *Letitia* arrives at Pier 21[58] in Halifax, Nova Scotia. It's Apr. 25, 1946, and it took Dorothy 10 days to cross the Atlantic. Pier 21was originally built as a cargo terminal but turned into immigration facilities. It's where immigrants, wartime evacuees, refugees, troops, war brides and their children first step foot into Canada.[59] The place will always be special to Dorothy because it's her first glimpse of her new country. It also means she never has to get on a boat again.

A band plays *Here Comes the Bride* as Dorothy, with Mike in her arms, walks briskly down the ramp of the *Letitia*, eager to get to land and her next set of instructions. There's a lot of action at the pier. Husbands kissing their wives. In-laws meeting their daughters-in-law for the first time — and for some, their grandchildren, too. There are tears, as a few husbands don't show up to welcome their war brides. These men maybe met someone else or were married before they left for the war. Dorothy isn't worried this will happen to her, although she hugs Mike a little closer in the chilly Halifax air.

The IODE, Imperial Order Daughters of the Empire, are out in full force to guide the war brides from ship to shore. The IODE is a national women's charitable organization and chapters in Nova Scotia raised money for the war effort. Now, post-war, they act as greeters for returning soldiers, war brides and immigrants at Pier 21. Women from the Salvation Army are there, too. The Nova Scotians take care of the children while the war brides get their paperwork in order. It takes Dorothy a while to fill out the immigration forms and get a Landed Immigrant stamp. However, she knows her bundle of joy is being well looked after.

Finally, with the "t" in Carleton crossed and a warm tea in her belly, Dorothy collects Mike. The next leg of their adventure will be by train. In her letter from V.N. Gill, Dorothy was told she'll take a train from Halifax, straight to Calgary, Alberta, where Ed will pick her up. She is not going to get a break from travelling except for short stops. If Dorothy decides to stay in Halifax or change trains and head somewhere else, she'll have to make her own arrangements and pay for them. That's definitely not her plan.

One kind woman takes Dorothy under her wing and escorts the war bride and her baby to the train. The massive effort to bring war brides and their children to Canada

58. Pier 21 is a historic site.

59. May Elizabeth Anscombe, a war bride, lands in Halifax on Apr. 11, 1945. She says she tries to catch some white balloons floating in the air for her children. However, the "balloons" are condoms blown up by sailors. May, originally from Sussex, U. K., married Calgary Highlander Nicholas Maley.

has been nicknamed Operation Daddy by the media. The press also takes to dubbing trains tasked with dropping off women across the country as the Diaper Special. For Dorothy, there's nothing special about Mike's diapers.

If Dorothy thought the ship's journey was arduous, the train is just as bad. The cars shake and rattle. Because children can't run around like they could on the ship decks, they're fussing and crying. Also, there are limited resources for cleaning diapers. There are no disposable nappies yet — and while some mums brought along Harrington Squares, a lighter weight gauze, to use as diapers, Dorothy has something else. Something much heavier and cumbersome. Dorothy's using bulky terrycloth diapers that her mother sewed for her. They certainly fit the budget, but they don't fit 10 days on a moving train. Clean water is hard to come by and the tiny washbasins aboard aren't ideal for washing diapers. It takes Dorothy forever to wash out one terrycloth diaper. Now, where does she put it? She hangs it on one of the endless strings crisscrossing the car. At least she doesn't have to cook. The women and children are provided three meals a day and Dorothy can enjoy all the fruit she wants.

Frustration is beginning to fray her nerves. If the train would just keep moving, that would be all right. Unfortunately, it stops and starts and stops and starts at every station. At each platform, women and children disembark. Dorothy watches as some are enveloped by bear hugs while others are greeted with awkward handshakes. She wonders what Ed's parents will be like. She has several days to think about it.

How big is Canada anyway? Shouldn't she be in Calgary after two days? Dorothy stares out the window and waits for the next stop that might be Calgary. She watches sunsets and sunrises with Mike in her arms. She sees trees and trees and trees slide by and then cities and lakes and rocks and later, dark fields checkering flat plains. The train halts multiple times in Saskatchewan, a name that makes Dorothy chuckle. There seem to be more women getting off in this province than anywhere else.

At last, after 10 days, the train rolls into Calgary. Where is Ed?

CHAPTER SEVEN

"HOME" IN BANFF

AN ENGLISH ROSE IN WILD ROSE COUNTRY

Somewhere on the crowded Calgary train platform ... is Ed. Dorothy searches for a face that's familiar at the Canadian Pacific Railway station. Could that man be her husband? No. How about that guy? That's not him, either.

It's Ed who spots Dorothy and Mike. She doesn't recognize him in civilian clothing. He's wearing a suit and a trilby hat (a soft felt hat with a narrow brim). To Dorothy, he looks like the American gangster Al Capone. Poor Ed. He's trying to be fashionably turned-out to greet his wife and meet his son. He kisses Dorothy and gently takes Mike from her. It's love at first sight.

Dorothy says goodbye to her friends from the train. A few of them are going all the way to the Pacific coast. Dorothy has only another hour to go before she's "home." From Calgary, Ed drives his family to Didsbury, where they'll live with his parents for a spell.

Once in the small town, Ed eagerly points out his former school, the church and the Didsbury Opera House. The opera house was where the townspeople held a Welcome Back celebration for service personnel on Dec. 28, 1945. The thank-you extended to Ed, Russ, Herb, Frank and Baillie was appreciated by Ollie and Millie. To have five out of nine children serve their country is certainly remarkable.

For Dorothy, Didsbury seems much slower than what she's used to. Although Reading isn't as big as London, there are always lots of shops open and people in the streets. Didsbury has a cinema, so that's good. There are many wide-open spaces and the houses are large. When Ed finally stops in front of the Carleton home, Dorothy is surprised at the size of the white wooden house – it's huge. Ed pats her on the knee and tells her everything will be fine and that Ollie and Millie are good people.

There's a big family welcome for Dorothy and Mike. Audrey, Ed's youngest sister, says her parents are supportive of their children, especially their sons who fought in the war. The door is always open for family.

Ed's parents and siblings are happy to meet Dorothy and Mike. Millie makes the Reading woman tea and Ollie asks about being on the ship and her train trip. Dorothy's English accent is a source of amusement for the younger people — but they don't dare laugh out of politeness. Mike has been ensconced in his father's arms on arrival at the house. Ed, proving himself a natural father, has four months of catch-up with his son.

LIFE IN DIDSBURY

The arrival of Russ' wife and daughter hits the news a couple of weeks after Dorothy and Mike land in Alberta. The *Didsbury Pioneer* makes the announcement on May 29, 1946.

Mrs. R.C. Carleton and daughter Maureen are expected to arrive in Calgary from Reading, Birkshire [sic] *this coming Friday.*

Russ has been working at the Payne-Freeman Company, a wholesale oil and gas agency, in Olds, a town about a 20-minute drive away from Didsbury. He's happy to have his English family in Alberta with him. Having a friend from back home is a comfort to Dorothy. Although she feels like a part of the Carleton family, it's nice to have someone to confide in, someone who knows what living in England is like. The one thing the Reading women notice about Canadian women is that they wear blue jeans. Dorothy has never worn jeans in her life! In fact, she had never heard of dungarees before moving to Didsbury. She has always worn skirts and dresses and hasn't packed one pair of trousers.

Jeans notwithstanding, Dorothy adapts to Ed's world. His family's home has no inside toilet and she bathes Mike in a dishpan in the kitchen. Ollie and Millie dote on Mike just as his English grandparents did. Mike isn't Ollie and Millie's first grandchild, but he's the first Carleton baby to have crossed the ocean and half of Canada.

Like Dorothy's mother Alice, Millie is a great cook. She does all the meals for the household and often barters Ollie's blacksmithing services in exchange for staples. Horseshoeing can be traded for eggs. She bakes many beautiful and spongy angel food cakes because she has so many eggs.

Ed continues to recover from his head injury. The metal plate in his forehead doesn't bother him too much. He takes on some surveying jobs and starts saving money. Soon, he has enough to move his family into a place of their own: a rental apartment on the top floor of a two-storey building. Dorothy has to leave the pram at the bottom of the stairs and carry Mike all the way up. As he gets older, he gets heavier. However, Dorothy's training with the Women's League of Exercise and Beauty comes in handy. She's in shape for those stairs and motivated to get out and walk with her baby whenever she can.

Strolling around town with Mike, Dorothy looks around her. Didsbury's streets are muddy and the walkways are made of wood. Nothing like her lovely paved English town. Of course, Didsbury also doesn't have centuries of history like Reading. The Alberta town was founded in 1894 because the prime minister at the time, Sir. John A Macdonald, began a drive to populate the West with settlers. The town has been in existence for just over 50 years. Fifty years! Palmer Park is older than this place. Be that as it may, Didsbury has its charms, with red brick stores and sandstone buildings. On a clear day, she can see the Rocky Mountains. They stick out like a spine in the Alberta landscape.

Most townsfolk are pleasant and Dorothy forms friendships – people she can sit beside at one of the many sporting and community events. One couple, Wilf and Audrey Skerry,[60] become close with the Carletons. Wilf is a printer at the *Didsbury Pioneer*. It's nice to have a couple to hang out with on long winter evenings.

Dorothy finds out that anyone can own a gopher[61] ranch in Didsbury: you just need a patch of soil. The vermin are everywhere and a nuisance to farmers because

60. When the Skerrys move to Mission, B.C., Ed and Dorothy keep in touch and visit them.

61. Most "gophers" found in Alberta are actually ground squirrels.

they damage tree roots and tunnel through fields. Even so, the idea that Dorothy moved to Canada because of Ed's "gopher ranch" becomes a running joke.

Snow doesn't hamper Dorothy's enthusiasm for walking. Winter doesn't keep her a prisoner inside. She gets geared up in boots and one of Ed's old coats and heads into the elements. She writes to her parents, as well as Marjorie and Fred Green, about her experiences in the cold north and also sends them parcels of food. Fred is still asking Dorothy, whom he calls Little Girl, to return home.

Dorothy is a wife and mother and in her mid-twenties, yet she doesn't mind her nickname. She loves receiving news of the EFA office about her colleagues and their work. Fred writes about the tree nursery's million seedlings and how proud he is of the thriving greenhouse. He gossips about some co-workers and it gives Dorothy a chuckle to think of him dishing about work. For instance, Fred tells her that Jill is going to get married and how she is a "damned fool in every way."

He also writes a few words about a couple of lads at the nursery.

Butler is just Butler – as deaf as ever and as obstinate. Rowe is never fat and is thinner than ever. I am about the same except for my eyes and a bit greyer.

Fred filling his pages with humour brings home a little closer to Dorothy. He asks her if she's started a League of Health and Beauty. In December of 1947, he writes that there is no way he would think of going to Canada when it is chilly enough in Reading.

It would be nice if Edmund and you packed up and returned to England. There is plenty of work even for you but housing is very difficult. I think I would buy one for you!

He offers to employ Dorothy as his chauffeur (Fred has bad eyes). Imagine that! He already has a good man, Cameron, whom he likes to poke fun at in his letters. The stories about Fred's driver make Dorothy laugh. Nevertheless, she tears up when her old friend writes that she should return home.

Well, little girl, I am sorry to say my eyes are not too good and I am so often alone in the evenings and cannot read for very long. I lack companionship and I often think of you and Ed and wish you are able to come to have a chat. If one of these days Ed and you are asked to come home, would you? I know your people at 55 [Grange Avenue] *would love you to do so. Besides, I should much like to see your wee laddie* [Mike].

Dorothy's first Christmas away from her English family is tough. She misses them and the carols they play on the piano at 55 Grange Avenue. However, this is Mike's very first Christmas and he's surrounded by his Canadian family. He'll turn one at the end of the month and it's been an exciting year for someone so young.

In January of 1947, Millie hosts a number of British war brides in her home. Dorothy, Phyllis and three other women talk and talk and talk about their past lives in the U.K. They sing songs like, *There'll Always be an England*, and eat to their heart's content.

This is the beginning of a long affiliation between Dorothy and war brides. Associations and groups are popping up all over Canada. It'll be a connection for Dorothy where she can share stories and sing the songs of her youth. For an hour or two, she's a girl back in England.

After a full year of living in Alberta, Dorothy still has her English accent. She takes on the role of wife and mother easily. She is often heard singing while washing the dishes, cleaning up Mike or walking around town. Sometimes, she'll dance a little, too.

Pack up your troubles in your old kit-bag
And smile, smile, smile

Summer breaks through the Alberta spring and on Dominion Day (Canada Day), Jul. 1, 1947, Ed and Russ prove they haven't lost their athleticism by winning the half-mile relay race at the Olds[62] Lions Club. The brothers make a great team although their differences are becoming more apparent. Ed, as we know, takes things as they come. He's more reserved while Russ is gregarious and doesn't mind living a bit on the edge. The two families spend a lot of time together when schedules allow. Ed has been working on building roads in southern Alberta and is often away. That changes on Apr. 1, 1948.

Ed gets a proper job in town. He's working at the Cassidy Lumber Yard.[63] The business started expanding in the war years and it sells kiln-dried coast fir, cedar posts and many other wood products. It's not Ed's dream job — he'd rather be in the woods than selling wood — but it's paying the bills.

Ed doesn't last long at the lumber yard. No, it's not what you think. He's not fired or laid off. He's going after a position that'll shape his family for generations to come. He applies to be a park warden.

Ed the Park Warden

An advertisement hanging in the Didsbury post office is the ticket to Ed and Dorothy's future. The ad is a job posting for an assistant park warden in Banff National Park, on the provincial boundary between Alberta and British Columbia (B.C.). As a nature lover who grew up in the wide-open spaces of central Alberta, it's everything Ed is looking for.

Ed and Dorothy discuss the possibilities of living in Banff, a park on the Continental Divide and a two-hour drive southwest of Didsbury. Ed travelled to Banff a few years back and says it's a beautiful place that would make a great home for their family.

The Canadian government wants veterans to have sustainable careers and encourages them to apply for warden postings. There's not a lot of information about the job but the Carletons would be given accommodation and Ed would be responsible for patrolling the backcountry. Dorothy has never heard that word before and wonders what being in the "backcountry" entails. The job would mean being away from the larger Carleton family. Phyllis is pregnant again and due in early summer, and Dorothy doesn't want to miss the occasion. Unfortunately, if Ed gets this job, she might have to leave with him before her friend gives birth.

Ed applies for the job and gets it. His news makes the paper on May 19, 1948.

Ed Carleton has secured a position with the Dominion Government in the Banff National Park and left Monday to take up his new duties as an assistant ranger.
Mrs. Carleton and Michael expect to leave shortly to reside at their park residence.

62. Olds is a small town in Alberta.
63. The Cassidy Lumber Yard is bought out by the Atlas Lumber Company in March of 1949.

Ed is thrilled at the prospect of moving to Banff. He'll be in the Rocky Mountains every day, breathing in the fresh air and living among the wildlife of western Canada. He'll be watching over the flora and fauna as well as nurturing his own family. It's going to be great. Ed kisses his wife and son goodbye and hops on a bus headed to Lake Louise, a small village west of the town of Banff. He'll do a couple of months of training and then send for Dorothy and Mike.

Banff National Park is famous for its tooth-like peaks as well as turquoise lakes, flowering meadows and abundant bears, elk, wolves, moose, squirrels and much more. Banff is Canada's first national park but Indigenous peoples,[64] such as the Îyãħé Nakoda (Stoney-Nakoda Nation), have been living and hunting there for centuries. They also consider the hot springs found on the land as sacred and use them for spiritual and healing purposes.

The hot springs' mineral waters vary from 37 and 40 degrees Celsius (98 and 104 Fahrenheit) and contain sulphate, calcium, bicarbonate, magnesium and sodium, great for your body's circulation and soothing sore muscles.[65] The Sulphur Mountain springs were "discovered" a few times. It's mentioned in Dr. James Hector's notes in 1859. Hector was a geologist, naturalist and surgeon who accompanied the Palliser Expedition, an exploration group led by John Palliser that surveyed parts of the West, including the southern Rockies. However, it wasn't until 1883 when some Canadian Pacific Railway (CPR) workers came across the springs, that they're noticed for their money-making potential.

After a dispute over ownership of the springs, the federal government created the Hot Springs Reserve in 1885. Together, the government and CPR turned the springs into a tourist destination, which brought people into the area via the railway. "If you can't export the scenery, we'll import the tourists," said CPR President Sir William Van Horne. The town of Banff was established in 1886 and offered some accommodations, but they weren't grand enough for Van Horne. He then built the Banff Springs Hotel and opened it on Jun. 1, 1888. The iconic landmark has stood by the Bow and Spray rivers ever since (although the original wooden structure burned to the ground in 1926).

The same year construction started on the hotel, 1887, the Hot Springs Reserve becomes Rocky Mountains Park, a name change through the Rocky Mountain Parks Act. The act heralds economic development through tourism, logging, mining and other activities. For the next 25 years, the majority of visitors arrive at the park by train. The feds had banned driving in the park until 1910, when the government realized roads meant tourists and tourists meant dollars.

Over the next several years, various federal government acts change the park to a "Dominion Park," a national area. The boundaries of Rocky Mountains Park change

---

64. Banff National Park is the traditional territory of the Siksikaitsitapi Confederacy including the nations of Siksika (Blackfoot), Piikani (Peigan) and Kainai (Blood) as well the îyârhe Nakodabi (Stoney-Nakoda Nation - Bearspaw, Chiniki and Wesley First Nations), Ktunaxa Ksanka (Kootenay Nation) and Tsuut'ina (Sarcee) Nation.
65. The hot springs remain a major tourist draw.

as well and grow due to the number of visitors. The park needs to build infrastructure to keep bringing people and businesses to the area and cheap labour is nearby. During the First World War, a seasonal tented internment camp is set up at the base of Castle Mountain. In winter, the camp moves to facilities near the Cave and Basin hot springs. The forced labour is by immigrants: prisoners of war from Austria-Hungary, Germany and Ukraine. They cut trails, construct bridges and build a new road to Lake Louise. The men are hungry and cold and some flee the camp despite the guards being told to shoot escapees.

In 1930, Rocky Mountains Park becomes Banff National Park when the feds regulate the protection of natural areas of national significance through the National Parks Act. The Great Depression of the 30s facilitates "make-work" projects for the unemployed and homeless, including further road development. At the same time, Prime Minister R. B. Bennett (1930–1935), cuts the budget of the National Parks Branch (as Parks Canada was then known). However, more cheap labour is soon about to become available.

Conscientious objectors, or "conchies," those who don't want to fight in the Second World War, along with citizens from enemy nations, are held at camps stationed at Lake Louise, Stoney Creek and Healy Creek. The parks branch needs the labour to expand and improve facilities for visitors. The internees are tasked with jobs such as building patrol cabins and repairing telephone lines in the park. They also chop down 18,000 beetle-infested trees in Banff.

With the war raging on, Banff National Park's budget is cut. Businesses in the park are also suffering. Times are tough and tourists just can't make summer trips to the mountains. The Banff Springs Hotel is forced to close in 1942 for three years.

The Banff Springs reopens in 1945 for the summer, thanks in part to veterans returning home to Canada. Former soldiers are finding the park a great honeymoon destination and a way to put their fighting days behind them. Not only are visitors packing their lunches in the summer to take with them to the hot springs or on fishing trips, they're enjoying Banff views in the winter, too.

Ed is going to be part of teaching tourists all about the wonder to be found in the park, as well as keeping wide-eyed visitors safe. For two months, he'll be schooled at Lake Louise by Percy "Beef" Woodworth, the district warden. (There are a couple of stories about how Beef got his nickname. One is that he liked to eat on the trail. The other is that he got portly as a youth when he wasn't doing a lot of physical work.) Meanwhile, Dorothy and two-and-a-half-year-old Mike continue their lives in Didsbury, waiting for the call to move to Banff.

Dorothy has heard from friends that Banff National Park is beautiful. She's heard that there are soaring mountains and bubbling streams and lots of wildlife. She thinks it'll be fine if she can get out every day and walk to the shops. She knows that the pace of life will be even slower than Didsbury but she's happy to support her husband. Ed has found more than a job, he's found a way of life.

More Banff History

John Connor was the Rocky Mountains National Park's first official "warden." He watched the park for fires and did some clerical work. The North-West Mounted Police also did some park patrolling in the summer months. Swiss guides, brought by CPR to take tourists into the mountains, often led rescues. In 1909, the Canadian government founded the Fire and Game Guardian Service. Men were hired as fire patrolmen and game wardens who looked for poachers and forest fires. Many of these game guardians were former trappers and mountain guides. Cabins were built in the backcountry so the wardens could spend weeks in the wilderness while patrolling on horseback. By the time Ed's hired as a Banff park warden in 1948, the service has changed.

Firefighting equipment has improved, there's a field forest telephone system and there are developed roads and trails. The park mandate has changed, too. For James B. Harkin, Canada's First Commissioner of National Parks (1911-1936) and "father of Canada's National Parks," a good predator was a dead predator.

Following Harkin was Frank H.H. Williamson (1936-1941). He decided it was better for nature to be in balance and so the apex of the park's food chain was allowed to live. Forest conservation was also stressed.

What has stayed the same since those CPR men stumbled upon the hot springs, is the desire for more visitors to come to Banff. James Smart, Controller of the National Parks Branch (1941-1953), starts development of the Trans-Canada Highway through Banff National Park. He improves alpine ski hills and expands campgrounds. The number of tourists drawn to Banff in the late 1940s is on the rise.

The town of Banff itself is an attraction – a little village surrounded by immense natural beauty. "Siding 29," Banff's original designation, was first a rail town that expanded in population and size right from its inception in November 1883. By 1907, there was electricity, water and sewage lines, established businesses and a newspaper. In 1933, Banff offered itself as a cultural hub by establishing the Banff School of Drama.

When Ed arrives in 1948, Banff is a close-knit community in a small mountain town that bursts with visitors from time-to-time. During the warm months and ski season, the streets fill with people gazing up at the mountains. In shoulder season —a few weeks in May and in the fall — Banff goes back to the townspeople.

Ed sees the importance of the town but prefers the mountains. He'll be spending ample time in the backcountry after his training. Through Beef, Ed learns about wildfires, predator and poaching control and first aid. Because of his military service, he doesn't have to spend time practicing shooting .270 rifles or .38 handguns. High mountain rescue techniques aren't a major part of his training either. Swiss guides do most of those missions.

Warden training means Ed is going to have to learn how to ride a horse. Despite his father being a farrier, Ed doesn't have a lot of experience with the animals. Being on horseback is a vital part of his job now. This is how wardens patrol their districts. Many of the men Ed trains with grew up on ranches and farms, but this isn't Ed's experience.

Besides Ed's new skills, he's equipped with a myriad of natural abilities: like not being scared of bears. You can't be a warden if you're afraid to go into the woods. A warden has to be able to keep his emotions on an even keel and not be provoked. He needs to be able to protect himself and the public under stressful circumstances. He needs to be able to deal with conflict and work under pressure. As a Calgary Highlander who fought in the Second World War, Ed's pretty sure he can do the warden job. No problem.

His time as a soldier was spent in a uniform and he'll have to wear one as a warden. Wardens were put into formal uniforms in 1938. They wear a dark green wool suit, a light brown Stetson hat and boots. The outfits are made by the Toronto company Tip Top Tailors. Ed's expected to wear his smart duds on duty. Now that he's suited up in more ways than one, it's time to bring the family down from Didsbury. Ed has worked in Lake Louise as an assistant warden for two months and has been awarded his own district.

Dorothy receives the call from Ed. It's been two months since she's seen her husband. He tells her to take the bus to Lake Louise and then district warden Ed will pick up her and Mike at the station. Dorothy wonders what to take to Banff for their new home. She doesn't know how large the house will be, so she leaves some things with Millie and Ollie. She can always send for items later.

Cabin Fever

Rushing to pick up his family at the Lake Louise station, Ed's vehicle fishtails and ends up in the ditch. It's rare for him to get so excited, but this is one of the few occasions where he is so worked up that he loses his usual levelheadedness. He can't wait to show Dorothy their new home. Luckily, he can drive out of the ditch and continues into town.

Dorothy has been sitting on the stuffy bus in the July heat for a few hours. She's not thinking about the weather, though, because the scenery is stunning. The distant mountain spine she could see from Didsbury grows into a grey leviathan. She can't believe her eyes. Mountains, large mountains, sharp mountains, grand mountains, rocky mountains, form right out of the ground. They get bigger and bigger as the bus gets closer and closer to Banff National Park. She asks Mike if he knew the peaks were as high as the heavens. Her toddler blinks a couple of times and then falls asleep.

Dorothy feels like a baby herself among the massive peaks that tower over the bus. She's tiny compared to the landscape. How is the vehicle traversing through the solid wall of grey? The mountains aren't frightening her, though: they're awing her. She wonders what secrets and adventures can be found in the midst of the crags and canyons.

In the Lake Louise parking lot, Dorothy and Mike reunite with Ed. He's back in uniform looking like the man she first met – complete with his wide smile. He leads his family to a 4x4 truck with big wheels. It's an old army vehicle with a cab placed on top so passengers don't get wet when it rains. There's also a large winch on the front.

"What is that used for?" Dorothy asks herself.

Mike and Ed with the Power Wagon at Bow Summit.
Photo: Carleton Family

She just drove a couple of hundred kilometres and hadn't encountered anything that needed to be towed. The roads are paved and in good shape. Perhaps in winter townsfolk need the winch to get their vehicles out of snowbanks.

"All aboard the Power Wagon,"[66] says Ed as he climbs behind the wheel. He can't stop smiling. The last time Dorothy saw him this happy was when he met his son for the first time. It's been almost two years since that day. Well, if Ed's happy then their new place must be nice.

The rubber hits the road and they're off. However, Ed's heading out of town. OK, they must be driving to the town of Banff then. But they're going north. Next, they're on a gravel road called the Banff Jasper Highway,[67] the road connecting Banff and Jasper national parks. They turn onto another dusty dirt road and are rattling around in the vehicle. Dorothy feels every bump as the truck hits a rut or large stone. She wraps her arms around Mike to make sure he doesn't fly out of the vehicle and into the woods.

The road switchbacks up a peak like one of the ones Dorothy spied coming into Lake Louise. There's no sign of other houses. No other buildings. No other people.

"Where are you taking us, Ed?" she asks her husband.

"Home!"

Just over half an hour on the isolated road, he stops the vehicle in front of an old shed in the middle of the woods.

66. Dodge starts manufacturing the Power Wagon for the military in the Second World War. Ed's Power Wagon isn't a Dodge. He just names his vehicle after the Dodge automobile.
67. Today, it's the Icefields Parkway.

"This is it," he says while getting out of the truck. "Bow Summit. This our home sweet home."

"What?" asks Dorothy. "You've got to be kidding me."

The small shack in front of her is no home. To Dorothy, it looks like a storage shed. How is she supposed to live in that? She shakes her head a couple of times to make sure she's not dreaming.

"Let's go in," says Ed, opening her vehicle door and taking Mike from her arms.

Once through the door of the log cabin, Dorothy sees the building is more spacious than it looks from the outside. It's not Buckingham Palace but the Bow Summit cabin's wooden plank floor feels sturdy beneath her feet, the walls are strong and the windows frame the best pictures she has ever seen. Nevertheless, her new home certainly is rustic. It's one room. There is no electricity. There is no inside toilet. There is no running water. Oh, yes, there is lots of running water – flowing past the cabin in the unnamed creek. Dorothy finally understands what backcountry means: wilderness.

They're living in the middle of it.

**The fishing is great at Bow Summit. Dorothy with her catch in 1948.
Photo: Carleton Family**

Crowfoot Glacier in Banff National Park.
Photo: Carleton Family

Chapter Eight

This is Backcountry Living

Bow Summit Life

Bow Summit is the high point on the Banff Jasper Highway and approximately 2042 m (6,700 ft) in elevation. It's north of Bow Lake and Bow Mountain and the cabin is just over the summit on the right-hand slope of Observation Peak. The mountains holding court over Bow Summit include Mount Chephren and Howse Peak. Nearby is Crowfoot Glacier, Peyto Lake, Waterfowl Lakes and lots of trees and boulders in between.

Besides the cabin, there's a corral and a small barn. Wardens patrol their districts on horseback and Ed has a saddle horse and a packhorse. There's not much pasture on Bow Summit but hay is brought in for the animals.

Once Dorothy gets over the shock of her new home, she starts setting up house. It certainly needs a woman's touch. She opens all the windows, sweeps the cobwebs from the rafters and the mouse droppings from the floor. As it's July in the Rockies, the late afternoon sun streams into the cabin, casting out all the shadows. Dorothy looks at Ed. He's happy and content here. Dorothy has never lived this close to nature. She was a big-city girl up until two years ago. However, the backcountry of Banff is nothing she can't handle. She is used to working hard, and has done so from the age of 14. She's strong from her Women's League of Health and Beauty. She was an Air Raid Warden during the Blitz. Most importantly, she loves her husband. There's nothing they can't handle together.

When night falls, it's dark outside. Very dark. The moon and millions of stars light up the sky but not the woods. The woods are where the outhouse is – down a little pathway away from the cabin. Away from Ed. Dorothy peers into the night. What's out there?

While Dorothy was in Didsbury, Ollie told her many a tale about the ferocious animals in the Alberta forests. Grizzly bears with claws as long as her arm. Wolves with teeth as sharp as knives. Cougars that you'll never see or hear until their fangs are in your neck. There is no way Dorothy is going to the toilet alone.

"Would you please escort me to the loo?" she asks Ed.

Ed grabs a flashlight and lights the way. Dorothy makes a mental note to make sure they always have fresh batteries on hand.

The next morning, Ed surprises Dorothy with a cup of tea in bed, made with water drawn from the creek. The tea in bed will become a daily ritual for the couple and Dorothy says it's the best cup of tea she's ever had. The creek water never fails to steep the tea leaves perfectly.

Ed's been up a while before Dorothy and Mike stir. He's got water, fed the horses, chopped some wood, lit the stove and made tea. Dorothy rises and breathes in the mountain air. She has a lot to do and a lot to learn.

First up, making breakfast. The kitchen in the cabin is little more than a nook. There is a counter and a sink and a wood stove. Dorothy puts her hands on her hips as she surveys what she's supposed to use to make meals for her family. This isn't an ordinary range, it's a wood-burning stove. Cooking is done on top of the stove and baking is done in the barrel oven built into a pipe extending off the main chimney. Besides worrying about recipes and burning things, she'll also have to stoke the fire. She won't be able to turn knobs to adjust the flames, she'll have to learn to cook by judging how hot her hand gets when it's near the heat. Heavy cast iron pots and pans or lighter enamel cookware is used on the stove and in the oven. Dorothy heaves an iron frying pan onto the stovetop and begins cooking her first meal. Bacon always tastes good no matter how it's done.

Ed is sticking close to home for the first couple of days as Dorothy jumps into backcountry life. She's glad her husband is there for the company and because she has so many questions.

"What's this?"

"What does that do?"

"Where do I go with these things?"

It's a big transition to go from not having lights at the flick of a switch or water straight from the tap. When the sun disappears behind a mountain, Dorothy reaches over to the wall to turn on the light. Of course, the room stays dark.

"You'll need to light the lamps," says Ed.

The hiss of Coleman lanterns is comforting to Dorothy. Unfortunately, they don't drown out all the noises in the bush. Ollie's stories of a bear behind every tree have been preying on Dorothy's imagination. When she hears something just outside the cabin door, she freezes in fear. She has another question for Ed, "What is that?!"

Ed cocks his head to one side. Then to the other. An animal is trying to gnaw through the cabin's wooden door.

"Is it a bear?" Dorothy asks.

Ed chuckles. "Oh, it's just a porcupine."

"A what?"

"Nothing for you to worry about. They're like hedgehogs[68] in England."

English hedgehogs are small spiny mammals that like to eat beetles, grubs, slugs and earthworms – not human flesh. (Most bears don't feast on humans either but Ed's father's stories made a major impact on Dorothy.) Porcupines in Canada are several times larger than hedgehogs, have longer quills and eat bark and other plants. Dorothy has never heard of one or seen one. Until tonight.

---

68. Hedgehog populations are actually being threatened in England. (2020)

Ed opens the door and shines the lamp on the porcupine.

"See!" he says. "Not a bear."

Ed uses his boot to shoo the slow-moving rodent off the front porch. He's careful not to get an ankle full of quills. It won't be the last time a porcupine visits the Carletons. It, or a revolving contingent of porcupines, comes back every night to chew on the cabin's wooden door. (They need to hone their continuously growing teeth.)

Dorothy collapses on the floor in relief. Then she starts laughing. Ed starts laughing, too. It's a good thing they can both see the humorous side of life. Otherwise, this living in the backcountry thing is going to get stale quickly.

To wash up in the evening, Dorothy fills an enamel basin from a bucket of water sitting on a washstand. There's a slop pail underneath so while she's brushing her teeth, she can spit into the pail. When the pail gets full, the waste is tossed into the woods.

That night, Ed escorts his wife to the biffy before they both hit the hay. Dorothy has survived her first full week as a warden's wife.

Warden and Wife Work

The first summer in Banff comes with a steep learning curve for both Dorothy and Ed. Thankfully, Dorothy gets some cooking lessons from Dorothy Black. Mrs. Black is also a district warden's wife. Her husband is Bill and like Ed, had been a Calgary Highlander. (It's thought he didn't serve overseas.) The couple lives at Saskatchewan River Crossing, north of Bow Summit.

Mrs. Black shows Dorothy how to make some meals on the woodstove. She teaches the young English woman that if she wants to cook fast, then she has to build a hotter fire. That means using the thin logs in the firebox instead of the thick ones. It also means Ed has to chop more wood as Dorothy goes through a lot. It's trial by fire.

While cooking on an electric or gas range, the pan doesn't have to be rotated. It heats evenly. That's not the case on the woodstove. Dorothy has to find the "sweet spot," where the heat is the hottest, all while stirring up a storm.

Another tip from Mrs. Black is to ignore recipes when it comes to cooking times. Everything is different when you're cooking with fire. Dorothy can't yet gauge warm from hot. Mrs. Black says a hot stove burns your food and a warm stove means you're cooking for hours. Dorothy realizes she's going to have to know her stove better than her husband. Otherwise, they might starve if she can't prepare a meal properly.

Baking is a whole new game, too. With no thermometer in the barrel oven, Mrs. Black shows Dorothy how to test the temperature of the woodstove by sticking her hand inside it. The first time she pulls her hand out too soon. Why would she want to catch on fire? But the second time, she hovers her palm until she feels the heat and understands what Mrs. Black is trying to teach her.

England is represented for a short while in the cabin kitchen through a recipe book Dorothy brought from home. She soon switches to a Canadian cookbook better suited for local ingredients. Her new *Purity Cookbook*, published by Purity Flour Mill Limited in Toronto, becomes her bible. But it doesn't perform any miracles when it comes to her first bread loaves. They go to the deer. Dorothy improves on her baking and soon, she's making spongy breads, as well as pies with the wild berries she's picked. Ed gobbles up the cookies she makes as quickly as they come out of the oven. Even though they're piping hot.

Dorothy and Ed have to be self-sufficient in the backcountry. There are no neighbours to borrow a cup of sugar from, nor any stores to run to if they need a refill of something. Banff is 85 km (just over 53 mi) away, so staples like flour and powdered milk are trucked in at the beginning of the season. Things are supposed to last until the next shopping trip. There are no summer treats like ice cream for Mike, as nothing can be frozen or refrigerated.

One thing that's available year-round is meat. Ed's allowed to harvest one elk a season and Dorothy has to learn how to process the edible parts. Mrs. Black shows her how to cut the meat up and put it in the oven for a short time so most of the blood is out of it. Then, Dorothy spoons the meat into the sealer jars and puts them in a heavy metal pressure cooker. (The pressure cooker can be used on the woodstove.) The jars are left for an hour while the meat cooks. Then, the jars can sit in the cupboard for months. Dorothy also does steaks by rolling them and putting them in the jars before the pressure cooker process.

If only the women from the League of Health and Beauty could see Dorothy now. They'd never believe how physical life at Bow Summit is. True to the league's motto, *Movement is Life*, she's getting a workout. Plus, she still has Mike to look after. When he's asleep, she does her stretches on the floor.

Ed's active in his job and home life, too. When not working in the field, he's cutting down dead trees with an axe. He brings the logs back to the cabin in the truck. He's also in charge of hauling water up from the creek and on wash day — several litres (gallons).

Washing is a full day's work. To wash clothing and linen, buckets of water are drawn from the stream. Dorothy heats the water on the stove before pouring it into a big washbasin. She hangs the sopping wet items on the clothesline strung between two tall and straight trees. The mountain breeze dries everything in no time. (In winter, it's a different story when shirts, pants and skirts will all turn into frozen bricks held up by clothespins.) Backcountry laundry is tedious and tiring and Dorothy hates it. Thankfully, washing day is only once a week.

Dorothy has to get her own water when Ed's out on patrol. The water pails are metal and heavy. She usually fills only one bucket to the half-way point. She can't wait until Mike gets older and he can do this job.

One job where Ed needs Dorothy's help is using the crosscut saw to buck off logs for firewood or to remove trees from trails or phone wires. The crosscut saw is better than an axe when tackling large timber. With two people, the saw is efficient, but only if the pair moves together. Otherwise, there's lots of starting and stopping as the saw teeth get snared in the wood. Dorothy says Ed is always telling her, "From me to you, from me to you," to get them into the proper rhythm.

The park is crisscrossed with telephone lines, haywires with insulators, connecting wardens in the field to the head office. Bow Summit cabin has a crank telephone (hand-cranked to produce electricity) but it's not for social calls. It's only for emergencies and checking in with headquarters twice a day. The phones are party lines (shared by multiple cabins) and Bow Summit's ring is a long ring, a short ring, followed by another long ring. It's Ed and Dorothy's only instant method of communicating with the world beyond themselves. However, it's never to be used for chitchatting, even though sometimes Dorothy wishes she could talk with the other wardens' wives.

The closest neighbour to Bow Summit is the Simpson family at Num-Ti-Jah Lodge near Bow Lake, about 6 km (4 mi) away. The lodge was a dream made into reality by Englishman Jimmy Simpson. It's quite an achievement for Justin James McCarthy (Jimmy) Simpson, who was supposedly considered a disgrace to his parents. He liked poaching and playing practical jokes among other "bad" qualities. His parents sent him to Canada in 1896 and he soon made a name for himself in Banff. In 1898, he fell in love with Bow Lake and knew he would one day build a home there near the water's edge. Meanwhile, he became a renowned guide and outfitter taking tourists through the Rockies.

In 1923, Jimmy and his wife, Williamina (Billie) Ross Reid, built a log cabin called the Rum Pasture near Bow Lake. Over a decade later, the Rum rooms grow into Num-Ti-Jah Lodge. (Num-Ti-Jah is an Îyãhé Nakoda word for pine marten, a small animal found in the Rockies.) People from far and wide came to stay at the wilderness hotel and hear Jimmy's legendary stories about his time in the mountains. In 1945, Jimmy Jr. is helping run the lodge and both father and son are around when the Carletons arrive at Bow Summit four years later.

Ed checks on the Simpsons from time-to-to-time but never with Dorothy in tow. The Carletons' next closest neighbours are both a good drive away, approximately 40 km (25 mi) on gravel roads. To the south and slightly east in Lake Louise, are Beef and his wife, Mac Woodworth. (Beef's wife's nickname is Mac.) To the north and slightly west are Bill and Dorothy Black. Mrs. Black and Dorothy meet a few times a month, often at the Blacks' Saskatchewan River Crossing home.

The Blacks have the Carletons over for supper and Dorothy appreciates the outings immensely. She likes the Blacks' frame house too because it's like a real home – albeit in the middle of the woods. It gets a basement one day and Dorothy discovers what the winch is for on Ed's big Power Wagon. He uses it to raise the Blacks' house so they can dig a basement. How's that for civilized living in the backcountry! Dorothy tells Mrs. Black she's lucky to have such a nice place.

Dorothy is never bored of life at Bow Summit and she's not lonely, but she is homesick. She longs for the companionship of her Women's League of Exercise and Beauty girls. She longs to sing songs with her family around the piano at 55 Grange Avenue. She longs to hop on her bike and visit Fred Green or Olive or any friend in cycling distance. Letters can only provide so much detail and she'd love to see the look on her father's face when he hears about the porcupine. She'd like to meet her nephew in Didsbury. Paul was born to Phyllis and Russ after Dorothy left for the backcountry. Even though her heart aches for home, Dorothy recognizes she would never have what she has in Alberta if it wasn't for meeting Ed during the war.

Because of Ed and Dorothy's close ties to the war; marking Remembrance Day is important to them. They begin attending Remembrance Day services and are involved with the Royal Canadian Legion and the Ladies Auxiliary. Despite this, Ed doesn't share any insights into his experiences as a Highlander although he does mention the long route marches the soldiers regularly endured. However, he doesn't talk about the actual combat, not even when old army mates or his brothers visit. Baillie Carleton still has a bottle of Champagne that he got when entering Paris. When his daughter asks him about going to war, he says he was shipped to Europe around D-Day and was scared stiff. He keeps his other stories to himself, too, like most other war veterans.

Bill Waterworth is a Banff boy who fought in the war. He enlisted in 1940 and was in the Royal Canadian Air Force. Bill was shot down over France in the fall of 1942 on his 33rd mission but escaped from his plane. He hid from the Nazis for two weeks until he was found by the Gestapo. He was kept for three years in a prisoner of war camp (Stalag VIIIB/344) before being forced to march from Poland to France in 1945. After the end of the war, he came home to Banff and it's here he meets Ed as well as Dorothy.

The Royal Canadian Legion in Banff is a place where veterans can see old friends (386 men and 25 women from Banff served in the Second World War), meet fellow veterans and have a drink. Ed went occasionally when Dorothy and Mike were living in Didsbury. Now that his family is at Bow Summit, he doesn't get many chances to get to the legion. It so happens that Ed and Dorothy are in town running errands one day when Ed thinks it's a great time to take her to the Colonel Moore Branch # 26.

Boy, oh, boy is Bill ever impressed by Dorothy! In fact, he says all the lads are really impressed by her. She's a "sweater girl" like the Hollywood actress Lana Turner … their curves hugged by their tight knitted tops. Of course, no one tells Dorothy about the comparison. It'll make her blush and besides, she's much too down to earth and modest to think she resembles a movie star.

Ed knows what a catch his wife is. Any other woman might have pulled up stakes and left when she got a glimpse of life as a warden's wife. Not Dorothy. The porcupines haven't chased her away either. One, in particular, has a penchant for toilet seats and chews one to sawdust. It's a crappy situation since Ed has to find a new one, but the Carletons roll with it.

Ed's a dedicated district warden. He cares greatly about nature and the animals and is good at dealing with everyone from colleagues, to tourists, to whomever. His duties take him all over the Mistaya Valley and include both land and water. He's responsible for stocking the lakes around Bow Summit. Banff's fish hatchery superintendent, Arthur "Art the Fish Guy" Colbeck, shows Ed how it's done.

Mike and Ed at the Bow Summit cabin in Mistaya River district, 1948. Photo: Carleton Family

Art is another veteran of the Second World War. Originally from Liverpool, England, he was living and working on a farm outside of Leduc, Alberta when war broke out. He joined the Loyal Edmonton Regiment (Loyal Eddies) and was sent, like Ed and his Highlander buddies, to the U.K. for training. Art met his wife Nancy there and they married in England a couple of years before Ed and Dorothy.

The Loyal Eddies fought in Sicily, where Art was wounded. He was sent back to Canada and spent time recovering at the Colonel Belcher Hospital in Calgary. His wife Nancy, a war bride like Dorothy, came to Calgary to be with him.

After his discharge from the Belcher, Art was looking for a job. He had a Grade 9 education, fighting skills and some experience farming and gold mining, but not much else. He did strike gold when he found employment at the Calgary Brewing and Malting Company but not doing what you'd expect. The brewery had a fish hatchery that opened in 1938 in cooperation with the Alberta Fish and Game Department. Art worked there for a couple of years before applying for a fish hatchery superintendent job in Banff. He got it.[69]

---

69. Art's son David says his father often marvelled that he got this position but he never looked back.

Art isn't a warden but he works closely with the Warden Service and Canadian Wildlife Service. He's in charge of the fish hatchery and the stocking program for lakes[70] in western national parks. Art and Ed spend many hours together collecting fish eggs from traps, talking about fish conservation and doing other general fish management.

Eggs are hatched into "fingerlings" in the fish hatchery. Rainbow trout, cutthroat trout, Yellowstone cutthroat, eastern brook trout, grayling and other species are among the fish raised for the National Parks Branch. The different types of fish won't all be swimming in the same lake but they all go into the water by the same method. The "fingerlings" are put into metal canisters strapped to the back of a horse or hiked by a warden to the park lakes. Getting the young fish to their new homes takes speed. Art straps the live fish to Ed's back and tells him to go as fast as he can. The fish need fresh water ASAP or else they'll go belly up. At the lake, the fingerlings are gently poured into their new home. Ed always sighs with relief when the fish are swimming. They'll eventually grow and be eagerly sought by anglers.

For all his long work hours, Ed gets only one day off a month. Even then, he's still in the mountains exploring trails and taking photos. His great curiousity for the park keeps him constantly updating his wilderness and mountaineering skills. He's always on the lookout for one of nature's greatest enemies in 1948: fire.

Fire is seen as destructive and must be extinguished.[71] It not only leaves ugly scars on the landscape but it also threatens infrastructure, wildlife and valuable timber. Earlier game and fire wardens and later park wardens patrolled areas looking for negligent campers who didn't put out their campfires, lightning strikes and brush close to the railway that could be sparked into an inferno. Wardens had lightweight portable water pumps and also used a fire retardant called Pyrox. The park also built fire roads and fire guards. In the 1940s, lookout men were stationed around the park on Tunnel Mountain, Castle Mountain and Beehive Mountain. The men telephoned headquarters at any whiff of danger.

Ed always has his firefighting tools at the ready. When someone reports smoke, he lashes his equipment to the horses and heads to wherever help is needed. Fortunately, the summer of '48 is a wet one.

Sometimes Dorothy phones headquarters on Ed's behalf with a report on fire conditions in the area. She's comfortable with that task, but the flames indoors have her frightened. When Ed goes away for the week, she's afraid she'll do something wrong with the wood stove and burn down the cabin. She doesn't dare leave her home for longer than it takes to go to the loo. Lighting the lantern is tricky, too. She pumps the fuel/vapour in the mixing chamber and then lights the match.

"Whoosh!"

The lantern flares bright and hot. Dorothy shrieks. She's uneasy with the burst of flame and wonders if she should stick to using the flashlight. No, that doesn't work. The torch is cumbersome and only spotlights one thing at a time. Dorothy takes the lamp outside to light it, just to be on the safe side. She has to admit, though, she enjoys the lantern on cool evenings. It gives off a lot of heat and makes the cabin cozy and warm.

70. Banff National Park stops stocking lakes and creeks with fish in 1988.

71. Fire is now considered a natural process and managed in the park. (2020)

Dorothy hangs the bright lamp on the ceiling hook and sits on the floor to play with Mike. In a couple of days, Ed will be home. Meanwhile, Dorothy has proven she can handle Bow Summit on her own. She has made it a home in the mountains.

Moving into Town

One morning, the earth has turned silver overnight. Frost paints the foliage and grass with its cool brush. The larches, too, are turning yellow, a sure sign of autumn. Cold comes earlier in the mountains and because the Bow Summit cabin isn't winterized, the Carletons will be moving into town.

Stan Peyto rents the Carletons a house in town on Muskrat Street. Stan works for the parks branch as a mechanic and heavy equipment operator and comes from a renowned Banff family. His father, Walter, was one of Banff's early wardens and his uncle, Bill, is a legend to this day, known by the moniker "Wild Bill." Peyto Lake, near Bow Summit, is named after Bill, who was renowned for his explorations, prospecting, mountaineering, trapping, guiding, geology studies as one of the first park wardens (1913 to 1936). Stan is impressive himself.

During the Second World War, Stan was stationed around Canada, including Vancouver Island, as a mechanic to "keep the tanks going." His wife, Inez, went with him until he was sent overseas. Stan is an explorer like his father and wild uncle, as well as an expert touring skier. He treats the Carletons with immense kindness and helps them get their footing in town. One of his sons, Paul, and Mike are around the same age so Mike has an instant buddy.

The Peyto family home is Wild Bill's former house on Banff Avenue. Stan and Inez have two other homes in Banff, one on Beaver Street and the other across from it on Muskrat Street. They rent this house to Ed, Dorothy and Mike.

Paul Peyto (left) and Mike (right) with Wild Bill Peyto (middle), Beaver Street, Banff, 1948.
Photo: Carleton Family

Dorothy has instant lights again. The house has electricity, running water and an indoor toilet. It's wonderful for a couple of days to be able to turn on the lights with a flick of the switch. Inez worries the Carletons aren't warm enough after seeing Ed collecting kindling and paper to start a fire in the furnace. She isn't concerned once she notices someone has opened a window to get some fresh air in.

The Peytos and Carletons spend time together over dinner and parties. Being in town means Dorothy can walk to the grocery store. She enjoys all the socializing among the community members. She likes receiving her letters at the post office from her parents, sister and Fred Green. But she's already missing the peace and quiet of the backcountry.

The family has been able to visit Didsbury. It's not all happy times. Russ and Phyllis are struggling. Phyllis is an only child and her parents are missing out on watching their two grandchildren grow. The Tuckers had a hard time saying goodbye to Maureen when Phyllis left for Canada on the *Queen Mary*. Phyllis's father asked her if she'd leave Maureen in Reading with them. Of course, that wasn't possible.

Living in small-town Alberta, Phyllis yearns for the busy Reading streets and the friends she has known since childhood. When Dorothy visits her in Didsbury, her energetic friend and sister-in-law lifts her spirits and makes her more homesick at the same time. Phyllis takes things day-by-day. When the year turns from 1948 to 1949, she holds on as winter passes. Maybe spring will be better. It's usually a season of renewal.

As the mountain streams start gushing with snowmelt, Dorothy and Ed are on the move again. They're not returning to Bow Summit. This time they're going to Stoney Creek. The Stoney Creek Warden Cabin is, well, by a stony creek, which flows into the Cascade River. The Carletons' new home is due north of Banff and west of the Ghost River wilderness, just over 14 km (9 mi) up the Cascade Fire Road. The road starts just west of Lake Minnewanka and follows the east side of Cascade Mountain.

The home by the edge of the creek is a bit of an upgrade from the Bow Summit cabin in Dorothy's opinion. There's still no electricity or running water — nor a biffy inside — but it's a nice little frame house. There's a chicken wire fence running around the cabin to keep out the porcupines and a narrow garden with a border of white rocks. Besides the hut, there's an outbuilding for the horses as well as a corral and a flagpole flying the Canadian Red Ensign.

The scenery outside parallels Bow Summit but it's vastly different. Stoney Creek isn't as tightly enclosed in mountains. Instead, there are wide open fields stretching to meet rocky slopes that lean back to meet the sky. The feeling of isolation is the same as Bow Summit though. Dorothy can see for miles and miles yet it's all rocks and trees and the occasional animal.

Dorothy, Ed and Mike settle into the cabin and nature's rhythm. By this time, Dorothy knows how to cook stews on top of the fire and bake cookies and bread in the barrel oven. With a wire grill, she crisps up the bread she's made and serves perfectly golden-brown toast to her family for breakfast. Then she's on to her next activity.

Dorothy always has something to do. Besides, days spent with three-year-olds are never boring. Mike asks tons of questions.

Why do birds fly?

Why are the mountains made of rocks?

How high is the moon?

At Stoney Creek, Dorothy and Mike go for long walks along the dusty Cascade Fire Road. They're soon accompanied by another friend, Chum. Chum's a cocker spaniel puppy when he comes to live with the Carletons. Mike runs and plays with Chum, and the pup keeps Dorothy company when Ed goes on his rounds.

At the entrance to the fire road, there's a swing gate with a lock on it. A permit and a key are needed to get past the barrier in the summer. After Labour Day in the fall, Banff residents can ask wardens at the Warden's Equipment Building in town for the key. There are plenty of fish to catch in the creek and nearby tarns.

A welcomed addition to Dorothy's home is a battery-operated radio. She taps her toes to her favourite music programs and hears news of the outside world. She says the radio is a godsend, especially when she's the only adult for miles.

Ed's patrols take him all over his district, sometimes for as long as two weeks at a time. He clears the deadfall off trails and telephone wires, and watches for poachers. He also records sightings of all wildlife including grizzlies and black bears. He marks down where he discovers wolf prints. Ed doesn't fear these predators after facing the worst one of all: humans.

While Ed is paid to be a warden, Dorothy never receives a dime for her work. She's often Ed's partner and has learned how to drive the Power Wagon on the rough and rocky road. Ed's a patient teacher and doesn't cover his eyes when Dorothy narrowly misses steering the vehicle into a tree or a large grey boulder. Now that Dorothy can get behind the wheel, she and Ed are a team lifting trees off wires and from the road.

It takes two people to operate the winch on the Power Wagon. One person has control in the vehicle while the other winds the cable around the tree. The apparatus is useful when ascending a steep hill. A particular spot near Lake Minnewanka is so precipitous that Dorothy feels like the vehicle will roll back down if they stop halfway up. With the winch, the Power Wagon, with Dorothy and Ed in it, is pulled up the slope and they can carry on their way.

Counting elk is another job where Dorothy pitches in. She and Ed drive around tallying the large ungulates for population surveys. One elk makes it into the supper pot. Fish are caught and add variety to the family meals. Ed sometimes finds shaggy mane mushrooms to complement a dish. Blueberries and tiny wild strawberries are great for pies and the whole family can help pick a bucketful.

After a long day, Dorothy and Ed relax in the glow of the lantern. They sing songs and chuckle about silly things and wonder what life would have been like without the war. Outside, the gurgle of Stoney Creek mixes in with the laughter as wildlife passes by the cabin under a starlit sky.

FALL AT STONEY CREEK

There are stories that float around the mountains of Banff like smoke. Ed only gets a whiff of a line or two about lost cabins built by Bill Peyto. Ebenezer William "Bill" Peyto came to Canada from England in 1887 when he was 18. After working in various places, decided he liked living in the mountains. Seven years later, he was a trail guide and a damn good one. He knew how to challenge hikers, giving them a taste of danger while keeping them safe.

The Boer War erupted in 1899 (1899–1902 – Canada's first foreign war) and a year later, Bill joined the Canadian army serving in Lord Strathcona's Horse Regiment. He survived and in 1913, became one of Banff's first national park wardens. A year later, the First World War began. Bill served with the 12th Mounted Regiment and Machine Gun Brigade and returned home wounded. He went back to his warden job. It seems that Bill, much like Ed, realized that there is no better place to be after hell, than in nature.

Bill's place in Banff history has been cemented because of his wilderness skills, exploration prowess and adventures. He was also a teacher and Jimmy Simpson benefited from learning the ropes from one of the best Rocky Mountain men. There are many stories about Jimmy Sr. and there are many legends about Bill. He supposedly went to a town bar with a live lynx strapped to his back. He looked "wild," too, with his large sombrero, a neckerchief, a gun and gun belt and big hunting knife. It's also said that while guiding groups around the park peaks, he'd go off on his own for the night. He liked his solitude and this is what might have pushed him to climb higher, hike deeper and find places no one had seen in a long time. He built cabins in these remote locations and was sure of seclusion.[72]

***

It has been Fred Green's mission to bring Dorothy and Ed back to England. Dorothy's friend and former boss writes letters to the couple and sends the mail addressed to the Wardens Service in Banff. Fred urges the pair to return to the U.K. He corresponds with the Fowlers, George and Alice, too. Dorothy's parents send him a photo of her, taken in Alberta, and he says she looks as young as ever.

On Sept. 13, 1949, the news from Fred is not good. He writes to Dorothy's parents and tells them that he is ill and could they please reach out to Dorothy.

When next you write to Canada will you please explain this to Dorothy as I feel I am just about breathing my last. Tell her we have not forgotten her in the office and I will certainly write to her when I am strong enough.

Dorothy's eyes fill with tears while she reads about her dear friend. She continues to write to him, telling him about her exploits. Autumn is a busy time around Stoney Creek. There are many visitors, which Dorothy enjoys. She gets to hear about what's going on outside her backcountry post, as well as sing with people as they're going on their way, often with a fishing rod. *Happy Trails* is a favourite song of Dorothy's.

Some trails are happy ones, Others are blue.
It's the way you ride the trail that counts, Here's a happy one for you.
Happy trails to you

72. One of Bill Peyto's cabins is now on the grounds of the Whyte Museum of the Canadian Rockies in Banff.

Horse wranglers also stop in for a visit and lunch at Stoney Creek. It's a stop-over point for warden wranglers herding horses on the return to Ya Ha Tinda Ranch for the winter. Ya Ha Tinda is a federal government ranch that trains the animals for work in western national parks. Park wardens use the horses to patrol their large districts but only in the summer. The animals spend winter at Ya Ha Tinda.

In the Ĩyãħé Nakoda language, Ya Ha Tinda means mountain prairie, and Indigenous peoples have used the area for centuries. William Twin, from Ĩyãħé Nakoda, introduced Bill and Jim Brewster, Banff businessmen, to the land. By the early 1900s, it was part of the Brewster Brothers Transfer Company and a ranch was established for guiding and outfitting purposes. Parks took over the ranch in 1917 to train horses as saddle and pack animals.

Horses are a good way for wardens to survey the backcountry. Well-trained, the animals don't spook easily nor do they scare wildlife. Horses are also an extra set of ears and eyes on the lookout for predators. Ed has a lot of respect for the horses that travel with him through the wilderness.

In the fall, the Ya Ha Tinda horses make the journey up the Cascade Fire Road to the ranch. Over two hundred horses gallop near the Carletons' cabin, on their way to their winter home. The first time Dorothy hears and sees this spectacle she's amazed at the power of the animals. Actually, it will always amaze her. She can hear the herd at the beginning. It's a faint rumble at first, almost like a Reading train a couple of miles from the station. Then, the sound turns to thunder. When the horses burst into the pasture at Stoney Creek, Dorothy puts her hands over Mike's ears. The sound is deafening as hundreds of hooves pound the earth. Dust fills the air as the horses slow their run by the cabin.

There are many wardens on the drive. If any of them needs a break, they'll stop at the cabin. Dorothy offers the men a drink of water. She brings the pail of water and the dipper over to them and each man takes a loud slurp. Water is the first thing any park warden or horse wrangler wants when they come to visit. They head straight over to the pail for a drink. The horses drink straight from Stoney Creek and then munch on the pastures near the cabin.

Mike has a couple of questions for the wranglers. They answer his queries good-naturedly before continuing on their journey to the ranch. He watches the men and horses disappear into the fall foliage knowing he'll see them again in late spring. Spring is the kickoff to a new season for the parks service. The horses will reverse their trip then and be distributed to the districts. Wardens look forward to getting their horses and finding out their likes and quirks. First, the park has to get through winter.

Backcountry Winter

With the first heavy snowfall, comes news of Fred's death. His wife Dora writes to Dorothy on Nov. 3, 1949, saying how Fred had been horribly ill during the last few months. Although his "little girl" (his nickname for Dorothy) misses him, she wouldn't wish him back because of all the pain he had been suffering.

Dorothy on horseback at Stoney Creek, 1949.
Photo: Carleton Family

Quite recently, he was talking of you and he did so appreciate your kindness in sending notes about the good things you did. My husband was very interested in you and your family – often talked of you and was very happy in association with you and thought perhaps one day you would be back here.

Yours very sincerely, Dora Green

Fred's obituary is included in the letter and he's called "one of the greatest authorities on forestry work in the country." He was once awarded a prestigious award (the Gillender Prize) by the Royal Forestry Society for an original written work on forestry. He was active in his community, too. He was on the Mapledurham Parish Council and when he resigned, Dora took his seat. With his death, England lost a valuable resource, Dora lost a husband, his son, Dr. Patrick Gordon Green, lost a father and Dorothy lost a dear friend.

She keeps some of Fred's letters. They are on thin beige air letter paper but the ink won't fade much over the years. She can still hear his voice when she reads his notes, a tie to the life she left behind.

More adventures await Dorothy. She's about to experience her first winter in the backcountry. She learns she always has to keep the fire stoked because Ed's often frozen to the bone when he comes in from his long patrols on snowshoes. For Ed, there's a fine balance between dressing too warmly for working outside and dressing too lightly. If Ed's too warm, he'll sweat. The downside is that the perspiration gets trapped in his

Ed and Mike skiing at Stoney Creek, 1951.
Photo: Carleton Family

clothing and will make him feel damp and chilled. If he dresses too lightly, he'll be constantly cold. Wool is the best way to keep Ed comfy in the outdoors. Thankfully, his warden uniform is wool.

Dresses and skirts (and those sweaters) are still Dorothy's preferred mode of dress. However, she is slowly coming around to the idea that trousers are better suited for a backcountry woman. Besides, she can't ride a horse or ski in a skirt.

Stoney Creek has a "ski hill" – an access road that slopes steeply down to the cabin from the Cascade Fire Road. It's where Dorothy straps two long wooden boards to her feet, grabs two long poles and attempts to glide over the snow for the first time. Ed laughs as his wife tumbles and lands on her butt.

"I'd rather be hiking," she says, brushing the snow off her legs.

Ed has learned how to ski tour and alpine (downhill) ski this year, too, during a warden snowcraft school at Yoho National Park in British Colombia. It's not like he was great at the beginning either. He doesn't come from a wealthy family that could shell out money for equipment and the flat land surrounding Didsbury isn't conducive to downhill skiing. However, his natural athleticism helps him improve quickly. Ski touring and alpine skiing are popular in Banff National Park. There have been skiing races held in the backcountry for more than a decade. Banff Sunshine Village is the first place to offer downhill skiing in the late 1920s. Mount Norquay gets the first chair-lift in 1948, the same year Ed got his job. Knowing how to ski isn't a warden prerequisite but opinions are slowly changing. Swiss guides, brought in by CPR to take tourists into the backcountry, often act as the leads on high mountain rescues — not wardens. However, a warden and accomplished local skier named Noel Gardner wants to change this. He thinks wardens should know how to ski as well as be avalanche aware and able to do high altitude rescues.

Bill Black has another option: snow machines. Why snowshoe or ski when a machine can get you over the deep snow quicker than on foot? He builds one that he demonstrates to Ed and young Mike.

Bill uses it around Saskatchewan River Crossing until he's told to park it by the park management. It's back to snowshoes.

Mike, at four years old, has his own little skis. He takes naturally to ski touring like his dad and loves to be outside with Chum kicking up the snow behind him. On warmer winter days, Mike and his mum snowshoe or toboggan. The sled picks up some good speed travelling down the road.

Stoney Creek Cabin in winter.
Photo: Carleton Family

The fire road is a nice escape from cabin life once a month during the chilly weather. If the road isn't blanketed with thick layers of snow, Ed, Dorothy and Mike drive to Banff. Dorothy and Mike get groceries, supplies, pick up the mail and have a quick visit with friends in town. Ed checks in at the office, meets with the chief warden, turns in his warden diary and picks up fuel. Then, it's back to the backcountry.

One stormy bleak morning, Ed kisses his wife and son goodbye. He's going on patrol. It's tough for him to leave the warmth of the cabin and start hiking into the cold but nothing can stop him from doing his duties. Darkness hovers while snow steadily accumulates on the ground. The wind howls at him as he forces the door open, pushing away a large pile of heavy snow. He puts on his snowshoes while Dorothy and Mike watch from the window. Then he treks into the blizzard and out of their sight. Dorothy prays her husband will be fine in the dreary weather.

The day passes slowly no matter what Dorothy does to keep her mind off Ed. She cooks. She bakes. She sings with Mike. She heads out in the elements once in a while to use the outhouse. It's freezing and she estimates the temperature is around -30. Brrrr.

Back inside the cabin, she warms up quickly by the woodstove. It's 4 p.m. and she'll have to start supper soon.

Bang! Bang!

She's almost shocked out of her skin. Something is thumping on the door. What could it be? There are no bears awake. She's not expecting visitors. Besides, the fire road is certainly impassable because of the storm. No one could possibly get here in weather like this.

The door is flung open and …

"Ed?!"

"Who else would it be?" he asks, covered head to foot in snow.

The elements had been too much for him. He struggled for hours climbing high drifts and shielding his face from the scouring wind. The cold snuck under his collar and poured down his back, making him shiver violently. The gale eventually pummelled him into submission. He had to use every ounce of strength to get back to his family.

Dorothy brushes the snow off her husband and seats him next to the blazing fire. She knows the perfect remedy for a cold man: a hot rum toddy.

Winter in the backcountry is not for the faint of heart when even getting to the toilet is a daunting task. The cold, snow, wind and isolation can wear a person down. But there's a beauty that can't be found anywhere else and the landscape is constantly changing. Dorothy is often struck by how different the mountains can look one moment to the next. On a sunny bluebird morning, the spires stick straight into the sky. On a blustery afternoon, snow is blown off the peaks and it looks like white sheets drying on a high, very high, clothesline.

There is a romance in the wilderness that can't be explained. Just outside the door of the cabin, is a world of snow and ice, while inside the cabin, everything is warm and cheerful. It's the perfect place to be for Christmas. Stan Peyto surprises the Carletons on Christmas Eve with a festive treat. Somehow, Stan manages to drive through the snow and delivers a 20-pound turkey to Dorothy.

"It sure beats elk meat for Christmas," she tells him while pouring him a festive drink of whisky.

The next day, Dorothy prepares a feast with the delicious turkey. To top off the meal, she bakes a pie made with canned fruit. The crust is flaky and the warm filling is rich.

"I bet even the Queen isn't served pie this perfect," says Ed, giving Dorothy a grin.

The family opens presents they've made for each other or bought on a trip to town. They sing carols and tell tales. Mike can now spin a yarn as well. The scene is almost repeated for New Year's Eve, except there are no gifts and the songs are different. There is also a drink or two of Bristol Cream sherry, Dorothy's favourite. The Carletons ring in 1950 with shouts and clapping and wishes for a banner year for family and friends.

***

In the spring of 1950, Dorothy is leaving Canada. She's sailing to England, where she'll stay for three months. It's her first trip back to the U. K. and she'll be bringing Mike along. Her parents have been asking for her to return home. They miss her and want to see their grandson. Dorothy also wants to see her family and friends.

After taking the train to Montreal, Mrs. D. Carleton and Master M.S. Carleton board *RMS Franconia* on Friday, Apr. 21, 1950. The ship is an ocean liner operated by the Cunard Line. She's a twin-screw turbine-like the *Letitia*, the ship that brought Dorothy and Mike to Canada four years ago. The *Franconia* had also been used to bring immigrants to North America. Sir Winston Churchill and a British delegation stayed on the Franconia during the Yalta conference in early February 1945.

Churchill had said that the ocean liner was a most comfortable ship. Dorothy agrees. It's certainly better than the last voyage she was on. This time, instead of falling off top bunks, dirty diapers and rampant seasickness, Dorothy has a bottom berth, a four-year-old and people to share conversations with over lovely dinners. Captain W. M. Stewart makes the transatlantic crossing to Liverpool in just about a week.

The train ride from Liverpool to Reading reminds Dorothy, briefly, of leaving home. She had thought it was forever and here she is, about to be reunited with her family. She's looking forward to the visit and banishes memories of the past. She points out landmarks and cows and sheep to Mike and wishes the train would go faster.

At 55 Grange Avenue, she is hugged and kissed. She can't believe how old her parents look. It hasn't been that long but there are wrinkles and lines in their faces that weren't there when she left. George is 61, Alice is 59 and Dorothy is 31. Mike, only a few months old when he was last in the small brick home, is four.

Dorothy is home but Mike is not. He is in a strange place with strangers who talk in a strange way. He's shy and misses his dad. Nevertheless, he warms up to his friendly grandparents and other relatives. He meets his Aunty Marjorie, Uncle Melbourne and his two cousins, Roger and Derek. His cousins run around with him in the English air as their parents catch up.

Fred Green's absence is felt by Dorothy. She keeps thinking she has to visit him. If she had more time, she might have gone by Mapledurham House. However, like most trips, the hours evaporate.

Olive and Dan Openshaw take Dorothy and Mike out for lunch. Olive and Dorothy sing and talk about their pals and raising children and Dorothy's toilet travails. She's a seasoned warden wife by now, but she likes to poke fun at herself and her unconventional (to the Brits) lifestyle. She also realizes that stolid city air cannot compete with Banff's fresh mountain air. It has been three months since she last kissed Ed. She's ready to go home.

The voyage back is aboard *RMS Ascania.* Dorothy and Mike board the ship in Liverpool on Jul. 13, 1950. The goodbyes in Reading were tearful, of course, but it was a great visit. Dorothy leaves England with her heart singing.

The *Ascania* is only recently back on the waves after reconditioning. Her first run on the sea was three months ago, on the very day Dorothy and Mike left for the U.K. on the *Franconia. Ascania* was originally built in the early 1920s as a "ship of innovations." It had stained glass windows, a dance floor, a library and many other home comforts. There was a nursery and even a gymnasium. The vessel was an armed merchant cruiser in the Second World War as well as a troop transport ship. It also repatriated Gibraltarians who were living in Northern Ireland during the war.

The ship is practically new and Dorothy likes this. The nursery has scenes from Alice in Wonderland painted on the walls and there's a little playhouse made in the shape of the shoe from the rhyme about the little old woman who lived in a shoe. Dorothy likes the Promenade deck and its sea air best and walks about the ship with Mike. Captain J. V. Locke forecasted nice weather for sailing and the trip is a breeze.

Back in Banff, Ed is slightly thinner. He's been out in the bush all alone and has had to cook for himself. Dorothy will fatten him up in no time with her cookies.

That summer, Russ, Phyllis, Maureen and Paul visit Stoney Creek. Russ and Phyllis are facing some relationship challenges. Nevertheless, both families have a great time in the backcountry. There's so much space for the cousins to run and shout while their parents catch up on news. Nights spent by the fire are for teaching the kids old English songs. When they're finally in bed, it's time for their parents to reminisce.

In a couple of months, Phyllis, pregnant with her third child, will leave Alberta. Her future is bleak in Didsbury with Russ drifting along in life. Her parents send her money to return to England with Maureen and Paul. The three board a ship for the U.K. and are gone from Russ' life.

How many war brides return home isn't known. It's thought that perhaps five to 10 per cent of approximately 48,000 war brides go back to their home countries. With Phyllis gone, Dorothy and Ed feel a bit adrift. The foundation of their relationship had been built through Russ and Phyllis. Both couples bonded through their courtships and their respective marriages had grown and been strengthened through shared experiences. Now one of those links is gone. It's upsetting for Dorothy, too, to lose a close friend and someone who knew her not just as a warden's wife and Mike's mother but as a young girl with a bright future.

Left to right: Russ Carleton, his daughter Maureen, Mike and Dorothy at Stoney Creek. Photo: Carleton Family

Dorothy does have other friends and makes them easily. People are drawn to her energy and cheerful spirit. She makes friends with other warden's wives through common backcountry problems. They talk and laugh about the outdoor plumbing, how to avoid getting soaked while getting water out of the creek and how to deal with all the mice that constantly get into everything. Their sharp rodent teeth can gnaw through any packaging (except tin) and they poop everywhere. Dorothy hates to admit that the little things frighten her with their high-pitched squeaks and frantic scurrying in the shadows. One way to get rid of them is by having a cat, so the Carletons get one. Ed names him Thomas L. Thomas (no one knows why) and the cat with two first names (or is that two last names?) feasts on Stoney Creek vermin. Once he eats all the mice there, Dorothy loans him out to another warden's wife. He takes care of her rodent problem, too.

Dorothy is always on the lookout for a way to help. She often records the wildlife she spots for Ed when she goes for a walk or a drive. On a sunny summer day, she and Mike take their brand new personal red pickup truck to Cuthead Cabin, about 11 km (7 mi) from Stoney Creek on the fire road. They're going to visit Vera Taylor, a woman who is staying at the hut.

On Dorothy and Mike's return, Dorothy spots a herd of brown and beige elk on a green slope. She is so intent on counting them all that she misses the curve in the road … and drives right over the bank and down into a gully.

What a pickle! After making sure Mike is fine and dandy, the pair scrambles up the bank. The new truck is deep in the ditch and Dorothy is sure it's not fine and dandy. The mum and son are about halfway home and will have to walk the rest of the way. Dorothy is upset. She can't believe she was so stupid.

"I know that bend in the road," she grumbles to herself. "How did I manage to miss it?"

After several minutes of marching, they hear a low rumble. It's Ed in the Power Wagon! He had been in town getting hay.

"What happened to the truck?" he asks.

"It's in the ditch and you'll never get it out," says Dorothy.

"We'll see about that."

The next day, a friend of Ed's brings his vehicle equipped with a heavy-duty winch and the pickup is pulled out of the gully. The truck needs some work before it runs again but it'll go. Afterwards, Dorothy teases Ed about how he was more concerned about the pickup than his family.

In August 1950, the federal government creates the Canadian Army Special Force to fight in the Korean War. Young men are being sent overseas but Ed isn't one of them. He isn't going to fight in this war. At 33 years old, he isn't too old to pick up a weapon again but he has a steady job and a family. Dorothy is glad he is staying home. She's also over the moon that Ed will be playing host to someone of the British aristocracy.

Ed has a very important meeting with a very important person. The VIP is Governor General Viscount Harold Alexander's wife, Lady Margaret Diana Bingham, Lady Alexander. Lady Alexander is the vice-regal consort of Canada and a daughter of British nobility.

Lord Alexander, the governor general of Canada, is considered a military genius and a hero of the Second World War by the British. In 1937, he was promoted to general at 45 years old and became the youngest general in the British army at that time. As the Korean War heats up, Lord Alexander is meeting with Canadian troops heading overseas and bolstering their courage. While he's doing that, his wife is coming to Banff to see the wildlife and wildflowers.

Before Ed's brush with the gentry, Dorothy fusses over his uniform and makes sure every crease is creased, his boots are polished and his tie is straight. When he returns that evening, she drinks in every detail of the day and wants to know what Lady Alexander wore, said and ate. Ed, smiling widely, happily tells his wife about the visit.

The warden, Lady Alexander and her entourage had a pleasant tour around Banff. They looked for bears and moose and Ed told Lady Alexander the names of the mountains ringing the town. He also took her along the Cascade River to fish.

On Sept. 7, 1950, Lady Alexander's lady-in-waiting writes a note to Ed. She sends along a penknife as a thank-you gift.

Her Excellency thoroughly enjoyed the day in the beautiful bit of country and was disappointed only that your grizzly bear did not show himself.

I am to send her Excellency's best wishes.

Yours sincerely, Lady-in-waiting Miss Anstice Gibbs

Chapter Nine

Nature Rules

Snowy Slopes

The spectacular scenery of Banff National Park can sometimes lull visitors into believing nothing bad can happen in a place this pretty. There are a variety of outdoor activities to choose from such as hiking, ski touring, alpine skiing and climbing. The mountains are alluring and people want to conquer them. Nevertheless, nature always rules.

The first recorded climbing accident in Banff was in 1890. An American, Yale University student Walter Wilcox, was ice climbing with Yandell Henderson and Lewis Frissell on Mount Lefroy, west of Lake Louise near the Alberta-B.C. boundary, when Frissell fell. When he landed, a boulder landed on him. Fortunately, he was alive but thought he had dislocated his hip. Wilcox ran to get help and found it among two Nakoda men, William Twin and Tom Chiniquay, and two others from a nearby CPR chalet. By the time the group got Frissell to the hotel, his hip injury was nothing more than a big bruise.

Wilcox went on to explore more of the Rockies, naming many of the areas around Lake Louise such as Paradise Valley. In 1896, he published *Camping in the Canadian Rockies: An Account of Camp Life in the Wilder Parts of the Canadian Rocky Mountains.* It was a best seller and an inspiration to many who read it.

The same year the book came out, there was another accident on Mount Lefroy. That August, Philip Stanley Abbot[73] fell during an ascent and died. The American lawyer's death is the first recorded climbing fatality in North America.

As mentioned in previous chapters, Swiss guides are often the ones plucking people off the mountains. In 1950, Walter Perren and Edmond Petrig (sometimes spelled Edmund Petrie) are brought to Canada as CPR Swiss Guides to take over from older guides such as Ernst Feuz. A few years into the future, Walter will play a large part in expanding the role of the parks branch in mountain rescues. Meanwhile, Noel Gardner is trying to convince the higher-ups that wardens need to take on more high altitude rescue duties, and that includes being proficient downhill skiers. It works and in 1951, Gardner puts on a ski school that Ed attends.

The ski school is held in Glacier National Park near Rogers Pass, B.C. Ed and four other wardens from various parks take the train to Rogers Pass and are handed the latest in ski gear. Then … they have to shape the "ski" hill. There are no fresh tracks for these guys. They have to stomp down the snow as they ascend the slope.

73. Abbot Pass and the Alpine Club of Canada's Abbot Pass Hut are named after Philip Stanley Abbot.

Then they practice snowplowing, the most basic manoeuvre of downhill skiing, on the way down.

Ed's legs burn as he shifts his weight from one side to the other, trying to make his turns while cruising down the slope. It's been a while since he's been physically challenged to this degree and he's enjoying it. He lets himself go a little bit faster. The wind whistles past his ears as he picks up speed and all of a sudden his ski tips cross and ….

"Ow!"

He's dumped deep into snow off the "piste" (a ski run of compacted snow). While he struggles to climb out of the hole he has made, he knows something is not right. It's his knee. He must have twisted it when he fell. Well, he won't be skiing for the rest of the week. He can, though, continue with the avalanche training.

When the wardens aren't on the slopes, they're learning about avalanches.[74] Snow slides can be catastrophic but they are also part of nature. In the late nineteenth and early twentieth centuries, many of the snow slides occurred at work sites like railroad lines. The 1910 Rogers Pass Avalanche was one such disaster.

Rogers Pass[75] is in the Selkirk Mountains and about a 70-km (43 mi) drive east of Revelstoke and about a 400-km (244 mi) drive west from Calgary. The pass was an important east-west route for CPR trains. The narrow valley edged by large mountains gets a ton of snow.

On Mar. 4, 1910, Canada's deadliest avalanche hit Rogers Pass. CPR workers were clearing snow from a slide when another one swept down into the valley. Fifty-eight people died, a locomotive and plow were found destroyed 15 m (49 ft) from the tracks and wooden cars were reduced to mere splinters.

By the start of 1930, avalanches were claiming the lives of people who were in the mountains for recreational purposes. An avalanche in February 1933 in Yoho National Park in B.C. kills two Banff brothers, Chris and Joe Daem. Their deaths were B.C.'s first recorded backcountry skiing fatalities. In April of the same year, Raymond "Kit" Paley was skiing alone and died after being caught in a slide on Fossil Mountain, near Lake Louise Ski Resort. His death was Alberta's first recorded backcountry skiing fatality. As the years move forward, avalanche victims start including snowshoers and mountaineers.

In the late 1940s and early 1950s, people are increasingly heading to the mountains for winter outdoor pursuits. Ski and backcountry lodges in the Rockies are extolling the virtues of being in the great outdoors during the colder months. However, many park wardens have limited avalanche knowledge. Gardner[76] hopes that by learning avalanche basics such as how they form and why the snowpack shifts, wardens will have more of a

74. Avalanche Canada, a national public avalanche safety organization, puts out avalanche forecasts and special courses on avalanche safety. Avalanche Canada: https://www.avalanche.ca.

75. The Trans-Canada Highway to and from Rogers Pass is dotted with snow sheds (roof structures built over the road) to keep slides from hitting vehicles. The Canadian Army's Avalanche Control Troop is also responsible for blasting away avalanche danger. At the end of 2019, the Canadian government was testing a new $3-million Swiss designed avalanche-detection system.

76. Through his work, Noel Gardner becomes known as the father of avalanche recording and forecasting in Canada.

role in preventing accidents. The wardens are at his ski school for nine days and then it's back to their regular routines.

Five-year-old Mike is thrilled to have his father home. Ed bounces his firstborn on his knee and sings him songs like *Keemo Kimo,* an old English nonsense rhyme turned into a tune. Mike watches his dad, who is always on the move. Ed takes care of the horses, gets water and fetches wood to fill the stove. On dark winter days, Ed is silhouetted by the Coleman lantern while he writes down his daily activities. His diary is an important aspect of his work and he jots down the jobs he has done, if he has seen any game and if there were any visitors.

Ed reads a lot to Mike and also gives him horse riding lessons. Just because Mike is young though, he's not exempt from chores. Ed has a couple of small jobs for his son, like hauling water and cutting kindling. Mike's next job is to be a big brother.

Here Comes Terry

For park warden wives, having a baby in the summer is a major no-no. It's fire season and they shouldn't be distracting their husband from their firefighting duties. Ed and Dorothy's baby will be arriving in the fall of 1951. Right on the park's schedule.

Before the new baby arrives, Dorothy and Mike move into Banff. Dorothy loves the backcountry but she is not going to deliver her infant in the wilderness. No, the baby will be born at Banff Mineral Springs Hospital.[77]

In October, Dorothy is the guest of warden Frank Bryant and his wife Beatrice. Mike stays with his friend Paul's family, Stan and Inez Peyto. While Mike misses his parents, he's treated to real milk! (Mike does NOT like the powdered milk he's served at home.) Ed stays at Stoney Creek, working as usual. Men aren't expected to be in the delivery room while their wives are in labour.

After Terence, shortened to Terry, comes into the world in early November, Ed heads into town and meets his new boy. He toasts the birth with a glass of whisky and then it's back to work. Mike, almost six, hopes Terry will make a good playmate. Dorothy is glad her infant is healthy and has a hearty set of lungs on him.

Terry's birth makes the Didsbury newspaper. The announcement on Nov. 21 spells his full name correctly. His birth certificate doesn't. "Terrance" will haunt Terence all of his life.

Dorothy stays with the Bryants for two weeks. Then, it's back to the bush and diapers. The Stoney Creek cabin is small but accommodates the growing family. Mike has the bedroom, Terry sleeps in a pram (which someone from Didsbury gave them) and Dorothy and Ed have their bed in the living room.

Infant Terry is not a great playmate for Mike. The older brother is a bit annoyed at the disruption his baby brother has brought to their backcountry home. Terry cries and then needs his diaper changed. Then he has to be fed. Then he has to be cuddled for hours and hours (or so it seems to Mike). Nevertheless, Terry is here to stay and the family of four celebrates a new year together: 1952.

---

77. The old hospital at 102 Spray Avenue is now a YWCA.

Mike greets his baby brother Terry and their mother at Stoney Creek.
Photo: Carleton Family

Dorothy and Ed make sure everyone at Stoney Creek has food, clean clothing and a song or two to keep them in good cheer. While Dorothy is as busy as ever in 1952, she manages to keep the household running and support her husband and his work. Ed, after a long day in the mountains, rocks baby Terry to sleep — and often, himself, too. There's no place like home.

Outside, winter has claimed every nook and cranny. Inside, the woodstove does a good job of chasing the cold out of the corners. First thing in the morning though, before the fire is roaring, it's chilly. Dorothy tells Mike it's time to get out of bed but he really doesn't want to leave his comfy nest. However, he listens to his mother and races to the stove to keep warm. He stands with his back to the fire and in no time, the back of his knees are toasty. Yet, the front of his knees are colder than ever. He has to turn around. Thus, the never-ending game of front-to-back starts until the whole cabin is cozy.

The Carletons run into a bit of trouble trying to return to Stoney Creek on a winter's evening. After a monthly outing into Banff, they're driving home in their family pickup truck. It's a frigid night, well below -40 C, and it's teeth-shattering cold. It's so cold the vehicle has a hard time keeping the heat up in the cab. Terry is only a few months old and is bundled in blankets to keep him warm. The condition of the fire road is fair and Ed's making good time. They'll be home in about 20 minutes.

They reach the Cascade River Bridge when the pickup starts losing speed.

"Cough," goes the engine.

"Sputter," goes the fuel pump.

Then the vehicle slows and … stops.

More than 6 km (4 mi) from home.

Ed tries to turn over the ignition but the engine only coughs and wheezes some more.

"That went over like a lead balloon," says Ed, using one of his common phrases.

The motor is frozen, much like they'll be if they stick around. The Carletons have no choice but to walk the rest of the way home. Ed picks up Terry and Dorothy takes Mike's hand. It's a clear night and the full moon lights the path for them. The freezing air turns their breath into ice. At least they're walking and will be warm. Dorothy's not too worried about her boys. She's worried about the produce they're leaving behind.

Ed had covered the groceries with a tarp but that probably won't stop the fresh vegetables from freezing. Dorothy is usually content with canned veggies, but when she goes into town, she prefers the fresh stuff. It's a treat to cook with them instead of the canned goods. Oh well. Not much they can do about it now.

When they finally reach home — a very cold home — Ed starts the woodstove. Soon the cabin warms enough so they can take off their mittens and gloves. Dorothy boils some water for tea and with some hot liquid in their bellies, they're finally thawed out enough for bed.

In the morning, Ed calls the warden office in Banff and a support vehicle comes to help him get the pickup started. As for the fresh vegetables, you could say they were flash frozen.

While Ed is working on the truck, Mike is working on his lessons. He's six and has to go to school. Except there is no school close enough for him to attend. Instead, Dorothy homeschools him in the winter through correspondence lessons. All the material for the Grade 1 student is mailed all at once to Mike from the provincial education office in Edmonton, Alberta. Since Dorothy can't go into Banff every week to pick up the mail, a huge stack of papers and books arrive on the same day.

Mike doesn't find the school work too onerous. It's only a few hours a day and when the weather starts getting nicer, he can sit in the sun and do his sums. He loves math and finds he has an aptitude for it. He also practices writing the letters of the alphabet and draws pictures of Chum, Thomas L. Thomas and other animals.

Although Mike lives in the backcountry with bears and wolves and pikas, there are some creatures that can only be found on a farm. Thus, when a lesson instructs him to draw a picture of a pig … he has no idea how. He's never seen one! Instead, Dorothy tells him to draw an elk. Mike starts his work and draws a big bull elk with majestic antlers. Dorothy adds a note to the illustration saying that pigs are few and far between at Stoney Creek.

Once Mike's completed his work, the pages are mailed back to Edmonton when the Carletons go to town. It'll be at least a month before his marked assignments are returned to him the same way.

The post is not only for learning the three Rs or mailing Dorothy's letters to family and friends: it's also a way to send food to an England that's still under ration orders. During the Second World War, Canada had rationing as well to make sure soldiers overseas were fed. Food was a "weapon of war." *Fat is Ammunition* boasted an ad. One pound of fat translated into glycerine to fire 150 bullets from a Bren gun.

Sugar was the first to be cut in 1942 in Canada. Other staples followed and soon, Canadians were coming up with some interesting concoctions like Tomato Soup Cake.[78] The soup is the liquid in the recipe, replacing rationed milk.

Canada also sent basics to the U.K. The Brits were estimated to have consumed 57 per cent of Canada's wheat and flour as well as 39 per cent of Canada's bacon, 15 per cent of its eggs, 24 per cent of cheese and 11 per cent of evaporated milk. Rationing officially ended in Canada in 1947.[79] Dorothy has been sending food parcels to her parents and her sister's family. Her relatives in Reading aren't starving but a little extra to eat or a treat here and there is very much appreciated. The lard is especially welcomed for pies and other baking.

In Banff, part of Ed's warden duties includes bringing food to warden line cabins in his district. He stocks hut larders with tinned meat, fruit and vegetables. Cuthead Cabin is on Ed's patrol route. The log hut is down the road from a camp for Second World War conscientious objectors where men were kept busy cutting wood and making trail signs in the early forties. After the war ended, the parks branch turned the camp buildings into a training centre for skiing and horse packing.

The Cuthead Warden Cabin[80] is at an important junction where you can head north to Panther River or west up to Flint's Park. Ed has ridden to Flint's Park with Mike. It's a fascinating place for the boy. Brothers George and Lou Smith of Banff have a logging operation on Flint Mountain. They set up a camp on a burnt slope for about six men. Mike is mesmerized by the horses dragging the cut logs down the slope and through the bush.

There are now two boys to introduce to the great outdoors. As Terry grows from a newborn to a sturdy five-month-old, the Carletons decide he's old enough to make a winter foray into the mountains. They plan a family ski trip in April to Cuthead, about 10 km (6 mi) away. The cabin is used by wardens who need to shelter overnight and Ed has to shovel snow off the roof and generally make sure the hut is habitable for anyone who needs it.

Ed, Dorothy and Mike can all ski. Terry can't even crawl. His parents think the pram (which also functions as Terry's bed) might be a good mode of transport for the baby. It's not. It's wheels barely turn when pushed through the deep snow.

---

78. People still make Tomato Soup Cake. Reviews of the recipe online say it's slighty spicy (in a good way).
79. Rationing doesn't end in England until 1954.
80. Cuthead Cabin is now a Recognized Federal Heritage Building in Banff National Park.

Tucking Terry into a backpack doesn't work either. They need that space for canned goods and other supplies. Finally, Ed finds a toboggan and Terry is bundled up and roped onto it. Along with him is Thomas L. Thomas, the cat. He snuggles up to the baby and falls fast asleep. The feline needs his rest now because he's expected to be busy over the next two days ridding Cuthead of mice.

There's a crust on the thick layers of snow and it helps speed up the journey for the Carletons. They glide over the skin instead of sinking down into powder. There are several uphills and they stop a few times for a drink of water, a snack or two and to let Mike and Chum rest. Arriving at the cabin, they find it in a less than livable shape. There are cobwebs hanging from every rafter and hook. Dust is thick in the air. The wooden floor planks are covered in mouse poop. Dorothy doesn't want to step one foot in the place until Thomas L. Thomas has had a good meal or twelve.

The family begins to clean up, sweeping and chucking things out and wiping things down. The reason for their trip was to drop off the canned food, so guess what they had for supper? A nice meal of tinned meat, tinned carrots, tinned peas and some tinned fruit cocktail for dessert.

They spend the night at Cuthead and the next morning, pack up for their journey home. The trip going back is a lot faster because of the downhills. They get home in time for lunch.

***

More and more people are coming to Banff for winter backcountry activities. In the spring, Banff, Yoho and Jasper parks administrators hold a conference to talk further about a possible ski and avalanche rescue program. Noel Gardner is tasked with heading the initiative and moving the program forward. Only wardens who want to be involved with the program will be brought on board. Ed is one of them. However, he'll have to wait until the snow flies again before working on his turns. Spring is in the air today.

As the snow recedes from the ground, Chum is out exploring. He isn't out long when Dorothy hears him yelping. She knows what happened. Those dastardly porcupines got him with their quills. He must be sniffing about them. Ed has to take some pliers and pull out the quills, one by one.

During summer at Stoney Creek, Dorothy takes both her boys for strolls. She's raising her sons with the *Movement is Life* philosophy. Mike walks beside his mother, who is pushing the pram with Terry in it. The three Carletons hike through the bumpy pasture with its lumps of rocks and dirt. Five of Ed's park horses join the humans as they walk towards the road. The animals neigh hello and run around, delighting Mike.

Once past the pasture, Dorothy and the boys connect with the fire road. They loop back to the cabin via the "ski hill." It's a good 2 km (over a mile) jaunt. When Mike and Dorothy return home, they put their toes in the cold Stoney Creek water. No one goes for a swim because the creek is freezing, even in summer.

Dorothy hauls water from the creek in the morning so it can warm up enough for evening baths. The order for baths goes: Mike, Terry, Dorothy and Ed. Then come the dishes.

Saturday night bath time for Mike at Stoney Creek 1949.
Photo: Carleton Family

Actually, doing the dishes in the dirty bathwater is just a joke Dorothy likes to tell. It always gets a chuckle. But Dorothy's serious about ensuring there's enough clean water left over for the job.

"You have to be economical," she says. "You don't want to always be running to the creek for water. There's no room for the dishes to pile up anyway."

Dorothy and Ed get some surprised guests one bath night. Inez and Stan drive up to see their friends, although maybe not to see so much of them. (That's a joke, too.) Everyone is decent and Inez watches how much work goes into filling the "Beatty tub," a round corrugated metal tub that was part of a "Beatty washing machine." (Named after the manufacturers, the Beatty Brothers Limited, a Canadian company.)

Another visitor is Jim Deegan. He stops in at the Carleton home for coffee from time to time. Jim isn't a warden but he works for the warden service on various tasks. He's done all sorts of jobs from being a radio dispatcher at the town warden office, to giving out tourist information, to signing out people going on climbs and backcountry trips, as well as selling fishing licences. Jim is a hoot to have around and a natural storyteller. (He has published a couple of books.) He once went into a bar and proclaimed, "When Jim Deegan drinks, everyone drinks!" The bar goes crazy thinking Jim's buying everyone a round. But when he's done, he says, much to everyone's consternation: "When Jim Deegan pays, everyone pays."

After a few years of living in the backcountry, Dorothy isn't fazed by much anymore. The grizzlies Ed's father told her were hiding in the bushes, don't make many appearances. When she does see a bear, it's usually a black bear. The Carletons are driving down the road one afternoon and Dorothy sees something big and brown in the distance. It's a grizzly! Actually, a grizzly mother and two cubs. The little ones are playing and when mum has had enough, she pats their behinds and they start walking into the woods.

Dorothy writes to her family and friends in England about it. She tells them about the "jolly good" sighting she had of the bear family.

Dorothy also tells her family about her trips on horseback to the warden cabins scattered around Ed's district of Stoney Creek. The first warden cabins were built when Banff was still Rocky Mountain Park. Huts were constructed at entry points into the park. The cabins weren't only for the wardens. If anyone was out in the back-country and needed a place for the night, he or she could open the door and roll out a sleeping bag. There were a couple of rules though: leave the cabin clean and don't take anything. There was a $100 fine for pocketing an item that belonged in the hut. In 1929, the cabins were closed to everyone except wardens. People had been using the cabins as storage lockers and not shelters.

Windy Cabin No. 3 was the third cabin to be built in the park and located in Ed's district. He goes there on horseback and manages to convince Dorothy to come along after a couple of riding lessons.

Riding a horse is not as easy as riding a bike. Horses have minds of their own and one, in particular, is a bit of a grumpypants. Dorothy often ends up with the cantankerous animal. They don't make a great pair and he has some unusual quirks. For instance, he doesn't like white shirts. He just doesn't. Dorothy has to be mindful of her fashion choices if she's going to ride him. A faux pas in the clothing department means she'll be bucked off.

On the trip to Windy, it's Dorothy who is not happy. The journey is long and she is getting a sore butt from the saddle. Thankfully, the horse isn't getting too ornery and it all ends well. It's another story during a trip to Dormer Pass Cabin on the same horse.

Ed and Dorothy are riding to Dormer Pass Cabin to stock it with food and other supplies. At the halfway point, Dorothy's horse bolts … galloping at full speed with Dorothy hanging on for dear life.

"Ed!" she screams. "Help!"

There's no use yelling at the animal. He's not going to listen to her. Ed has to!

In a flash, he's there. He grabs the horse's reins and it slows down. Dorothy jumps off the saddle to catch her breath.

"He must have smelled another horse," says Ed. "That's why he took off."

"I hope she smelled pretty," says Dorothy.

She has no choice but to get back in the saddle and continue the ride. Arriving at the cabin, she ties her ride to a tree. Soon he's jumping and whinnying and not at all in a good mood. No wonder. Unbeknownst to Dorothy, she had picked a tree full of hornets. Karma stings.

By Far the Worst Letter

There's an ebb and flow to life at Stoney Creek. The Carletons have lived here for almost four years. Dorothy says they're "living the dream." The children are thriving in the fresh mountain air and Dorothy and Ed are busy and content with their daily duties. There haven't been too many surprises throughout their time near the babbling brook.

Ed repairing a telephone line at Stoney Creek, a critical job for the wardens in isolated districts. Photo: Carleton Family

Men and boys always surround Dorothy. In town, however, she finds some all-women's groups to join. She is initiated as a member of the Banff Rebekah Lodge No. 34. The lodge is part of the women's branch of the Independent Order of Odd Fellows, an international service-oriented fraternal organization. She also becomes part of the Royal Canadian Legion Ladies' Auxiliary in Banff. She likes being part of groups that combine social time with supporting veterans and raising money for good causes. It connects her not only to other women but also to the community as a whole.

There's always food on the table and her family is healthy, but being a warden's wife is often isolating and lonely. There's a saying about the park being the first wife and Dorothy feels this when Ed is out on patrol and she's all alone with the children in the backcountry.

Ed's job in the winter is to make sure the telephone lines, — a vital lifeline for wardens — are working. In a bad storm, some of the lines come down or are taken down by falling trees. To check where the break is, Ed carries a field phone powered by batteries. He calls Dorothy at different locations until he discovers the outage. (Stoney Creek, Ya Ha Tinda, Scotch Camp and Windy Cabins all share the same line.

The ring at Stoney is a long, a short and a long.) Once Ed knows where the break is, he clambers up the telephone pole or tree to re-string the line.

Ed climbs up trunks with spurs he attaches to his boots. He becomes proficient at scaling trees and can get to the top in a matter of seconds. It's exciting for Mike to see his father scrambling like a black bear, but it gives Dorothy a bit of anxiety. However, it's not just the height of the pole that's causing her to worry.

Her father is ill back in England and there's nothing she can do about it. George is unconscious when he's admitted to the Reading hospital in early December 1952. He has some sort of abscess and the doctors are having a hard time figuring out where it is. In a letter, Marjorie says their father is awake now but the family is told to stick close to home.

Thursday, Dec. 11, 1952 I was going home to Crawley in Oxfordshire for a few days but the Sister of the Ward said she would not if she was me. So it seems they are expecting some change.

I am sorry about your Christmas parcel but I am afraid it will be a New Year one. I hope you all have a nice Christmas. Mum is a bit worried over you as she has not heard from you for over a fortnight. I guess it is the Christmas post. Well, cheerio. We are just off to the hospital again. Lots of love to all, Marjorie.

Marjorie keeps Dorothy apprised of what's happening but letters can only do so much. Letters can't give Dorothy the most up-to-the-moment information or hold her hand while she reads the latest about how her father is doing. The news is grim in the new year.

Jan. 21, 1953 Melbourne and I have been up at the hospital all night. We were sent for at a half-past eight last evening. Dad was unconscious and just breathing but at 2 a.m. he came to and knew us both and said he felt wonderful and it was a hard job to keep him from chattering. His pulse became quite strong and he drank a cup of milk. He is feeding himself and I think he has not done that for days. Thank you very much for the ham. It arrived Saturday, Jan. 17 but it had the wrong address: Manor Farm, Cowley, Witney. We are in Crawley. Cowley is nearby.

For Alice, putting pen to paper is difficult but she wants to thank Dorothy for a £5 cheque that she calls "a Godsend." Alice is struggling with money while her husband is ill.

Jan. 28, 1953 Dad is still in the hospital and it is just a matter of time. He is in no pain but he does want to come home to finish but it is quite impossible to move him. I was with him yesterday and he had a hard job to talk. I wish some miracle could happen. I hope you are all well and the boys are growing fine. I am wanting to see their photo and hope it will be here in time to show dad. He says he wants to see his other boys in Canada. Best love and kisses to all, Mum

A couple of weeks later, the letter Dorothy knew was coming, arrives. She wishes she could send it back, unopened. Perhaps then, the news wouldn't become a reality.

Her father has died. Marjorie's letter is dated Dec. 16, Ed's birthday. In her grief, she had put the wrong date. The actual date is Feb. 16. No matter which day it is or isn't, it is by far the worst letter Dorothy has ever received.

Well, I find this difficult to write but Dad passed away 10 o'clock last night. (Sunday 15th). Mum came home from the hospital at 9 o'clock and Melbourne and I went down at

half-past ten but he was gone. We were able to tell mum ourselves.
She is really taking it much better than we thought. He is being cremated as he wished.
Try to think of it as a happy release Dorothy for he suffered terribly and the drugs are little help.
Lots of love, Marjorie.

Dorothy's tears for her father are wiped away by little hands wondering why she's crying. Ed holds his wife after the kids are in bed and listens to her as she tells him stories of her dad bringing home Digestive biscuits. She sings songs of her childhood and cries some more. She's so far away from her mother and sister and aches to be with them when they say goodbye to a wonderful man.

Marjorie tells Dorothy that their father didn't want white flowers at his service. White flowers mean death. George had wanted a celebration of life. The Carletons send pink carnations that Marjorie mixes in with mauve and red tulips and yellow daffodils at his service.

Feb. 23, 1953 Dad told me just how he wanted it and I carried it out. He wanted gay flowers and of all the flowers, there was not one white one. We are having Dad's name and the words 'His valiant spirit rests' put in the Book of Remembrance. Mum says she cannot realize dad's not coming home anymore. Thanks very much for the boy's photo. It arrived on my birthday and I was thrilled with it. I think Terence is more like his mum. Love to all, Marjorie

All Dorothy can do from Canada is send letters to her sister and mother and tell them she wishes she were there. Alice writes about the many people who are sending her flowers and cards and thoughts of George.

Feb. 24, 1953 I have not felt like writing I can tell you for it seems awful to think dad is not coming home again. This morning I had a nice letter from the hospital matron. She told me I had been a brave little woman as she has seen me come to see dad every day for the last 5 weeks after we had the bad news about dad. She said he is such a good patient and the staff said it was a pleasure. He is so thankful for what they did for him but I could have done with him a few more years but it is not to be. I had a cremation for the service and all was great. Rev. Smales did it as he went to see and talk with dad three times a week. He is the chaplain for the hospital. I will go to Marjorie's for a week or two. Do write to me as often as you can. I expect I told you what your dad said about what two nice boys you had and the little one looks full of beans. Best love and kisses to all from, Mum

Dorothy's sister says their mother's heart was strained throughout the ordeal with their father and Dorothy's not to let on she knows about this. The next hurdle for Alice is the rent on 55 Grange Avenue. When George died, Alice stopped receiving his pension from Huntley & Palmers. Her only income now is her old-age pension and it leaves little to live on after the £13 a week rent comes out.

It's unfathomable to Dorothy that her family home might not be her family home soon. The small house holds a mountain of memories. She can't lose her father and her home in the same year. Thankfully, Marjorie might have a solution.

Mar. 10, 1953 While mum is with us she can manage all right. I cannot see her living on her own yet a while but I want her to make her own decision over giving up her home and living with us. If she decides to carry on her own, Melbourne says he will pay the rent so I think we have been as fair as possible to her. Lots of love, Marjorie

Indeed, it's the right thing to do for Alice. She says all she wants to do is sit and cry. She hopes she'll feel better when the sunshine and warmer weather appears.

Mar. 11, 1953 When I'm cold I feel just miserable. Melbourne wants me to make up my mind and settle with them but I don't quite want that. I still got my home and don't want to give it up. My pension is £32 a week and I can pay the £13 a week for rent. Melbourne thinks I could live cheaper if I live with them but my life is not his.

I will try and write a bit more cheerful next time. Love to the boys, Mum.

The row house on 55 Grange Avenue continues to be the home of the Fowlers. Alice stays.

While Dorothy had been dealing with her father's illness and then death, Princess Elizabeth was also experiencing grief. King George VI of Great Britain and Northern Ireland died on Feb. 6. Life stopped in England for the day and even the BBC cancelled its programs. Elizabeth is crowned Queen on Jun. 2, 1953, and Dorothy, who is fond of the Royals, thinks she'll do a good job for England. At any rate, life goes on.

A Penniless Quest for Love

By 1953, Banff National Park is well known by tourists all around the world. Even Hollywood star Marilyn Monroe is checking out the mountaintops and rushing rivers of the Rockies. She arrives to film *River of No Return* in August and spend quality time with her boyfriend Joe DiMaggio. (She sprains her ankle while shooting the movie and so in some photographs, she is using crutches.) Of course, Dorothy and Ed know the glamorous movie star and baseball icon are in their midst and get all the details when they see warden friends.

The Trans-Canada Highway is about to bring more visitors to Banff. The Trans-Canada is a coast-to-coast road that has been in the works since 1949. While the park already has established routes, the Trans-Canada will link the Rockies to the rest of the country via one long highway. Negotiations on the land for the major roadway begin under National Parks Director James Smart (1941-1953). (Smart is also the director who was convinced that wardens need to develop better skiing and avalanche skills.)

Family from Didsbury often make the trek to Stoney Creek, especially Russ. He's at loose ends. His wife and children have disappeared from his life and he is adrift. Russ is an adult but Ollie and Millie think he needs a talking-to. Ollie sits him down and tells him to shape up.

"Go back to Phyllis," he says, "or else get a divorce and move on."

The words spur Russ on an epic quest to win back Phyllis and their children. With no money to his name, he hitchhikes across Canada. The last time he had been this way, his trip had been paid for by the Canadian army. He was just a kid then and hadn't known if he was going to live or die. That train ride seems far in the past. Now he's 34 and a father to three children, one he has never met.

Russ gets to Halifax and due to his gregarious nature, makes a couple of friends in the port city. One of his new buddies arranges for him to stow away on a cattleship destined for England. He's provided with food and a place to sleep aboard the vessel. After landing in England, he thumbs a ride to Reading.

There's a knock at the door at the Tuckers' home on Battle Street. Phyllis peers out of the curtains and sees a man down on his luck. His hair is unkempt and his clothing is old and worn. He looks like he doesn't have a penny to his name. Perhaps he is just looking for something to eat. Phyllis will give the homeless man a slice of bread with jam and then send him on his way. Except … there is something familiar about him.

"Russ!"

The door swings open and he's embraced. Despite everything that happened in Alberta, Phyllis loves him. He meets his third child, Christine, and the father moves in with his family and parents-in-law. Russ finds a job with the Ford car company near London and will never call Canada home again.

A Buffalo Paddock Birth

After four years of living at Stoney Creek, Ed is given the job of assistant town warden. The Carletons are then transferred to a house near the buffalo paddock at the end of summer in 1953. Bison (commonly called buffalo) used to roam wild across western Canada. The large snorting animals were important to Indigenous people and a mainstay of their diet. In the early days of the European exploration of Alberta (late eighteen and early nineteenth centuries), more bison were seen than deer. However, in the late 1800s, uncontrolled hunting by settlers, rail workers, miners and others in the Banff area almost decimated the bison. When Banff became a national park in 1887, there weren't any wild grazers thought to be left in the Canadian prairies.

Ten years later, a Toronto lawyer had an interesting gift for the Canadian government: three wild bison. T.G. Blackstock had the animals shipped from Texas to Banff. A year later, Donald Smith, (Lord Strathcona and co-founder of the Canadian Pacific Railway), sent 13 bison to join the bull and two cows already at the park. One of the new bulls is named Sir Donald. Howard Douglas, superintendent of the park at that time, saw the bison as a tourist draw and created a "buffalo park" by fencing in 500 acres of land at the base of Cascade Mountain. He also built a zoo around the bison and included Persian sheep, a timber wolf, cougars and other animals. Later, there was an addition of a polar bear cub and in 1914, the zoo was home to 50 mammals and 36 birds. The zoo closed in 1937 but the bison were allowed to stay in their enclosure. This is the buffalo paddock where the Carletons now live.

Syd Meezer and his dog at the gate to the Buffalo Paddock, 1954.
Photo: Carleton Family

Ed and Dorothy aren't in the backcountry anymore.

A bison behind the fence at the Buffalo Paddock.
Photo: Carleton Family

They're just over 3 km (2 mi) from town, near the visitor entrance to the park. Their new home is at the corner of the turnoff to the buffalo compound. The warden's cabin here is no hut: it's a former CPR frame house and it's massive compared to the Stoney Creek home. The new house is close to the train tracks, about 30 m (100 ft) away and the family will have to get used to the rumbling thunder of frequent trains heading east or west.

For the first time in several years, the Carletons have an inside toilet, electricity and tap water. These are all luxuries to them — and with a baby due in the spring, Dorothy is glad of the running water and the ability to wash the baby, diapers and dishes in instant hot water. (Not all at once though.)

The buffalo paddock is open in the summer to anyone in a vehicle who wants to see the big hairy bison. The entrance is through a big gate controlled by Sid (or Syd) Meezer. He lives in a small hut on the grounds and when visitors arrive, he reminds them of the rules. They're posted on a large wooden sign at the entrance but nevertheless, he emphasizes that sightseers must stay in their cars. Bison might look like slow lumbering beasts but they are not. They can throw you in the air in a blink of an eye.

There's no way Mike is going to tangle with a bison. His dad has taught him to respect wild animals and especially wild animals that are as large as bison. Ed isn't a harsh disciplinarian and never spanks his sons. Ed rarely raises his voice, yet Mike never wants to disappoint him. So, the young boy hangs out by the fence between his house and the paddock gate and watches the vehicles drive by.

As cars and trucks crunch up the gravel road, Mike loves spotting all the different makes and models. There were few vehicles at Stoney Creek, but here there are many, and it's an enjoyable pastime counting the out-of-province licence plates, especially ones from the U.S. It's a fun lesson in geography.

Another pastime for Mike is riding his bicycle. He learns from Dorothy, who remembers how much freedom and fun a bike gives a kid (and grown-up kids). She holds the seat, keeping the bike steady, while Mike climbs on. Once he gets his balance, she tells him to push the pedals. She starts jogging and then running alongside while still holding on at the back. Mike gets faster and faster and soon, she can't keep up (she is pregnant) and lets go. Mike cycles away.

He often bikes by the maintenance grounds, about 500 m from his home. The "camp" is where government workers, seasonal crews assigned to various jobs in the park, live for the summer. They're fed in a cookhouse/dining room building by Don and his wife Mrs. Graham. Mike calls Mrs. Graham "Mum" because that's what everyone calls her. While Don is small and stooped, Mum Graham is big and tall and they both make fine meals.

Mum Graham and Don are close to Ed and Dorothy. The two women are often found deep in conversation. Dorothy pats her friend on the arm and nods in agreement. No one knows what they're talking about but what is for sure is that Dorothy cares about her. Dorothy is a confidant to many and will cheer you up in a matter of minutes with a song and a cup of tea.

Mum Graham always has a treat for Mike. When he rides by the cookhouse, his mouth starts to water. He has to stop. He also knows that Don will tell him stories of cooking adventures past. One day, Don tells Mike about the time he put bear grease in the frying pan and it flew out the window. The pair howl in laughter until they get a stern look from Mum Graham. You don't want to mess with her. Mike hops back on his bicycle and pedals home.

Ed and Dorothy take their sons to Banff Indian Days, a tourist attraction, in July. The event has been held in town since the late 19th century. While the Indigenous people had been forced off the land years ago and not allowed to hunt in the national park, visitors wanted a glimpse of the First Peoples. Banff Indian Days was intended to showcase the Îyãhé Nakoda people to the tourists, though the event's non-Indigenous organizers impose tight restrictions on the Indigenous participants.[81]

The true origins of Indian Days are lost but a couple of stories remain. One is that the event began between 1889 and 1897 when the CPR tracks were flooded. Guests staying at the Banff Springs Hotel weren't going anywhere. To entertain the tourists, a guide suggested bringing in some Îyãhé Nakoda people from Morley, a First Nation settlement near Banff. Another story says people from Morley were participating in many of the Victoria Day and Dominion Day sporting events, such as horse racing, and Indian Days grew out of that.

81. The original incarnation of Indian Days, as a tourist attraction, ended in the 1970s. The Îyãhé Nakoda revived Indian Days in the early 2000s but there's a different focus now: with the exception of a powwow and some other cultural events for the public, it's mainly a private gathering for members of the nation to celebrate and pass on traditional knowledge.

Rocky mountain romance: Dorothy and Ed at Buffalo Paddock, 1953.
Photo: Carleton Family

Dorothy at Buffalo Paddock, 1953.
Photo: Carleton Family

No one really knows which story is the real deal but the fact was, the tourists flocked to Banff Indian Days.

Indian Days kicks off with the Grande Parade, a parade of horses and riders dressed in traditional garments of beautifully beaded buckskin and other attire. There are also sporting events such as roping and bow and arrows competitions. Visitors can get up close to tipis at the Îyãħé Nakoda camp. It's a surface-level introduction to a people who have an immense history in the Banff area and an intricate and complex culture that was forced underground by early European settlers and Canadian laws of assimilation. Mike and Terry, though, are young boys and don't understand any of this yet.

On a hot summer day, the brothers watch in awe as the Grande Parade passes by. Then, they check out the tipis. They play with some friends as Ed talks to a couple of the men from the Îyãħé Nakoda Nation. They know each other through park business and seeing each other at different events in Banff.

Summer means visitors for Dorothy and Ed, too. Relatives from Didsbury make the drive to Buffalo Paddock and stay for a few days. Frank and Dorothy Carleton drop their children, Danny and Stephen, at their cousins' place and the four boys have a great time. There are acres of space for the kids to run, bike and get dirty. Dorothy doesn't have a fight on her hands when it comes to telling the boys to go to bed. They're all tuckered out from the fresh air and gladly hit the hay.

That July of 1953, the Korean War ends for Canada. More than 26,000 Canadians served in the conflict over the Land of the Morning Calm and 516 Canadians are dead. There's an uneasy truce between South and North Korea.

Summer comes to a close. Mike is in for a big change in September. He's starting school – with other students. His first day of Grade 2 is not the best experience. He's dropped off at the door of the Banff School on Banff Avenue by his father and not given much instruction about where to go and what to do. He feels lost in the unknown corridors of the large (to him) brick building. He also feels alone.

There's a difference between being by yourself and being alone. Mike was often by himself in the backcountry and he felt perfectly fine. However, in his class, he's surrounded by a bunch of strangers. Mike is the youngest in his grade and shy. He knows no one. His town friend Paul Peyto hasn't started school yet and his other buddy David Colbeck (Art the Fish Guy's son), moved to Waterton[82] in southern Alberta with his family.[83]

---

82. The Colbecks moved when Art became Waterton Lakes National Park's fish hatchery superintendent, a job he held for eight years.

83. David Colbeck remembers living in Banff in the hatchery house (still standing) on the way to Bow Falls. *"There was a huge viewing pond in the front of the hatchery and another set of ponds going up the side. I know all three hatchery's ponds as I somehow fell in all three of them. There was an artist, Mr. Wride, who used to sit in front of the hatchery and do pastel paintings from pictures in the area. He was working one day when a bear came up behind him and looked over his shoulder. Visitors to the hatchery saw it all."* (2019)

Mike's classmates have grown up together. Not counting the summer and skiing tourists, Banff's population is less than 2,000. These kids have played in Whiskey Creek and hung out at the hot springs together. At recess, they start poking fun at the new kid. There's strength in numbers and with Mike all alone, the other kids sense his weakness. Some bullies push him around and call him names including one that sticks: "Warden." It'll be his nickname for life.

Despite the rough first day, Ed and Dorothy send Mike back to school under the tutelage of his teacher, Miss J. Wonnacott. There's no way he's going to stay home. It takes some time but he eventually makes friends and looks forward to each day. He eats his lunch with buddies and they trade sandwiches and fruit. Mike will never swap his favourite sandwich of peanut butter and banana for anything.

On warm spring and fall days, Mike rides his bike to school. Otherwise, his parents drive him into Banff. Dorothy sometimes drops him off on her way to run errands in town. She always leaves him with a cheerful, "Enjoy the day, good luck with whatever and see you later." When the snow starts falling, Ed takes his son to school. The elder warden is often reserved in the vehicle, no doubt thinking about his day's work. His sense of duty is strong.

Mike isn't the only one who has had some adjustments to make. As the assistant town warden, Ed has had to make changes, too. Banff has facilities and activities to monitor, as well as visitors to give directions to and maybe scold from time-to-time (especially when they're feeding the bears). From the backcountry, to the front country, Ed's job now consists of dealing with tourists, animals straying into Banff, supporting the fire lookout on Tunnel Mountain, helping out with special events like the Banff Winter Carnival on top of patrolling the town and Mount Norquay.

Being a short drive away from the ski hill means the Carletons have access to a ski lift. No more trudging up the hill at the Stoney Creek cabin to get some speed! Before Mike (and Terry a couple of years later) can take off for the black diamond runs, he's relegated to the bunny hill. He attempts to ride the Memorial Hill rope tow – and is thrown off before reaching the top. Soon though, it's all downhill and Mike wins a Mount Norquay event in the Peewee boys category on Mar. 19, 1954.

Ed, along with other wardens, is refining his downhill skiing, avalanche training such as terrain evaluation, and mountain rescue. Noel Gardner's vision of wardens being emergency first responders on the peaks, instead of relying solely on Swiss Guides, became a reality a year earlier, in 1953. Cuthead College, near Cuthead Cabin, is their base for practice. There's even a fun competition held at the end of the week to see who can travel the fastest over a marked route – snowshoers or skiers?

When Ed first started winter patrols in 1949, he used snowshoes, like many of the wardens. Then, the branch moved to skis and Ed learned to tour on downhill skis with bear trap bindings. Warden Bill Vroom "discovers" Norwegian wood skis. He buys a pair from Bernie Mason in Calgary. Bernie has started importing the wood skis, early renditions of modern cross-country skis, and selling them out of his basement. Bill thinks these skis are better suited for backcountry travel because they're light and you can travel faster. Ed tries the "skinny skis" but thinks they're too fragile.

Baby Brian crawling on the lawn at the Buffalo Paddock.
Photo: Carleton Family

Ed is an average downhill skier and he likes to be on the slopes with his son if he has time. Mike likes to kid Ed about his "snowplow-like" method of getting down the hill. It means dad is slow. That's probably best when Ed has a rescue toboggan hitched to him but when he's on the hill, Mike doesn't find him any fun. Dorothy likes to get in some runs too but she's expecting again and so stays off the piste. Chum the dog and Thomas the cat keep her company.

When the Bow River ices over, Mike skates on it with his friends at Mather's boat house. The Mather family built the Bow River Boat House to accommodate summer visitors sailing on the Mountain Belle, a steamboat offering pleasure cruises. In winter, there was an ice skating business. The property was sold to Ed Mader in 1951 and the skating rink remains a popular winter pastime for both kids and adults. Terry's too little to join the big boys on the ice but soon, he won't be the youngest child.

That April of 1954, Brian is born — thus spawning a family joke that Dorothy and Ed's third and last child was born in a buffalo paddock. That's not the case. Brian is born at the Banff hospital. He's Mike and Terry's newest best friend.

Russ and Phyllis also add to their family in Reading. They welcome their fourth child, Lorna, in June. The park service in Banff is getting an addition too, someone Ed knows well: Bert Pittaway. Bert is transferred from Waterton Lakes National Park and becomes Ed's supervisor. Bert and Ed are former Calgary Highlander soldiers who were both part of the Dieppe raid and Normandy. They now share the duty of keeping the park safe. They might also share a penchant for solitude. The many hours alone in nature gives them time to contemplate their war years.

Bert joined the Second World War because of his father, a First World War veteran. Bert was living at Waterton Lake and had to go to Pincher Creek, the closest large town, to enlist.

Also just like Ed, Bert married an English girl. Pam met Bert when he was on guard in Port Slade, U.K. She was having a debate with her mother over the location of a brewery so she cycled over to where she thought they made beer. Instead, she found some Highlanders stationed there. She started talking to Bert and he thought she was very nice … and very young. Pam was sixteen the day she arrived at the brewery.

The pair later married in England and Pam became a war and warden bride. She moved to Waterton Lakes National park, at the far south end of Alberta, in March 1946 to be with Bert.

Her first two winters here were spent at Belly River Ranger station,
the most isolated warden's district in Waterton Park.
Since then she and her warden husband lived at the Waterton River District cabin for two years and are now living in the townsite where Mr. Pittaway is in charge of the Waterton Lakes district.

Lethbridge Herald Newspaper Archives

Pam and Dorothy are becoming fast friends. It's a boon in the summer to be able to walk into town for a visit. Dorothy pushes Brian in the pram along the gravel road while Terry walks and Mike rides his bike. They all have their own friends in Banff to see. Chum is usually following the pack. He doesn't want to be left behind.

Chapter Ten

Tragedies and Changes

High Mountain Rescues

Rock climbers had discovered the beauty and challenge of the Rocky Mountains in the nineteenth century. Recorded first ascents for early explorers almost always include British members of the Alpine Club and American members of the Appalachian Mountaineering Club of Boston. Now, in the 1950s, people are coming from all over to scale the Banff peaks.

The sight of the Rocky Mountains from the ground is spectacular enough. To climb them is something altogether different. Some summits, such as Mount Temple, are around 3,544 m (11,627 ft) up. Imagine the view!

The first recorded climbing fatality in Banff was in 1896 when Philip Stanley Abbot fell in his attempt at the first ascent of Mount Lefroy. Other mountaineering accidents followed each year on the crags. In 1921, Margaret Stone, the wife of Dr. Winthrop Ellsworth Stone, saw him fly past her as he plummeted down Mount Eon. She survived on the mountain for a week before being rescued. The couple had been planning the first ascent of Eon, which has an elevation of 3,305 m (10,843 ft).

On Jul. 25, 1954, Ronald Butler dies on Grotto Mountain, near Canmore and outside of Banff National Park. The 18-year-old was from Calgary and is the first of three high-altitude accidents that happen within weeks of each other in the Rockies.

Five days after Butler's death, a group of Mexican climbers are hoping to climb Mount Victoria, a peak at the western end of Lake Louise in the park. There are seven women in the group who are being guided by Eduardo San Vicente, an experienced climber from Mexico. The women's spokesperson, Ofelia Fernandez, bills her crew as *"the first feminine expedition organized in the whole world to conquer peaks in other country* [sic] *thousands of miles away."*

Abbot Hut climber's logbook

The group is fully equipped with modern climbing gear such as crampons on their boots for purchase on ice. The Mexicans ask Ernst Feuz, a retired Swiss Guide, for advice on tackling Victoria's south peak. He gives them some suggestions before they start climbing.

The crew gets to the Abbot Hut, between Victoria and Lefroy, and rest a day. On the morning of Jul. 30, they begin their quest to the top. One woman is feeling ill and stays back while the others push on. The group reaches the peak but instead of making the safer choice to go back the same way, they decide to take a different route — one that Ernst had warned them was difficult.

The group's decision is to descend from a ridge on a steep and snowy slope. The Mexicans are roped together in two separate parties. It's tough going since the snow is rotten and the climbers can't get good traction. While belaying down the mountain face, one woman loses her footing and falls, taking three of the climbers with her, including their guide. They land on Lefroy Glacier, more than 600 m (approximately 2,000 ft) below. The three other climbers can't move off the slope for fear they'll end up like their friends. They're in need of rescue.

Fortunately, people at the Chateau Lake Louise had been watching the climb through binoculars, including employees of Brewster Transportation and Ernst Feuz's brother, Walter. The men spring into action and quickly arrange a rescue party with Ernst at the helm. Ernst and Charles Rowland, a Chateau summer employee, make the final pitch to rescue the climbers in 35 minutes. It usually takes an hour. They bring the surviving four women (including the woman at the alpine hut) down the mountain and to safety. Ofelia is one of them.

There's another mountaineering accident in early August and Ed is involved in one of the recovery missions. Seventeen-year-old Jack Nelson[84] was climbing Mount Rundle, a 2,948 m (9671.9 ft) peak overlooking Banff and Canmore, with Barry Nixon of Regina. It was the first time Jack had climbed a mountain and he decided to jump over a small cliff. He slipped after landing on loose shale and fell almost 244 m (800 ft.).

Ed, Bert, RCMP Const. Howard Shrigley and John Morrow are tasked with getting the Winnipeg man's body out of a canyon. It takes around four days to retrieve the University of Manitoba engineering student because he's in a hard-to-reach canyon.

The shale, crags, cliffs and vertically dropping precipices of Mount Rundle made recovery efforts a torturous experience for the crew.

Crag & Canyon – Aug. 13, 1954

Ed can deal with the steep rock and the sharp angles he has to contour his body around and over. But he's troubled by the loss of such a young life. He has seen young men die on the battlefield but somehow, today, he sees something different. It's because he's a father and bringing up three sons who are active and adventurous, just like Jack. He resolves to teach them everything he knows.

Ed's rescue skills and efforts are praised by park superintendent B.I.M. "Bim" Strong. He says Ed showed a strong knowledge of climbing and didn't back down despite the obstacles. Ed tells Dorothy of the recognition but doesn't mention it to anyone else. Not even his children.

Dorothy is also an indispensable cog in the rescue efforts. Ed is a calming presence out in the field amidst the tumult, chaos and horror of climbing accidents, highway collisions or avalanche tragedies. Dorothy is the same for families and friends who wait to be told the outcome of a rescue operation. She always knows the right thing to say and the right thing to do.

Walter Perren and Edmond Petrig's guiding contracts with CPR are about to run out. The Swiss Guides, who have been shaping Canadian mountain culture for years, are becoming extinct in Banff National Park. Summer guests staying at CP Hotels don't

84. Winnipeg Free Press reported Jack Nelson's age as 18.

Ed (left) at the Rundle Mountain fatality recovery in 1954.
(Note footwear and equipment of that time.)
Photo: Carleton Family

While on mountain ridges, Walter Perren would tell his wardens, “Stand up boys, you won’t bump your heads!”

need licensed guides to show them the ropes anymore. Not only that, but former guides are getting older. Ernst Feuz, the guide who helped rescue the Mexican climbers, is in his mid-sixtics, as is his brother Edward. However, the number of rescues is only going up and the number of those who know what to do is going down. The park wardens are going to assume full responsibility for mountain rescues. But first, they're going to have to learn proper search and rescue skills.

Cuthead College - Stan Peyto instructs the wardens on how to operate the fire pump 1954.
Photo: Bruno Engler

Noel Gardner had begun building the parks' mountain rescue program but he has resigned. He has a position with the National Research Council in Rogers Pass studying avalanches. Noel's replacement is Walter Perren, a diminutive man with tons of expertise. Walter is hired in the fall of 1954 to further develop the mountain rescue program for wardens. His first official title, though, is janitor since there's no position set up yet and the post of janitor is vacant. However, Walter will soon become known as the father of modern mountain rescue.

In both Switzerland and Canada, Walter has an incredible reputation. He was born into a poor family in Zermatt, near the Matterhorn, one of the highest summits in the Alps. The first time Walter climbed the Matterhorn was when he was 12 or 13. As a young teen, he was a porter and went up the mountain with a guide and his two clients. There was a snowstorm and they were stuck so they hunkered down in a hut for the night. That evening in town, when no one came off the mountain, the people thought all four had perished. The next morning, Walter wandered into the parish church where people were saying prayers for him and the other three "departed." Since then, he has scaled the Matterhorn over 140 times.

Walter's reputation as an excellent mountaineering man and his unflappable attitude make him a sought-after guide in both Europe and Canada. He is someone Ed and the other wardens can learn from as well as respect.

Mount Temple Tragedy

Three Banff National Park wardens are sent to the U.S. in January 1955. They're attending an advanced snow and avalanche training school. Among those heading to Alta, Utah for the week is Banff's Bert Pittaway. The Canadian wardens impress the American parks services in their new olive green skiing uniform of a peaked cap, ski pants, and unlined hooded parka. The men are also good skiers and understand the elements of safety planning with ease.

J.A. Hutchison, the director of the National Parks Branch who took over from James Smart in 1953, receives a letter from Monty Atwater, a U.S. instructor on the course and renowned snow researcher. Atwater proclaims the Canadians as capable men, who no doubt have the skills needed for winter mountain rescues.

In early February, Ed's at Cuthead College under Walter's instruction. Ed, along with several wardens, a ski patrolman and an RCMP member, are being pushed to the limit. Training is physically intense and the men are ski touring, snowshoeing, ski mountaineering as well as learning ski patrol first aid, avalanche forecasting and control, mountain rescue and winter survival. It's a jam-packed nine days.

Looking out the window of her Buffalo Lodge home in March 1955, Dorothy spots some bare patches of ground, places where the snow has melted away. Spring has arrived earlier than usual and with it, the race to visit the Rockies will be starting soon. Tourists will come for the views, the wildlife and to hike, fish and climb.

Climbing is popular and if any climber needs help, it's the wardens to the rescue. The men travel on horseback as far as the animals can take them. Then, they climb to those in need and bring them down the rocky slopes. The wardens learn how to do this safely during Walter's public safety training courses.

On Jun. 4, 1955, Walter brings some of the wardens to Cuthead College to teach them rope skills, climbing techniques and other life-saving methods. When the wardens are facing a particularly daunting task or trail, Walter often finds a way to lighten the mood. He spreads horse manure on a steep and narrow mountain ridge so the men think the animals walked all the way up there. His wry sense of humour often has the wardens laughing, or at least not thinking about the sheer drop into the abyss below ... for a second or two anyway.

To add to the wardens' skill sets, Walter brings on Hans Gmoser[85] to help teach some of the mountain rescue sessions at national parks around Alberta. Hans is a young Austrian man who has been living in Canada for a few years. Ed finds him an agreeable fellow and is impressed with his exploits in the Rockies. Hans is an expert climber and is

85. Hans Gmoser is known as the father of modern heli-skiing.

making a name for himself by finding routes up pitches that are thought to be physically impossible. Walter hopes Hans will build the wardens' confidence on the crag. Walter needs the men to do rescue missions without relying on him, Hans or anyone else for instruction. The wardens need to be the experts. On Jun. 22, a group of 22 American kids, ages 12 to 16, and their two counsellors leave Philadelphia, Pennsylvania, in a Ford station wagon, a-hearse-turned-minibus and two trailers. They are part of the Wilderness Travel Camp, an expedition taking the boys on an outdoor adventure scheduled to last more than two months.

The crew travels to Minnesota, North Dakota and Montana. In Montana's Glacier National Park, on the border with Alberta's Waterton Lakes National Park, the group does a bit of hiking. By Jul. 7, the boys are camping in Banff National Park. One boy, Billy Watts, describes the area in a letter to his sister as beautiful but cold.

The group is two weeks into their tour with teacher Don Dickerson as their leader. At the park information office in Banff on Jul. 9, he registers the group to climb Mount Rundle. He then asks Catherine Thompson, who is staffing the information desk, about the peak. She finds him curt and not interested in what she tells him. She advises Dickerson to talk to another woman in the office who is knowledgeable about the mountains in the area. He doesn't.

Dickerson isn't well-informed about the routes or the conditions of many of the mountains in Banff. Wardens like Ed or Bert or Walter would have told him to avoid climbing areas like Mount Temple. They would have told him that the early spring is causing avalanches as the warm sun and wind turns the snow into slush. The slush doesn't stick together like snow and it eventually slides off the slopes. Nevertheless, Dickerson gives the nod to a plan that has the boys doing a scramble on the south face of Mount Temple, near where they are camping at Moraine Lake.

While both scrambling and climbing mean going up a steep gradient, with scrambling you don't need technical climbing abilities or equipment. At 3,544 m (11,627 ft), Temple is considered a difficult scramble even in the best conditions. On Jul. 11, the weather is hot and sunny. (If it was going to be a dreary day, the group would have taken in the sights at the 43rd annual Calgary Stampede.) Sixteen boys and the second in command, teacher William "Bill" Oeser, head up the side of the peak, many of them in cleated sneakers and summer T-shirts. Their equipment is two cords of manila rope (made from Manila hemp) and one ice axe.

On the way up, they meet Thomas Dunn, who works at Moraine Lake Lodge. He's sawing logs around 9:30 a.m. when the group asks him if they're on Wenkchemna-Sentinel Pass Trail. He says yes and the crew keeps moving.

Around 2,590 m (8,500 ft), Oeser stops. The teacher has a blister and doesn't want to ascend any higher. He says the rest can go on if they want and leave their lunches with him for when they return. Five boys stay with the teacher and 11 keep going. As they climb higher and higher, the snow gets deeper and deeper and wetter and wetter. The boys are cold and can see and hear avalanches swooshing down the sides of peaks around them. They're scared and decide to descend. They are at 3,020 m (10,000 ft). It's 4 p.m.

The trail is slippery and steep and the boys flail about trying to get a good foothold in the snow. They slide down the snowy slope, running into each other. Towny Baylis, whose twin brother is also on the scramble, is slight and can't dig his feet into the snow for traction. It's frightening as someone could slide away. That's when they decide to rope themselves together like their counsellor, Don Dickerson, had taught them. The boys think this is a good safety measure. This way, they can stop each other from falling.

The tied-together crew takes a shortcut across an open snowfield leading into a couloir. The stony ditch looks like an easy way down but it's actually an avalanche chute. Then, more than 200 m (700 ft) above them, the snow lets go.

"Avalanche!" cries Tony Woodfield. "Head for cover!"

Almost all the boys are immediately buried by tons of wet snow. Tony, holding the only ice axe, plunges it into the ground. He holds on for dear life as the rope at his waist connecting him to 10 boys, pulls at him. It's shredded away and in mere strands in seconds, leaving him untethered from the others. The avalanche continues to pour and roar down the peak for two minutes. After it stops, Tony starts helping the friends who aren't buried and tries to dig out those who are stuck in the concrete-like mass of snow.

When the avalanche struck, Peter Smith managed to hold onto the side of the mountain for a few seconds. Then, the slide carried him down the slope. The rope that had been tied around his waist for safety slipped around his throat, almost choking him to death. Thankfully, he is alive. His first reaction is to look around and see who needs help. He realizes it's nearly everyone.

After tending to a couple of the injured, Peter starts walking down the mountain. He gets to the meeting place and Oeser and the others who had stayed behind. He tells the counsellor what had happened. Oeser had watched the boys ascend before his attention wandered away. He had heard a noise like running water and had got up to look for the source of the strange sound but hadn't noticed anything amiss. The avalanche is unexpected news and Oeser sends Peter and another boy down the peak for help. He'll go up to the scene with Tom Jones, a man who just happens to be hiking by.

Oeser and Jones quickly get to the accident site. A couple of the boys are not badly injured, a couple are unconscious, another one is calling for help, one is clearly dead and two are nowhere to be found. Meanwhile, Peter and the other boy get to Moraine Lake about an hour after they started down the mountain. They find Dickerson and give him the news. Peter also tells Moraine Lake Lodge manager Myrtle Shaw about the accident. Shaw calls the emergency into the Chateau Lake Louise, her headquarters, and the news is relayed to Parks.

Warden Beef Woodworth's district includes Moraine Lake. He's told about the accident over the phone. He grabs his assistant wardens Wes Gilstorf and Jack Schauerte and they drive to the lodge to talk to Peter. Then the rescue mission is put into high gear. It's 7 p.m.

Beef gathers other wardens and volunteers, including the Chateau Lake Louise physician, Dr. Geoffrey Victor Sutton, and the camp leader Dickerson. They take horses up the mountainside in the growing darkness to dig the boys out. It starts to rain hard and the temperature drops.

By this time, the snowpack is stable. The men search for the missing boys and treat the injuries of boys who are still alive and who are all in shock. There are multiple lacerations, rope burns, bone breaks but no life-threatening injuries. Lights are spotted coming up the mountain and Walter, Bert Pittaway and some RCMP members join the rescue mission. With them is a bellhop from the Chateau, Bruce Lee. The group carries mine rescue baskets used in steep terrain rescues, along with stretchers, ropes and food. Other groups arrive on the scene with more stretchers and supplies. The injured are taken to the horses and then loaded on the animals to be brought down the slope. Towny Baylis, one of the twins, dies just as he's about to be put onto a stretcher.

By daybreak, seven boys are dead: Miles Marble, 12, Luther (Buzzy) Seddon, 13, twins Ricky (Richard) and Towny (Townsend) Baylis, 13, David Chapin, 15, Billy (William) Watts, 16, and Willie Wise, 16. Five of them died from exposure. All of their bodies are taken off the mountain by horses.

Three days later, there's another high mountain rescue, this time on Mount Field in Yoho National Park. A woman is stranded on a 30-cm (12 in) ledge that drops 183 m (600 ft) straight down. The wardens take her off the ledge, at night no less, and prove that they have the abilities and skills to work without the direct guidance of Walter Perren. It's a small victory in a terrible time.

***

There's a hearing into the deaths of the seven Philadelphia boys. The inquest begins on Jul. 15, a day after what would have been Miles Marble's 13th birthday. Six male jurors are in the Banff Masonic Hall to listen to the three boys who survived the accident, Peter Smith, 13, is there along with Ricky (Frederic) Ballard, 13, and Tony (Anthony) Woodfield, 16. As well, the two camp counsellors, Bill Oeser and Don Dickerson, are testifying while lawyers listen closely.

Tony had seen the avalanche coming. In the aftermath, he had tried to dig out his friends for an hour and a half before Oeser and Tom Jones, the Good Samaritan, got to the site. Oeser told Tony to get help and tell officials to find a helicopter that can fly to the scene.

Peter tried to help his friend Buzzy Seddon. Buzzy was in a lot of pain because of a broken leg.

"I tried to help him but I couldn't," testifies Peter.

Ricky doesn't remember the slide. He was knocked out. Oeser and Jones found him and moved him off the snow and onto the rocks. When he woke up, he was wrapped in heavy shirts. He could walk under his own power and told Buzzy Seddon, now unconscious, that he was going to "try and hurry the rescuers up."

On his way down the mountainside, Ricky met assistant warden Wes Gilstorf. Wes carried the boy down to where the group had left their lunches. Wes dropped him off there and went on to the accident scene. After Ricky ate three of the lunches, he walked further down the mountain. The 13-year-old then ran into counsellor Dickerson and another rescuer named Wilfred, who carried Ricky to the lodge.

Under examination on Day 2 of the inquest, Bert Pittaway says the heat of the afternoon sun probably triggered the slide. As well, the Philadelphia crew had made a number of mistakes, including not being aware of conditions, being unprepared, being tied together and using the Manila rope.

"It tightens, you won't get it undone," says Bert, "and it's very coarse to your skin if it were to catch you, it is not strong, it's got no tensile strength. There are special qualifications of a climbing rope, particularly nylon, which takes precedence over hemp, in that when one is climbing and he falls it is elastic and therefore, prevents choking a person or really injuring them."

Later, Bert adds that Dickerson and Oeser are not leaders.

"In an emergency, a leader should go to the fore and do everything he can."

The coroner's inquest wraps up on Aug.11 with a verdict from the jury.

"We find that all leadership and equipment ... was inadequate for this type of climbing," says jury foreman Cyril Paris.

No criminal charges are laid in the event. Nevertheless, the tragedy leaves an indelible mark on Parks management, staff and Banff. Despite the jury absolving the parks service of all blame and commending it for the efficiency of its rescue work, it finds the Parks registration system outdated and unreliable.

One of the results of the inquiry is the mandatory registering of those heading into the backcountry. Climbers, ski tourers, packhorse parties and others have to register in advance and give an estimated time of return.

Mount Eisenhower Move

There's no doubt that the deaths of the seven boys impacted the community of Banff National Parks and surrounding national parks. Walter Perren is a professional whose mandate is to make the park safe for anyone wanting to venture into its peaks and valleys, even if they don't know what they're doing. District wardens like Ed are now allowed to give climbers warnings about their planned routes and if anyone hasn't registered properly, he can send them back to town.

Besides the new guidelines in the field, Ed, Dorothy and their three boys are getting a new place to live: Eisenhower Lodge. After two years at the Buffalo Paddock, Ed is given another district: Mount Eisenhower.

The Eisenhower district is unique. It has all the backcountry features but is also very much front country. Banff is the closest town and it's a 30-km (20 m) drive away. Being at the junction of the Banff-Lake Louise highway and the Banff-Windermere highway, the Eisenhower Lodge is a busy place, especially in the summer months with many tourists coming to the park.

At Mount Eisenhower, the district office doubles as the warden's home. The office, known as the station or lodge, is equipped with a telephone switchboard and radio communication to the fire lookout. As well, tourists, climbers and anglers stop here to register and get information.

Ed, Dorothy, Mike, Terry and Brian leave Buffalo Paddock and stay in Banff for one night in the summer of 1955. Then, they move their belongings to the office/

Mount Eisenhower.
Photo: Carleton Family

lodge/station near Mount Eisenhower. Before settlers arrived in the Banff area, the peak was known as Miistukskoowa by the Siksikaitsitapi (also known as the Blackfoot Confederacy).

In the mid-nineteenth century, Scottish geologist James Hector named it Castle Mountain. In 1946, 24 hours before U.S. Gen. Dwight D. Eisenhower, Supreme Commander of the Allied forces in Europe, visited Canada, Prime Minister William Lyon Mackenzie King decided Castle Mountain needed to be Mount Eisenhower. The name change wasn't popular with many Albertans, although some Calgary Highlanders, including Ed, remember Ike as a capable general.

Dorothy is happy to find that the Eisenhower Lodge has an indoor toilet. There's also running water … of sorts. Silverton Creek flows right by the house and there's a long pipe leading from the creek right into the house! It's the best of both worlds: running water and fresh creek water delivered straight into the kettle.

The lodge, a large log cabin, is big and there is a veranda. Dorothy loves that! On warm summer days, she'll be able to bring a chair out onto the porch and enjoy the breeze. The house has a large kitchen with the usual wood stove. Besides burning wood, coal is used. It's stored in big bags. Kindling and wood are used to start the fire and keep it going for the most part. The coal is added to the hot fire to extend the warmth, but that's mostly in the winter.

The first morning Ed reprises his tea-making role. He gets the fire going, turns on the faucet and fills up the kettle with water straight from the source. He steeps a cuppa for his wife and hands it to her while she lies in bed. She has to admit, it's a joy to be served tea this way. A crackling fire isn't bad either.

The boys like their new home, too. They are eager to hear stories from the visitors who come to the lodge for information or the anglers who need fishing licences. As well, there's a vast unexplored wilderness steps away from the young boys' backyard.

Ed isn't the sole warden at Mount Eisenhower. There's an assistant warden who stays with his family in a separate house. There's also a small trailer for the seasonal summer assistant. In addition to the warden homes, there is a barn, corral, garage, saddle shed, woodpile and a small building for the generator that powers the lights in the lodge.

There are several trails on Mount Eisenhower and one leads to a fire tower. An elderly fellow in his eighties and a veteran of the Boer War, Charlie Phillips, inhabits the lookout in summer, surveying the land for puffs of smoke and trees on fire. The mountain is dry, there's no creek running nearby. Charlie tries to trap some rainwater in a barrel so he can wash his clothes. Otherwise, Ed is his only source for water.

Every few days, Ed brings water to Charlie on horseback. The pack animals are loaded with metal containers full of water. Then, they trot up the trail to Charlie where he and the warden chat about the weather.

"How many lightning strikes were there last night?" asks Ed.

"I counted about thirty," says Charlie.

"That slope burned a couple of years ago," says, Ed, pointing south. "How much re-growth is there to fuel a fire?"

"I don't think we have to worry yet. The brush and scrub are slow to return."

Ed will also ask if Charlie has seen any grizzlies from his isolated perch. When the chinwag is over, Ed and his horses head back down the trail. Charlie waves them off.

As Dorothy likes to say, every day is different when you're a warden's wife. If she isn't in the kitchen baking bread, she's looking after the big garden or washing clothes or keeping the fire going or the children in line. She is also selling fishing licences and answering questions from the many tourists who stop at the lodge asking for information. She writes letters to her family and friends in Canada and abroad. She gives her sister advice and lends an ear to her mother, who misses her husband so, so much. When Dorothy was younger, people admired her spirit. As she ages, people admire her kindness, too. She is there for anyone and everyone who needs her.

***

Ed, with Mike along for the ride, is heading home for lunch after patrolling the roads. They're both looking forward to a hearty meal after a morning of work. They walk into the lodge expecting to take a load off, but someone is sitting at the kitchen table in Ed's chair. It's a scruffy-bearded man eagerly chomping down on a cheese and onion sandwich that Dorothy had just made. Cheese and onion is one of Ed's favourites and although he doesn't say a word about having to wait for his meal or seat, his wide grin isn't so wide.

Mount Eisenhower handymen Terry (left) and Brian.
Photo: Carleton Family

"The poor man was hungry," says Dorothy after the hobo had left.

"Well, you made this poor man hungry in the process!" Ed responds.

The summer community at Mount Eisenhower is much larger than Buffalo Paddock. There's the parks crew made up of the district warden, the assistant warden and the summer warden. The district warden is in charge of the district and the assistant warden. The assistant warden is full-time and works under Ed's supervision. The seasonal summer warden does a lot of trail maintenance work, feeds and attends to the horses in the corral and other odd jobs around the station. The seasonal warden also has to be ready to be called upon in case of emergencies like fires or rescues. As well, there's a revolving contingent of travellers at the Eisenhower Youth Hostel (also known as Ike Inn) across the highway from Eisenhower Lodge.

The hostel has a grand view of the craggy, castle-shaped mountain and the fresh air gives many a young person a great night's sleep no matter who's snoring in a nearby bunk. The inn was converted from a former Second World War prisoner-of-war camp to a cozy place to rest after a day of adventure. The communal kitchen and wood-fireplace lounge is a draw for anyone looking for the quintessential Banff experience.

The woman in charge of the hostel is Mrs. Flo Spear. She has been the housemother there since 1951. She runs the inn when it's open during the summer and during holidays like Christmas, Easter and teacher convention breaks. Two of her children, Peter and Caroline, spend time there, too. Peter is six years older than Mike but they pal around. Mrs. Spear is a friend of Dorothy's and they spend many hours talking over cups of tea. Mrs. Spear is a great angler and catches trout in the Bow River, many of which end up on the Carletons' dinner table.

Ed and Dorothy's house turns into the summer social centre. There's always a pot of tea ready for guests and the front door is never locked. Eisenhower Lodge is, unofficially, open all the time. Besides those living in the vicinity, government workers stop in to say hello as do friends from the federal forestry camp located a few kilometres away. The forestry professionals are studying bugs like the mountain pine beetle, which causes a lot of damage to trees. Mike dubs the entomologists "bugologists."

Some of the bugologists like to have a tipple or two with Dorothy and Ed. Robbie Reid's wife Betty is from England and after a few drinks, she's singing away with Dorothy. Even Chum gets into the busy social scene around the lodge: A litter of cocker spaniel/English setters shows up after he's been visiting a female dog at the field station.

The bugologists see a budding entomologist in Mike and encourage him to collect insects. He puts a lot of effort into his research and has two wooden boxes filled with pinned and labelled insects. He submits his collection to a science competition and receives an honorary mention for his dedicated work. He also takes a stab at writing poetry about the fascinating creatures. The following are a couple of lines about ground beetles. You might larva it.

This is the classification of the Cicindelladae,
The first abdominal sternite is divided by the hind coxae.

The entomologists see Dorothy when they're going hiking and give her a wave. Mike heads out with them if he's not watching his brothers. He makes friends with Herbert "Herb" Cerezke, a young University of Alberta student who is hired to work at the field station for the summer. Mike follows Herb into the field often and learns a lot from the bugologist.

Not far down the road are the Baker Creek Bungalows and the Johnston's Canyon Lodge and Bungalows. Baker Creek and the Johnston's Canyon Lodge both offer accommodations for visitors. Walter and Marguerite Camp own the Johnston's Canyon property and are well acquainted with Ed and Dorothy by the end of the summer.

In the fall of 1955, Ed reunites a few wayfarers after they've been waylaid. Some anglers who had been fishing on Twin Lakes, get separated. One man is lost and Ed is called out to find him.

In the dark, Ed and two assistant wardens comb the woods and the rocks looking for the missing tourist. They find him the next day, cold but otherwise fine.

Ed undergoes more high terrain rescue training at Cuthead College. Some wardens grumble at the prospect of spending time learning new skills to get tourists off the mountain. Ed is not one of these men. It's partly because it's his job and partly because he cares about people. If one of his sons is stuck on a precipice high on a peak, he wants to be sure that the wardens will be able to get him down.

Dorothy plays a role in the rescues, too. As she's done at Ed's other postings, she does her part by giving waiting families someone to talk to and a shoulder to cry on. She brews pots of tea and listens as grief-stricken mothers, fathers, husbands and wives wonder what's happening high on a mountaintop or down the road.

Dorothy's also the main line of communication between Banff National Park and Kootenay National Park (in southeastern B.C.). She works the telephone switchboard in the Eisenhower Lodge kitchen. It's a party line and the lodge's call signal is three longs on the west forestry line. The best thing about the job is Dorothy gets paid! It's not much but it's better than a kick in the pants.

Dorothy likes her job of operating the switches and plugging them in and pulling them out. If Aileen Harmon from the Parks office in town wants to know the weather in the Kootenay park, Dorothy hails someone and then relays the information back to Banff. She passes on food orders, too, from the family running the Kootenay Park Lodge and Cabins at Vermilion Crossing, on Highway 93 between Banff and Radium.

Along with the mosquitos and bugologists, most of the tourists disappear in autumn. The mountains that shone warmly in the summer sun look cold and grim when the clouds move in. The change in season doesn't mean Mike is going back to the classroom; he'll do correspondence courses again. School is too far away. Terry, at three years old, isn't given any schoolwork yet but he can sing the ABCs and count. He is also old enough to wonder how Santa is going to find him out here in the dark forest. There are no lights close by to point out his home.

A few weeks before Christmas, Ed comes up with the perfect idea: a Santa beacon. He winds a string of battery-operated outdoor lights around a small spruce tree growing near the cabin. The lights are blue to show Santa that this is where the three Carleton boys live.

Another potential problem for Santa could be that the lodge doesn't have a fireplace, only a wood stove. Dorothy tells her boys that it'll be no problem for Father Christmas.

"He is filled with lots of jolly good magic."

Christmas magic also comes in the form of Dorothy's baking. Eisenhower Lodge is filled with the scents of gingerbread boys (not men), mince tarts and pies made in the wood stove. With all her baking, the fire needs constant stoking. Mike and Terry are eager to help. They want to impress the Big Man in Red. The children bring in kindling and dry logs from the woodshed anytime their mother asks. No complaints. They're making the "good boys" list for sure.

Ike Inn is going to be open in time for Santa's visit. Mrs. Spear and her two children take the train from Calgary and are dropped off at the Mount Eisenhower siding near the Department of Public Works (DPW) camp, about a kilometre (.6 mi) from the hostel. They lug all the supplies, packages, food and gifts up to the road and through the snow on a toboggan.

On Christmas Eve, Mike and Terry each hang one of Ed's grey wool socks from the end of their beds in the hope that Santa realizes the heavy-duty woollens are stockings. In the morning, the boys find mandarin oranges, nuts in their shells, candies and a little Dinky Toy (miniature car) stuffed into each of the socks.

That Christmas Day, the Carleton home is filled to the brim with holiday cheer. Ed and Dorothy bought a record player as a family gift. It's well-received and the family listens to favourites like Wilf Carter and Marty Robbins crooning good old cowboy songs. Of course, the Carletons also sing some carols.

Before dinner, Ed takes Mike and Terry skating. Their dad has made a rink for them and the boys are zipping here, there and everywhere. Dorothy and Brian are inside preparing supper. Dorothy, in her everyday white-and-red apron over her Christmas clothing, has her battery-operated radio turned up as loud as it will go. She's playing all the festive tunes and singing along merrily. When the turkey and trimmings are done, she waves all her boys inside.

"It's time to eat!" she says, giving each of them a kiss on their cold cheek as they walk through the door.

New Year's Eve is a dress-up affair for the adults. Dorothy has a nice taffeta dress with a yellow bodice and Ed puts on a suit. They'd make a glamorous pair anywhere in the world. Dorothy turns on the radio and they start following the celebrations starting on Canada's East Coast. They toast the New Year, 1956, with almost every province except for British Columbia, which is an hour behind Alberta. By then, the Carletons are knackered and go to bed.

Mount Eisenhower Lodge.
Photo: Carleton Family

WINTER AT MOUNT EISENHOWER

There's a steep hill at the base of Mount Eisenhower that makes the perfect toboggan run for boys and girls in winter. The slope doesn't have many mature trees growing on it because it was once the site of a personal ski hill. Ulysses LaCasse created it for his daughter, Ila.

Ulysses was the district warden at Mount Eisenhower a few years back. Before that, he was a guide for Jimmy Simpson. Ila was an up-and-coming downhill skier in the 1930s and she needed a place to train. Her father knew the right spot: a slope about 350 m (400 yds.) away from the lodge, their home. The newspaper has a record of some of Ila's races, including a giant slalom event held at Mount Norquay in 1946. She was the only woman who finished in the top ten in the chase for the inaugural Ski Runners Memorial trophy. She was sixth.

A small creek flows by the base of the Eisenhower hill and dead willows are laid down in the creek bed in the summer to provide a smoother descent when the snow flies. Guests from the Eisenhower Youth Hostel use the ski hill and so does Peter Spear, the son of the hostel's house parent, Flo Spear. Before learning how to turn on skis, he takes a stick and marks a location on the hill. Then, he skis straight down to see how far he coasts out at the bottom. As he gets braver, his marked location gets higher and higher.

The little ski hill is close enough for Mike and Terry to go on their own. They climb up the slope and slide down it on pure powder. It transitions nicely into a sledding run, too. Sometimes Ed tags along with his sons to see how well they're doing with their skiing. They're better than him on two boards and he's proud of that and of all the other things his children do. They're good little workers and he can depend on them to help him and Dorothy at any time.

Mike, at 10, is an especially great support for his parents. He doesn't get an allowance for his various chores but he feels like one of the "big guys" who can pitch in. He keeps a diary of what he's done, just like his dad. On Feb. 2, 1956, Mike writes down all the work he did during the day (all chores are completed while looking after his two brothers):

- make toast
- bring cups of tea to mum and dad in bed
- puts Eurax (cream) on Brian's rash
- gets brothers ready for the day
- wash the dishes
- chop wood
- make kindling
- pile wood
- bring wood into the lodge
- get coal
- stoke the fire in the lodge
- stoke Smokey Guttman's fire while he's away on patrol

- tidy woodshed
- shovel snow
- answer phone
- straighten the rug
- feed the goldfish
- make dinner
- set the table
- wash the children, and
- put them to bed

Entries in Ed's 1956 diary include going on ski patrols and checking on his area. He's inspecting and maintaining the telephone lines and shovelling snow off the shelter roofs. Some evenings after work, Ed has time to skate with Mike and Terry on the outdoor rink he made. It's the perfect way to wind down a busy day. If there are no clouds, the moon and the stars light up the ice. When the boys' feet get cold, they all go into the cabin to warm up with a cup of hot chocolate made with that dastardly powdered milk. The boys hate it because they think it tastes like chalk and it's both watery and lumpy at the same time. For Dorothy though, it's a practical solution. She can't go to the grocery store every week for fresh milk. She can bake cookies every week and the kids get one with their cocoa. Ed has three.

Terry (left) and Brian panning for gold.
Photo: Carleton Family

Cowboys, Thunderstorms and Getting Schooled

Spring comes to Mount Eisenhower and Dorothy heads to the garden. In June, she plants flats of pansies and other flowers that will bloom until the first week of September. She attempts to coax some vegetables to grow out of the rocky mountain soil but not even potatoes will sprout.

Freckles do sprout on Mike. Not enough, though, to win the Freckles Contest at the Banff sports day held in June. Rosalie McCallum brings home the ribbon for her speckled cheeks.

Life at Mount Eisenhower becomes a little more lively when the tourists arrive in the park. When Dorothy is busy with her telephone switchboard work, she shoos her three sons outside to play.

"Keep an eye on Brian," Dorothy tells the oldest two boys.

Mike is the unofficial babysitter of his siblings. They run in the forest, splash in the creek and chase each other around the buildings. Brian toddles after his older brothers, wanting to do everything they do. Sometimes though, he's happy to sit and play in the sandbox. In the evenings, Terry shows Brian picture books and keeps him company while he drifts to sleep.

Joining the warden crew this summer is John Laut, Ed's seasonal assistant. John was unemployed in the spring of 1956, sitting at home in Calgary when he saw a flyer announcing summer job opportunities with the National Parks Branch. He filled out an application and a short time later, was told to report to Banff National Park for a seasonal job with the warden service. He had a job for the summer.

In Banff, Ed kits out John and takes him to the Mount Eisenhower warden station. He's set up in the bunkhouse, where he'll live until he's moved to a cabin at Hillsdale Meadows. The wardens first call-out together is to the Johnston Canyon campground, where a bear has been caught in a culvert trap, a barrel-shaped device. The pair hook the trap, with the bear inside, to the pickup truck and drive it to a meadow in the Lake Louise district. Ed hands his assistant some whitewash paint and a brush and then hoists himself on top of the tube.

"When I open the gate and the bear comes out," says Ed, "you paint its flank."

This is John's first encounter with a bear, an animal that has sharp teeth and claws and is not going to wag its tail when it's let out. The paintbrush in John's hand quivers.

"On three," says Ed. "One, two, three!"

Ed lifts the door and the bear runs into the wild. Not before John covers its side with white paint.

John's horse for the season is Annie. She's an older, gentle mare with a smooth gait. Ed teaches John how to pack and throw both a two-man and one-man diamond hitch (a lashing technique used to hold loads on packhorses). John masters the knots after several tries.

The wardens and their horses ride up to the fire lookout. It's a dry summer and during the first week of June, the park trails are shut down. Ed and John bring water to Charlie Phillips at the tower. It's a long ride. The men and their horses travel along the railroad right of way until reaching the lookout trailhead at the site of a First World War internment camp. Then, they go up the trail to the lookout.

Besides riding the trails, Ed has also been climbing a lot on the mountain. Climbing Mount Eisenhower can be difficult depending on the route and experience of the climber. There are lots of gullies and wide ranges of exposure. The first recorded climb to the top of Eisenhower was in 1885 by Arthur P. Coleman, a geology professor from the University of Toronto. The Eisenhower Tower, a pinnacle on the eastern side of the peak, was first climbed in August of 1926 by Lawrence Grassi and Peter Cerutti, who lived in Canmore. The tower is popular with modern mountaineers, especially those staying at Ike Inn. Thankfully, there are no major incidents this year in Ed's district.

***

Old mines and cabins scattered around Banff National Park have caught Ed's attention. The lost sites of the Queen of the Hills mine and Bill Peyto's cabins ignite a passion in him. On duty and off, he searches for overgrown trails and remnants of log cabins deep in the bush or high on a peak. While it's not an obsession, looking for lost sites becomes one of Ed's missions.

The Queen of the Hills was supposed to be around Mount Eisenhower and was supposed to be filled with silver or copper. The mine partly gave rise to Silver City, a settlement that was established sometime in 1883 just over 1.5 km (1 mi) east of Eisenhower Junction. The boomtown grew in a year to include saloons, hotels, pool halls and a population of about 2,000 who were watched over by two North-West Mounted Police. In 1885, the place became a ghost town when no precious metals were discovered.

Whenever Ed hikes up a Mount Eisenhower slope, he takes out his binoculars and searches for dips and breaks and bumps in the landscape. He finds at least three locations with evidence of digging or old shafts but no proof that one of them is his queen. The mystery continues.

Ed has company during a backcountry trip on horseback to Taylor Lake, northwest of Mount Eisenhower. Mike and assistant warden Jack Schulte have come along for the ride. Jack is a young warden who can ride a horse anywhere no matter the terrain. He and his steed put the trail into Rockbound Lake, a steep climb, before there was ever a path.

The trail to Taylor Lake isn't as difficult but it is secluded and not many people get up there. That means the lake is teeming with fish. No one is around when the trio arrives at the tarn. Mike sees countless cutthroat trout jumping to grab bugs or swimming under the calm, clear surface. Ed has his fly fishing rod with him but Jack has another idea of how to catch a trout. He rides his horse into the water, gets out his rifle, takes aim and ... shoots a fish right between the eyes.

"Wow!" says Mike.

"Don't ever do that again," says Ed. He's not angry but he's none too pleased. Wardens are caretakers of the park and not supposed to be shooting the wildlife. According to Ed, Jack is living in the wrong time period.

"You should have been born a hundred years ago," Ed says, "as a cowboy."

Mike at Twin Lakes with a catch of native cutthroat.
Photo: William Dekur

For little Terry, Jack is the epitome of a cowboy. He is almost always on a horse and has the hat to go along with his "get it done any way possible" attitude. The hat he wears is not a warden-issue hat. No, it's a beat-up cowboy hat.

When Taylor Lake Trail needs some work and a check needs to be done on campers and anglers there, it's seasonal assistant John Laut who is on the job that morning. Mike wants to tag along with him and Ed and Dorothy are fine with the 10-year-old "helping." Ed drives the pair to the trailhead and tells them he'll be back for them in the afternoon.

John starts work and Mike starts fishing once they reach the lake, about a 7-km (4 mi) hike in. The seasonal warden later decides he should scout Larch Lake nearby and won't be able to meet Ed at their scheduled spot. Mike says that's OK, he'll hike out to his dad by himself.

It all goes as planned. Nevertheless, that hadn't been Ed's plan for Mike. In a rare show of anger, Ed flies into John. He is furious that he let Mike walk out alone.

Mike and his friend Peter often go with Ed on patrol in the truck. Ed is responsible for the telephone lines in his district. He has the only line between Banff and Jasper and Kootenay Park and Radium.

Ed keeps an eye on the lines, spotting problems like when a tree falls across the wire or an insulator comes unattached. Just like at Stoney Creek, Ed puts on his climbing spurs and clambers up the pole to make repairs. The telephone poles aren't short either, they're just under 5 m (15 ft) tall. The boys watch as Ed does his work and when he's finished, he'll explain what he did. On the drive, he'll talk about other interesting things he has seen and done as a warden. In a rare moment, he talks about the seven boys who died on Mount Temple. The tragedy shouldn't have happened and yet it did, right on Ed's doorstep. More than ever, he feels a responsibility to those heading out into the backcountry.

Smokey Guttman is another warden who is keeping an eye on park visitors and the park. The young "cowboy" warden is a colourful man. He's the life of the party and loves an impromptu guitar jam.

Smokey is a tall rangy fellow with thick black hair. He dresses in western gear whether he is on duty or not. He had been a forest ranger in Ontario for five years before moving to Alberta the previous year. One afternoon, he's out on patrol with Ed and seasonal warden Bill Dekur when they come across a tree that has fallen onto one of the phone lines. It has broken one of the glass insulators. The sky that had been full of sunshine a few minutes ago, is now swirling with dark clouds. The wind is picking up, pushing large trees from side to side. A rumble of thunder passes over the men like a wave.

"Smokey," says Ed. "Get up there and fix that insulator."

"Now?"

"There's no time like the present."

"But … it's thundering and lightning!"

"I haven't seen any lightning."

Smokey puts on his climbing spurs and sprints up the pole. He's working away as thunder claps around him. The storm is almost upon them. He throws a cut wire (it's not live) down to the ground to Bill. Bill grabs it to put a sleeve on it — but just as he's

Brian (left), Bill and Terry at Mount Eisenhower Lodge, 1959.
Photo: Carleton Family

about to do just that, lightning strikes. It travels through the wire Bill is holding and shoots out his hand.

"Ahhhhhhhhhhhhhhhhhh!"

That's from Bill. He's been knocked flat on the ground.

He gets up and starts running around like a chicken with its head cut off.

"Ahhhhhhhhhhhhhhhhhh!"

He falls down.

He gets up and repeats the hollering, screaming and falling again until Smokey climbs down and helps him to his feet. Ed, who has been watching, scratches his head.

"I guess we could wait to hook this line back up after the storm is over."

No doubt Smokey will tell this story in years to come. He's a great entertainer and has a penchant for spinning a yarn or two around the supper table. He is often accompanied by his guitar, which he plays as Dorothy sings along. Smokey also strums some of Ed's favourite country tunes from Johnny Horton and Johnny Cash. If there's enough room, Ed will take Dorothy for a spin on the "dance floor." Their love for each other is obvious after over a decade of marriage.

Back in England, Russ and Phyllis have their fifth child, Andrew. He completes their family in August 1956. The British Carletons then say farewell to Reading and move to Birmingham, a large industrial city. Russ gets a job with Land Rover, a British auto company.

Dorothy has a few more funny Banff stories to tell them. She writes to England about Bill, the bull elk. He's been hanging around the warden station for years. He's not a pet but he's also not completely wild. The other day, Dorothy threw potato peelings into the compost pile. The smell attracted Bill and he was munching away when something spooked him. He ran right through the clothesline that had clothing on it and carried everything away on his antlers. Dorothy has to giggle but she is a little upset that Bill took a pair of Ed's socks that she had just darned. Darn! The autumn leaves will soon cover up the ground and they won't be able to find the clothes that Bill dropped in the woods.

This fall, there's exciting news for the older boys. Well, for Mike. He's going back to the classroom in Banff! Terry, although a couple months shy of turning five, will attend school too. Banff is not close by. A round trip from the lodge to the school, twice a day, totals around 129 km (80 mi). That's a lot of driving. Nevertheless, Dorothy and Ed think the boys need to mix with other children.

Mike is excited about returning to his friends at school. Terry doesn't know what's about to come. After a kiss and a hug from Dorothy, the boys pile into the truck with Ed. He'll take his sons for their first day of school on Sept. 1, 1956.

The boys are dropped off at the front of the elementary school. Mike heads through the doors to find his Grade 6 friends. Terry? Terry isn't sure what he's supposed to do. Except that he's not going to school. All the children bother him. Why are there so many kids here? Terry knows where there are no kids.

He walks to the Warden Equipment Building, where he's been with his dad several times. Inside it's quiet and semi-dark but it's perfect for Terry. The hay for the wardens' horses makes a soft spot to sit and the smell of the leather saddles is comforting. Terry isn't going to go hungry either. He has the lunch Dorothy prepared for him in his giant lunch bucket: a baloney sandwich and treats.

Terry is used to entertaining himself. He looks around the building, discovers hiding spots and has a nap or two. When the door opens a few hours later, it's his father. Highly unimpressed.

Ed's usual smile is turned upside down. He points outside and Terry gets up and walks out the door and into the waiting vehicle.

"I'm taking you back to school," says Ed.

He marches Terry through the entrance and right into his classroom. The other students are in awe of Ed. He's dressed in his full warden uniform and must look pretty sharp to them. To Terry, it's his father's words that are sharp. However, the little boy knows he's safe from a spanking. When he gets home, Dorothy tells Terry he has to go to school. He can't play hooky again.

A few weeks later, Dorothy receives a phone call from Terry's teacher.

"Your son is playing in the sandbox when he's supposed to be in the classroom."

Dorothy sighs. She is realizing Terry is having trouble being around other children. However, if this is the only problem Terry is having in school, she'll count her blessings.

***

On Ed's rare days off, the whole family goes for a ride into the backcountry. Those days off are not too frequent. There is no such thing as 9 to 5 for a warden. However, when there is a spare moment, Ed returns to nature. He likes to paint what he has seen. The vistas Ed has visited, the flora and fauna he's studied and the wildlife he's encountered are things that even an ordinary Banff resident might never see. He's been privileged to tread on such unspoiled land. To capture memories of the places he has been, Ed takes pictures in his mind and transfers them to the canvas.

Painting gives Ed a chance to share his work in a creative way. He takes photographs around his district but they're in black and white. Painting adds colour, depth and brings the scenery alive. To do this, Ed uses watercolours or oil-based paints. A couple of art classes in high school taught him the basics of sketching and he uses that knowledge to draw out a place or animal before getting out the paintbrush. He shows Terry how to draw a horse using a circle and line technique. Horses figure into many of Ed's works because they are the warden's constant companion on the trail. Another one of man's best friends ends up frozen in time. Ed paints a picture of a springer spaniel, similar to Chum, the family's dog. The dog in the watercolour is white, though. Chum is mostly black.

Other art pieces by Ed feature Mount Eisenhower, Windy Cabin and Peyto Lake. Ed does an oil painting of Bill Peyto overlooking the bright azure lake named after him. Bill's horse is off to the side grazing while Bill kneels on the mountaintop, smoking his pipe. Ed says since he didn't know how tall Bill was, he didn't know how big to make him next to his horse. That's why Bill is crouched down. Ed wants the details in his paintings to be exact. He'll often cut out pictures of animals and birds from magazines like Western Horseman to capture the finer points.

Every year, one special picture gets pride of place on the Carletons' Christmas card, such as Ed's *Mountain Men* painting of Banff wardens sitting around a campfire in the Stoney Creek District. Ed takes the artwork to a printer and gets a few cards made for family and friends. Russ and Phyllis in the U.K. look forward to receiving the holiday greeting from Banff, as does Dorothy's family in Reading. Alice, who is 64, is still in her home and visits with her daughter Marjorie when she gets a chance. Dorothy receives their news when the weekly letters arrive at the Banff post office. Lives are busy everywhere.

In December, Ed puts the blue lights up on the little tree outside the lodge. Mike and Terry insist on the lights being blue. This is the only way Santa Claus can recognize their home. Brian isn't old enough to know Santa yet but he knows his brothers must be right.

One evening Dorothy and Ed take the family out to visit neighbours. On the way home, Dorothy catches sight of the tree with the blue lights. A lump forms in her throat as she takes in the beauty welcoming her return to Eisenhower Lodge.

Christmas and New Year's pass with the traditional gifts and goodies. They spend time with friends at the Mount Eisenhower Lodge as well as in Banff. There is singing and skating and skiing and hot chocolate and of course, a glass of Bristol Cream sherry to ring in 1957.

Brian and Chum at the Mount Eisenhower skating rink, 1958.
Photo: Carleton Family

Ed's painting of Bill Peyto.
Photo: Carleton Family

Chapter Eleven

A Time Capsule, Royalty and Lots of Wildlife

The Man and the Mountain

The snow is piling up and up in the winter of 1957. Ed and Smokey Guttman need to get out to the Johnston Creek cabin and shovel off the roof. They put on their snowshoes for this trip and travel several kilometres in the powder and cold. It's hard work. It is this hard work, though, that Ed thrives on.

Smokey says Ed is a good boss. He's experienced and doesn't complain and rarely loses his temper. He's athletic and can be counted on to do things efficiently and safely, although he likes to do things himself. Smokey has witnessed this while attending one of Walter Perren's Public Safety Training sessions.

Walter doesn't play around with his rescue scenarios. He wants the men to behave like they're in a true life-or-death situation despite it being a dry run. Sometimes, reality does end up smack dab in the middle.

During one practice on a mountain, rocks of all sizes are tumbling down slopes and narrowly avoid hitting wardens. Smokey almost gets smoked while pretending to be a victim. Seconds after being unstrapped from a mine basket that the men are using to lower the injured off the peak, a large rock slams into it.

Another time, the wardens are simulating a rescue that has the men crossing a canyon via a rope. The drop to the rushing water below is about 60 m (200 ft): a bone-shattering height. The wardens are using a system of pulleys, carabiners and climbing harnesses to get themselves, their equipment and the "wounded" across. The wardens almost lose their first victim, Bill Hollingsworth, when the mining basket he's in comes untied from the rope spanning the river. Fortunately, he holds on for dear life as he's pulled to safety.

It's things like this that give Ed pause. He'll tie his own knots thank you very much. That's very well and good but he gets stuck halfway across the canyon. Ole Hermanrude watches as Ed gets himself out of the mess and safely to the other side. Ole is more unnerved over it than Ed.

"I made it, didn't I?" says Ed.

Ole and Ed have been practicing their life-saving and skiing skills together for many years. They were at Noel Gardner's first ski school in 1951. Later, they attended Walter's ski, climbing and mountain rescue sessions. Now they're paired on some regular warden patrols.

Ole and Ed are on a mountain ridge one day when a thunderstorm breaks out. The silver plate that was put in Ed's skull after his war injury, starts reacting with the electrical charges in the air. Sparks start flying ... inside and outside Ed's head. Ed and Ole get off the mountain rim as quickly as they can.

Ed, in the basket, being "rescued" during search and rescue training. Andy Anderson (right) is smoking his pipe while guiding the basket. Photo: Bruno Engler

During the various rescue training sessions over the years, the wardens have built up a wealth of experience. Walter introduces the willing learners to difficult climbing manoeuvres and rescue techniques. Also on the mountain, is photographer Bruno Engler. Engler has snapped many pictures of Walter and the wardens on the rocks.

Walter and Bruno have many things in common. They are both Swiss, were Swiss Guides, worked with Ernst Feuz and are knowledgeable about the Banff park mountains any time of the year. During the Second World War, Bruno was a mountain warfare instructor for the Canadian Army. He's at home hanging off cliffs or hurtling down steep slopes on his skis. Another one of his great talents is photography.

Bruno is a high-altitude photographer and filmmaker and creates Alpine Films. Besides taking pictures of Hollywood stars like Paul Newman, some of Bruno's subjects are the park wardens and Ed is in a few shots over the years. Ed has great respect for Bruno and his picture-taking expertise. Both Ed and Dorothy think the photographer has the charm of the Swiss and a good sense of humour. He also is a mountain goat and goes pretty much anywhere he wants. He scrambles up cliffs and gullies and over many obstacles to get the perfect shot. Once in a while, he has to abandon his photo plans, especially when he's charged by a bull moose that doesn't want his picture taken.

Mike and his cousin Baillie (named after her father, Ed's brother) are recruited for a less adventurous, more low-key shoot in town. Mike and Baillie have to run up to the Bow River and then throw rocks into it.

Bruno's often at Cuthead College during public safety training for the wardens and takes many great pictures. There's another iconic image of Walter and Ole on a rock. Walter has some rope coiled around his arm and it looks like he's about to trek up the mountain with Ole following.

With Ed away training, it's up to Dorothy to take Mike and Terry to school. There are two constants on the drive: tedium and the moose that is almost always at 17 Mile Flats.[86] The Carletons sometimes carpool with other families in the area. Ole Hermanrude has four children, Karen, Margaret, Rob and Larry, and there are the two Lebourgeois children who live at the CP rail siding. One parent will shuttle a carload so the other parents can have a day off. Madame Lebourgeois has a tiny Renault but manages to fit everyone in.

When Dorothy returns home, she bakes bread, does housework and then it's back in the vehicle to pick up the boys from school. When Mike and Terry return home, they have chores to do after their homework is finished. Mike chops wood and Terry cuts kindling. They both entertain Brian as he walks about, asking questions.

There are other kids to play with at Mount Eisenhower. The assistant warden and his wife, Jim and Alice Robertson, have a few children. There's another Michael, although a couple of years younger than Mike, and his sisters Kathy, Marilyn and Yvonne. Mike and Michael love to tease the younger girls.

Jim Robertson always has a cigarette hanging on his lip. The assistant warden is amazingly skilled with horses and it's a boon in his job. The horses used by the wardens

86. Now called Moose Meadows.

are owned by Parks. Ed thinks it's time his family has a horse to call their own and buys one from a farmer friend. Chiquita comes to stay in the barn near the lodge. She's named after a song that Dorothy and Mike both like to sing: Chiquita Banana by Edmundo Ros and His Rumba Band.

Chiquita is a fairly small buckskin horse with a white face She's mild-mannered and a well-suited ride for the Carleton kids and their cousins who come to visit. Mike is the most frequent rider, taking Chiquita on backcountry patrols with his dad.

During one trip, Mike and Chiquita are going over Pulsatilla Pass, part of the Johnston Creek -Luellen Lake-Pulsatilla Pass-Baker Creek trip. There's a grizzly living out there and Chiquita can smell the bear. She gets nervous, putting her ears back, making Mike nervous. He feels her body shaking and trembling underneath him and he holds tight to her reins. She could bolt at the snap of a twig. Mike says a few soothing words and Chiquita loosens up. They never see the griz.

John Laut is back at Eisenhower as a seasonal warden. Last year, Ed and Dorothy had encouraged him to return to his studies at the University of Idaho. He's doing a Bachelor of Science in biology and botany with a minor in forestry. He ran out of money at the end of the school year and is in Banff again to build up his bank account.

Dorothy and the boys look forward to weekends and summer holidays. No driving! Mike and Terry invite their buddies out to the lodge during time off school. (Terry has made friends after warming up to the other children in his class.) The kids race logs on the creek, ride horses and stare at the stars. The brothers and their friends are never bored.

Peter Spear[87] doesn't have too much time for child's play. He's working at Johnston Canyon for Parks under Ed. Ed had told him about a summer maintenance job there. It was open because the man Parks originally hired drank too much and was unreliable.

"But I'm only 17," says Peter. "I'm too young to be hired."

"Don't let that stand in your way," says Ed.

He suggests Peter get a Social Insurance Number (SIN) and fudge his age on it.

"That's all you'll need to do," says Ed.

Peter gets the job and spends many hours re-decking the bridges in the canyon and replacing broken railings. It's strenuous work bringing the new wood into the canyon, through the narrow path, and getting the old wood out. One day, Peter sees a tree leaning over the canyon. He reports it, as it could topple onto the trail and hurt someone.

There's a rushing creek spewing through Johnston Canyon and getting to the tree isn't easy. Ed calls in Walter Perren and he belays a fellow down the slippery rocks to cut the tree, which crashes and splashes into the canyon. Peter's role is to guard the trailhead and stop tourists from hiking up until the operation is complete.

---

87. Peter Spear is an accomplished skier and ski patroller who is highly respected by his peers. He is also an experienced climber and was one of the 16-members of Canada's first-ever Mount Everest expedition in 1982.

Teddy Bear, Terry, Brian and unknown woman with Chiquita, Mount Eisenhower, 1955. Photo: Carleton Family

Peter stays at a small Parks cabin north of the Johnston Canyon Bungalow Camp while working for the summer. He's a frequent viewer of Walter Camp's evening shows, entertainment for the guests. Walter, the owner of the bungalow camp, is a natural per former and loves telling jokes and stories to the tourists.

"How did Pilot Mountain get its name?" he asks the crowd. "Well, when they were building the railway they had to dig out all the rocks to make a smooth base for the track, they had to put all those diggings somewhere. So they asked the foreman what to do with the rocks and he said, 'Pile it.'"

Everyone roars with laughter.

Rescue work is not in Peter's official job description but it's something he picks up. Late one evening, a young girl tells him that her friend has sprained an ankle on a trail and can't walk out on her own. Peter knows what to do. He takes an old wheelbarrow and after carrying it up 30 stairs and pushing it almost 2 km (just over 1 mi), he finds the injured girl. He picks her up and puts her in the wheelbarrow with her legs dangling over the front, and starts the return trip. At the canyon stairs, he piggybacks her down the steps while someone else carries the wheelbarrow. He then delivers her via the wheelbarrow to the family car.

For an end of the summer break, Ed gives Peter permission to use the Johnston Creek cabin, about a 12-km (8 mi) hike from Johnston Canyon towards Luellen Lake. There has been early snow, making the fire hazard low, and there aren't many tourists around. Peter takes off for his solo trip and along the way, spots a spruce grouse. He knows he's not supposed to hunt in the park but those "chickens" are tasty!

Whack!

Peter takes the grouse to the cabin and plucks off the feathers before roasting the bird in the barrel oven. He hides all the evidence of his yummy meal by burying the feathers and bones near the cabin. No one will miss one little grouse.

***

It's late August 1957 when Ed and Walter Perren are tasked with helping two Americans with an errand that Ed thinks is a bit foolish. He has to bring Jacob and Agnes Verwoerd up to the summit of Mount Eisenhower so they can pay tribute to the American president with a rocket-shaped time capsule.

Ed knows Jacob and Agnes. They've been coming to Banff National Park for a few years now and have met Dorothy, too. While Ed likes the Californians, he doesn't think they're up for the trip. Jacob and Agnes are known as adventurers, explorers, photographers and filmmakers in their state of California. Jacob is originally from the Netherlands and has lived in Vancouver, B.C. Agnes is from B.C., and they both like to hike and snap pictures of the Rockies and its wildlife. However, their definition of "adventure" and Ed's definition are not the same. The Californians do not have much experience climbing to summits.

The Verwoerds want to honour Eisenhower the man, who became president in 1953. They call him *a leader in the cause of peace*. They'll recognize him with a torpedo-shaped time capsule that will be filled with maps of North America, as well as microfilm and documents on the histories of both Eisenhowers – the man and the mountain. The White House gave the Verwoerds a U.S. flag that has flown over Washington D.C. to put with the capsule, Eisenhower gave them an autographed photo and a letter. Canada, including former prime ministers William Lyon Mackenzie King and Louis St. Laurent, gave the couple the OK for the mission.

Stateside, the Verwoerds herald their quest as the first since Castle Mountain was renamed Mount Eisenhower in 1946. But anyone who has been on the peak in the last 10 years knows that's not true. The Californians are also marking the centennial of the Palliser expedition, the British North American Exploring Expedition that first surveyed the Rockies from 1857 to 1860.

Although Ed is not fond of the Verwoerds' expedition, he and Walter head up the peak along with Jacob and Agnes on Aug. 28. They are not travelling light. They pack the time capsule, a three-pound hammer, a rock drill, sand, cement, water, camera equipment and food on horses. Jacob is on John Laut's horse, Annie. The seasonal warden knows that Annie doesn't like a tight rein and passes on this bit of information to Jacob.

On the trip up to the back of the mountain, Annie stops at a creek for a drink. Jacob ends up in the drink because he didn't loosen the reins. John warned him.

The group goes as far as it can on horseback. Then they hike the rest of the way ... with Ed and Walter hauling most of the heavy supplies and gear. A cumbersome wooden sign has already been left behind, pounded into a tree. Jacob and Agnes had planned to erect the sign at the top of Mount Eisenhower. It's staying down here.

It's already taking way too long to get to the summit. The Verwoerds are struggling in the scree and finding the physical work of scrambling up the side of the mountain taxing. Blisters, blood and huffing and puffing have slowed the foursome. Usually, the mountain trek is a seven-hour return trip. It's been that long by the time the group gets to the peak.

Ed and Walter drill holes into the rock and bury the time capsule. Then, it's all covered with two inches of concrete. Walter had managed to "snag" the bag of cement on the ascent and so there isn't much left to put over the capsule. A cairn is then placed over that. Cheers are shouted and photos are taken. Then, with the American and Canadian flags finally flying on Mount Eisenhower, the four begin their descent. It's dark by the time they get to the lodge. When Dorothy catches sight of Ed, she breathes a sigh of relief. She had been thinking the worst. Agnes, though, looks like she's been in some

Ed (left) with Jacob and Agnes Verwoerd at the main peak of Mount Eisenhower just before burying the time capsule, August 1957.
Photo: Walter Perren

sort of accident. Her legs are bruised and bloody and she can barely stand because of exhaustion. Dorothy brings her into the kitchen and makes her a cup of tea to wash away the weariness and celebrate her return.

The time capsule is supposed to be opened in one hundred years, 2057. But like Banff's lost cabins and mines, the Verwoerds' time capsule fades from memory. There are too many other things to occupy the mind and body and people, like John Laut, move on. The entomologists tell him about a federal posting for forest biology technician positions in Calgary. He applies and is successful. With mixed feelings, he leaves the warden service.

September means getting all the firewood to keep the Carletons warm and fed over the winter. The firewood usually comes from dead pine trees, which are trailered to the lodge. Then, parks employees bring a portable sawmill worked by two men. One fellow makes the cut with a large armsaw while the second man feeds the logs into the mill. Ed's job is to move the cut blocks to the woodpile for splitting into firewood and kindling. Then the wood is stacked and all the kids help, including Brian. At three years old, he carries the littlest pieces.

Once the woodpile is full, winter can come. And it does. The Carletons spend their evenings in 1957 doing homework and playing cribbage and Rummoli. It's a contented home and one where music and laughter reign.

The usually cheerful family is hit hard with news that Ed's father has died. Right before Mike's birthday in December, Ollie passes away at the Holy Cross Hospital in Calgary. He was 69.

Ed, Dorothy and their children get into the truck and drive to Didsbury, where they attend the funeral at St. Cyprian's Church. Russ, Phyllis and their children can't be there as they're in England but other family and friends gather to say goodbye. It's a sad day for Ed. However, he knows his father lived a good life. He had been ill for a while so his death isn't unexpected. Ollie's legacy is seen in the hardworking, honest and kind people Ed calls brothers and sisters.

Campers and a Wild Child

The Banff area gets a spectacular light show on Wednesday, Feb. 12, 1958. The Northern Lights dance in the sky and long-time residents say they've never seen anything like it. The red glow in the sky is so vivid that some people think there's a fire on Mount Norquay. Dorothy's never seen anything like it. She watches the red, blue and green lights snake across the sky. They move so fast that she thinks she should hear them crackling. Yet they are silent. It's a once in a lifetime show.

The Rundle Junior Boys' Choir is putting on a performance this spring. Dorothy has been singing to her children all their lives. They've also heard her stories about being on the Reading stage. Now it's Mike's turn in the spotlight and Dorothy couldn't be prouder. Her son is performing a solo with the choir and she's been his voice coach.

On May 7, Mike sings a folk song about a knight fighting a dragon. It has some rather tongue-twisting lyrics!

Sir Eglamore that valiant knight
With his fa, la, lanky down dilly
He fetched his sword and he went to fight
With his fa, la, lanky down dilly

Mike wears a jacket and tie and when he looks out at the crowd gathered in the church, spots Dorothy with a smile as wide as Ed's. Mike is happy to have made his mother happy but he hates every second of it. He'd rather be singing something by Johnny Horton, Marty Robbins or Wilf Carter. Those guys aren't slaying mythical creatures. No, they're singing about being on the road, going to the rodeo or playing cards! Real man stuff.

Ed has been known to break out in song. It's often when he's hiking with Mike that his son hears him belt out that old Calgary Highlanders tune, *Glenwhorple.* It's the only connection his son has to his father and the war. Otherwise, Ed remains tight-lipped about fighting overseas.

There's a new man around Mount Eisenhower Station in the spring of 1958. Stan Murray starts doing odd jobs around the lodge and then in June, moves to the fire tower. He's taking over from the elderly Charlie Phillips. Fire is an ongoing issue in Banff National Park. The construction of the Trans-Canada Highway through the park continues and it continues to spark fires. Slash piles being burned are fanning the flames. Wardens become responsible for making sure contractors don't create any fire hazards along the new national route.

Dorothy and her summer blooms at Mount Eisenhower Lodge.
Photo: Carleton Family

The men working on the highway stay at a Department of Public Works (DPW) camp about a kilometre from Eisenhower Lodge. Hillsdale Meadows is where Cubs and Scout groups tent while another group sets up trailers in the area. That crew is known as the Wally Byam Caravan Club. Wally Byam founded the Airstream company. He led tours in his caravans all over North America. The club comes annually to Banff and stays for a couple of weekends in the summer. The Carletons like to visit with the members and see who's returned for the season and hear about what they've been doing since their last trip to the meadows.

Remember that grouse that Peter Spear killed and ate last summer? He had buried the carcass near the Johnston Creek cabin. Well, he didn't bury it well enough. Ed comes across the bones during a visit to the hut.

"How did you like that grouse?" he asks Peter when he sees him next.

"Uh, what do you mean?" says Peter.

Ed stares down at Peter until the young man confesses.

"OK," he says. "But it was only one. How did you find out?"

Ed tells him that some rodents had ratted him out. They dug up the remains and scattered them all over the grounds.

Ed and Dorothy are doing a lot of hiking while living near Mount Eisenhower. One of their favourite trips is Arnica Lake. The fishing is excellent there and the views of the colourful green water are worth the 9.2-km (5.7 mi) return trip. There are steep sections, muddy spots and snow in the early summer and early autumn. The mosquitoes can get pretty thick and this is one thing Dorothy doesn't like. She swats at the buzzing insects as they whine around her ears.

***

The Carletons buy a new home in Banff. It's a huge financial decision for them. Their mortgage payment is $10 a month more than what they'd pay for the rental of a government house. The couple wonders if they can afford it. They decide they want to own instead of rent.

Up until a couple of years ago, wardens in Crown-owned housing (owned by the federal government) had their accommodation as a benefit. That all changed in 1956. The federal government wanted to have equal accommodation for all wardens since some were in free housing and others paid for it.

Ed and Dorothy's new house is at 139 Rainbow Avenue. They realize it's an investment in many ways, including time. While living at Eisenhower Lodge, Ed and Dorothy drive into town almost every day of the week including Sunday when they take their children to Sunday school. Their sons are spending more and more time in town, too. The boys have school events and skiing at Mount Norquay, not to mention Ed and Dorothy's own legion meetings and other commitments. A home in Banff is going to pay off in more ways than one.

At the start of July 1958, Ed helps bring a little girl home after she's lost on Mount Eisenhower. Four-year-old Leola Barry wanders off from her parents while they're making supper at a cabin. It's discovered she's gone around 7 p.m. Twenty hours later, she is found. Walter Perren organized the search for the little girl from

Camrose, Alberta and had more than 200 people, including Ed, looking for her during the rainy night. Walter hears crying from some bushes and there she is. She is taken to the new Mineral Springs Hospital for treatment.

The hospital is a new one. It officially opens on Jul. 26, 1958. The one where two of the three Carleton boys were born is too old and closes. The modern building on Spray Avenue includes a kitchen, dining rooms, cafeteria and a physiotherapy room along with X-ray, surgery and maternity wards.

Princess Margaret, Countess of Snowdon, visits Banff from the U.K. in August. She's not the Queen and a bit of a "wild child" but for Dorothy, that doesn't matter. Margaret, Queen Elizabeth's younger sister and only sibling, is in town. Almost 40 years old, Dorothy has never given up her British roots and supporting the English monarchy is something she'll always do. She is delighted to hear that the princess rode a horse along Lake Minnewanka, a place Dorothy knows well – it's on the way to Stoney Creek.

"I doubt she'll have a cup of tea made from the creek water," says Dorothy to Ed, "but if she does, she won't find any better in the world, even at Buckingham Palace."

Dorothy is also happy that her Royal Highness has a trip out to the buffalo paddock. Dorothy agrees with Ed that the bison are impressive animals and bound to impress the princess. Besides a look at the natural world, Margaret tours the Banff School of Fine Arts and inspects the National Army Cadet Camp. She also attends a dinner in her honour hosted by the province at the Banff Springs Hotel.

The official opening of the Banff Windermere highway, 1961. Left to right: Ed, Honorable W. G. Dinsdale and Glen Fagan.
Photo: Carleton Family

The next day, she leaves for Calgary. On her way to the city, she can see the mountain named after her, Princess Margaret Mountain. It's just outside of Canmore.

A rare event occurs in November: Ed is taking Dorothy on a trip that doesn't involve hiking or tenting or an outdoor bathroom. They're going stateside for 10 whole days. It's their first trip to the U.S.

Some fun with a bear.
Photo: Carleton Family

Ed's mother Millie comes to take care of her grandchildren while Ed and Dorothy drive to the town of Radium Hot Springs, near Kootenay National Park, to meet up with Glen and Edith Fagan. Glen is another Banff warden and a war vet. The foursome head to Spokane, Washington, stopping in the Idaho city of Coeur d'Alene on their way. The ladies do a lot of shopping and the men do a lot of sitting. Without beer. The pubs are all closed because of the U.S. senate election on Nov. 4.

Back in Banff, some tourists take an 8mm film of themselves feeding bear cubs at Lake Louise. The cubs stand on their hind legs begging for scraps that two men hold in a brown paper bag. There are more films like this one featuring visitors feeding animals in the park.

It's disturbing to Ed that the wildlife is being used for entertainment. His children know better than those nincompoop adults. A few weeks ago, Ed and Terry were on patrol when they stopped to watch a grizzly on the side of the road. The bear charged the truck and then reared up on its hind legs. The animal was huge and so were the front paws that slammed down on the hood of the vehicle. Terry was shaking and grabbed on to his dad's sleeve.

"Don't worry," Ed said to his seven-year-old son. "It's OK."

Ed calmly put the vehicle in reverse and backed away. Once they were home, they checked the front of the truck. It had scratch marks on it. The grizzly taught Terry an important lesson about respect.

The completion of the Trans-Canada Highway is only going to increase the number of people coming to Banff and the number of hazards for animals. Conservation and ecology practices have been evolving in the park. In the early days of game guardians, that meant killing predators like grizzlies and wolves to safeguard other animals like moose and sheep. Now wardens are involved in the natural management of animals, and part of their job is to gather various data in the field such as animal numbers and the health of the different species. Ed, Dorothy and their sons are always counting the wildlife. Ed collects the numbers and files them with his reports to head office.

Ian McTaggart-Cowan did one of the first ecological surveys in Banff and Jasper national parks back in 1943 and 1944. Then, it wasn't a vital part of a warden's job to note species and their numbers. McTaggart-Cowan, a Provincial Museum[88] biologist in Victoria, B.C., was hired by Parks to inventory the wildlife. Officials were especially concerned about the number of wolves and thought they might be a threat to other animal populations.

When the early settlers came to Banff, wolves ate their livestock. A bounty was placed on the animals and by 1907, the Western Stock Growers Association, an organization that promoted and protected ranching, had paid out hundreds of dollars for the deaths of almost 3,000 wolves. The province then took over the bounty program and the wolf population dwindled. In 1931, only one pair of wolves is spotted in Banff National Park and the province ends the bounty call. However, it only took a few years for the wolf population to rebound but Parks didn't know how many were actually in the area.

McTaggart-Cowan, with Jimmy Simpson as his guide, crisscrossed the peaks, valleys and rivers over two summers doing research. The ecologist took copious notes detailing what he and other people living and working in the park had seen.

Windy Cabin, Panther R. [River] July 4/43. [1943]
Saw fresh wolf tracks on Snow Cr. [creek] trail.
Yaha [Ya Ha] Tinda Ranch. July 7/43. [1943]
[Warden Clifford] Murphy saw 2 black + 2 gray wolves here last winter
Warden Wm [William] Nish [sic] *heard wolves at Scotch camp in 1932.*

Ian McTaggart-Cowan field notes (1943)

In his study, McTaggart-Cowan estimated that there was one wolf between 87 and 111 square miles of potential range. He wrote in his 1947 report, *The Timber Wolf In The Rocky Mountain National Parks Of Canada*, that the wolves weren't a threat to other species in the area. Leave them alone.

McTaggart-Cowan didn't think the same thing about the elk.[89] Elk damaged park ranges by feeding on seedlings and saplings. Before 1918, it was rare to catch a glimpse of the large herbivores. Then between 1918 and 1920, 235 elk were translocated from Yellowstone National Park in Wyoming, to Banff. This was when their population began to grow.

Twenty bulls were killed in 1937 and starting in 1942, elk slaughters were done annually every winter. In 1946, McTaggart-Cowan backed the parks branch's elk management plan of controlling the ungulate population and proposed 800 animals be exterminated.

In 1958, the elk are thriving and still on the kill list. Terry and Brian hear the gunshots from the lodge on winter days. Mike writes a postcard to his grandmother in England telling her about the cull.

---

88. Now the Royal B.C. Museum in Victoria, B.C.

89. In an interview in 2010, Ian McTaggart-Cowan says he wouldn't make the same decision about the elk if he had to do it all over again.

These are animals we see quite frequently throughout the year. In the fall, the bull elk will fight for possession of the cow. In winter, the wardens must kill some or there is a shortage of food for all of them.

The animals are shot and then skinned and gutted at an abattoir. Some of the meat and hides are given to Indigenous peoples and some of the meat goes to wardens like Ed. Elk has been a staple of the Carleton family's diet since they arrived in the backcountry over eight years ago. Dorothy cooks almost every part of the animal including the kidneys, heart and tongue. Preparing meals is often a parent's recurring nightmare and Dorothy attempts to please her family's palate and pocketbook. She makes elk stews and elk liver and onions. She takes the elk kidney and rolls it in flour and fries it in a pan. She thinks elk tongue is easy to cook and it can be eaten either warm with a dollop of mashed potatoes, or cold -- sliced and put into a sandwich.

Terry and Brian can't stand the organ meats and they definitely do not like the tongue. To them, it's the worst. Brian makes up the word "grimsely" to describe the taste. The definition of grimsely is: not good or unfavourable. But Brian takes care to use the term in jest, because he doesn't want his mother to feel bad about her cooking. It's not her, it's the meat.

Ed (left) and Jack Blomquist at the original site of Windy Cabin, Panther River District, 1949.
Photo: Whyte Museum of the Canadian Rockies

The Carletons have a reprieve from elk and the backcountry at Christmastime. They leave their blue lights twinkling at Eisenhower Lodge and move into their new home, 139 Rainbow Avenue, for the week. They open gifts in the Banff house and celebrate the holiday with a turkey dinner. On Boxing Day, they visit new neighbours and get acquainted with their families. It's back to Eisenhower to ring in the new year. It's 1959.

A Royal Wave

Skiing is playing a larger and larger role in the Carleton kids' lives. The little hill that Ila LaCasse used for training is not cutting it for Mike anymore. He's at Mount Norquay with his friend Paul Peyto.[90] They are both on the Banff ski team, the Banff Ski Runners of the Canadian Rockies, and take part in four-way competitions. Mike and Paul challenge each other and skiers from Lake Louise, Calgary, and Revelstoke, B.C., in four events: ski jumping, cross-country skiing, downhill skiing and slalom. Mike's favourites are jumping and downhill. It's the thrill of launching himself into the air or hurtling down the slope at full speed that he likes. Cross-country skiing is boring. Urgh. It's so much work having to shuffle along rolling terrain while swinging your arms and trying to get into some sort of rhythm. Not to mention, finding the right wax to fit the conditions. Slalom is just as tedious. Mike hates practising over and over through the gates. Hitting the gate (a pole) kind of hurts, too and leaves a mark.

The girls race against the boys in some events. Stephanie Townsend beats Paul in November in the slalom. Her two-run total is 51.8 seconds on Norquay. Paul's is 52.2. He's second.

The "Big Three" ski hills in the park are Mount Norquay, Sunshine and Lake Louise. Louise opens a ski school and gondola in winter 1959. That's great news for Banff. Some hardcore alpine skiers don't think the area is doing enough to bring skiers to the park and now with the Trans-Canada Highway being built through Rogers Pass, skiers are going to take the road all the way to B.C.'s wonderful resorts.

Clearly, we have to get busy and improve conditions hereabouts if we are to capture and hold our share of the "skiers' market."

Crag & Canyon editorial, *Action Needed*, Sept. 16, 1959

There had been some attempts at building a practice slope on Sulphur Mountain in 1951 and the 1959 editorial brings up the idea again. The mountain is close to town and people wouldn't have to go too far for a run or two. There had also been attempts to bolster Banff's reputation in the ski arena in 1953. Alberta ski clubs vied for the 1958 World Ski Championships and started improving Norquay's course in anticipation of the event. The championships ended up going to Salzburg, Austria.

The editorial garners praise and two comments are that Banff should begin to develop accommodations and better roads to the hills so skiers have places to stop while on their way to British Columbia.

90. Paul Peyto is a two-time winner of the Canadian four-way junior championship in the 1960s.

To introduce a steady winter sport business Banff, Lake Louise and Sunshine must further develop and pool their attractions as one big unit.

John Jaeggi, *Letters to the Editor* Sept. 23, 1959

Sulphur Mountain isn't turned into a ski hill. Banff National Park Superintendent BIM Strong says there is no money in the budget. Funds are already designated for highways and camping and picnic facilities.

From 1947 to 1957, the number of tourists has steadily risen from 300,000 to 800,000 a year. Some visitors think Banff is already overcrowded. A tourist from Victoria, B.C. writes *Banff is wonderful but too commercialized* in the register at the Government Information Bureau. (Someone from Texas writes: TEXAS!) Ed and Dorothy have watched their small mountain town get descended upon in the summer and winter. What never changes are the sentinels surrounding Banff. The mountains, like Eisenhower, stand watch day after day, season after season.

The human guardians of the park still see people using animals as roadside attractions. When Field Marshal Bernard Law Montgomery, 1st Viscount Montgomery of Alamein, was in Banff a few years earlier, he did not respect park rules. Monty was a Second World War British Army officer and gave the Allies their first major land victory against Nazi Germany at El Alamein, Egypt in 1942. (He is the same man who thought Calgary Highlander Lt.-Col. Donald MacLauchlan didn't know what he was doing as a battalion commander.) While in the park in 1956, Monty saw a bear cub near the Timberline Hotel. The viscount fed it sugar cubes and when he had none left, he called for the hotel attendants for more food. The staff knew it was against regulations to feed wildlife, however, someone produced a meringue pie.

How can the wardens be expected to stop the tourists from such bad behaviour when a precedent is set by a distinguished guest? It's this year, 1959, that the wardens start prosecuting people who are feeding or harassing animals. Four tourists are fined and given "a stiff lecture" from Parks after giving some bears a couple of snacks.

Eisenhower Lodge is fortunate it doesn't have to deal with bears in the garbage or prowling around the horse barn. However, There is a time when Dorothy is walking with Evalyn Gautreau, a bugologist's wife, and Chum chases away a black bear and trees her cub. Mama bear comes running back and Dorothy and Evalyn go running the other way.

Most problem black bears or grizzlies are trapped and released in remote areas of the park. Ed does have to shoot an animal if it is hurt or a danger to humans. In some cases when Ed is forced to put down a bear, he removes its gall bladder and trades it for vegetables with a family of Chinese descent that has a huge garden a few kilometres east of town.

Coyotes and wild dogs are causing some concerns in the park. They chase deer and elk and other wildlife, sometimes forcing a deer through a homeowner's fence. Some Banff residents think Parks should be footing the bill for property damage by large animals, but this doesn't happen.

Left to right: Brian, Terry and their cousin Jack Carleton displaying the catch.
Photos: Carleton Family

Before he was hired by Parks, the closest to wildlife that a young Bill Crabbe gets is mould on cheese. In the summer of 1959, 20-year-old Bill is introduced to Ed at the Cuthead warden school, where the young assistant is working as a cook's flunky. Bill thinks Ed is smart, outgoing and down-to-earth and is impressed with the man. It is obvious that Ed is highly respected by the other wardens, too. Later in the season, Bill is sent to Johnston Canyon in Ed's district.

Ed explains what's expected of Bill and the pair forges a great relationship. Bill comes to respect Ed more for the person he is than the position he holds. But listen, there's never any doubt about who's the boss: Ed just goes about it in the most friendly of ways. Although Bill is hardly out of his teens, Ed treats him like an adult and never talks down to him.

At one point in the summer, some canyon stairs are washed out and Bill can't get to his post. While the repairs are being done, he does some chores at Eisenhower, where he meets Dorothy. Bill can't imagine a kinder and nicer person. She treats everyone with respect and Bill feels almost like one of the family.

A new family moves into the assistant warden home at Eisenhower Station: Hugh and Meta Jennings, and their sons Robert and Randell. The boys, Robert and Randell, are tots, and around five years younger than Terry. He plays hide-and-seek with the kids and Brian. Mike babysits for the Jennings when Hugh and Meta go into town.

Dorothy is in town when she hears some news that makes her do a little dance on the spot. The Queen is coming to Banff! The royal couple is travelling across Canada and stopping in every province and territory. Ed's interest is piqued too: Queen Elizabeth is the Calgary Highlanders' colonel-in-chief.

On Jun. 10, the *Crag & Canyon* publishes an article saying that Her Majesty Queen Elizabeth II and His Royal Highness Prince Philip, Duke of Edinburgh, will be in town for two hours.

According to the official programme, the Royal Party will arrive at Banff at 10:00 a.m. on Friday, July 10th, by train from Calgary and depart from Lake Louise at 12:55 p.m. by road for Field, B.C.

Crag & Canyon, Jun. 10, 1959

The Queen will do some of the same things her sister Princess Margaret did. She'll tour the Banff Centre campus and the Banff Cadet Camp.

Before the Queen's visit, famous crooner Bing Crosby stops in town. He plays a round of golf under the "Blue Skies" at the Banff Springs Golf Club. Two days before the royals come to the park, a grizzly mauls two men and one of their sons. The Banff residents had been on a fishing trip at Chephren Lake, at the base of Mount Chephren in the Bow Summit district, about 48 km (30 mi) north of Lake Louise. The anglers, Frank Winchester along with Tom Semochuk and his son Alex, climb trees and wait for the mama bear to retreat. Then, the least injured of the three, Frank, runs for help. They are rescued and treated in hospital for their injuries. Dorothy is appalled the incident happened so close to the Queen's visit. Ed shrugs his shoulders.

"Wild animals are wild," he says. "Besides, you'd do the same to protect your 'cubs."

Dorothy's cubs, Mike, Terry and Brian, are scrubbed and put in their best clothes on Jul. 10. Dorothy puts on a nice dress and herds her crew out the door for the drive to town. Ed's in his formal warden uniform but he won't be squiring the royals around, much to Dorothy's chagrin. G.H.L. Dempster, superintendent of Banff National Park, is one of the hosts along with Donald Cameron, a senator and director of the Banff School of Fine Art, and his wife Stella.

It's a sunny day and the Banff streets are crowded with royal watchers. Queen Elizabeth and Prince Philip arrive on the train and are greeted by 200 children from Girl Guides, Scouts, Brownies and Cubs groups. The royal couple is then driven into Banff and past the hospital, where patients stand and sit near windows to catch a glimpse of Elizabeth and Philip. On Banff Avenue, Dorothy cranes her neck to look down the street. The cavalcade is coming!

The mother, who still speaks with a British accent, pushes her sons to the edge of the sidewalk.

"Wave boys!" she says. "That's our Queen."

In a flash, she's gone. At least Dorothy got a peek at Elizabeth's hat. The Carleton boys find friends in the crowd and they're off to pretend they're John Wayne in *Rio Bravo,* a movie set in the Wild West pitting a sheriff against some outlaws. Dorothy lets her kids go and chats with her friends. The ones who are war brides from England like Dorothy are happy that a piece of home has come to them.

The Queen will miss the opening of the Sulphur Mountain gondola by about a week. Instead of a ski hill, Sulphur got a cable car in 1959 that takes visitors from the bottom of Banff, right to the top. Town officials and businesses hope it'll draw tourists who will not only go to take in the views, but dine and shop as well. The gondola is featured on the CBC news with footage from Bruno Engler.

The weather is terrible on Labour Day weekend yet the winds and rain don't scare away the visitors. Around 3,500 people take the gondola up Sulphur Mountain. The cable car is a boon and keeps visitors occupied.

The new gondola lift certainly helped to minimize the feeling that, due to the unpredictable weather, this year's Labour Day visit to Banff was a complete loss.

Crag & Canyon, Sept. 9, 1959

The weather hasn't been good since July. August was rainy and cold. Ed had helped out with a Girl Guide camp at Hillsdale and had hoped the weather would warm up for them. However, nature never does what you want. Ed knows this well by now. It has been almost a decade since Ed became a warden. For Beef Woodward, it's been over 25 years.

Beef received his 25-year service button from the federal government the previous year. The 61-year-old has worked with some of Banff's renowned old-timers like Jimmy Simpson. Banff born and bred, Beef has seen the town transform from a mountain village to a tourist attraction. There's even a coin-operated laundry and streets that used to be full of horses and pedestrians are now lined with vehicles.

That used to be the same for Silver City. It was once a booming place. It's nothing but sticks and rocks now, yet some things remain. Emile Gautreau, a forest insect and disease survey technician (a bugologist) originally from New Brunswick, discovers an old log cabin. The cabin, still capped with its sod roof, is in good shape for its age. Emile knows Ed through his patrols and the two often talk about the history of the area. Emile knows the warden will be interested in the find. Along with Parks naturalist and historian Aileen Harmon, they hike to the location of the ghost town: past Smith Lake on the lower slopes of Copper Mountain.

There it is.

Aileen takes photos and Ed studies the site. He says he thinks the hut was probably built in the 1880s for a prospector. He pulls some artifacts out from around the area, including glass bottles, tins, picks and a 76-year-old newspaper. The illustration on the front page of the paper from 1883 is the Statue of Liberty. Edouard de Laboulaye's creation, Liberty Enlightening the World, was just being manufactured in France.

Left to right: Mike, Ed and Emile Gautreau at the Silver City log cabin, 1960. Photo: Herbert Cerezke

Chapter Twelve

A Year in the Life of a Warden and His Family

Patrols, Fires and Worry

People love to get outdoors. Recreation opportunities abound in Banff National Park and it's getting more accessible every year. It's the start of the 1960s and travel is cheaper than it's ever been and equipment is getting lighter and less cumbersome. Hans Gmoser is pivotal in bringing adventurers to the park. Some of his clients took footage of their trips chasing powder or bagging peaks with him. Hans puts the film together into movies and shows them in the U.S. and abroad.

Hans gives people a glimpse of places where long lift-lines and crowded slopes are miles away. He presents a pristine wilderness with pillowy snow and challenging crags that jut into the blue sky. For anyone looking for a sporting paradise, Hans's films are their inspiration.

Bruno Engler makes films, too, and his photographs are certainly a draw for those wanting to see what he has seen. Iconic images from the park capture people on skis, elk, bears eating from the palms of tourists, and the Banff Springs Hotel. One photo even features Ed, west of the Bourgeau Lake trailhead. The black-and-white picture shows Ed surveying the land with binoculars while dressed in his uniform.

Ed is in his forties and remains committed to working hard. He writes down everything he does while on duty and hands it in as a month-end report to the warden office. It includes daily weather observations and gas and mileage for the Parks vehicles he drives. That's not all: In the winter of 1960, he compiles a list of his long and varied jobs.

He runs regular patrols in his vehicle to various places like Baker Creek, the Divide (the Alberta / B.C. boundary), Moraine Creek, while making stops en route. He records game he sees as well as animal tracks he has found in the mud or snow. He inspects and maintains the telephone lines. He does snow removal around the station and from the roofs of several shelters such as Johnston Canyon and Baker Creek. He cuts wood for his family's stove, as well as for the bunkhouse and garage. He does maintenance of the power plant generator, hauls garbage to the dump at DPW Camp and picks up supplies like gas and camp fuel in Banff.

When the elk slaughtering crew is in the Eisenhower district, Ed heads out to oversee the operation. It's here he makes a sad discovery on Jan. 20. Old Bill, the elk, along with another almost tame bull, Harry, were done in by the cull. They were shot.

"Oh no!" says Dorothy when she hears the news. She remembers Bill running around the woods with her clean laundry wrapped around his antlers. He definitely wasn't her favourite then, but she feels a bit sad that he's gone to the stew pot.

Ed keeps in close touch with the wardens in neighbouring districts: Ole Hermanrude is in Healy Creek, Einar Bjorkman is in Marble Canyon and Beef Woodworth is in Lake Louise. A call comes in for Beef and Ed to trap a lynx. They get their cat.

Dealing with people and paperwork aren't jobs Ed loves but he gets them done. The Trans-Canada Highway remains under construction and he monitors the operations at the Standard Gravel quarry, a company working on the road. He lies in a snowshoe track and acts as a guide when the men go on a dragline crossing of the Bow River. (The dragline is a series of pulleys and ropes that pull a small wooden car suspended on the cables across the water. The car takes equipment, supplies and men to the other bank.)

There are a bunch of Walt Disney Company personnel in the park shooting footage for movies including *Nikki, Wild Dog of the North*. Ed ensures the Disney folk don't get lost or do something contrary to park guidelines.

With all the traffic in and out of the park, Ed responds to vehicle collisions and animal incidents on the road. At 11 p.m. one night, he cleans up after a moose was hit and killed by a vehicle. It had been decapitated. A few months later, he picks up a frozen cougar that had been killed by a diesel locomotive.

Some days, Ed works in the mountains. He does ski patrol into Boom Lake, Johnston Canyon and Baker Creek. Walter Perren's training camps are always on a warden's schedule and Ed attends ski school for a week of learning how to use a rescue toboggan and prepare for avalanche rescues. The wardens hit the slopes at Mount Norquay, Lake Louise and Sunshine to carve out better downhill techniques. The week wraps up with a written test and then a film by Bruno Engler. Then the men are treated to a slalom race and they reward themselves afterward with a few beers in Banff.

Ed's on traffic duty during the 1960 North American Nordic Ski Championships in March. There is an idea being floated about Banff hosting the 1964 Winter Olympics. The Calgary Olympic Development Association (CODA) hopes that by holding the Nordic championships at Mount Norquay, the area's potential for the games will shine.

Dorothy has been keeping the home fires burning, literally and figuratively, while Ed's at work. If she can't drive the kids to their activities in Banff like skiing at Mount Norquay or hockey games, Ed does pitch in. As well, he gets up early to drop the boys off at the hill.

Another one of his many hats is as the Legion Youth Club volunteer boxing instructor. It's thanks to the Calgary Highlanders that Ed learned what he calls the "Manly Art of Self-Defense," borrowing the title of a popular boxing manual published in the early 20th century. Ed stresses that his boxers never pick fights but they must be prepared to defend themselves. He teaches his sons the same thing.

Spring 1960 arrives with the opening of Ike Inn by Mrs. Spear and her children. Mrs. Spear is an industrious woman and spends a lot of time clearing out the forest around the hostel. She makes an arrangement with Parks to pick up her brush waste on a weekly basis. On occasion, after a muscle-burning day, Mrs. Spear goes across the road to the Carletons for a bath. The hot water is more soothing than the only option at the inn: a basin and a sponge. She gets a chance to soak in the thermal waters of the Cave and Basin hot springs when Ed takes her, Terry and Brian for a swim. The natural springs are what drew explorers and eventually led to the establishment of Canada's first park.

When Dorothy returns from a shopping trip to Calgary, Mrs. Spear goes over to see what she bought in the city. The Carleton boys have outgrown their clothes and need new items for the summer but it's basically an excuse for Mrs. Spear to visit with Dorothy.

Around the end of May, Dorothy digs her garden and plants her flowers and starts selling fishing licences. That's Ed's signal to start sprucing up Eisenhower Station.

The grounds are cleared of debris like broken branches. The inside of the main lodge is painted by Ed and Dorothy. They cover the walls with two coats of pale yellow paint. Thankfully, the spring air isn't too cold and the windows are opened wide to air the place out. Ed also builds a fire hose drying rack and does inventories of equipment and tools at campgrounds and the station along with Neddy Hume, a Parks inventory worker.

The Ya Ha Tinda Ranch horses are driven into town and the animals are farmed out to the districts. Trixie, Deuce, Kate, Chief and Nick are the station's horses for the summer. Ed puts the animals out to pasture. He'll use the horses to take water up to the Mount Eisenhower fire lookout. Brian goes with him on one trip. On the way back, Ed has some unwanted guests: 25 ticks.

Besides tick bites, a dog chomps a young boy in the face. The child is Jean-Pierre Lebourgeois, a neighbour and the son of Madame Lebourgeois. Ed takes Jean-Pierre to the Banff hospital. The youngster needs four stitches.

A group of kayakers also requires Ed's support when they run into trouble on the Bow River. The eight men are struggling with their thirteen kayaks on the water. Three boats are swamped and everything goes into the river: cameras, clothing and food. Ed gets them safely to shore.

The warden inspects the Johnston Canyon trail. Some branches are across the path and he cuts them in half. He repairs a few guardrails that were damaged either by the weight of heavy snow or trees coming down on them.

The roads always need patrolling. A tourist in a Ford Thunderbird convertible hits an elk. The elk damaged the vehicle's windshield but is nowhere to be found. Ed scouts the animal and then puts it down.

Ed helps Bruno film some wildlife for the National Film Board of Canada. The pair captures footage of goats and sheep — and get cinematic gold when a pair of sheep rams start fighting. Heads cracking, horns locking and lots of snorting. It's all on camera.

Mike and Peter Spear are in the backcountry, too. They're travelling to mountain lakes and fishing. The best places to catch cutthroat trout are Twin Lakes, Taylor Lake and Larch Lake. Sometimes the boys are so wrapped up in fishing that they're late getting to the trailhead to catch their ride home. That means hours of waiting for Ed or Dorothy to return. The boys learn to greet grumpy adults with a peace offering of trout ready for the pan.

Between Mike and Peter, they'll do over 320 km (200 mi) on Banff trails and catch more than 200 fish over the summer. Mike hitches a ride from the bugologists after hiking over 25 km (16 mi) in a day. He could have walked the whole way home but he doesn't want to worry Dorothy. She expects him in before dark.

To fish in the park, you need a licence. Although some try to get away with not having one. Ed's assistant warden, Hugh Jennings, lays charges against a man and a woman he catches fishing without a licence. They're fined $5.

High winds on Jun. 1, 1960 topple some phone lines. Ed's out there on his one day off repairing them. Then, a few days later, a pipe elbow at the Mount Eisenhower campground breaks, causing a flood. Thankfully, Ed isn't responsible for the cleanup, just reporting it to the Banff office to get a maintenance crew out. He is responsible for preparing trailhead signs and installing them in his district.

He works on a new trail from Altrude Lakes to Vista Lake. On Jul. 7, he climbs Mount Louis, near Mount Eisenhower, with Walter Perren and three other wardens. The crew are up at 4 a.m. and drive to Edith Pass trailhead. They go by horseback to the start of the climb. The route they're taking has very loose rock on it and a tough chimney climb to the summit. It's a long way to the top and they're slowed by the gravel and possibility of falling boulders. The worst thing is, they didn't pack enough water. All of them are parched.

They don't make it down to their horses until 9 p.m. and when Ed gets home to Dorothy, he drinks glass after glass of water.

"Guess you're thirsty," says Dorothy.

July has been dry and hot. Ed puts out a fire on Jul. 18 at a Johnston Canyon cabin. It went up in smoke from an overheated stove.

The next day, Ed and Mike are supposed to go on a trip. It's postponed because Ed gets called out as a firefighter. The fire hazard is at "extreme" and Parks officials are worried about several areas. Mike writes in his diary that there are 250 forest fires burning in B.C., including one raging across 1,200 acres in Yoho National Park near the Amiskwi River.

Jul. 19, 1960 AM: Dad and I were ready to go into Luellen Lake with Roy Hawkins when Dad was called to go fighting the Yoho park fire. Trip is cancelled until later.
PM: Helped Roy make some signs to put at the start of the trails –
TRAIL CLOSED, EXTREME HAZARD. Then I worked on my bike.

Meanwhile, Ed is on the scene of the fire after driving from Banff. He picked up some recruits in town on his way to Yoho, about an hour's drive west of Banff. Ed is detailed to handle the fire crew on the east side of a sawmill that's on the Amiskwi River. The flames are so intense at one point that the heat pushes the men back.

At home at the lodge, Dorothy is worried. She has been here before and it never gets any easier. She's keeping an ear on radio communications between Parks crews when she hears something that stops her heart cold.

Ed and 50 other men are missing. Their situation appears to be bleak. She doesn't dare move away from the radio. There has got to be more news coming about her husband. It has got to be a mistake. Her children know what's happening and they're also worried.

Ed packing up at Johnson Creek cabin.
Photo: Bruno Engler

At the fire zone, Ed makes it back to fire headquarters and finds almost everyone has pulled out. However, it's great to see Ed! The radio report lets Dorothy, Mike, Terry and Brian know he's safe and sound.

Ed battles all night against the flames. He shows the driver of the Cat (a Caterpillar D9 - a bulldozer and a piece of heavy equipment), where to cut a fireguard. (Taking down and removing natural fuels for the fire.) Some of the work is in swampy areas and Ed watches to ensure the Cats aren't swallowed up by the bog.

He's given another crew to manage and at 3:30 a.m., they too are pushed back. They withdraw to headquarters and lay out firelines until they're relieved at 8:30 a.m. Ed has been severely tested by nature. He thinks about the power of the fire and how it galloped over rocks and ridges and gobbled up trees and vegetation with such ease. The thing that is some comfort to him is that fire is a natural process and the land usually rebounds. Albeit with scars.

Dorothy lunges for Ed when he walks through the door. He smells terribly of smoke and sweat and is covered in soot, but she doesn't care. He's home. Mike notes in his diary that the day is pretty much ordinary after that.

Jul. 20, 1960 Dad arrived home at 10:30 AM, had a bath and went to bed. I rode over to friends and visited. In the evening, I snuck away when company arrived and Mum had to entertain them by herself. (Dad had driven back over to Yoho to have a look at the smoke and check on progress with the fire).

It's back to work for Ed the next day. When he checks on the Wally Byam caravan group, which is back in Banff for its annual visit, someone hands him a tin of pure maple syrup. That's a sweet deal!

The fight against the Amiskwi fire is not over. On Jul. 24, Ed's back in Yoho and stays there for several hours. That same day, Dorothy is called into action. There's a bad collision on Radium Road, just south of Storm Mountain, and a man is injured. Dorothy phones for police and ambulance to send help. She's sad to learn that the man died in hospital.

Mike is following in his mother's footsteps. He not only gets a job as a 14-year-old but he bikes to and from it. He applied to Johnston Canyon bungalow camp on the morning of Jul. 27 and was told to report for work that afternoon. His job entails everything from pumping gas, peeling potatoes (which Mike hates), to washing car windows so the tourists have a clear view of nature. Mike's boss, Bennett Camp (the son of Walter Camp), tells him over and over again that window washing is the most important job. Mike shrugs. He's grown up with these mountain vistas.

The gas pumps are very busy on Jul. 31. Mike serves 16 cars. He also has to go around to all the cabins to tell guests about the films and lecture that night. For all his hard work, Mike earns $1.75 a day. He knows this isn't much but it's something. He bikes several kilometres each way, dripping with sweat because of the heat.

The fire hazard in Banff is still high. Fire crews extinguish the Amiskwi fire but not before it eats 2,000 acres. The cause was human. Someone at the mill site had ignited it through a careless action. Meanwhile, some other humans ignite Ed's fairly cool temper when they don't understand why they can't hike the mountain trails. The paths are closed due to the dry and unusually hot weather. Ed, first in his mild-mannered way, tries to tell the tourists about the fire hazards. Nevertheless, they try to convince him to let them go and talk at him for half an hour. That does not bode well for the visitors.

"I lost my temper," Ed says to Dorothy. "I said 'fiddlesticks.'"

His wife knows that it takes a lot to push Ed to "swear." He never snaps at his kids, although they have certainly tried his patience. Those tourists must have been infuriating.

August is quieter. Ed assists with the poisoning of Vista Lake. It's a drastic attempt to keep invasive fish from taking over from the local species. The last month of summer is a good time for family: Ed goes up Copper Mountain with Dorothy, their sons and Emile Gautreau and Herb Cerezke to view an old copper mine site from Silver City days. Emile and Herb have heard some yarns about the mine, including one about a "salted mine."

Salting means planting valuable ore, such as silver, about a claim so the value of it goes up. Apparently, says Herb, this happened at Silver City.

"One or two people ran off with a considerable sum of money taken from several gullible folks who invested unknowingly in the mine scam," he says.

The treasure on the slopes of Copper Mountain today is strawberries. Dorothy and the kids pick a bunch along the way to put in Dorothy's tasty pie.

Another day, the family goes fishing at Taylor Lake. They have one horse, Trixie, between them and somehow it's not the youngest kids, Terry or Brian, who get to ride her. It's Mike. The hike from the station to the nearby lake tuckers Terry and Brian right out. They can barely keep their eyes open at the annual corn roast the entomologists throw at the Forest Biology station.

Ed gets to visit with an artist staying at Johnston Canyon. William "Bill" Harisch is originally from Czechoslovakia but lives in Calgary. He paints the scenery in his "back yard," much like Ed. They have a lot to talk about and Ed's interested in Bill's techniques. Bill gives the warden an oil painting done with a knife and Dorothy hangs it on the wall in their home. It's a conversation piece when the Colbecks drop in for a visit. Art, Nancy and David are living in Jasper now.

"Art is still the same old joker," says Ed to Dorothy when the Colbecks leave.

Mrs. Lebourgeois stops in that same day to talk about carpooling to school in a couple of weeks. Mike isn't looking forward to going anywhere with her in the tiny Renault. She wears an absurd amount of perfume for his liking and he can't breathe.

The day before Dorothy's 41st birthday, Sept. 4, 1960, the family hikes in the rain to the Eldon mine. The trip is mostly for curiosity, but there's a hint of excitement: What if one of the boys discovers something that hasn't been seen in 70 years?

The Carletons reach the site at 1 p.m. in the drizzle and search around for an hour. They find a rock with copper ore, one pick and some shovels. Once back home, the boys get a hot bath each and everyone gets a hot meal. They're all cold, wet and hungry.

Left to right: Art Colbeck, Nancy Colbeck, Millie Carleton and Dorothy on Vermilion Lakes Road in the 60s.
Photo: Carleton Family

The day of Dorothy's birthday, she is pampered. Ed takes her to a show in town. He likes the adventure films of the day – Westerns like *The Alamo* with John Wayne or *The Unforgiven* with John Huston. These are not Dorothy's favourites but even on her birthday, she'll see whatever her husband wants to see.

Ed does have a gift for Dorothy: an electric toaster. She never has to use the tongs over an open flame again. (Unless she wants to.) Her sons give her thoughtful gifts. She opens a tea serving set from Mike, a sparkling brooch from Terry and a bar of sweet-smelling soap from Brian. Then, they eat Fanny the rabbit for dinner.

For a couple of years, the family has kept a rabbit pen at Mount Eisenhower. There are coyotes and other predators around but they don't seem to be attracted to the rabbits. There are around nine rabbits and Dorothy gave a couple of them names. Fanny makes it to the birthday celebration, albeit in a pot.

With fall, comes canning for Dorothy. She makes dill pickles, bread-and-butter pickles and pickled beets. Ed lends a hand in the kitchen on a night he's not on duty. Tomorrow he's heading out with assistant warden Hugh Jennings to the fire lookout to pack out the operator and close the tower for the season.

Every day is recorded in Ed's diary. Terry watches his father make entries about everything from birds he sees, to hikers he meets. Keeping a journal lets Ed keep track of the months. The diaries are always passed into the administration office in Banff, nevertheless, by writing things down, it lets Ed process them. His war wound hasn't affected him much over the years except for the occasional trip to Calgary to see the doctor.

Ed and Dorothy out for a ride in Banff National Park.
Photo: Carleton Family

Ed's work speaks for itself. The signposts he made in his former district of Stoney Creek are still standing a few years later. The family sees them when they drive up the Cascade Fire Road and on their way to Ya Ha Tinda Ranch. The road is dusty but the scenery is wonderful and Dorothy remembers all the great times they had at Stoney Creek. Mike echoes her sentiment.

"It hasn't changed at all," he says during a visit.

Neither have Ed and Dorothy's socializing spirits. They host a party with people from the area and they dance and sing until 2 a.m. That's not the latest they've stayed up. They go to many social events with warden families and other friends in town and sometimes get home at 4 a.m … right before the sun rises.

As the leaves turn yellow, the summer population takes its leave. Stella, Bill and Jill Nokes, the current owners of the bungalow camp at Johnston Canyon, stop in to say farewell. It's also time for Dorothy to start driving her sons to school again.

Eisenhower District is quiet in October and it's the perfect time to visit Jasper National Park, where the Colbecks are living. The Carletons surprise Art, Nancy and David and get a warm welcome. They stay overnight and sing songs, tell stories and play games. The parents clobber Mike and David at crokinole: 130-15.

The next morning, Ed, Dorothy and the gang stop at the Sigurdsens, friends who used to live in Banff. The Carletons arrive so early they get them out of bed. It's OK, because that day, Oct. 10, 1960, the Pittsburgh Pirates are playing the New York Yankees in Game 5 of baseball's World Series. The series is knotted at two games apiece — and there's an opportunity to watch the game on TV at the Sigurdsens'. The Yankees are Terry's favourite team, but no amount of cheering helps them. The Pirates win.

It's a luxury to watch television. Living at Eisenhower Station means living far away from TV towers. That doesn't stop Terry from knowing the names of almost all the players in Major League Baseball (MLB), the National Hockey League (NHL) and the Canadian Football League (CFL). He memorizes the standings and statistics of his top teams: the Calgary Stampeders (football), New York Rangers (hockey) and of course, the New York Yankees. Dorothy also likes watching sports and is a fan of the Stampeders like Terry.

Einar and Margaret Bjorkman at Marble Canyon, down the Windermere highway, have a daughter who is a big TV fan and so Ed helps them try to get reception at their home. The sound is fine but the picture is like Mount Eisenhower in winter: snowy.

It's almost Halloween 1960 when Ed drives into Calgary for a reunion of the Calgary Highlanders at the Palliser Hotel. Ed sees many of his old mates and chats about the "good old days."

Some of his colleagues are wardens, like Bert Pittaway, and it's not long before they're discussing wildlife along with life. Some of his friends have aged well and some, not so well. Ed's fortunate he has a wife as a partner to lean on and three boys who are healthy and active.

He remembers this as he carves Halloween props for his two young children's costumes. Ed is whittling a cutlass for pirate Brian and a broadsword for Robin Hood (a.k.a. Terry). Ed is on the job All Hallows Eve and reports for duty at the RCMP barracks for the special Halloween patrol. The seven-hour shift goes off without any ghosts or goblins getting into much trouble. Dorothy says she would have dressed up when she was a child if Halloween had been a big deal in England. The U.K. marks Guy Fawkes Night, also called Bonfire Night, on Nov. 5. That's the day in 1605 that Guido (Guy) tried to blow up King James I and his government in the Gunpowder Plot. In the 1960s, Brits have fires but they don't dress up.

"It's a shame Bonfire Night isn't the same as Halloween," Dorothy says.

***

Just like Dorothy's family, Ed's family loves hearing about their mountain life. Ed takes Dorothy to Calgary to visit his mother, who moved to the city with Ollie in 1954. The younger Carletons then drive on to Medicine Hat, about three hours southeast of Calgary, to see their elderly Aunt Nell. Before going home, Ed and Dorothy drive to the small southern Alberta town of Claresholm to visit Baillie and his wife Patricia. Ed's relatives are always impressed with his family's healthy and active life in the backcountry.

Dorothy enjoys seeing her in-laws but she loves returning home. She appreciates the peace and quiet of Eisenhower Station after several days in noisy cities and busy towns. Sure, you can get gourmet food and fancy clothing a few steps away, but you'll never get this view of a magnificent stone peak right outside your door.

Backcountry to Town

The Trans-Canada Highway was supposed to go all the way to Revelstoke National Park by the end of 1960. It's 1961 and the road hasn't reached Rogers Pass yet. Former warden Noel Gardner, along with other engineers and federal employees, is working on an avalanche control system to keep the slides from hitting motorists on the route. Rogers Pass is well-known for its avalanches.

Mike is on the road now. He's 16 and has his licence. He actually started driving at age 14 when Ed took him out for lessons on the gravel roads. Dorothy also let Mike take the wheel of their family vehicle, a Vauxhall. He scared her a couple of times with some close calls, like sliding around corners or going a bit too fast for her liking.

It'll be a while until Terry and Brian learn to drive but in the meantime, they have friends from town whose parents will drive them to Eisenhower Lodge. In summer, the kids splash about in Silverton Creek. They build wood boats to float down the river or try to pole vault across to the other bank. They hike a few minutes to see nearby Silverton Falls. In every season, they explore their surroundings by bushwhacking into the forest to find secret hiding places. The brothers and friends are outside all day until, Dorothy calls them inside for supper.

Dorothy has ingrained the Women's League of Health and Beauty motto *Movement is Life* in her own children. However, she knows the importance of a good education and Ed is the same. The couple read voraciously and Ed likes to recite passages from the classics, like Charles Dickens, to his kids while they're hiking up a peak or driving down the highway in the warden truck. Ed and Dorothy never miss a parent-teacher meeting and when Terry's marks need improvement, Dorothy and Ed don't criticize him. They ask him to try a bit harder.

Mike is a superb student and is doing particularly well in high school. He wins numerous awards for high marks in math and science. He's a hard worker and in the summer of '61, he gets a job with the group he called bugologists as a child: the entomologists. The forestry professionals are studying insects like the spruce budworm and mountain pine beetle among other research projects at the Eisenhower Field Station. Herb Cerezke is there too, as he's doing work for his studies at the University of Alberta. His Master of Science graduate thesis is *The Morphology and Functions of the Reproductive Systems of Dendroctonus monticolae Hopk. (Coleoptera: Scolytidae).* Or: The Sex Life of the Mountain Pine Beetle.

The Eisenhower Field Station is almost brand new. It was built in the mid-1950s and has a laboratory and accommodations. The Forest Entomology and Pathology Branch, Department of Agriculture, was responsible for the lab and field station from 1958-59. A year later, the branch was transferred to the Canada Department of Forestry.

Understanding bugs is not only important for the forestry industry but for Parks, too. There's an emphasis on the mountain pine beetle. These beetles lay eggs under the bark of lodgepole pine trees, where their larvae subsequently feed and sever the bark, which leads to the death of the tree. The insects are massively destructive to Alberta's forests and could create ghost forests – acres upon acres of dead trees.

Dr. Philp Thomas, director of forest entomology and pathology at the Forest Biology Laboratory in Calgary, often gives tours of the field station to visiting groups, such as botanists. Mike's job is to keep the place looking fresh and he has to stain the wood cabins that make up the accommodations for the researchers. The cabins have some interesting history. They're structures by Pan-Abode, a Canadian company that sells easily-assembled wooden buildings. In 1954, the field scientists actually helped construct their lab and other quarters on evenings and weekends when they weren't working. Not much of this impresses Mike. All he cares about right now is getting the job done. On his downtime, he hikes with his friend Herb and other scientists at the field station. Some researchers are here from as far away as the University of California.

Dorothy and Ed's boys are growing up. During the bugologists' annual corn roast, Mike gets into the drink, the drink being sake. Someone (as in John Watson, one of the entomologists), makes his own Japanese fermented rice drink. Mike has way too much.

Part of the Eisenhower Field Station.
Photo: Herb Cerezke

Considering it's Mike's first experience with alcohol, he's groaning and moaning in the morning. The hangover is crushing. It feels like all of Mount Eisenhower is sitting on Mike's head.

Terry feels great and heads out with Ed and Walter Perren to Block Lake, near Windy Cabin and Panther River. It's a tough climbing day but the tussle to get up to the lake is worth it. The fishing is amazing since hardly anyone fishes there. Terry reels in some monster cutthroat trout that Dorothy proudly cooks for supper.

Ed takes Terry on another backcountry trip. They're off to Mount Cory, renowned for its cave that locals refer to as the "Hole in the Wall." It's a tough scramble on some rocky ridges with sheer drops. Terry is glad when they reach the cave. He is not glad when his father takes off. "Stay here," says Ed. "I'll be back soon."

Soon isn't fast enough for Terry. The cave floor is carpeted with bat droppings and Terry is pretty sure he hears a mouse squeak over in the corner — a corner covered in darkness. It is not a comfy spot to wait.

Sitting at the mouth of the cave, Terry sees the sun slide down in the sky. Where is his dad? Is he coming to get him? What happens if he doesn't? Terry thinks about how he's going to rescue himself. He's sure he can hike down to the trailhead alone if he takes it slowly. What does he do after that? He can't drive home. He's only 9.

Thankfully, Ed shows up in time for the pair to get off the mountain before dark. When Dorothy asks how the day went, Terry grumbles to her.

"It was not fun."

Although the trip had been excruciatingly long and terrible for Terry, he never passes up a trip with his dad. They head out to camp on a summer's evening in the backcountry. Terry soon finds out that Ed can sleep anywhere.

That night in the park was pitch-black with only the stars and the moon to prove that Terry isn't deep in a cave. Then, the clouds covered the lights in the sky and he couldn't see a thing. But oh, he could hear everything. A twig snap. Dead leaves rustling. A thump. A cough — or is that a growl? Terry's eyes are wide open and he's sweating buckets. There's no way he can sleep when a monster bear could descend on them at any moment. How is it that his father is fast sleep? A snarling grizzly probably couldn't even wake him up.

Dorothy's nightmare is made up of smaller beasts when she goes along on patrol with Ed later in the week. They're riding to Taylor Lake and while they spot a black bear, it's the flies that are ferocious. They're terrible and biting every patch of uncovered skin. Dorothy had thought getting out into the backcountry would be a nice change from handling the lodge office. She has Terry hard at work there now looking after the phones. At nine years old, he's capable of running the office.

***

Ed is looking forward to some shuteye. He's getting ready for bed after a busy day. Earlier in the evening of Aug. 14, 1961, he had helped two tired climbers off a mountain in Lake Louise. But sleep is going to have to wait.

At 10:10 p.m., two distraught climbers, Adolf Bauer and Louise Carter, walk through the Eisenhower Lodge door. Their friend has died on Mount Eisenhower.

He was killed while climbing the southeast tower.

Dorothy tends to the climbers at the lodge while Ed reports the accident to his chief, Jim Sime, and the RCMP. Then, he arranges the horses and equipment for a recovery party that'll head to the scene early the next morning.

At 4 a.m., Ed, Jim, Hugh Jennings and Roy Hawkins pack up the horses and by 5:30, the men are on the trail. Also along are other wardens including Ole Hermanrude, Bob Woods and George Balding, as well as an RCMP officer and Adolf Bauer, one of the surviving climbers. They leave the horses in the back of the southeast tower and along with a rescue basket, begin the first part of the mission, a scramble.

Once they reach the Goat Plateau, a large ledge between Eisenhower's upper and lower cliff faces, Ed asks Ole to stay with Bauer. Then, Ed and four others continue up the pitch. They find the man's body, as well as a camera and backpack, and start their descent.

The route down the pinnacle is somewhat easy but exposed with some scree bowl traverses. Ed and the rescuers take their time but it's a tricky balancing act. They reach their horses by 2 p.m. The climber's body is put on a packhorse that Ed leads to the lodge.

A couple of days later, Dorothy receives a note from Louise Carter in Calgary.

Aug. 16, 1961,

Dear Mrs. Carleton, I don't know how I can ever thank you sufficiently for all the kindness you showed Adolf and me at such a difficult time. You will never know how much a soft word, a gentle touch and a hot cup of tea meant to us. Sincerely, Louise Carter

The climbing accident was in Ed's backyard and another accident hit close to home. Ed's brother Garry is seriously injured in a car crash. Ed drives into Calgary to see him at the Holy Cross Hospital. He's in bad shape and months of recovery ahead.

August is a trying month for Ed. On the afternoon of Aug. 22, he receives a phone call at the lodge. A man has drowned and Ed has to find the body. Ed and the RCMP find the man about half a mile upstream in the Pipestone River, near Lake Louise. They recover the body and it's sent to Banff in an ambulance.

On Aug. 27, Ed is part of another rescue mission that is one for the history books. He has driven into the town of Banff that morning for work when he gets a phone call about a climbing accident on Mount Blane. Blane is a 2,993-m (9,820-ft) peak southeast of Banff. It's not in the national park but nestled in the Kananaskis Forest Reserve and under the jurisdiction of provincial rangers.

Ed, along with Walter Perren and warden George Balding, make the half-hour drive to Canmore, where they get an overview of what happened from Provincial Ranger M. Verhaege. Then they head to King Creek, near the base of Mount Blane and hear the whole story from Dieter Raubach, who has made it to safety.

Raubach and Gordon Crocker are members of a new group, the Calgary Mountain Club, and had been climbing Mount Blane the day before. The pair was pioneering a route on the west face. It was a great day for climbing: dry and cloudy in the morning, clear in the afternoon with not much of a breeze. Nevertheless, Crocker slipped on the wall, plummeting about 16 m (60 ft). He was hurt and Raubach received nasty rope burns stopping his fall.

Crocker was hanging over a gully but managed to get to solid ground. However, he was unable to get down the peak. There was something wrong with his ankles and he was bleeding from his head. He was stuck almost at the top, at an elevation of 2,865 m (9,400 ft). It's 6 p.m. when Raubach, the uninjured climber, starts his descent. It'll be morning before he finds anyone who can help.

Walter knows rescuers will need to get to the injured man before another nightfall. However, the terrain is incredibly technical and challenging. He decides a helicopter would be a great asset in this rescue. It'll speed up things by delivering supplies, equipment and men to the mountain instead of the men having to haul everything in on horseback.

Walter calls Foothills Aviation in Calgary and asks for a chopper. He also calls in other recruits, including Hans Gmoser and Klaus Hahn. Hans has assisted Walter before and he is an experienced climber. (Hans and Klaus are also Calgary Mountain Club members.) Then, Walter starts the ascent, along with Raubach, to the injured man.

George stays on the radio while Ed and Windy District warden Hal Shepherd[91] begin building a landing platform for the helicopter at the base of the mountain. Walter and Raubach reach Crocker, perform first aid and wrap him up in a sleeping bag. Raubach spends the night beside him while Walter goes back to his men.

Meanwhile, the helipad is completed and the bird has dropped off supplies and men including Hans, Klaus and RCMP officer Gerry Johnson at the mountain base. Ed spends the night in a tent at the foot of Mount Blane.

At 5 a.m. the next morning, Ed, Walter, Hal, Hans and Klaus and some others start up the pitch. The steep terrain is made more difficult by precarious rocks and gullies. It's slow going. On a ledge 121 m (400 ft) below Crocker and Raubach, some of the men stop as planned. Ed, Walter, Hans and Klaus push on to the climbers.

Morning turns to afternoon and Hans piggybacks Crocker down the rock wall until he can be belayed to the men waiting on the ledge. Crocker is going to have to spend a third night on Mount Blane. It's getting late and the sunlight is disappearing. Ed volunteers to stay with Crocker and the rest of the men climb down to base.

Ed and Crocker bivouac for the night. They "sleep" on the ledge – a narrow shelf on the side of a vertical wall that plunges down, down, down. Ed does get some shuteye and is glad he's not a sleepwalker.

At 8:30 a.m., Walter, George, Hans, Klaus, Hal, Gerry and a second RCMP officer reach Ed and Crocker. They load the injured man into a rescue basket and bring him down the pitch. They get Crocker to the helicopter pad at 3 p.m. and he's rushed to the Banff hospital. At 9 p.m., Ed's rescue duties are over for now. He goes home. The past three days have been hard but he has been part of making history. It's one of the first times a helicopter has been used for a high-altitude rescue in the region.

Mike brings news of another accident in early September. He had been fishing at Luellen Lake, near Lake Louise, when Sid Hall, an angler, accidentally cut his leg

91. Hal Shepherd is also a Second World War veteran. He was with the Royal Rifles of Canada and taken as a Prisoner of War in Hong Kong in December 1941.

with a hatchet, badly injuring his calf. Mike runs almost 19 km (12 mi) from the scene to alert Ed. The warden gets the horses ready and rides out to help. He administers first aid, puts Hall on the spare horse and the pair ride out to Johnston Canyon.

Responding to emergencies in the backcountry is often a matter of life or death. It's a regular occurrence and part of the job of a warden. That doesn't mean Ed doesn't need a break from it all. To de-stress, he stays overnight with his wife … in the backcountry. Dorothy and Ed hike and camp all over the park. They even have a special lake that they've called Carleton Lake. It's a small tarn that Ed believes to be unnamed. It now bears his family's name.

The couple also likes to visit Kootenay National Park. Ed carries an old canvas tent for them. The tent is heavy but he is strong. His physical strength comes from his outdoor duties and his mental and emotional strength comes from his closeness to Dorothy. She is his whole support system.

This is the Carleton family's last summer at Mount Eisenhower. They're going to be moving to the "House at the End of the Rainbow," their place on Rainbow Avenue in Banff, soon. The house has been rented out for the past three years to good tenants, Ken Millions and his family. Now it's time for the Carletons to live in their own home. Chiquita the horse finds a new home, too. She's sold to a family friend in the Windermere Valley.

Dorothy and Ed know that their children need to be in town for extracurricular activities. The drive is getting to Dorothy as well. She feels like she lives in the Vauxhall. If they move into their house in Banff, Mike can ski all he wants, Terry can have the accordion lessons he's been asking for and Brian, well, Brian can have his pick of things.

Terry and Brian think town living will be great. They both have many friends in town and — wait for it — there will be instant access to television!

A slightly cool autumn wind blows past Dorothy as she shuts the door of the Eisenhower Station house for the last time. She'll be back, sure, but it won't be her home anymore. Living in Banff has its perks. She'll be closer to friends.

Ed is now a town warden. His work in Banff is different from his work in the backcountry. It's not as physically demanding and he has more interaction with people, like telling them to put their dogs on a leash. He also has more time for historical research, one of his many passions. On his own time, he collects and writes about fires in the park during the 1920s and 1930s.

Dorothy and Ed attend regular Legion and Ladies Auxiliary meetings and join other groups. Ed is a volunteer with Scouts Canada. He got involved when Mike was a Cub scout. Terry and Brian are in the scouting movement as well. Ed helps out when Calgary scout groups have their camps at Hillsdale. He talks to the boys about nature and wildlife and warden life. One troop makes him a small wooden plaque with the words *A Scouting Thanks* burned into it.

Mike was a Cub for a couple of years while the Carletons were living at Buffalo Paddock but he never went on to Scouts. Instead, he became a cadet while at Mount Eisenhower. Mike particularly likes target practice and firing the .22 rifles. Ed finds a community with the Calgary Highlander Cadets. He passes down his army training as well as his warden skills. He takes groups on hikes in the summer and snowshoe tours in winter.

All moved in to the House at the End of the Rainbow!
Left to right: Terry, Dorothy, Ed, Mike and Brian.
Photo: Carleton Family

Banff has been holding an annual winter carnival for more than 40 years but it has never been a big draw for the Carleton boys, especially Mike. He'd much rather be hanging out on the ski slopes with friends. Mike is skiing all the time at Norquay with his buddies. When he's not in school, he's on the hill.

As a member of the Banff High School ski team, Mike gets some time off classes to practice. It's a thrill to throw himself into the air during ski jumping and he tries to go as fast as he can down the slopes and beat his friends. However, he isn't dreaming about medals and podium finishes. He simply loves the sport, hanging out with his teammates and being in the snow.

Last year, during cold winter days at Eisenhower, Dorothy could open the wood stove and put her feet on it to warm up her toes. She can't do that in Banff with the electrical oven in her new house. Does she ever miss that wood heat. She also misses the way it talked to her, telling her stories with its crackling and sizzling. It was alive, unlike her modern appliance. There's a romance to being in the backcountry and having mountains and wild things at your door. There are bright stars on clear nights and the howl of wolves at clouds. Streams chortle along at their own pace and tree branches rustle in the wind. For all the loveliness of nature though, it could be lonely. Dorothy wipes her hands on her red-and-white apron and tries to remember that. With all the luxuries town provides now, she probably couldn't go back to living in the woods.

Being in town brings Dorothy into close proximity to some of Banff's top entertainment acts. Louis Trono is from Bankhead, a town a couple of minutes away by car. Bankhead, nicknamed the *Twenty Year Town*, was a boomtown thanks to a mining operation at Lake Minnewanka in the early 1900s. At one point in Bankhead's life, it had been busier than Banff. It's a ghost town by 1961.

In 1903, the Canadian Pacific Railway established the Bankhead Mine, digging out its valuable coal. It did well for a few years, but there was trouble: Its coal was brittle, its miners were striking, digging was tough and the whole operation became too expensive. The town died around 1922.

Louis was born in Bankhead in 1909 and he becomes a Parks employee as well as a trombonist and the orchestra leader of the Louis Trono Trio. The musical group performs at the Banff Springs Hotel often and Dorothy and Ed dance many a night away while the trio plays music from the Glenn Miller Orchestra and other music from the swing era (1933–1947).

Dorothy and Ed are more social in Banff because they have the chance to be. They can walk everywhere instead of driving. That makes Dorothy very, very happy.

Just because Ed is in town, it doesn't mean he's exempt from avalanche and rescue training. Walter Perren is providing Banff National Park with many self-sufficient, capable and skilled wardens who can take on any mission. He runs programs for Parks employees and RCMP members in the spring and fall of 1961. Because of the introduction of the helicopter in missions, Walter adapts the warden training and equipment. His men are prepared for anything.

Goodbyes and Hellos

Banff loses its bid for the 1964 Olympics to Austria, but hopes to host the 1968 Winter Olympics. The ski hills have been attracting skiers from all over the world for many years. Flights from Europe, the U.K. and Eastern Canada land in Calgary for the sole purpose of bringing tourists to the slopes of Alberta. With the completion of the Trans-Canada in the summer of 1962, B.C. powder hounds can drive from Revelstoke to Banff in a few hours.

Hans Gmoser has been looking at the mountains and pondering a way to get fresh tracks without standing in line or trudging up a ridge. Hans, along with Art Patterson, thought: What about heli-skiing? It's not an original idea. In 1948, Skyways Services Ltd., a helicopter company, had flown some skiers to a peak. Hans wants to commercialize heli-skiing. In 1963, he, Art and 20 clients try to ski down a slope in the Banff park after being dropped off on a glacier. It's too wet, but the experience is enough to convince Hans to keep pursuing the concept.

Skiing is fine but the wardens want to show off their equestrian skills. The first annual warden gymkhana — don't call it a rodeo! — is held in the fall of 1963 at Ya Ha Tinda Ranch. It's a result of the "horsing" around by the wardens during the seasonal roundup. Who is the best rider? Who has the fastest horse? Banff warden Wally McPhee thinks the only way to find out is by holding a competition. The all-day event is open to wardens and government employees and is a chance for everyone to let off some steam and demonstrate their expertise.

Ed doesn't mind a bit of sport. He enters the pole bending competition. There's a series of poles in a row and Ed has to ride his horse through them. Together, they weave in and out until they get to the end. Then they turn around and weave in and out again. The horse and rider with the fastest time win.

Dorothy cheers on her husband and gets the kids to shout some words of encouragement. Ed does well but doesn't win. His former assistant at Eisenhower, Jim Robertson, always cleans up at the gymkhana. There's not much he can't do with a horse … though Jim always does it with his trademark cigarette dangling from his lip.

By this time, there's one less person at the House at the End of the Rainbow. Mike moved to Edmonton in September. He's going to the University of Alberta (U of A). Dorothy and Ed drove their eldest son to the Alberta capital. They're pleased he's furthering his education. Ed sees it as an opportunity and one that wasn't available to him. Dorothy and Ed are in awe of the campus, all the buildings and classrooms and the number of students milling about. There are probably more people at the university than the entire population of Banff.

Mike is dropped off at Athabasca Hall, a residence, where he is paired up with a random roommate from Manitoba, Phil Cove. Their room is in the basement and it's frequently visited by insects the guys call silverfish. The bugs scamper about on the floor until they're whacked by a spare slipper kept handy for killing squirmy things.

The roommates have their meals in a communal dining hall and Mike misses his mum's home cooking. Edmonton is a large city; nevertheless, the U of A campus is

Rider Jim Burles at a Hillsdale Gymkana.
Photo: Carleton Family

on the quieter side. (Until the weekends.) Mike doesn't have any specific career goals other than to dive into his studies. He's registered for math, science and computer courses.

Dorothy is realizing that that old cliché, time speeds up as we age, is true. Although she no longer has to feed the fire while cooking and baking, manage phone lines or do the washing in a big tub, she is always on the go. It's non-stop as she gets her boys off to school, prepares meals and walks downtown for many, many meetings.

Ed and her sons never hear her complain about being tired. That's for old people. Besides, Terry and Brian chip in with the housework. They get an allowance for their chores, which range from shovelling snow to doing the dishes. It's not much, no more than a dollar a week, but Dorothy tells Terry it's the "going rate" when he asks for a raise. He doesn't bother asking his dad. Dorothy has the final say.

Having a father as a warden isn't a big deal for the Carleton boys. Many of their friends have parents in the parks service. Kids of all ages like Ed. He has that wide smile and is friendly. He always has a hello for them when he's out and about on patrols, especially on Halloween.

On one memorable Hallows Eve, Ed catches a prowler. Ed and a police officer are making sure the Banff streets are safe for trick-or-treaters and making sure the trick-or-treaters aren't pulling any big pranks. While checking on Rainbow Avenue, Ed sees something suspicious at his own home. It's a break and enter in progress. Someone is trying to squeeze through a window!

Ed and the officer run and grab the man before he can do anything else criminal.

"Terry?"

"Hi, dad."

Terry had come home early and found all the doors locked. He thought he would climb through an open window and get in that way. Oops. He ends up getting into the back of a patrol car and being driven around until Ed's shift is over.

The middle child does prove he's just as responsible as his older brother and his mum at 14-years-old. Terry has a job at the Hi-way Gulf service station for the summer. He sees many tourists on road trips in the park. There are picnickers, hikers, climbers and those who only want to shoot a picture of the famous Banff mountains.

For Ed, work in the bush is preferable over work in town. He's given the Bryant Creek district with the Spray River in the south of Banff. He travels back and forth to the area from his home. When he has to stay overnight, the remote cabins there provide shelter from the elements.

It's 1964 when the Canadian government comes out with an official National Parks Policy that includes a townsite development plan. New zoning systems are put in place so commercial developments don't overwhelm park towns. The towns are supposed to blend in with the scenery, not be the main attraction. Are the Olympics exempt?

CODA put its hat in the ring for the 1968 Winter Games but Banff won't be part of those either. In the spring, the world finds out that Grenoble, France will be the home of the Games. CODA refocuses and shoots for 1972.

The warden summer games, the gymkhana, moves to Hillsdale Meadows in 1965. It's getting popular and some wives are competing in events, too. Women have been working for the parks service since it was established. Some of the labour was unpaid, like Dorothy's work with Ed, and some of the jobs were paid, like being a gatekeeper. Annie Staple was the Rocky Mountains Park gatekeeper in 1916. Her job was to gather information from motorists going into the park and collect fees. It was a dollar to be able to enjoy the park for a day or $4 for the month. Nevertheless, women are not in the warden ranks. They can explore and hike and climb mountains but not be formal guardians of the park. That's considered a man's job.

Daring Rescue on Mount Babel

Charlie Locke and Brian Greenwood are two young climbers pushing the limits. They belong to the Calgary Mountain Club and have been putting in new routes on the crags around Banff. One of two things usually happens when these men are on the cliffs: they're successful or they get into trouble. When they get into trouble, the wardens pluck them off the rock. In August 1966, Locke and Greenwood are on Mount Babel, and in need of heroics.

Babel is in the Consolation Valley near Moraine Lake and has an incredibly steep east face. It's one big leaning slab of rock. Locke, around 21, and Greenwood, around 32, are hoping to bag the first ascent. They're near the top of the 3,101 m (10,175 ft) peak after the second day of climbing when Locke, leading, falls and breaks his wrist.

Locke needs his hand to get down and Greenwood needs him to put in the anchors. Before they had left for their climb, Locke and Greenwood had done the proper paperwork and signed out. However, they had signed out for a few days, so no one is going to be looking for them just yet.

They're stuck. On a ledge with sharp rocks pressing into their skin.

Greenwood starts yelling for help. Thankfully, his pleas carry to hikers below and they rush to tell the Lake Louise district warden, Wally McPhee, about the climbers. Wally gets his assistant, Jay Morton, to scout it out. What he sees is almost unspeakable.

There is no way these men are getting off the rock alive. Locke and Greenwood are in a position that's impossible for any human, or helicopter, to reach. The narrow perch is below an overhang that slopes beyond the vertical. It's in the shape of a wave.

Walter Perren knows what to do. The always-watching, always-learning mountain rescue specialist has been reading about using cables and winches in rescues. He saw the technique explained in a European magazine and he realizes this is what the wardens must do. It's going to be a top-down operation.

Ed isn't at the rescue but he's following it with interest. He knows all those involved and the hazards of that area. It has to be a team effort to get Locke and Greenwood down to the ground and the wardens are going to be using equipment that's brand new, practically invented on the spot.

Walter needs Stan Peyto's metal expertise and hands him a sketch of a tripod pulley. The pulley is central to the whole operation. It'll be used to lower the rescuer and then raise him with a person strapped to his back. Without the pulley, the cable will get caught on the crag.

High above the rescuers, Locke and Greenwood read a message Jay fashioned out of toilet paper on the ground. It says the climbers are going to have to spend the night on the mountain but help is coming. Stan gets to work on the pulley. He fabricates it overnight and it's ready to go in the morning. Jim Davies,[92] with an underpowered helicopter, flies a handful of wardens to the top of Babel. Walter wants to be the one to be winched down with a Gramminger seat (a type of harness chair) but it needs to be the slightest and lightest man. That's Bill Vroom.

Bill is being slowly lowered to the climbers on a braided cable. He is going to take a more detailed look at the rock and the men below. He has a radio and is in contact with the men above. Bill is hanging in the air, suspended over a drop so long that if he falls, he can think about a few things on the way down. However, he starts spinning! That's not supposed to happen. There's no swivel on the pulley and the cable is unbraiding — turning Bill around and around and around. Nevertheless, the rock wall halts his twirling and he spots Locke and Greenwood. They talk about the situation and Bill explains he'll put the men, one at a time, on his back and then they'll be pulled up to the top. Bill is then spun up to the summit to relay information to Walter.

Then, Bill repeats the twisted scenario.

Spin down, get Locke, spin up.

Walter says Bill doesn't have to get Greenwood, another warden can do it. Bill says he knows the way now. He'll go.

Spin down, get Greenwood, spin up.

All men are safe and choppered off the precipice in the early afternoon. It's been a collective effort by all wardens, and Bill has shown tireless strength and commitment to his job of saving lives.

***

The wardens say goodbye to Beef Woodworth when he dies in 1966. Percy George Woodworth was born on Feb. 14, 1900, into a pioneer family in the Banff and Canmore area. With Beef, goes a treasure trove of stories and memories of Banff National Park, particularly Lake Louise.

Beef guided many of the wardens through their first years and Ed thinks about his beginnings on the job 17 years ago. Ed's closing in on age 49. He's physically strong from his work but his mind is moving a bit slower. Dorothy thinks it's because of his war wound. The old piece of metal in his head is taking its toll. Nevertheless, Ed's still a better worker than those young guys at the Parks regional office.

"I call them postmen," says Ed to Dorothy, "because it's like they're working in the post office. All they do all day is shuffle papers."

Dorothy tells her husband not to say that to anyone else. She would like to tell him to slow down, but it's not like she's about to take it easy either. The English Rose has been in Canada for 20 years. Banff is her home. She wouldn't go back to England for anything, even for a lifetime supply of Digestive biscuits.

92. Jim Davies is a local helicopter pilot and one of the pioneers of Rockies flight. He could land his Piper Super Cub on glaciers.

In the summer of 1966, Dorothy has a flourishing garden. Alongside Ed, they plant potatoes, onions, carrots, radish and beets. Flowers are put into beds in the backyard. There are many blue and yellow sprigs of pansies (Dorothy's favourite) and splashes of pink geraniums. Roses of all colours dominate the front yard and they're a source of pride for Dorothy. The elk and deer are thorns in her side and she wages a constant war against them. They have a taste for the pretty buds and Dorothy has to run outside and chase them away.

In all seasons, she visits with Banff seniors and residents at the Mineral Springs Hospital. She volunteers at the legion and is in close contact with war bride associations. Dorothy has never lost contact with her friends in the U.K., and she regularly exchanges letters with Olive Openshaw. There's no way they're 47 years old. Dorothy feels like she's in her twenties.

It doesn't matter the age of the tourists coming to Banff, young or middle-aged or old. They've turned the town and campgrounds into giant parties. In 1887, the visitor count was three thousand. In 1912, it was just over seventy-three thousand. By 1966, it's two million.

Visitors are the reason Terry has a job at the Sulphur Gondola Lift. He catches the cars when they reach the bottom. He makes 90 cents an hour. Twelve-year-old Brian makes money off the tourists as well, selling the *Calgary Herald* newspaper at the Tunnel Mountain Campground.

Tourists are what built Banff, yet Banff is a wilderness area. It's a catch-22. Some residents and business owners like that the mountain town is popular. Others don't share their sentiment. CODA (Calgary Olympic Development Association) would like to introduce more visitors to Banff and Calgary via the 1972 Olympics. They're touting the region as an alpine destination and the games as a way to bring money to southern Alberta. Alas, it's not meant to be. Sapporo, Japan will be the host.

The news is a boon for conservationists. Nevertheless, the 1964 national townsite development policy for Parks that was supposed to provide a measure of environmental protection for Banff, doesn't. Construction and expansion of accommodations and recreational facilities are ongoing in the park. Campgrounds need to be expanded and Tunnel Mountain is one of them. A new trailer park is built in 1967 so row upon row of people can admire the scenery.

Those in charge of protecting the natural world of Banff are morphing into a new species. In the past, the men hired to be wardens were usually outdoorsmen with an abundance of outdoor skills and knowledge, but no formal education. The wardens coming on board today have at least a high school diploma and some science courses, but less backcountry experience. A series of studies are being done by the federal government across its parks system to determine how to shape the service into an efficient workforce.

A report prepared by Bert Pittaway gives some insight into what western chief wardens think needs to be done. The Sime-Schuler study (named after researchers Jim Sime and Don Schuler) provides additional fodder for Parks administrators to consider, calling for the dissolution of districts. The era of wardens living year-round in the areas they work in, is over.

Parks' first alpine specialist, Walter Perren, is an athletic 53 years old in 1967. However, a few days before Christmas, he is hospitalized. On the morning of Dec. 29, his wife Pamela is summoned to his bedside. She asks Ed and Dorothy to stay with her three sons at the Perren home.

The families know each other through warden connections and events but they are not close friends. Nevertheless, Dorothy and Ed are with the Perren boys when their father passes away. Out of that devastating news, a new relationship sprouts. Dorothy and Ed regularly stop round to see the boys and their mother.

Ed greatly respected Walter and he's glad a peak is eventually named in Walter's honour. Mount Sapta in Kootenay National Park is re-named Mount Perren. The 3,051-m (10,010 ft) mountain is part of the Valley of the Ten Peaks overlooking Moraine Lake.

***

Ed and Mike go climbing to Gonda Traverse, a common climbing area on Tunnel Mountain and a regular training spot for guides. Mike appreciates the fact that his dad is willing to go out with him on his day off. The father and son climbers are making good time on the pitch. The 22-year-old Mike is leading and working his way across the traverse to get to the main belay point. Ed, in his fifties, starts to follow. Mike ties into the bolt and then … Ed falls.

Mac Elder (left) and Ed (right) during search and rescue training on the summit of Mount Victoria (elevation 3,464 m / 11, 365 ft.), 1966. Photo: Mac Elder

Mike grabs the rope with his bare hands and breaks his father's fall. It's a hair-standing-on-end moment as they're 182 m (600 ft) above ground.

"Are you OK?" Mike shouts down to Ed.

Ed waves up at him.

Mike has a burning and bleeding right palm from holding the rope. It's going to be rough getting off of this rock.

Fortunately, Rudi Gertsch, a Banff guide, appears on the scene. Rudi is in the midst of certifying a crew of six climbers as guides. They help Ed and Mike down the crag and get them to the hospital. Mike's hand is dressed and Ed stays overnight for observation.

Reconstructing the accident in his head, Mike realizes they both could have been killed. He had no idea if the bolt he had anchored himself to, was indeed a strong anchor. It could have been loose and then....

The next morning Mike goes to see Ed at the hospital.

"Anything hurt?" he asks his dad.

"Only my pride," says Ed.

This is a turning point for Mike. He recognizes that his strong and agile father is fallible. It's all part of growing up but as well, it's a warning sign that Ed is starting to have difficulty with certain aspects of his job. He's having a harder and harder time with physical tasks. He's also under emotional strain: Ed and many other wardens have taken Walter's death to heart. He was still in his prime and had so much to give.

***

The backcountry of Banff National Park is becoming safer for everyone. Visitors are increasingly moving past the park gates and into the wilds. In 1963, 650 groups registered for backcountry trips in the summer. Four years later, that number is 1,700 groups, about 4,000 visitors. Ski touring is 828 parties, about 3,000 people.

Ski touring is a big draw to the Banff area. Walter's former climbing instructor, Hans Gmoser, has turned choppering tourists to snow-covered peaks into a heli-skiing business. The headquarters of Canadian Mountain Holidays is in Banff. Meanwhile, resort skiing gets a huge boost thanks to the 1968 Olympics and Canadian Nancy Greene. She wins a gold medal in giant slalom and a silver medal in slalom.

The hills of Banff come alive with new skiers. In the early days, the development of ski hills like Mount Norquay, Sunshine Valley and Lake Louise was encouraged by national parks administration. Highways, recreational facilities and the town of Banff itself were seen as pivotal for the park to profit. Now there is a new voice highlighting several concerns about such activities — including the Olympics — in national parks: conservationists.

Conservationists are looking to preserve the natural beauty of the national parks. The National and Provincial Parks Association of Canada,[93] founded in 1963, is one such environmental voice. It sponsors a conference in October 1968.

---

93. Now the Canadian Parks and Wilderness Society.

The Canadian National Parks: today and tomorrow conference held in Calgary discusses several issues, including creating more parks in Canada and learning how to preserve the existing ones. John I. (Jack) Nicol, director of the National and Historic Parks Branch of the Department of Indian Affairs and Northern Development,[94] says that although tourist traffic was a natural revenue stream many years ago, it shouldn't be the way forward. There must be a clarification of the role of national parks in outdoor recreation.

The conference calls for stricter policies on development, clearer wording and more say from the public, among other initiatives.

The Banff wardens are reading the room. They already know about the restructuring of the warden service and see their jobs changing. The Sime-Schuler report is basically the blueprint for the realignment however, tweaks are made as the new functions are discussed and changes are rolled out. The start of centralizing services in 1968 and 1969 means wardens are taking on more specialized roles in areas like resource management, search and rescue, public relations and public and park safety instead of doing a little bit of everything.

To Ed, some of the changes look more like jumping off a cliff. The work is going from being qualified to be outdoors, to being qualified to talk to the public. He is disappointed that many of the bureaucrats in Ottawa are making decisions without consulting Parks people on the ground. He understands communication skills are valuable and ecology and biology are important to resource management, but so is actual wilderness experience. Ed doesn't agree with the centralization, but since he's located in town, it won't be as much of an adjustment for him.

Ian McTaggart-Cowan is stressing the "role of ecological science in the design and operation of parks" and says ecologists should be included in Parks ranks. These are the people who understand the interrelationships between organisms and their environments.

Elk remain a "problem animal." McTaggart-Cowan, who had backed Banff National Parks plan of culling of 800 elk in 1946,[95] is now suggesting moving the park boundary so the large ungulate's winter range is on public property. This way, hunters can shoot the animals. This was done in Waterton Lakes National Park and the elk population decreased. He thinks live-trapping should be continued too.

The Banff elk cull is ceased in 1969. The animals are safe from a warden's rifle but not other human hazards. Vehicles on the highway pose a threat to elk and the other wildlife that call Banff National Park home. Cargo and passenger trains cause wildlife mortality, too. Environmental concerns hadn't been priorities when the railroad tracks and the Trans-Canada were constructed.

---

94. The federal government at the time placed national parks in the conservation program area in the Department of Indian Affairs and Northern Development.
95. The most elk slaughtered was 352 in 1945-1946.

***

Terry, like Brian, has also inherited his mother's penchant for music. He saves up his money to buy a 1968 Gibson J-50 guitar, his "pride and joy." He had the instrument shipped to Banff from the factory in Kalamazoo, Michigan.

He plays the guitar non-stop, strumming country and western songs much to his father's pleasure. Terry teams up with two other musicians, brothers Kelly and Murray Grittner, and the trio perform at the Legion in Exshaw, a town about a half-hour drive east, many Friday nights.

Dancing at the show is not very popular. Most people stick to drinking. Dorothy and Ed see at least one of Terry's performances. Ed approves of the song list, with numbers from Merle Haggard, Johnny Cash and Johnny Horton. Dorothy would like the tunes to be livelier but she'll sing along anyway.

Although Ed sang Brian to sleep with country songs, the youngest son has turned into more of a rock and roll man. He discovers Led Zeppelin, the British band that's only getting started in North America in the late 60s. As well, he falls in love with drumming.

Brian plays the snare drum in the junior high band and likes it so much he buys a drum set. He and two friends form a power rock trio and they often practise in the basement at 139 Rainbow. At 15 years old, Brian and his band, *Three Way Street*, have already performed some paid gigs in Banff and the surrounding area. They've actually made some good money. With the cash, they've bought a new microphone so Brian can sing back-up vocals.

The musicians are learning a new song that Brian can lend his voice to and have run through it a couple of times. It's not working. Mainly because of Brian's singing. The guitarist, Bill, says they should take a break and try later. That's when Brian hears the pitter-patter of feet coming down the stairs.

It's his mother.

"Brian," says Dorothy, "you're not singing that right. You're off-key. Try it again."

The band strikes up and Brian belts out the words. Across the room, Dorothy and Bill are rolling their eyes at each other.

"Listen to me," Dorothy says to Brian while reaching for the mic.

She nails it on her first try.

Needless to say, that's the end of Brian's singing career.

Chapter Thirteen

Conservation and Concerns

A Thank You for Ed and Adventures For Terry

Terry trades small-town life for one in the big city when he starts at the University of Calgary (U of C)[96] in the fall, studying economics. Brian is the only Carleton son left at home. Dorothy and Ed move their middle child into their oldest child's home in 1969. Mike has a house near the university on Charleswood Drive. The parents wish Terry all the best with his studies and know he'll be OK. Besides, he has his big brother looking out for him.

Terry has some trepidation about the big city and attending classes on a huge, almost new, campus. He can't hide anywhere this time. It's a volatile year for him.

The Banff Springs Hotel swings from the sixties and into the seventies with enough occupancy in the summer AND winter to stay open all year round — a first.

Jacob and Agnes Verwoerd, the California couple that buried a time capsule on Mount Eisenhower, return to Banff in 1970 to check on it. Part of their mission 13 years earlier was to honour U. S. President Eisenhower with the capsule. He died last spring.

The Verwoerds climb Mount Eisenhower to see their tribute to Eisenhower. It has spent years being pounded by the wind, swallowed by heavy snow and hit with strong sunlight. The cairn has shifted and the cement encasing the capsule is crumbling but it remains embedded in the rock even as it slips from memory.

***

A new ski resort is in the works for Banff National Park. It's 1971 and Parks is partnering with Village Lake Louise Ltd. (jointly owned by Lake Louise Lift Ltd. and Imperial Oil) on a planned alpine tourist town that will serve almost 3,000 people.

Ed appreciates the history of ski areas, hotels and other attractions in the park. He supports what is already established, nevertheless, he wants to preserve the wilderness aspects of the area. Commercial development does not align with his values.

Skifaris (ski + safari) to Banff and area are being advertised all over the world. Air Canada, the ski hills, transportation companies and hotels team up to offer tourists Alberta verticals. Almost three thousand skiers take them up on their offer. Those who want to stay away from the crowds can book some time heli-skiing thanks to Hans Gmoser's company, Canadian Mountain Holidays.

In Calgary, Mike is staying on the ground and doing a lot of ski touring and socializing with the Foothills Nordic Ski Club (FNSC). It's through the club he meets

96. The University of Calgary becomes an institution independent from the University of Alberta in 1966.

Ruedi Setz. Ruedi, who is from Switzerland like Walter Perren, is a leader in many ways, too. He is called the "father of biathlon in North America" and brings biathlon, cross-country skiing and loppets to the Rockies. It's Ruedi who encourages Mike to get involved in cross-country ski racing both as a competitor and a volunteer official.

Mike and his girlfriend Sylvia Hellberg become friends with Ruedi and his wife Valerie. When they're ski touring in the national parks with FNSC, they almost always have to break trail through fresh snow. There aren't many people out and if they do meet someone, it's usually someone they know.

It was on a ski trip to Lake O'Hara in Yoho National Park where Mike first met Sylvia. He thought she looked great in a ski suit and then found out that she was one of the stronger skiers. He was smitten. Ed and Dorothy like Sylvia as well. She's Swedish and grew up cross-country skiing, putting wood on the stove and being active in nature – a real outdoors girl. That certainly appeals to Ed. Sylvia also knows how to knit, sew and cook – great skills to have as a mother. That certainly appeals to Dorothy.

Calgary is not appealing to Terry. He stays at U of C for the school year but his time there is not a rousing success. His grades are marginal at best and he isn't sure if he wants to be in university. He returns to Banff in May and picks up a gas jockey job again at the Hi-way Gulf station at the west entrance to the Banff townsite.

It's spring and Terry thinks about taking a long break from school. Perhaps he needs to get out of Canada and see the world, get a different perspective. Hey, what about the British Isles? He has family there and could meet them. They would also be a kind of safety net for him – people looking out for him while he's away from home. He decides to stop in England and meet his grandmother Alice and then see Russ and his family in November.

"I think that's a jolly good idea!" says Dorothy.

Although she doesn't think skipping a year of education is wise, she's eager to have Terry meet his grandmother. Dorothy has told him stories about Alice and George and 55 Grange Avenue over the years and is excited that Terry is going to see her homeland. She is worried that he is travelling solo but Ed reminds her that lads Terry's age, around 20, had been shipped off to war.

Dorothy gives Terry a tight hug before he boards the plane in Calgary for Gatwick Airport, near London. Dorothy wishes she could join him and see her mother, too. However, Dorothy is busy. Brian is still at home finishing high school.

When Terry arrives at 55 Grange Avenue in Reading, he can't believe how tiny it is. His mother had told him stories about it and he had imagined it differently. In his mind, it was a large house. Not this small home with all sorts of knickknacks and dishes hanging on the wall as decorations.

Alice is 80 years old and interested in everything and anything Terry has to tell her about Dorothy, Ed, his brothers and Canada. She cooks a great meal and Terry is happy to be able to spend some time with his grandmother. She points out the Huntley & Palmers biscuit factory and he sees the tall red brick building where his grandfather used to work. It's old but still standing and he'll write to his mum about it. Now he has to leave Reading. It's a short visit and he's gone again before nightfall.

Russ and Phyllis are in Birmingham and Terry stays with them for a couple of months. Terry's uncle has five children and they're all eager to meet their Canadian cousin. Terry and Russ get along very well and they head to the Bluebell Pub together.

The only beverage the bar serves is cider and it's terrible stuff at that. It hits Terry rather hard and he's packed out of there at night's end. It takes him two or three days to feel better.

When Terry is up and about, it's time for Russ to introduce his nephew to gambling. Ed and Dorothy never gamble. Not on anything. They've told Terry it's like throwing your money away. Phyllis says that Russ would bet on two flies climbing up a wall if he could.

"He loves horse racing," she adds.

Russ takes his nephew to the betting shop and shows him how to make all different types of wagers on the horses. That's the moment Terry also falls in love with horse racing. Russ somehow has uncanny luck with his bets and wins some money. Terry, not so much. After the horse race tutorial, the pair goes to the dog track the following evening.

Terry's next destination is North Africa. His luck here is on par with his luck on the English horses. He's solo when he boards a boat in Gibraltar for the voyage to Morocco. It is not smooth sailing on the choppy Mediterranean Sea. He can barely move a muscle he's so sick. Meanwhile, there are women around him balancing baskets laden with fruit on their heads.

"How can they do that when I can't even blink?" he says to himself while on his hands and knees, trying not to puke.

He feels slightly better when his feet hit solid ground in Tangier. A customs agent runs up to him and puts a yellow X on his one piece of luggage, a blue and white flight bag. Two men approach him and say they'll take him to the Kasbah, a museum in old town.

"These are friendly guys," Terry thinks and so he follows them through the maze of streets. They end up in a room with a wrinkled elderly man. The man has a huge knife stabbed into the table in front of him and he's holding out his hand. He doesn't say anything, he just keeps his arm straight out until Terry realizes something.

"Oh, these are not friendly guys."

Terry gives him everything. Quickly. He's feeling pretty stupid but he has actually done something very smart. The rest of his traveller's cheques are in his shoes, not in his bag. At the first chance he gets, he runs out of the room and into the street. He has no idea where he is going and walks and walks and walks until he meets a police officer.

The man speaks some English and understands Terry when he asks for a bank.

"There's one in the new town," the officer says. "Follow me."

Terry is relieved. He's not going to be stranded in Morocco with no money, no clothes and no place to stay. He won't have to call his parents and worry his mother.

The police officer stops at some beautiful marble steps leading into a building.

The bank looks like a palace! It's fit for a prince. As Terry is pulling his cheques out of his shoe, the officer holds out his hand.

"I'll take those," he says.

And he does. Now Terry has nothing. Not even his pride because he's been taken not once, but twice. His shoulders slump when he thinks about sleeping on the streets. He is lost and alone. The prince is a pauper again.

He catches some English being spoken by a group of young people passing by. They're from Kansas, U.S. and become Terry's lifeline. They take him in and help him out while he's waiting for money. He makes a call to Russ, who wires him some cash. Terry also writes to Dorothy and Ed and asks for money.

It's almost the end of the road for Terry but he does see Marrakech through the windows of an ancient rattling bus. He returns to England via Malaga, Spain and Amsterdam, Holland. He also travels to Shannon in the Republic of Ireland before returning to Canada in March. It's 1972.

***

Brian catches the travel bug from his brother and goes on a four-month overseas backpacking trip with a buddy, Peter Ferrari. Brian's only 18 and Dorothy frets about him being away. While Terry had been away, she'd take his beloved guitar out of the case to let it know it was loved. While Brian is away, she talks about him constantly and hopes he's taking care of himself.

Brian is using the English Carletons' home in Birmingham as a base. On his way to the city from London, he gets lost. He's taking the train and supposed to get off at a particular station. He doesn't. He overshot it and ends up in, well, he doesn't know where. He has Olive Openshaw's phone number and so he rings her.

"Where are you?" she asks.

"I don't know!"

They eventually figure it out and Olive and her husband Danny fetch young, lost Brian from the station. They drive him to the Carletons' home and he's in good hands with Russ and Phyllis. In fact, Brian has a riot with Russ. Terry had told his brother that Russ is a punter (gambler) and of course, off Brian and Russ go to the betting shop to put some wagers on the horses.

Russ also takes Brian and Andrew, Russ's son, to a professional soccer game (football in England). Dorothy says Birmingham City Football Club is rubbish. She's a Reading Football Club (Reading FC) supporter so she's going to say that. (She also says her own team's rubbish when it's relegated from the top division to the second division — and then, down to the third tier.) The Birmingham football match is a fun time for Brian. There are 40,000 people packed into St Andrew's and the crowd is alive with football fever. It's a party atmosphere for sure.

Brian and his uncle go for a pint of cider at the Bluebell Pub. Brian fares slightly better than Terry the next morning. There's nothing wrong with Russ and he is off to work as a mechanic at Land Rover. He's in awesome shape, a lean machine, and has lots of energy. Brian can barely keep up with the man who is more than 35 years his senior.

Ed talking to a rapt audience of young Calgary Highlander cadets. Peppi the dog is sitting beside Ed.
Photo: Carleton Family

Returning to Banff after sowing some wild oats, Brian enrols at Mount Royal College in Calgary for a two-year program.

For the past three years, Ed has been assisting the Highlander cadets. The cadets of today aren't solely focused on military training but also on physical fitness and outdoor skills. Captain T.D. McCargar of the 2137 Calgary Highlanders Cadet Corps wants to thank Ed for his contributions and has written a letter to the superintendent of Banff National Park, Steve Kun, to ask if Ed can have a day off in June to come into the city and accept a plaque.

We would like Warden Carleton to be in his park warden's uniform in recognition of both his services to the Corps and the parks department's excellent cooperation.

Yours very truly, Captain T.D. McCargar

The superintendent responds to the captain and gives Ed the day off, adding,

We would also like to thank you for your kind gesture as Ed is truly a credit to our service.

Yours sincerely, S. F. Kun

For Ed, a thank you isn't necessary. Nevertheless, it's touching. Dorothy is proud to see Ed's contributions to the cadets be recognized. He is dedicated to the young boys and tells them stories of living and working in the park. His accounts of the mountain rescues he has assisted on captivate the cadets. The cadets listen in awe as he describes sheer rock walls, climbers falling and the types of injuries he has seen.

He also talks about encounters with bears and what to do and what not to do. Ed doesn't want to scare the boys, he wants to educate them so they respect the animals and won't be afraid of going into the backcountry.

On the morning of Jun. 4, 1972, the cadet corps has its annual inspection at Mewata Armoury. It's where Ed signed up to be a Highlander and today he's at the cadets' ceremonial parade with Dorothy. He cuts a dashing figure in his formal Parks garb and is smiling ear-to-ear when handed the plaque. The small wooden gift has the Calgary Highlanders crest on it and below that, Ed's name and the date. Later in the day, there's a coffee party in the Officers Mess with a dram of something stronger than caffeine.

"Nothing better than a wee drop of the craythur (whisky)," says Ed.

A wee break from university has been good for Terry. He's back at U of C in the autumn and living in Harry and Alice Lord's home. Terry knows the Lords through Mike, who also spent some time at the Lords' house. Harry is Al Bradley's uncle, another good friend of Mike's. Al, Harry and Mike get to know each other really well at the bar of the St. Louis Hotel in downtown Calgary. The bar is a well-known hangout of Ralph Klein,[97] a reporter. It's also a place to debate the 1972 Summit Series that's taking over Canada in September.

It's Team Canada versus the Soviet Union and they're both playing to win for their nation's pride. It's an eight-game series with four games in Canada and four in the Union of Soviet Socialist Republics (U.S.S.R.). The Canadian hockey team had sat out the 1972 Winter Olympics hosted by Sapporo, Japan. It was a federal decision made in 1970 by Canadian Health and Wellness Minister John Munro, in protest of rules banning professional hockey players from international competitions. Canadian officials and fans were frustrated because this rule meant Canada couldn't ice its best players — pros playing in the NHL — against Communist-bloc countries like the Soviet Union and Czechoslovakia, whose elite players were technically considered amateurs because they played domestically for teams that represented the military or state-owned enterprises.

The 1972 Summit Series is supposed to settle the score once and for all, with a true best-on-best competition: Canadian NHL players against the Big Red Machine for ultimate bragging rights.

Bobby Orr, Brian's hockey hero, isn't on the ice for Team Canada. He's injured. There's another hero in the making, though. Terry and Alice are glued to the TV screen. Terry has even missed a few university classes because he's been watching hockey but this is important! The series is tied with one game left to go. Many Canadians initially thought Canada was going to easily beat the Soviets, but the Russians make them think again. Game 8 is in the U.S.S.R. and it's a nail biter. Russia is up two goals. Canada rallies and ties it up. Terry and Alice have their fingers and toes crossed. Can Canada do it? It's the final seconds ... and Paul Henderson shoots and scores the winning goal for Canada. He is immediately a national hero.

97. Ralph Klein goes on to become the mayor of Calgary and then the premier of Alberta.

***

The Carleton family has been a family of five for many years. It's expanding to six in 1973. Mike and Sylvia are engaged around Christmas time. Ed's smile can't get any wider when he hears the news. Mike's parents think it's time for him to settle down. He's 28, around the age Ed was married, and has a good job. He's been employed by the City of Calgary as a computer programmer in its data processing department. Mike got that job right out of university in 1967.

Sylvia is much loved by the Carletons, especially for her handmade burgers. Ed and his hearty appetite gobble down four at a family picnic.

There's a family reunion in Reading when Mike sees his grandmother again. The last time Alice saw Mike was in 1950. Mike is sporting a beard and Alice does not think it suits him. She tells him to shave it off. It's the 1970s, though, and Mike doesn't want to be a square.

Back in Banff, Ed and Dorothy are on the legion dance floor every Saturday night. The ladies like when Ed shows up because he'll dance, unlike the partners they've brought along. Many years of waltzing and two-stepping with Dorothy have polished Ed's dancing skills.

Terry is working at the Hi-way Gulf station on weekends. Besides pumping gas, he's doing a fair amount of oil changes and other mechanical work, like changing tires and lube jobs. After having driven several larger, gas-guzzling vehicles, which are always in need of repair, he picks up a blue 1973 Datsun 510. The $2,910 purchase is co-signed by Ed and Dorothy and they pay the insurance, too. Terry appreciates it and he appreciates the block heater, radio and freedom it gives him while he's at university. Nevertheless, almost every weekend he drives home to Banff to take advantage of his mother's home-cooked meals and work at the gas station.

Mike and Sylvia tie the knot in June 1974. The ceremony is held in Banff at the Rundle United Church with the reception at the Banff Legion. Dorothy and Ed beam at the newlyweds as they toast a happy future. The elder couple has been together for more than 30 years, married for 29 and counting.

***

It has taken almost 90 years but finally, women are joining the ranks of Parks Canada wardens, as the National Parks Branch is officially known now. Jen Cadieux was hired as a seasonal warden in 1973 and stationed at Yoho. In 1974, another woman begins working in Yoho for the warden service, Kathy Calvert.[98] Three more women are on the roster at other national parks, including Banff. Ed supports giving women roles as wardens. His wife did her fair share of work in the park alongside him.

"Good for them," says Dorothy when she hears the news. She remembers all the years she helped Ed on the job. For free. She wouldn't change a thing, although she's glad women are getting paid now.

---

98. Kathy Calvert is also an author and has written several books including one about Ya Ha Tinda Ranch: https://rmbooks.com/book-author/kathy-calvert.

The national parks are evolving and the relationship between people and the great outdoors is shifting. The proposed Lake Louise resort isn't getting a good response from the public. Conservation groups are opposed to it and the deal is struck down by the federal government. Ottawa wants to keep the mountain village from being inundated with tourists. Jean Chrétien, minister of Indian Affairs and Northern Development, adds that the issues remain on how to deal with current visitors as well as future commercial enterprises and the environment.

The Sime-Schuler report had called for better research, monitoring and reporting of wildlife — something Ed has been doing of his own initiative since he began his job as a warden. He's been writing fishing bulletins on his own time for years. Now he's seeing his responsibilities and his schedule change.

Centralizing the Banff National Park wardens has brought in a regular 9 to 5 work week with overtime pay and union dues. A warden's law-enforcement role is waning while resource conservation activities are picking up. As well, wardens are working all over the park instead of in single districts.

Even though the old system of districts no longer exists, some of Ed's duties have him working around his old stomping grounds. He patrols the area around Mount Eisenhower as well as Stoney Creek.

Joining Ed in the field is Halle Flygare. Halle has been a warden since 1972. The Swedish import is Ed's assistant in 1975. Halle fell in love with Canada when he was an exchange student in forestry in 1959. He was working in the bush then for the B.C. forestry service. He returned to Sweden when his visa ran out and headed back for good in 1962. On his travels through Banff National Park, he was in the backcountry and saw cabins in the area. He was told park wardens lived in them and he knew what he was meant to be: a warden.

Halle and Ed cover Egypt Lake, an area near the Alberta British Columbia boundary. With names like Pharaoh Peaks, Scarab Peak and Mummy Lake, the region is filled with wildflowers in the summer and has staggering views any time of year. The mosquitoes can be terrible and whine and bite as the wardens hike up the trail. They don't take the horses since they destroy the terrain. The wardens are working to keep the park pristine and as untouched by humans (and horses) as possible.

Getting the Shot

Ed has been in Banff for over 25 years and he knows every tree, rock and stream. He's a great note taker and there's nothing he doesn't notice. Ed and Halle Flygare hike to Egypt Lake and discover some other wardens have been there ahead of them. The other crew has written in a logbook what kind of animals they had seen, including an ivory-billed woodpecker.

"That's not right," Ed says. "It's a pileated woodpecker that lives out here."

Ed and Halle talk about how some wardens don't have an interest in the animals they protect. The men only want to ride their horses all day long. That's not Ed. He's always interested in the flora and fauna and wildlife and mythical mines and cabins with stories. He finds a solid workmate in Halle, who is also interested in flowers and animals and birds.

Ed checking for game.
Photo: Bruno Engler

Together, they fix up the Redearth Creek Warden Cabin before it's replaced with a modern one. The pair also go on trips with their wives as well. Ed, Dorothy, Halle and his wife Linda go on an overnight to the cabin near Egypt Lake.

"Is that a mouse?" asks Linda, pointing to a dark corner.

"No, no," says Ed, "there are no mice here."

After a restful night, Linda takes a cup off the cabin shelf. She looks in it before filling it with coffee. There's mouse poop sitting on the bottom.

"Uh, Ed?" she says. "There's a turd in here."

"That's dirt."

***

Ed and Halle are called to the dump every once in a while. The site is a few kilometres east of Banff, around Two Jack Lake off Lake Minnewanka. The waste station attracts grizzly bears and they'll dig under the fence to get at the garbage. Ed is walking around the fenced enclosure when Halle spots a big griz laying on the ground, having a good look at Ed. Halle doesn't know if the bear is sizing up Ed for a meal or only lounging, but he knows Ed has to get out of there.

"Ed," says Halle softly. "Back up. Slowly."

One evening, Halle and Linda check out the dump around 11 p.m. They pull up in their pick-up truck and see the gate has been left open. There are at least six bears milling around. Halle fires a cracker shell from his shotgun to scare them and the grizzlies bolt and take off through the gate. One big bruin speeds past the truck. The grizzly is the same height as the truck's side-view mirror.

Halle has seen the carcass of a black bear that had its face bitten off by a grizzly. Bears are large and powerful and the wardens treat them with respect. Halle and Ed carry guns and will use them if they have too. Rifles remain a component of a warden's kit. They can use shotguns and bear bangers, too. However, both men like to shoot photos more than animals.

Parks officials send Ed and Halle to see what's going on at a campground near Banff. There have been reports of blood on the road. The wardens go to check it out. Sure enough, there's blood as well as drag marks. Ed scratches his head. It could be a poacher who killed a mule deer. He follows the track in about 30 m (100 ft) and finds the deer … with a cougar beside it.

The large muscular cat disappears into the bushes.

Ed and Halle return later in the day. They don't bring a gun; they think they can kick the cat away from the carcass. The cougar does take off again — until a cheeky magpie flies to peck off a piece of flesh from the deer carcass. Then the cougar charges at it. The black and white bird stays put and the cougar doesn't pounce. It stops and settles down beside the kill.

The wardens monitor the doe and every day, it gets closer to being only bones. By the end of the week, there's hardly anything left of the deer. The cougar has been chowing down heartily on its meal.

"Let's try and get a photo of the cat," says Halle to Ed. "I'll walk down the trail and you spook the cougar my way."

The big cat.
Photo: Halle Flygare

The animal has beaten a nice path in the snow from the carcass into the woods. Halle walks 20 m (21 yds.) down the trail and waits for Ed to do his part.

There's the cougar. It stops and sits down 5 m (just over 5 yds.) in front of Halle and his camera.

Click.

He's got the shot.

The deer is a skeleton in a couple more days and then there's nothing left except for the hide. The cat scraped everything off that he could eat. He comes back the next year and kills a dog. That's when Parks calls in a professional cougar hunter from the States. He brings hounds with him that tree the cat after about an hour.

The animal is shot with a tranquillizer gun and then put into a crate to be relocated.

Helicopter pilot Jim Davies flies Ed, Halle and the cougar to White Rabbit Pass, a remote area in the Cascade Valley. Jim drops the crate onto an open snowfield. The large cat springs out and is gone in a flash. For good, the wardens hope.

A couple of weeks later, the cougar is in Banff again.

***

Ed and Halle take their guns with them into the high country. They're looking for poachers. An Exshaw guide has been taking people in the park to shoot bighorn sheep. It's illegal to hunt in national parks and the wardens are flown by helicopter into the mountains to find their man.

Hiking around the area, they find a dense grove of spruce trees that's thick with horse dung. The poop marks the spot. Ed and Halle camp out, waiting for the horse and hunter to show up. Three days later, they spot a rider with his gun. The wardens have a clear view of him because he's silhouetted on the ridge. He's in provincial territory though and before crossing into the park, he spies the wardens. He rides off.

The wardens aren't trained to arrest people. Ed and Halle don't carry handcuffs. They are told that when they stop people speeding down the highway, they have to radio for the RCMP. The Mounties, though, aren't supposed to shoot animals. That's left to the wardens. However, sometimes the wardens don't have their rifles with them. Ed and Halle are on the scene of an accident on the Trans-Canada. A Volkswagen hit a sheep. It has a broken leg and the wardens don't have a gun. They have a two-by-four piece of wood and hit the animal over the head.

Ed and Halle are called out for a wounded elk. The animal is a big one with an impressive rack of antlers. It's lying in the ditch and still alive. The Mounties had fired six bullets into it but didn't kill it. The wardens finish it off with their rifles.

On a winter midnight shift near Mount Eisenhower, someone reports seeing a moose with broken front legs on the road. Ed and Halle investigate and discover the moose is lying down on the road, licking salt off the asphalt.

Snow machines aren't allowed in Banff National Park, although the wardens use them from time to time. Ed and Halle are on a sled looking for poachers around the Bryant Creek area, southwest of Banff. Halle is driving the machine with Ed holding on behind. Halle tells Ed not to lean into the corners but he does anyway.

There they go! They tip over into the deep and cold snow. Ed keeps leaning the wrong way and the pair keeps ending up in the powder. Arriving at a cabin near Spray Lakes, Halle tells Ed to stay put. He will lay out a track to Bryant Creek warden cabin.

It's not exactly a fine day. It's snowing hard and the wind is blowing. Halle is driving on what he thinks, and prays, is the trail. It's whiteout conditions and he can't see much ahead of him. All of a sudden, he and the sled are suspended in the air. Where's the ground?

Boom.

Halle's body slams into the earth, along with the snow machine. He has dropped about 3 m (just over 3 yds.) off a small hill. Halle pushes ahead and gets to Bryant Creek. After picking up Ed, they shovel snow off the warden cabin roof and look for signs of poachers' sleds. The tracks would be hard to find in the storm but they wouldn't be erased. The new snow would settle into the indentations and grooves made by other sleds. Nevertheless, Halle sees no signs of human activity.

Out in the bush in February, a grizzly emerges from a den. It's far too early for the bear to be out of hibernation. There's something wrong with this animal. It's skin and bones, obviously ill. Ed has to shoot it. A necropsy is done on the carcass and a large tumour is found in the bear's stomach.

Ed is firm with illegal campers at the Egypt Lake cabin who can gain access to the remote hut from trails in the area. It's a pain in the neck dealing with this sort of "people" stuff. To camp at the hut, visitors need a permit. When the wardens show up and ask for proof of permission and the campers don't have it, the wardens have to ask them to leave. Ed makes sure they understand why they're being told to go. He isn't always hard on visitors. Halle experiences this when the wardens are in a valley near Egypt Lake. A group of campers have cut down a few trees and started a fire. Halle tells Ed he's going to write them a ticket and is surprised when Ed says not to bother.

"I've been talking to them and they're nice people," says Ed. "We won't write them up."

After a kid goes missing at the Sulphur Mountain Gondola, Ed and Halle arrive at the scene first. The boy and his father took the gondola up the mountain and the kid said he was going to hike down. Well, he never made it to the bottom of the hill. It's now evening.

Ed and Halle start trekking up the trail around 8 p.m. when they hear someone screaming for help. It's the boy. Ed and Halle find him with a broken arm. He thought he'd take a shortcut and was sliding in the snow when he started speeding down the mountain. He lost control and hit a tree. The wardens load the kid into a toboggan and get him off the mountain and to the hospital.

***

Someone has reported a fire on the top of Banff's iconic Mount Rundle. There's nothing there when Ed and Halle look. However, there is a campfire on Tunnel Mountain. It's getting dark and Ed and Halle can see flames. They hike to the fire and find it along with a man and a woman lying on a large bed with a thick mattress. The man is dancing around the flames and when Halle talks to him, he says he's dancing for his father's ghost. The phantom is telling him to take over the national park.

Ed and Halle aren't impressed with his story or the fire but they are impressed that the fellow managed to carry such a big bed up to the peak. The wardens extinguish the blaze and help the people off the mountain. The man will have to get his bed down himself.

The next morning, a bunch of cadets are hiking on Mount Rundle and find an injured woman. She had broken her leg and started a fire the night before as a call for help. There had been flames on Rundle! The cadets save the day and bring her down.

Since the terrible incident with the Philadelphia boys in 1955, Parks has a strict policy of signing in and out for those heading up mountains and going on trails. Hikers, climbers, skiers and the like are supposed to sign up at the warden office, tell the wardens where they're going, and leave a slip at the trailhead. After they return, they let the wardens know they're back. However, the woman hadn't followed any of those procedures. She's lucky the cadets discovered her.

Ed and Halle are explorers as well as wardens. Ed has found someone who also likes to search for old trails, mines and cabins. They uncover an almost lost path from Sulphur Mountain to Mount Assiniboine to Sunshine Village. In the Simpson Pass area, they find one of Bill Peyto's many cabins is being dismantled piece by piece. People are taking bits of it and Ed takes a pane of glass from a window where Bill had doodled a self-portrait. Ed donates it to the Whyte Museum, a Banff institution preserving the area's history.

In the bush, both Ed and Halle feel at home. Halle notices that Ed isn't afraid of anything. He's a natural warden, however, he does keep alert and hollers every once in a while to let the bears know he's visiting. The mountain ranges are Ed's close friends and maybe because he feels comfortable in the landscape as well as in his job and with his partner, he begins to open up to Halle about his war years.

Halle has been noticing Ed's becoming a bit forgetful but the older warden will sometimes talk about his experiences overseas. He remembers when he was shot in the head. Ed says he didn't feel a thing.

"Someone said to me, 'Ed, you're bleeding.' I hadn't noticed. Someone poured me a drink in the trenches while I was being looked at. I don't remember what it was but it must have been a stiff drink."

Halle listens but he doesn't ask questions. He simply lets Ed tell his stories. On May 3, 1976, Ed is given the Dieppe medal by the Montreal Chapter of the Dieppe Veterans and Prisoners of War Association (a group representing those who fought and were captured at Dieppe). The medal honours Ed's participation in the raid and commemorates the 30th anniversary of the Aug. 19, 1942 event.

Once Young Men

In 1977, there's an official Calgary Highlanders reunion. Ed gazes at the old men in the room. He himself is teetering on the edge of 60. How can it be that these lads were once young men who survived amazing and atrocious things? The veterans toss around old jokes and tell their war stories. They ask one another: Would today's hippies rise up for democracy?

The main speaker for the event talks about the nostalgia for the days when the country was united in the fight against evil. He says part of that is because of the hippies, who are challenging social norms. However, differences with the following generation shouldn't mean prejudice and struggles: it should mean listening and accepting our differences.

You always got along with the Maisonneuve and recognized the fact that they did things differently – even riding home from an exercise on the bus – but there was never any indication that an attempt should be made to change or mould them in our image – an attempt to stifle their ambitions and aspirations.

Ed thoroughly enjoys Highlanders reunions over the years and swapping anecdotes with his mates. The older warden never shares any Second World War stories with Jim Murphy, another of Ed's young assistants. Jim and Ed have been working alongside each other for several years. Jim has never seen Ed get seriously angry, although he could be a stickler for details.

During a backcountry trip, a warden dropped an orange peel on the trail. Ed found it and gives the man a stern talking-to. Ed also found fault with wardens who shaved in the morning instead of at night. Shaving in the morning means wasting precious daylight and time.

Ed passes down his knowledge of the ranges and the wildlife environment in the park. He knows where the goats hang out and where the prime sheep habitats are located. Jim and Ed have many in-depth chats about the idiosyncrasies of the area. Why do the bighorn sheep like this mountain over that mountain?

Being an older warden isn't easy. Ed can keep up with the younger lads and guide them through the trails that crisscross Banff and teach them about the intricacies of the land and wildlife. However, he is stumbling over his words and has memory troubles. Dorothy is worried about him and has a private conversation with Jim.

"Look after him, Jim, please," she asks the younger man.

The larches are turning yellow when Jim and Ed ride to the park boundary on Dormer Trail. Jim is on Casper, Ed on Whack and the "deadheaded" Boston is the packhorse. They're out in the backcountry for at least a week and on the first day, are joined by another warden, John Wackerle. John, originally from Austria, is a good warden and an excellent skier. He started as a ski patroller at Mount Norquay and then got a job with the warden service. Right now he bears some concerns. There's a grizzly in the area.

John radios the sighting into headquarters and advises the trail be closed. At least the griz isn't hungry. She killed an old bull elk. John doesn't want any hikers to come along and surprise her while she's eating her large meal. She might see people as a threat.

The days go by while Ed and the wardens ride around the area, clearing downed trees and counting wildlife as they go. They see nine bighorn sheep and 78 elk.

At Windy Cabin, Ed stays overnight with Jim and a trail crew who are already there. Ed goes out and fishes for his supper, hooking a Dolly Varden. The next day, the trail crew moves on and Jim has to leave Ed alone for 24 hours. He feels bad about not keeping his word to Dorothy but he has to go into town for an employee review. He can't miss it.

Ed waves Jim off and then saddles up Whack for a ride downstream of the Panther River to "the Corners" – the junction of the Dormer and Panther rivers. There's an old cabin there, the Corners Cabin, and it brings back memories of Ole Hermanrude and when they patrolled the district. Later, Ed heads to Barrier Cabin, chops some wood for his evening fire and settles in for the night.

Bright and early, Ed is up and tidying up the cabin. He saddles Whack and waits for Jim. Jim is trying to get back to Ed as fast as he can. He is worried about letting Dorothy down. Along with him is Don Warner, the timekeeper for the warden service. Don is getting a "break" from his regular routine at the Warden's Equipment Building. However, he's rethinking his decision to hit the trail with Jim. Jim didn't adjust the stirrup straps on Don's horse properly. Don is a very sore man.

When Jim sees Ed through the yellow leaves he lets out a loud "whoop!"

All is well and Dorothy's man is fine.

***

Peter Fuhrmann is in Walter Perren's public safety and mountain rescue role for Banff, Kootenay, Yoho and Pacific Rim parks while Willie Pfisterer has Jasper, Waterton, Revelstoke/Glacier and Kluane parks. They're part of a large group working on improving helicopter sling rescue systems that includes Jim Davies, the helicopter pilot who was part of the Mount Babel rescue team in 1966, and Tim Auger, a climber and search and rescue technician. Parks Canada is taking some of its material from the International Kommision of Alpine Rescue (IKAR) and using it to improve first aid, avalanche rescues and other lifesaving techniques.

Skiing magazine's January issue has an ad for Banff ski hills. Come ski the greatest snow on earth it touts.

Canada – so much to go for.
Ski Banff 7 days, from $159 from Calgary
Includes a stay at the Banff Springs Hotel,
lift tickets to Norquay, Louise or Sunshine
and round trip transportation to and from Calgary.
Skiing Jan. 1977

It's not only tourists from far away coming to Banff; it's also day-trippers from Calgary. The city has exploded since Alberta's petroleum industry is booming. The oil embargo in the Middle East has been great for Cowtown. Alberta's population increases by a third.

Some of the old cabins are considered too small for the numbers of people using them. Windy Cabin, in the Panther River district, is one of them. Windy was built in 1911 by Scotty Wright, a warden, and sheltered many in the backcountry. It's falling apart though: logs rotting, splitting, cracks, holes and not to mention, the door has fallen off. The door was essentially a calling card and autographing it was a rite of passage. Whoever passed by the cabin, signed the door. Many of the wardens taking horses to and from Ya Ha Tinda Ranch used Windy on their stopovers and inscribed their names on the wood. Ed is also familiar with the hut as it was part of his patrols when he was at Stoney Creek.

The old cabin is hauled into town over the Cascade Fire Road and set up on the property of the Whyte Museum. While Ed's sad that the Windy he once knew will no longer greet wardens and hikers in the backcountry, he appreciates that it'll be an example of warden life in the past.

The next generation of Carletons is born in Calgary in the summer of 1976. The first grandchild is a girl and Dorothy is thrilled. She tells Mike it's nice to have a girl in the family. Dorothy and Ed babysit Ingrid a lot, starting when she's eight and half months old while Mike and Sylvia go on a ski camp in the Eremites (Wates Gibson hut) in Jasper. Sylvia writes "instructions" for the grandparents who will be looking after baby Ingrid.

Ingrid's brother, Erik Edmond, is born in the winter of 1978. Sylvia is two weeks overdue and Erik is quite a large infant.

"Poor Sylvia!" says Dorothy.

She and Ed have been looking after Ingrid while her parents were in the hospital in the city. In the afternoon, the grandparents and their granddaughter go on a wintery walk around the Fenland Trail in town. Ed pulls Ingrid in the toboggan with Peppi, his little sheltie dog, leading. They run into friends Jack and Em with Morley (their dog). After supper, Ed and Dorothy drive out to Canmore for Halle and Linda's house warming party with Ingrid in tow. There are a lot of people at the gathering there and they make a big fuss over the toddler.

Mike's family makes the drive from Calgary to the mountains many times. They ski in the winter, often pulling a Norwegian pulk (a sled) with a baby and toddler tucked warmly inside. In summer, they go hiking and fishing, carrying Erik in the snugly that Sylvia made. It's always a happy moment to stop in at the Rainbow House after being out in the fresh air. Dorothy and Ed greet their family warmly and everyone (except for the children) relaxes with a drink. Yes, Dorothy has her sherry. They'll chat about the day and hear the latest news from Banff. Brian often visits at the same time and shares his latest exploits. Dorothy breaks out the treats and offers up some of her famous Rocky Roads chocolaty squares. The visits to the House at the End of the Rainbow mean so much to Mike and he's glad his daughter and son share in the moments.

As grandparents, Ed and Dorothy are great. They love their grandchildren and the children love them. They're going to have more time to spend with Ingrid and Erik soon: Ed is thinking about retiring.

Ed has seven "stripes" on his official warden jacket, each for five years of service and his wartime service is included. That adds up to over 35 years. He thinks that's long enough. He's also wary of the new management system in the parks – his job is definitely different from the good old days with the districts. Another factor is that Ed has been forgetting things and having trouble with words. It's thought the cause is Ed's war wound. It's time to say farewell to the warden life.

Dorothy is pleased. She can stop worrying about her husband when he's out on the job. She's looking forward to their retirement years together. They can travel, garden and do things they couldn't do while he was working. May 17, 1978, is Ed's last day with the Banff National Park warden service. A few weeks later, there's a huge party to celebrate the milestone.

Dorothy and Ed leading the dancing at Ed's retirment party, Banff Springs Hotel, 1978. Photo: Bruno Engler

The Party of a Lifetime

The Banff Springs Hotel is the site of Ed's retirement party, thrown by co-workers and friends on Jun. 9, 1978. It's a large event and around 250 people, including the who's-who of Parks Canada and the warden service, are there to celebrate Ed's achievements. Ed's smiling so much his mouth hurts, but he forgets about the pain when he's dancing with Dorothy. Of course, they're the first ones to hit the dance floor to the tunes of Louis Trono.

At over 80 years of age, Ed's mum Millie is there and having fun. She is getting tired though and Brian drives her to Rainbow House to rest. Her grandson returns to the party. He, on the other hand, is not tired!

Other families at the event include Ed's siblings Frank, Baillie, Garry and Joan, and their spouses. Mike gives a "congratulations you're retired speech" and the rest of the night, he and Sylvia are trying to keep their family content. They have a four-month-old baby and a toddler. Terry isn't at the party. He has been living in Calgary and working as an assistant manager at the Westbrook Gulf service centre. It's not his job keeping him away though: he is attending a wedding.

Representatives from parks all across the West, from Riding Mountain in Manitoba to Pacific Rim on Vancouver Island, and friends from all corners of Ed's life help him celebrate. The Peytos, Hermanrudes, Peter and Barb Spear and Peter's mum Flo, Nancy and Art Colbeck, Jack and Em Chisholm, Scott and Wanda Ward, Halle and Linda Flygare, Alice Robertson and Stella Camp (from Johnston Canyon), Bill Nokes, Pam Perren and her son Mark and Slim Haugen from Ya Ha Tinda Ranch are at the festivities. Bert Pittaway is not at the party. He's already retired and living in Victoria, B.C. with his wife Pam. They send a card of congratulations, with a note saying they hope Ed and Dorothy enjoy retirement as much as they do.

Ed and Dorothy are enjoying the food, drinks, music and laughter of the evening. The stories are rolling out about Ed and his penchant for order and economy. However, on some occasions, he has got himself into a pickle. Someone tells a tale about Ed driving the warden patrol boat into a boathouse. He got confused which way to move the throttle and rocked the boat right through the place.

Halle talks about travelling through the park with Ed. Many times when they'd get to a trail sign, Ed wanted to go one way and Halle the other.

There's another story about Ed and Halle. A warden remembers going to the Redearth warden cabin on a beautiful sunny day. He stepped through the hut door and there were Ed and Halle, dissecting a mouse.

For his years of service, Ed is given a plaque from Banff park superintendent Paul Lange. Bruno Engler snaps photos of the moment: Ed is wearing a three-piece suit and a big smile; Dorothy has a long gown on and the same grin. Ed's surprised with some gifts, including a belt buckle made by Canmore silversmith Steve Cody. As well, he's given a piece of art made by Paul Peyto, some of Halle Flygare's photos and a handcrafted wooden coffee table. Carved into the table is Ed with his horse while on patrol at Windy Cabin. Henning Sorensen, a Parks carpenter, created the piece of furniture that is instantly beloved by Ed and admired by all.

Ed says he has had a rewarding career and is proud of the work he has done and the work the wardens will continue to do without him. He's not one to show deep emotions and well up, but those who know him, know he's getting teary inside. Dorothy tears up for him at the end of the night. It has been a beautiful yet emotional evening. She can't believe all the friends and colleagues who have turned out to wish Ed, and her, well. The retirement event is heralded in the local newspaper, the *Crag & Canyon*, with Bruno's photos.

There isn't much time for rest or to get hungry again. Dorothy has planned a smaller gathering at Rainbow House the next day. Retired wardens, their wives and other park employees and friends talk about last night's grand event and what's to come now that the "good old days" are over.

The director-general of Parks, J. I. Nicol, steps down in 1978, too. Under his tenure as the head of the national parks program, 10 national parks have been created, conservation strengthened and Canadians are playing a larger role in what's happening to their natural resource. Al Davidson takes over from Nicol.

Retirement for Ed doesn't mean lazing around the house. He and Dorothy do their favourite hike to Arnica Lake. For the first time, they don't have to rush it. They take their time and drink in the scenery. They eat lunch by the greenish-blue water sheltered by a wall of rock on one side. The couple could have had a nap if they wanted but Dorothy is only 59 and not a senior citizen. She'll never rest!

Dorothy and Ed hike together a lot in the park now, like when they started their backcountry adventures at Bow Summit. Many of their excursions today are to search for the lost mines that haunt Ed. He thinks the Queen of the Hills mine might be somewhere on Mount Eisenhower. Ed gets his friend Jack Chisholm fired up about finding the queen with him. Jack is a Parks employee and maintains the grounds and all the flowers at the Banff Administration Building. Jack and Ed are often bushwhacking up mountainsides and creating new trails with their wives following behind.

Dorothy and Em Chisholm are lifelong friends and like to joke that they bonded while stepping over, ducking under and going around trees. Searching for the mine makes for some long, tiring hikes but there's usually a favourable outcome: a cookout where they toast the day with a glass of wine.

"Where are we going next time?" asks Dorothy.

Well, the next time they find the Queen of the Hills mine. Right there on Mount Eisenhower. No doubt others have stumbled upon it too but it makes Ed ecstatic to have discovered it at last.

Finally, There's Time to Spare

Mount Eisenhower has a name change in 1979. It becomes Castle Mountain again. It really does look like a castle with towers, battlements and thick walls. Besides, President Eisenhower is American and dead.

The "new" name is something that's been brewing for a while. The Historical Society of Alberta in 1975 had suggested that only the most prominent peak on Mount

Eisenhower should be named after Eisenhower. It looked like Parks Canada was fine with this move but nope. Canadians, including former prime minister John Diefenbaker (born in Ontario), made a fuss. They insinuated a name change would be insulting to Americans, especially since the U.S. was celebrating its bicentennial in 1976. Three years later, Prime Minister Joe Clark, born in High River, Alberta, endorsed Castle Mountain. Eisenhower's name remains only on Eisenhower Tower, at the southeast end of the mountain.

Dorothy, Ed and Olive Openshaw have a visit at Olive's home on Stanton Close, Earley, U.K., 1979.
Photo: Carleton Family

With leisure time on Ed's hands, he's using it to paint. He has been picking up pointers from his old Didsbury friend, Earl Cummins. Earl gave an untitled picture to Ed. It's a painting of birch trees and it contains amazing colours. Earl is a bonafide watercolour artist and has been selling his works in galleries. He's self-taught and a realist landscape painter who is familiar with the areas Ed is depicting in his pieces. Earl had a job working on the dam around Spray Lakes, a few kilometres south of Banff National Park. The two share a passion for the Rockies and capturing their spires and couloirs with brushstrokes.

A trip "home" is in store for Dorothy. Ed has all the time in the world to accompany her. On Apr. 7, 1979, Brian drives his parents to Mike and Sylvia's in Calgary. They all have lunch together before dropping Dorothy and Ed off at the airport.

Dorothy is excited about the voyage but it's going to take some extra time to get to London. Their flight, which is supposed to leave at 8:15 p.m., doesn't. They end up sleeping on the hard chairs at the airport until 3 a.m. because of a suspected fire in the airplane cargo hold.

Eight hours late landing at Heathrow Airport, the Carletons have a joyous reunion at the arrivals gate with Dorothy's sister Marjorie, her son Derek and friends Olive and Danny Openshaw. The dreary English rain that's falling can't dampen any of their spirits as they head to Marjorie and Melbourne's home in Hailey, near Oxford.

The next day, Dorothy and Ed catch the bus to Woodstock to see Dorothy's mum. Alice isn't at 55 Grange Avenue anymore. She moved to be closer to Marjorie and Melbourne and is now in a seniors home. Alice is going to be 95 in a couple of weeks and Dorothy will be there for the party. She hugs her mother and notices she's not a fragile old woman. Her grasp and voice are strong and she is looking sharp in a new outfit. Like mother, like daughter, Alice has some homemade cookies ready to serve. After several hours of talking, it's time for Dorothy and Ed to say see you soon.

The weather stays damp for the next few days. Dorothy and Ed are busy anyway with friends and stops in pubs and strolls along the English streets. Of course, there's a meal of fish and chips.

"Delicious!" says Dorothy.

The sun is out on Apr. 15. That's also the day they're leaving to see Russ and Phyllis. Danny Openshaw is driving the Canadians from Reading to Birmingham, about a two-hour trip. They arrive at 3 p.m. to a whole gang of U.K. Carletons. It's a cheerful evening and a late one at that.

The next few days of sightseeing and pub visits with Russ and Phyllis have Dorothy and Ed tuckered out but content. It's then back to Hailey, where Marjorie is preparing for Alice's milestone birthday. On the big day, the party is attended by almost 40 "old" people with all the food done by Marjorie. Of course, there's cake. Over a slice of chocolate swirl, Dorothy marvels at how well Alice is doing.

"Imagine, being 95 years old," Dorothy says to Ed.

Amid a trip full of family and friends, Dorothy and Ed take some days for themselves. They walk along the seaside in Conwy, a walled town in Wales, and do some shopping. They buy some souvenirs for the grandkids before going back to Hailey and more visiting with Alice and Marjorie. On May 6, Dorothy and Ed are getting ready for their flight back to Canada. Dorothy tells Ed she's glad they spent the time and the money to cross the pond. It was important to her to show her mother that she's appreciative of everything she's done for her.

There's a turn of events on the plane: Ed is the one who doesn't stop talking! He has bumped into an old army buddy and they chat the whole way home. Dorothy flips through a magazine and hopes Ed tires out soon. She'd like a nap.

Mike, Terry and Brian greet their parents at the airport. The sons are a sight for sore eyes. When Dorothy and Ed arrive home in Banff, their furry family member Peppi looks just as good.

That 1979 visit is the last time Dorothy sees her mother. Alice dies in 1980. With her, goes any information about Dorothy's biological parents. In any case, Dorothy has never given much thought to being adopted. It was, what it was. Alice had been the only mother Dorothy had ever known. She isn't yearning over unanswered questions about her birth parents.

Family means everything to Dorothy and Ed, and they are there for the Perren family that same year. Pamela Perren, Walter's wife and the mother of Peter, Martin and Mark, passes away. Dorothy tells the three brothers that she and Ed will be adoptive grandparents to any of their babies.

Mike and Sylvia add to their family when Patrick is born in the fall of 1980. Dorothy and Ed are, of course, happy with the news. Dorothy calls Brian and tells him he is an uncle – again. She offers to come to Calgary to help Mike and his wife but they're doing fine. It's their third and last child.

A young man running across Canada has caught the interest of Dorothy. She's following Terry Fox's Marathon of Hope. Terrance "Terry" Stanley Fox is running across Canada raising money for cancer research. He had one leg amputated due to cancer and is using a prosthetic leg for his epic journey, called the Marathon of Hope. Dorothy and Ed call the young man "a brave lad" for the distance he puts in every day: 42 km (26 mi).

Unfortunately, Terry's cancer returns and his run ends on Sept. 1, 1980, in Thunder Bay, Ontario. The 22-year-old dies on Jun. 28, 1981 but his dream of finding a cure lives on. A fundraiser in his name has been started, continuing his work. Terry Fox Runs are organized in Canada and other countries and Dorothy and Ed are eager participants in the Banff-area event. It'll be an annual tradition for the couple.

Dorothy and Ed at Lake O'Hara.
Photo: Carleton Family

Chapter Fourteen

Making New Memories While Remembering the Old

Don't Forget Your Long-Johns and Warm Jackets

For decades, CODA (Calgary Olympic Development Association) has been bidding for the Winter Olympics. The dream comes true in 1981 when Calgary is awarded the 1988 Winter Games. The XV Olympic Winter Games Organizing Committee, OCO '88, begins to coordinate and plan. It starts looking across Canada for experienced officials. Mike's Nordic sports experience with the Foothills Nordic Ski Club (FNSC) gets him noticed. He's named as one of many volunteer "chiefs" for the Olympics and is the Chief of Timekeeping for cross-country skiing.

For the next seven years, Mike will be in training, immersed in all the preparations to make sure the Olympics go smoothly. He has to gain experience by hosting events such as national events, North American championships and World Cups. This all has to be done through coordination with the international federations, national sport organizations, the provincial government, the Town of Canmore (where cross-country races will be held), cultural groups, and of course, OCO '88. It is a major long-term commitment.

A chance meeting at a Banff high school reunion leads Terry to make a long-term commitment of his own: he meets his future wife. In August 1981, classes from the years 1969, 1970 and 1971 gather to catch up with one another. They've only been out of school for a decade and some have stuck around town. Terry has been in Calgary and a couple of years ago, started a career at Safeway.

A classmate of Terry's, Wendy Hall, lives in Granum, a town in southern Alberta and around a three-hour drive from Banff. She convinces her friend Mary Lou to join her for the weekend. (Who can pass up a trip to the Rockies?) At the mixer on Friday night, Mary Lou and Terry start talking. They become friends, too.

Terry likes Mary Lou's gregarious nature and how she puts him at ease. Nevertheless, Mary Lou has a different life than him. In 1982, Mary Lou moves to High River with her two children, La Rae and Darryl. Terry is living and working in Calgary, about an hour and a half drive north. Terry and Mary Lou talk on the phone from time-to-time and see each other occasionally until finally, things get serious in 1982.

Terry could do the drive to Mary Lou's home and back with his eyes closed. He knows every little bump on that route. The next year, he moves to High River, commuting to his Safeway job in Calgary from High River.

Terry and Mary Lou are married in May 1984 at the St. Francis de Sales Catholic Church in High River. Ed and Dorothy are there and couldn't be happier to see Terry so happy. The older Carletons can't believe they've just celebrated 36 years of marriage. It seems like only yesterday that Ed had to haul Terry out of the equipment building and take him to school.

At the reception, Ed and Dorothy are the hit of the party when they hit the dance floor as soon as they hear the strains of Johnny Horton. They spin the night away, leaving the younger guests in their dancing dust. People can't believe how much energy Dorothy and Ed have – they're the last ones standing at the party.

Peter and Chris Perren have their first child in 1984. A daughter, Heidi, is born. True to their word, Dorothy and Ed make sure Heidi is doted on as their second granddaughter.

Ed's mother Millie passes away in August of 1984 in Calgary. She was 89. Her children and grandchildren gather in the city to say goodbye. Ed, Dorothy and their sons talk with many relatives they haven't seen in years.

Another grandchild is born in late spring. Terry and Mary Lou's son Kevin arrives in June 1985 in High River. There will be many birthdays for the Carletons to celebrate as the family grows.

The National Parks Centennial in 1985 is a great excuse for an old-time warden get-together in the backcountry. Ed and Dorothy are part of the pack of wardens and wives who worked and lived in the park before 1975. A whole weekend of events is planned and Ed and Dorothy are looking forward to it.

On Oct. 4, there's an autographing party at the Banff Public Library for a recently published book. *Silent partners: Wives of National Park Wardens* was written by Ann Dixon, the wife of warden Fred Dixon. She collected anecdotes and photos from wardens' wives and compiled them into an anthology along with artwork. Dorothy's story is included and she's excited her life story is going to be published. She has one page in the 205-page book where she talks about coming to Canada from England, porcupines and Stoney Creek. She and Ed are actually heading to Stoney tomorrow with the reunion crew.

The next day, the group leaves for Stoney Creek cabin, once the Carleton family cabin, via horse and wagon or horseback. Dorothy is thrilled to see Ed on horseback again. He's riding with the younger wardens while Dorothy is in the wagon. They'll both be staying under canvas overnight and the organizer, Barb Anderson of the Warden Service Planning Committee, says, "Don't forget your long-johns and warm jackets."

It's autumn in the mountains and the sun isn't doing much to warm the air. It doesn't matter, the flames of friendship counter the chill. The Carletons are talking to many of their backcountry buddies like Jim Deegan, Bruno Engler, Halle Flygare, Smokey Guttman, Ole Hermanrude, Inez Peyto and Bert Pittaway. In the evening, the tents are filled with stories and songs. Dorothy leads an impromptu choir singing *Happy Trails* and other tunes she used to hum while working in the mountains. If she could, she'd grab Ed and head outside to look at the stars and listen to the water flow by. However, tonight there are clouds in the sky and it's much too cold to leave the cozy canvas.

It snows on the return home. The horses, their riders, the trees and the rocks are covered in a soft blanket. The snow muffles sounds and it's a good time for introspection. Ed has been retired for seven years and as he knows, things don't always stay the same.

Warden Smokey Guttman in earlier days, Tonquin Valley, Jasper National Park, spring 1956.
Photo: Carleton Family

Windy Cabin looks very much as it did 20 years ago. Bill Vroom, who has been a warden for 30 years, restored Windy Cabin in time for the centennial. It's open for inspection at the Whyte Museum. Ed and Dorothy are impressed. Snowshoes and lanterns hang on the wall, the woodstove has the oven in the pipe, the telephone looks like it could ring at any moment and there are enamel dishes ready to be used. Dorothy has a few of those dishes in the cupboards of Rainbow House. They're leftover souvenirs from her family's time in the backcountry.

War Bride Reunions

Memories are made and relived during war bride reunions. The Alberta War Brides Association is putting together a European tour for 160 war brides and their spouses. Dorothy and Ed have signed up for the May 1986 trip arranged by Rostad Tours in Calgary.

It's a trip of a lifetime and they're both looking forward to seeing family and some familiar places. Other familiar places will be harder to visit, especially the battlefields.

On May 7, Brian drives his parents into Calgary. The trip is beginning with a flourish: a reception held at city hall and hosted by Ralph Klein, the reporter who once hung out at the St. Louis Hotel is now the mayor of Calgary. Brian swears a little at the mayor as he tries to find parking along the busy city streets. So much traffic!

Mayor Klein shakes hands with Ed and Dorothy and tells them to enjoy the sandwiches and cake. The British consul general is there as well. After the treats and meeting fellow travellers, Ed and Dorothy are put on a bus for the Calgary International Airport. In the evening, around 8 p.m., the Carletons are on board KLM. First stop: Amsterdam. Dorothy and Ed sit together and enjoy a meal of airplane meat – tenderloin steak. It's about as good as elk tongue. With the meal over, Ed snoozes away. As we know, he can sleep anywhere. Dorothy, well, Dorothy has a lot to think about. She's returning to her homeland but a home without her parents. Things are going to be different.

The plane lands in the Netherlands at noon. Tour buses pick up the group and take them to Arnhem, about an hour's drive southeast of Amsterdam. The Battle of Arnhem was fought here during the Second World War and the 1977 film *A Bridge Too Far* is based on the events of the British 1st Airborne Division. It was supposed to be securing the bridge at Arnhem but couldn't. The bridge was captured by the Nazis.

Ed hadn't fought in the Netherlands but other Calgary Highlanders had. They were instrumental in the Battle of the Scheldt. Here in Arnhem, two Highlanders were captured while they were on loan to Britain. Lt.-Col. James (Jim) Taylor and Lieut. Lawrence (Larry) Kane were part of CANLOAN. Towards the end of the war, Canada had a surplus of army officers. The Second British Army was short. Officers from Canada were "loaned" to the Brits. Four Highlanders in total were loaned to the British. Taylor and Kane were with 7th Battalion Kings Own Scottish Borderers in Arnhem in September 1944.

Arnhem is built on the banks of the rivers Nederrijn and Sint-Jansbeek and Dorothy and Ed take a boat ride through the canals. It's a peaceful cruise through a town that had seen brutal action in the fall of 1944. It's a lot to take in and by the time Ed and Dorothy get to their hotel, Dorothy is hungry and tired. She climbs into bed with Ed at midnight.

There is no rest for the wicked and at 6 a.m., Dorothy is up and at it. She goes for a brisk walk and earns her breakfast of bread, hardboiled eggs, meat and cheese. It fills her up for the bus to Germany.

"Germany's countryside is beautiful," says Dorothy to Ed. "Everything is neat and tidy."

Ed nods. He never fought in Germany but he remembers the stories his Highlander mates told him at reunions. Germany wasn't so neat and tidy 40 years ago. He won't say anything to Dorothy. He doesn't want to dampen his wife's spirits with his war tales.

The tour bus arrives in Koln and the visitors go sightseeing. Dorothy is trying to spot the loo. She finds one but is told she has to pay to pee. No amount of pleading softens the toilet attendant and Dorothy dashes to find the money. It's a relief after she finds a couple of coins.

The tour continues into the Rhine Valley. They see castles and cathedrals and grapes. In a wine-making town, Ed and Dorothy drink a glass of good white wein (wine in German).

Before they tuck themselves into bed, Dorothy goes for a walk around the block. She hopes the exercise helps her sleep.

The evening walk didn't lead to a good night. Dorothy is up early. The hotel is too warm and she needs to get out. On her stroll, she discovers a lovely little market with eggs and flowers. She buys some apples for the journey to the Black Forest.

Touring about the Schwarzwald (Black Forest), they stop in Titisee, a town famous for making cuckoo clocks. At home, Dorothy knows the song of all the birds that sing in Banff. The birds here only sing every 30 minutes.

That evening, the Canadians cross into Switzerland. The group is staying at the Belle Vie Hotel near Lac Lucerne. On her evening stroll, Dorothy runs into a wedding party parading through the streets. They have a band playing and there's singing and dancing. Dorothy claps her hands and spins around as the music surrounds her. Once the revellers pass, the streets quiet down and Dorothy continues her walk. The lake is calm and stars shimmer on the water, reflections of the night sky. She is tired and heads to the hotel, looking forward to a good night's sleep.

Unfortunately, sleep is not going to happen here. The bed is the hardest, most uncomfortable thing in the world. It's worse than a backcountry bunk that's made with logs and spare fire hoses. Oh well.

Today, May 12, is Mother's Day in Canada. Dorothy takes her morning constitutional and wonders what her sons are doing. She hopes Mike and Terry are being especially nice to the mothers of their children today. For Dorothy, there's yet another cruise and a delicious meal. She dives into the cheese fondue appetizer. The main course is a veal stew with vegetables.

"This almost tastes like elk!" she jokes with Ed.

Ice cream is for dessert and then the entertainment comes out. Dorothy tries to blow an alpine horn, a several-metres-long traditional Swiss instrument. She takes a big breath in and lets it out and … nothing happens. She can't toot her horn about that, then. It's nightcap time anyway. She is up until 1 a.m.

The journey then takes Ed and Dorothy to Basel, where sixteenth-century philosopher Erasmus is buried, and then into France. The weather is getting warm and a tad uncomfortable for Canadians used to spring in the mountains, where you can have cold, wind, rain and snow all at once. Ed trips on a curb while getting off the bus in Colmar, France. Dorothy rushes over to him and administers first aid. He has a couple of scrapes on his hands.

To many travellers, France is a romantic country of champagne and lavender and well-dressed men and women. Indeed, the town of Colmar is easy to fall in love with, thanks to its narrow streets, tiny canals and quaint houses. For Ed though, the last time he was in France, he was a fighting soldier. He experienced things he can't describe, nor ever wants to talk about. We all know Ed as an easy-going, laid back man and he's not going to break out into dramatics now about life and death in the Second

World War. Nevertheless, thoughts of returning to France have been floating around in his mind for a while. How would he feel being here? Perhaps a piece of Quiche Lorraine and a glass of wine to wash it down with will wash away any lingering bad feelings. First, they have to order their lunch in French.

Dorothy and Ed get their Quiche Lorraine in Alsace Lorraine, where the French pie was created. The pastry is perfect and crumbles in their mouths like shortbread. The cheese is creamy with just the right amount of sharpness and the bacon, well, it's all *par-fait*. Ed is enjoying the meal with his wife. Life moves on no matter where he is.

Strasbourg is next and so is beer. It's too hot in France! Dorothy and Ed have supper with a war bride from Edinburgh. She now lives in Red Deer with her husband.

At breakfast, Ed spills juice all down the front of himself. Dorothy cleans him up and hopes his jacket will dry on the bus. They're driving to Paris and Dorothy wants Ed to look dapper in the City of Fashion. Along the way, they stop at the Champagne caves. Unfortunately, a war bride's purse is stolen there. (Not something to toast about.) This means a trip to the police station for everyone. An hour later, they're on their way to Paris. Without the handbag.

Of course, there's an evening cruise on the River Seine. Dorothy doesn't find it interesting and would rather be tucked in her hotel bed. The next morning, the tourists traipse all over Paris and see the usual attractions such as the Notre Dame Cathedral, Avenue des Champs-Élysées, Mona Lisa's smile and Napoleon's tomb. The prices in Paris are high but it doesn't stop Dorothy and Ed from enjoying wine and ice cream. (Not at the same time.)

The traffic in Paris seems to always be heavy and Dorothy thinks the bus driver is doing a great job of getting them around the crammed boulevards. She also notices a crazy amount of sex and peep shows being offered at different venues. Rows upon rows of neon signs advertising sex blink in the night, calling out to people.

"It's quite a sexy city," she says to Ed.

"I haven't noticed," he says.

Good answer.

Dorothy goes for a walk in the Paris rain in the morning. It's Thursday, May 16 and on the agenda is the Palace of Versailles. Louis XIV's magnificent home and gardens are way too busy for Dorothy and Ed. Tourists are shoulder to shoulder trying to get a look at where Marie Antoinette ate cake and sipped wine. Dorothy is incensed that it costs 2.50 francs to go to the bathroom. Only a queen could afford to sit on that throne at those prices!

Before arriving in Lille, the bus stops at the Canadian National Vimy Memorial at Vimy Ridge. The Battle of Vimy Ridge was fought in the First World War from Apr. 9 to 12, 1917. The Canadian victory here has been called a defining moment for Canada – Canada became a country in its own right, stepping away from Mother Britain. But it came at a steep cost. Around 11,285 Canadians lost their lives in France, 3,598 at Vimy.

Ed and Dorothy know people who fought in the Great War. Dorothy's father George is one of them. There aren't many First World War veterans left in the world. Their ranks get smaller and smaller every Remembrance Day parade.

The Holiday Day Inn in Vimy hosts the tour group. Dorothy and Ed have supper with Saskatchewan friends and wait an hour to be served their meals. Is this the French way? There's instant access to croissants for breakfast and Dorothy eats one with jam. Her appetite has been waning. Lack of sleep, the crowds of people at tourist sites, and the constant noise of the city are wearing her down. It's a good thing the war brides are going to England today.

In Calais, the group says an emotional goodbye to their bus driver. He got them everywhere, in every weather and traffic condition imaginable. Dorothy buys a bottle of duty-free sherry and some little gifts before boarding the hovercraft destined for England. She steps onto the amphibious vehicle and asks Ed to pinch her.

"Am I really going home?"

England has a surprise for the war brides. The Royal Marine Band is playing for them at the Dover terminal. It brings tears to Dorothy's eyes and Ed gives her a little hug. The mayor of Dover greets the group and they get a free glass of sherry. Dorothy can't believe the welcome and loves the attention. She hums along with the band as she sips her drink. Ed smiles at her. Now onto a new bus with a new driver. Southampton is their destination.

Ed last saw Southampton from a boat. That was when he was part of the 1942 Dieppe Raid. He shakes his head. He was just a kid then. His youngest son Brian, at 32, is older than Ed was that dark August morning. It's been a long time since Ed has thought about that day. He has worked through some of his war memories during his many hours in the backcountry. However, little tufts of painful thoughts still stick to his skin. Coming back to Europe proves they can't be brushed off easily. Meanwhile, Dorothy is rejoicing at being "home" and Ed realizes that for her, this is an amazing chance to reconnect with her own past.

At the Southampton Guildhall that Friday evening, May 16, there's a "do" with a Second World War theme: Dugout Evening. The air raid sirens are screaming and Dorothy and Ed get ration books. They have to exchange a coupon for a fish and chip meal wrapped in newspaper – just as Dorothy likes it. For entertainment, there are short plays and re-broadcasts of radio speeches and a band with a choir. The Southampton Musical Society is singing wartime songs. Dorothy is in her glory crooning her heart out and dancing the night away with Ed. It's a wonderful time and Ed appreciates the new memories he's making in Southampton.

The Banff couple is making all new memories during the next half of the trip. Dorothy and Ed are visiting places they've never been to before. Stonehenge, Worcester (where Worcestershire sauce was invented) and Carlisle Castle, where Mary Queen of Scots was imprisoned. Just over the border in Scotland, Dorothy and Ed play bridesmaid and groomsman to a couple getting "married" in Gretna Green.

Gretna Green is infamous for marrying young "runaway" English couples in the 18th-century. That's when English law changed and couples had to be 21 before they could marry without their parents' consent. As well, their marriage had to take place in a church. In Scotland, the law was different. All the young lovers had to do here was show up with two witnesses to be married. Dorothy and Ed have so much fun at the mock wedding at the Gretna Green Blacksmith Shop and giggle about it in their Glasgow hotel room.

The last time Ed was passing by Glasgow, the River Clyde had large silver balloons sprouting from it. The Clyde now looks like a regular river. The train ride through the Scottish countryside in the fall of 1940 had been a blur. The bus ride in 1986 is a delight! Ed wonders if the sheep he sees are descendants of the ones he saw a long time ago. Soon, he's counting them. He's much more relaxed than at the start of the trip and nods off.

The last half of the U.K. journey begins in Edinburgh. A good English breakfast of eggs, bacon, sausage, beans, tomatoes, fried bread and a strong cup of tea powers Dorothy through the city. The group returns to England with a stop in York. Dorothy and Ed are enjoying a piece of shepherd's pie at their hotel restaurant when Phyllis and her family walk in. What a surprise!

"I can't believe it!" Dorothy says, giving her sister-in-law and old friend a big squeeze.

"Russ isn't feeling well," says Phyllis, "so he's staying home in Birmingham."

It's like no time has passed. It's a great visit and the evening passes in an instant. Before both Carleton families know it, it's time to say goodbye. However, they'll have time together after the tour wraps up.

The trip is winding down. There are only three days left on the tour. The group hits Stratford and Oxford before travelling through Henley-on-Thames, northeast of Reading, on the way to London.

The Henley countryside is familiar to Dorothy. It's good to see it again. She thinks about her parents and her sister and wonders what she might be doing now if she hadn't met Ed. She wonders if she would have been as happy. These thoughts don't linger because they reach London, the city where Dorothy was born.

There's not much nostalgia here. London is busy, expensive and the food is terrible. Ed doesn't have a great time and can't find a loo when he really needs one. They take the Underground and have trouble finding the right trains going the right way. It's the last day of the war brides' trip and nerves are shot. The travellers are grumpy and tired. However, the big wind-up party on Sunday, May 25 rejuvenates them.

Everyone is dressed up for the evening event and there are cocktails and soup, roast beef for dinner with cream puffs for dessert. Then, the band starts up and the dancing begins with Dorothy and Ed leading the charge to the floor. Everyone is happy and sad at the end of the night. The journey is over and tomorrow, many of the war brides will fly home to Canada. For many of them, including Dorothy, Canada has been home for almost 40 years.

The Carletons' trip isn't over. They're staying a couple of days later than the group. Marjorie and her family are meeting them today and bringing them home to Witney. Dorothy can't wait to see her sister, brother-in-law and nephews. Nephew Derek picks them up and takes his aunt and uncle to his parents' home. There are hugs and kisses and pats on the cheek. Marjorie is 74 but Dorothy doesn't think she's changed a bit. Sadly, Melbourne has. He had heart surgery a few months ago and is moving slowly. Nevertheless, he has a glass of sherry when they toast their family reunion.

Nephew Roger and his wife Audrey arrive with their children later in the afternoon. Everyone sits down to an early afternoon dinner of turkey with all the trimmings. Marjorie is a great cook like their mother. The sisters keep the Fowler family tradition of a long stroll after supper. They chat during their walk into town. They peer into the shop windows before turning around for home and more food.

Being surrounded by family after a couple of weeks of being on the go helps Dorothy unwind. She sleeps in for the first time on the trip. Ed delivers her a cup of tea in bed. What a prince. The next couple of days are filled with pints at pubs, walks and talks. When there's a knock at Marjorie's door, it's Olive Openshaw. She has come to bring Dorothy and Ed to Reading.

Olive and her husband Dan open their home to their Canadian friends. They take the pair around the town, which has outgrown Dorothy's memory. In her mind, it's a small, quaint place. However, large housing projects have expanded Reading's borders. Olive drives her friend past her former home and 55 Grange Avenue is smaller than Dorothy remembers. The Fowler home is tiny yet the love that was cultivated there is as big as a mountain.

Dorothy is more of an "in the moment" person. She has had to be while living in Alberta. Nothing was routine in the backcountry. Here in Reading, she's allowing herself to look back. She's taking a few moments and thinking about the past, her past: a place without a husband or kids. She is grateful the Fowlers adopted her and gave her everything she needed. They believed in her and taught her she could do anything.

In the evening, Dorothy and Olive prove they still have it when it comes to performing. The women break out the songs and dance moves from the 40s. They can still kick as high and step to the quick beat, though a few glasses of sherry does grease the joints a little. Dorothy has made sure she's stayed in shape on the trip by walking in the mornings and evenings. Tomorrow, she'll be sitting on an airplane all day.

Olive and Dan drop off Dorothy and Ed at the airport. The Carletons have had a wonderful time on their trip but home is calling them. They have grandchildren to see and gardens to plant. Peter Perren and his wife Chris have added to the grandchild count with another girl. Dorothy is glad to be back at the House at the End of the Rainbow so Ed can rest. The voyage across the ocean has tired him and he's getting more and more confused. He's also getting headaches. That old war wound is making its presence felt.

Calgary Olympic Winter Games

Opening ceremonies for the Winter Olympics take place at Calgary's McMahon Stadium on Valentine's Day, Feb. 14, 1988. The world is watching as 1,423 athletes from 57 countries descend on the city. Not only are the Olympics memorable for the athletes, but for Mike and Sylvia, too.

Mike has been training for seven years to take his spot as an Olympic volunteer. He had helped develop the venues, including the Canmore Nordic Centre and a backup site at Mount Shark, as well as helped build an experienced team of volunteer chiefs. The chiefs eventually form a separate organization called Georgetown Event

Management and the friends became known as the Georgetown Old Boys. Through most of the preparations, Mike was chief of timekeeping. In the last year, he's been appointed chairman, cross-country skiing.

There are 295 volunteers on the cross-country skiing committee.

Sylvia is also a volunteer but she's naturally more suited to be a hostess of international teams. She's friendly, easy-going and speaks Swedish so this is why she starts out hosting the Swedish teams. She eventually becomes the hosting chairman for the Canmore Nordic Centre, coordinating hostesses for the various teams.

The volunteers have spent countless hours at the Olympic Volunteer Centre at McMahon Stadium, especially in the last year. Mike has a full-time job and most of his volunteer obligations occur in the evening or on weekends.

Through all of this, his children prevail. Pizza is a good bribe. There's a local pie joint called Coast to Coast near the Carletons' home and on many occasions, supper is from Coast to Coast. Ingrid, Erik and Patrick are involved in the opening ceremonies at the Canmore Nordic Centre. They're "jackrabbits" that parade into the stadium.

Ed and Dorothy don't go to any Olympic events. Ed doesn't like large crowds of unfamiliar people or being out in the cold for a long time. They did watch the Olympic torch relay when it came through Banff. The grandparents are also a huge help to Mike and Sylvia throughout the Olympics and during the lead up. The grandparents drive their three grandchildren to Canmore for their opening ceremony rehearsals as well as keep the kids for most of the 16 days of the Games. (Uncle Brian also does his share of looking after the children.) Patrick, Mike's youngest, is happy to have grandma's cooking for the two weeks and not attend school. When he returns to class at Brentwood Elementary in northwest Calgary, the other students are envious of his long break.

Banff is not hosting any Olympic events. CODA's previous attempt to hold events in the national park had been met with opposition from conservation groups. Canmore, a mountain town outside the park, becomes the venue for Nordic sports. Alpine skiing is being held at the Nakiska ski resort, in Kananaskis, also outside of the park. Karen Percy, a Banff-born skier, wins Canada's first medal, a bronze in downhill. Some last-place finishes also make headlines around the world. Eddie "the Eagle" Edwards, a British ski-jumper, and the Jamaican bobsled team are fan favourites. Overall, Canada ranks 12th in the medal standings when the Calgary Olympics end.

The Games leave a lasting impression on Mike. There were many stressful moments related to weather or protocol but otherwise, he calls the Olympics a highlight of his life. He met so many people from all over the world and made many new and good friends. Mike says the volunteers on the cross-country skiing committee did an amazing job. Many of them continued with their commitment to the sport and became the heart of the enduring legacy of the Canmore Nordic Centre.

***

The Canadian National Parks Act is undergoing an amendment. Ecological integrity is being added to the legislation as a formal policy objective. Despite not being employed by Parks Canada anymore, Ed thinks it's a step in the right direction. He sees limiting commercial development in the parks as a good thing. The Canadian Rockies have also been recognized as a UNESCO (United Nations Educational, Scientific and Cultural Organization) World Heritage Site. A World Heritage status designation is an honour and also a tourist draw. Sites can be delisted if not properly managed or protected.

Dorothy is worried that major developments will descend on Banff National Park if Banff residents vote for self-government. The Town of Banff has been weighing the issue in 1988. Dorothy favours the status quo, and thinks Parks Canada should maintain control over projects.

Ed is having second thoughts. He has seen how much time Parks puts into managing town business. In fact, 40 per cent of the superintendent's attention goes to matters involving the townsite. Self-government would allow Parks officials to focus on issues in the park.

The couple votes on Jun. 13, 1988, in a plebiscite calling for incorporation. Sixty-five per cent of Banff residents want to be self-governing and the process moves ahead to the next stage.

***

The Whyte Museum is hosting an open house in November 1989 and Dorothy is asked to bake cookies in Windy Cabin's woodstove oven. She claps her hands and says she would love to show people how to make cookies the old fashioned way.

The fire is crackling and the smell of chocolate and vanilla wafts through the air on Saturday, Nov. 21. Windy Cabin reminds Dorothy so much of her Bow Summit home, her first home in the backcountry, that she almost forgets she's in the middle of Banff. She sings Happy Trails while tending to the stove and her cookies. Ed is there, too and dressed in his formal warden uniform for the occasion. Two hundred and fifty people visit the cabin and get a chocolate chip cookie, a song and many, many stories from Dorothy. She is in her element and glows from the conversation and attention. (As well as from the heat of the stove.)

Dorothy's baking session during the open house is so popular she's invited to bake cookies the next year. The museum's membership coordinator writes her a letter and says Dorothy is the highlight of the weekend.

It is time like that that the visitors have the opportunity to have a very special, memorable experience with the museum. Thank you for providing the opportunity.

Sincerely, Barbara Parker

Dorothy continues hosting cookie demos at Windy Cabin for the Whyte Museum and it becomes an annual tradition during Back to Banff Days. She bakes for her grandchildren as well.

As of 1990, Dorothy and Ed have numerous Carleton and Perren grandkids. They all like coming over to Rainbow House for goodies, a walk and their grandmother's accent. Dorothy has kept a touch of her English lilt.

Dorothy and Ed baking cookies in Windy Cabin at the Whyte Museum, August, 1989. Photo: Carleton Family

A Mountain Town and Personal Shift

Dorothy has never lost her reverence for the British monarchy. She has the chance to see Queen Elizabeth in person in June 1990 when a fancy note arrives in the mail addressed to Ed. He and Dorothy have been invited to Calgary for the Calgary Highlanders Grand Reunion on Jun. 30. The Calgary Highlanders and the King's Own Calgary Regiment are going to be presented with a new Queen's Colour at a Trooping the Colour ceremony. Dorothy cannot contain her excitement and breaks out into song: *God Save the Queen.*

A day before the event, Friday, Jun. 29, Ed and Dorothy drive into Calgary. They attend an elegant gala dinner at Mewata Armoury and have a great time talking to military friends. The next day, Dorothy, Mike, Sylvia, Terry and Brian drive to McMahon Stadium while Ed is bused over to the event. He sits in a special section reserved for the "old guard."

"Is the Queen calling my husband old?" Dorothy laughs. She glances at Ed's thick white hair and runs a hand through her own mane, which is brown with a few grey "highlights."

Dorothy and Ed the day of the Calgary Higlanders 80th Anniversary and Queen's visit. Photo: Carleton Family

It's brutally hot in Calgary — in the '30s (over 86 F). Terry is worried about his dad and the heat. Is Ed going to be able to parade in front of the Queen without toppling over? Dorothy is worried that Ed won't be able to find his way to the field from the stands. She speaks to a young Highlander and tells him to "keep an eye on Ed."

A new Queen's Colour marks a special anniversary or event in a regiment's history. Queen Elizabeth is the Colonel-in-Chief of the Highlanders and she'll be presenting the unit along with the King's Own Calgary Regiment with new regimental flags (colours) to celebrate the inception of the first Calgary unit, the 103rd Regiment (Calgary Rifles) 80 years previously.

The Carletons are only a handful of the 35,000 people at the stadium in the bright sunlight watching the parade and the Queen's inspection. She gives a speech highlighting the military history of the regiments and talks about the First World War and Second World War.

Forty-five years have passed since the victory celebrations of 1945.
All of you participating in the parade today and in the dedication of this new Colour are taking part in another significant event in your regimental histories.

The chain of history that links the past and the present is remarkably strong here today and will be well illustrated in the Museum of the Regiments, which I was happy to open this morning.

You young men and women of the King's Own Calgary Regiment and the Calgary Highlanders will, I know, be proud inheritors of the honours and traditions of your regiments.

I share your pride in being part of two such distinguished Canadian militia regiments.

Queen Elizabeth

Ed parades past the Queen with his back straight and his head high. The early summer heat is no match for the Calgary Highlander veteran. He's got this.

Her royal highness doesn't go to Banff this tour. She's off to celebrate Canada Day in Ottawa. Since her last visit to Banff several years ago, the town has been officially incorporated as a municipality (Jan. 1, 1990). It's the first of its kind in Canada – a town in the middle of a national park. Because of this, the townsite boundaries are limited, there's a commercial development cap and its population is capped at 8,000 residents. Not capped: the elk population.

Elk are moving into town to escape the jaws of wolves. (More elk are actually being killed by trains and vehicles on the roads in the park.) A group of local people in Banff have formed an elk advisory committee to consult with Parks Canada about the extraordinary amount of ungulates. Dorothy counts 28 elk on her lawn in one day. She doesn't like when the animals make holes in the grass, eat her prized roses and leave droppings everywhere. She has to watch her step when she goes outside to make sure her foot doesn't end up in a pile of round, brown, squishy marbles.

Dorothy picks up the "elk nuts" with a large metal dustpan. However, when the bull elk are around, she needs help — especially in the fall. Elk breed in autumn and the bulls get territorial. They can be aggressive and charge and kick. Ed knows how to chase the testosterone-fueled animals away.

In his early 70s, Ed is not one to loll at home. He walks with Dorothy into town and loves to attend parties and be social. He really enjoys his painting and works through numerous sketches and drafts until he's happy with the final result. He helps at Windy Cabin during open houses, still looking handsome in his warden uniform while his wife hums around baking cookies. Nevertheless, he is not doing well physically. His memory is not what it used to be and he is increasingly having trouble getting around. It's good he has Dorothy — his rock. He can count on her for anything. The two are often seen strolling slowly together, Dorothy holding on to Ed's arm, on the sidewalks of Banff.

There's one part of Ed that never changes: his smile. Dorothy knows how to get him to grin. Friends drop in to see him and know that to spark a chat, all they need to do is bring up the lost mines and cabins. Ed has found a few mines and cabins and counts the Queen of the Hills discovery as a high point for him.

***

It's the middle of 1991 and Ed is slowing down. His emotions are coming close to the surface. Never one to cry in the past, Ed tears up at a Remembrance Day display. Local school kids have done illustrations to mark Nov. 11 and the art is hanging at the legion. Ed can't maintain his usual calm, cool and collected demeanour. It's another sign the shadows of dementia are creeping into his mind. By 1994, he's basically non-verbal.

He can't form words and is frustrated when he tries to talk. Dorothy can always make him smile though.

Dorothy is Ed's caregiver. She is with him from morning until bedtime. She dresses him and undresses him, helps him with shaving and feeds him all while maintaining her own daily routine required to run a household and keep her community contacts. Terry and Mary Lou spell off Dorothy once in a while so she can do other things outside of the home. Of course, Brian spends innumerable hours with his mother and father and Mike and Sylvia come when they can.

Dementia erodes Ed's ability to write. For a man who made such copious notes and wrote pages upon pages of diary entries throughout his career, it's heartbreaking. Dorothy prompts and encourages him to write things down on a note pad. On sunny days, she brings Ed outside to listen to the birds or look at all the colours in the garden. He nods his head to acknowledge what's being said to him. In June 1994, Ed is placed in the Banff Hospital. He never comes home.

On the evening of Aug. 7, Brian and Dorothy are at the hospital with Ed. He's not doing well. When he shakes Brian's hand at the end of the visit, Brian is astounded at the strength of his father's grip – strong. Despite being ill and bedridden, Ed is still a powerful man.

Terry and Mary Lou are on vacation in the States when they get the call that Ed's health is failing. They had just arrived in Sandpoint, Idaho with their son Kevin and his friend. Terry immediately turns around and heads back to Alberta by himself. He's too late.

Ed dies on Aug. 8, 1994. He was 76. He was predeceased by Russ, who died in July 1992.

Mike was with Ed the day before he passed away. The son's final recollection of being with his father was talking to him at his bedside in the hospital. Mike described the scene outside to Ed: the birds, the mountains and how nice everything looked. Ed couldn't speak but Mike could tell from his eyes and expression that he knew he was loved.

Goodbye to a Very Fine Man

Dorothy is totally distraught over Ed's passing, as is Brian. Ed didn't suffer too long and no doubt Dorothy is glad of that. It's small consolation in a time of grief.

"He's at peace now," says Terry.

For Terry, the loss of his father leaves a huge hole in his heart. He'll miss him and his movie-star smile each and every day.

The local newspaper, *The Banff Crag & Canyon*, writes that Banff has lost a friend. With him – goes a wealth of local history. There are many tears shed for Ed and many hugs for his family.

More than 200 people are at the funeral at Banff Park Church on Aug. 12 to say goodbye to the "very fine man," as Peter Perren calls him. Peter delivers the eulogy while his brother, Reverend Martin Perren, leads the ceremony. The pallbearers are men of the Banff Park Warden Service including Bill Vroom, Don Mickle and

Ed, Peppi and Dorothy at the House at the End of the Rainbow in 1990. Photo: Carleton Family

Tim Auger. A cadet piper plays as a tribute to Ed's Calgary Highlander ties and there's a Colour Guard. The Last Post is played by Louis Trono. A reception is held at the Banff Legion afterwards.

The loss of Ed is felt acutely by his sons. Mike is thankful for the practical skills his father handed down to him at a young age. These included chopping wood, starting a fire, tying a fish hook and using a knife for wood carving. He also taught Mike to have respect for the horses and respect for nature. Mike loved his dad and admired him as a man. Ed showed Mike how to respect others through his interactions with other people.

Terry admired his father, too. They had a good relationship and Terry learned to take pride in himself no matter what he's doing.

Brian is no different than his older brothers. Respect and love of nature are ingrained in Brian because of Ed. No one will be able to replace him. Brian followed his dad into Parks and is on staff in Banff. His first job with Parks Canada was as a sign fabricator and silk screener. Parks closed the sign shop and he was then hired in the painting department. After three years of seasonal work, he moved to Lake Louise for a year until a full-time Parks job came up in Banff.

George Morasch, Ed's longtime childhood friend and fellow Calgary Highlander veteran, is at the funeral along with his wife Fern. The couple meets Ed's sons and isn't surprised at all that they are like their father. George tells Dorothy how much Ed's friendship meant to him. He will miss him.

Dorothy is comforted by the words people say to her after the funeral. They tell her Ed was a great man who loved his family and the outdoors. He helped save lives on the park peaks and roads. If someone needed a hand, he was there. He knew every nook and cranny of the land and every old cabin and mine. He was a part of Banff during an era like no other.

If it wasn't for Ed, John Laut doesn't know what he'd be doing. John says Ed was the strongest influence on his career as a forester. Ed suggested John return to college in the late 1950s and he eventually becomes a research forest pathologist. Ed also nurtured John's love of the Alberta Rockies.

Four days after the funeral Mike and his family, along with Brian, scramble Temple Mountain. There's not much talking as they go up the rock but it's a good time for reflection. Another place to think in peace is found along the Sundance Trail. There, you'll find a memorial bench overlooking an arm of the Bow River. This is for Ed. As a warden in 1973, he spent a lot of time in this area. The resting spot sits about a kilometre and a half from the Cave and Basin trailhead. Brian likes to bike out here in nice weather. It's a great place to remember Ed.

Dorothy and Brian at Ed's bench: *In Loving Memory Of Park Warden Ed Carleton 1917-1994 The Carleton Family.*
Photo: Carleton Family

CHAPTER FIFTEEN

LIFE MOVES ON

ADAPTING AND NEW WAYS OF THINKING

The House at the End of the Rainbow is quieter for several months. Dorothy is finding her way without Ed. They had been together for almost 50 years and Dorothy is learning how to live life on her own. Towards the end of Ed's life, Dorothy and her husband were inseparable as she cared for him. It was tough to see such a strong man go downhill. She has many wonderful memories to keep her going.

It's the memories of the Calgary Highlanders who are buried overseas that tug on George Morasch's heart. When the Highlanders returned from the Second World War, there was no PTSD (post-traumatic stress disorder) diagnosis and no one really talked about their feelings despite seeing, hearing and experiencing great tragedies. George knows all of this. He says they grieved in silence. He doesn't open up until 1995, after returning from a trip to Europe with his wife Fern. The pair visits many of the places George had been during the war – including Normandy. It's then he decides to tell his story. Ed's experiences are long gone but George's stories are a living link to a history that might otherwise be lost.

After Ed's death, the Carletons lay a wreath in his memory at the Remembrance Day ceremony in Banff. This year, and for many years to follow, it's Dorothy who arranges it with the legion as well as picks the family member who will place it on the Banff Legion cenotaph. After the service, the public is welcomed into the legion. There's always a seat reserved for Dorothy. She's a VIP, dressed smartly in her Ladies Auxiliary uniform. Many people come and talk to her and she chats away with them. All conversation ceases though when the Calgary Police Service Pipe Band begins to play.

Music fills the air and Dorothy sways along to the marches and the reels. There's one person in particular who she loves to watch play. His name is Bill Crabbe. Bill worked with Ed one summer over 35 years ago. They kept up their friendship and Bill made many trips to Banff to visit Ed and Dorothy —and later, just Dorothy.

Bill has been playing the bagpipes for many years. He grew up listening to his mother's Scottish music and her stories of Scotland. It developed into a pride for his Scottish heritage. In the mid-1960s, Bill had a chance to learn to play the bagpipes and he jumped at it. His instructor was Jock Ritchie, a chief-inspector with Calgary police. Bill started playing with the Calgary Highlanders but in 1973, realized that Calgary was the only police department in Western Canada without a pipe band. Bill was granted permission from Calgary police Chief Brian Sawyer to form a police pipe band.

In April 1973, Bill recruited "wannabe" pipers, drummers and instructors and two years later, the Calgary City Police Pipe Band made its debut in the 1975 Stampede parade. (The band won "best pipe band" honours.)

Dorothy and Bill Crabbe at the Royal Canadian Legion Branch 26 in Banff on Remembrance Day, 2005. Photo: Carleton Family

About seven years later, Bill got a call from the Banff Legion telling him that the Calgary Highlanders Pipe Band had to cancel its Remembrance Day appearance and asking if the police band could perform instead. Bill says the band happily said yes and that's how it started playing in the Banff Legion Remembrance Day parade. It's also a chance to visit with Dorothy, someone he thinks is a wonderful person. Dorothy thinks highly of Bill, too.

"I hope Bill Crabbe is here," she says each Nov. 11.

***

Lately, Dorothy needs a hand here and there at home. Her sons and friends help with certain chores and tasks. Brian pitches in and does a lot of the yard maintenance. When the bulls are hanging out on the lawn in the fall, Dorothy calls the wardens to chase away the elk.

The Banff National Park Elk Management Strategy is rolled out in 1995 by Parks and the elk advisory committee. One of the initiatives is to lessen elk-human conflicts. In the rutting season, bulls can charge not only people but cars, trucks and bicycles. Dorothy knows all this and stays at least the recommended distance, 30 m (98 ft), from the animals when she's out and about on foot.

Dorothy has been keeping active but when Peter Perren zips by on his motorcycle, she can't say no to a lift. Peter is no longer a warden, he's a lawyer. In 1980, he had a 620-m (2,000 ft) fall while on a Parks Canada training climb on Mount Logan in the Yukon. That fall prompted a career change for him.

Today, he's driving a Honda Gold Wing touring motorcycle. He says a "midlife crisis" coerced him into buying it. However, being a family man, Peter bought a bike that has a full backrest and armrests so he can put his kids on the back and they're not going to fall off. When Peter asks 77-year-old Dorothy if she wants to hop on, she can't resist.

The pair drive down Banff Avenue and Dorothy, with a helmet on, is waving madly at all her friends. Of course, they don't know who the rebel senior is on the motorcycle. Dorothy is chuckling away at the puzzled looks she's getting. She bets her friends will soon be telling her stories about the stranger waving to them from a roaring bike.

Peter takes Dorothy a few kilometres outside of town and to the Lake Minnewanka Loop. It's a scenic drive and passes by the Cascade Fire Road, the road Dorothy took many times with Ed to get to Stoney Creek. She wonders what Ed would say if he saw her on the motorcycle. He'd probably laugh.

Peter asks Dorothy if she wants to go up Mount Norquay. She sure does! They zoom down the highway and then wind their way up the hill, flying around the switchbacks. It's exhilarating in both speed and dar ing. Dorothy has never done anything like this before.

***

The Canadian Parks and Wilderness Society (CPAWS)[99] is worried about the commercial exploitation of Banff National Park. It has asked UNESCO to strike Banff's World Heritage status. CPAWS believes that the park's ecological integrity isn't being considered due to the planning of commercial developments, the widening of the Trans-Canada Highway and Sunshine Village's ski hill expansion.

In 1996, the Banff-Bow Valley Study, a comprehensive study authored by a team of independent experts commissioned by the federal government, is released. It admits to the struggle between preservation and development. More than five million visitors came to Banff National Park in 1995. There are just over 9,000 people who live in Banff and Lake Louise and 1,300 businesses are licensed to operate in the park. All the use is causing stress on the land and to wildlife. The study, considered a landmark document, makes 500 recommendations allowing for the long-term management of Banff while maintaining ecological integrity and appropriate levels of development and continued access for visitors. The study also establishes these as baselines for all national parks, not only Banff.

It isn't easy to marry development and ecology. There are many different stakeholders, groups, organizations and opinions. Parks Canada and interest groups study managing ecological integrity over the next few years.

The Banff townsite brings dollars to the region: $700 million annually and 18,000 jobs. However, wildlife doesn't go to the bars like in Wild Bill's time (remember he carried in a live lynx). Animals need habitat — and it's disappearing.

Ways of life are disappearing in the park, too. Wardens don't live full-time in the backcountry. Dorothy is a living link to another time and she's in demand. She's asked to talk to students at Banff Elementary and in June 1999, she is featured in the newspaper.

The *Banff Crag & Canyon's* headline is "Banff Senior Living Life as an Adventure." Dorothy tells the stories of her youth and how she became a shorthand typist at age 14. She talks about the broken biscuits her father brought home to her and Marjorie in Reading.

---

99. CPAWS was formally the National and Provincial Parks Association of Canada.

She says she was an Air Raid Warden in the Second World War and then explains how the war brought her and Ed together. She says she fell in love with the Canadian wild and couldn't imagine her life any other way. She is always living life to the fullest.

It's true. During celebrations in the Bow Valley to mark the United Nations International Year of the Older Persons, Dorothy was part of a musical production in December. She taught those "older persons" to sing from their bellies and not be afraid of their own voices. She's again featured in the newspaper and called the *Pride of Banff*.

On her 80th birthday, she takes the family hiking up Sunshine Meadows. Everyone is there: Mike, Terry and Peter and their families, as well as Brian and friends. Dorothy's as perky as ever and, as always, singing her lungs out to the bears and the squirrels.

There's another milestone to celebrate: Castle Mountain Hostel, aka the Ike Inn, is marking 50 years in October. The hostel, now under Hostelling International management, still shelters visitors to the mountains. The majority of people staying at the hostel are Canadians but tourists from the U.K. and Australia are also frequent visitors.

Telling Stories and Being a Friend

Depending on where you stand in the long-running calendar debate, the year 2000 either ushers in a new millennium or the celebrations are one year too early. Either way, the streets of Banff are teeming with revellers and many are outside of Wild Bill's Legendary Saloon (how apropos) watching the big clock tick down 1999.

The Y2K bug has some people worried that the world is going to end or at least come to a screeching halt because computers around the globe are going to stop working. Dorothy, humming Auld Lang Syne in between sherry sips, is having none of this nonsense. She lived through the Second World War. However, this new era will be without Ed.

Ed is not forgotten. He remains in his family's memories, warden stories and his discoveries. He's also mentioned in a book of poems, Mid-river, published in 1981. Canadian writer David Zieroth wrote the poem, *Death of a Warden*, about a warden dying from a horse kick to the kidneys. Ed is not the man dying but was supposedly also kicked by a horse.

The author says he wrote the poem many years ago when he was working as a park naturalist in Kootenay National Park. Ed's story was common knowledge and a legend passed down from warden to warden.

The warden service had a certain aura back then (and perhaps still does - I've not been connected with the parks now for many decades), and legends and myths were part of their charm and power. Whether Mr. Carleton was actually kicked is perhaps open to debate although the story was accepted as true among those who told it.

David Zieroth

Banff wardens and their wives keep in touch with Dorothy and she's invited to socials and reunions. They'll always be a part of her extended family. The park has taught her so much and she is invited to talk about her experiences for a Parks Canada project.

Twelve Banff-area seniors are asked for their stories in 2000. Parks is doing an oral history project on the industrial history of the Bow Valley. It is looking for information on past practices and knowledge about the area and recording the histories. Carleton friends Jack Chisholm and Bruno Engler are among the people providing anecdotes.

At a thank-you lunch Parks holds for the storytellers, Dorothy is given a copy of a plaque that is going to go on Stoney Creek cabin, Dorothy's former home. The monument is to the Carletons and there's a photo of her in front of the cabin and a write up about the family. The warden hut has been recently restored by volunteers.

It isn't until Jun. 3, 2001 that the commemorative plaque is unveiled at Stoney Creek. Dorothy, 81, is there to see her family and other backcountry warden families honoured. The event is not only a celebration but a reunion. Dorothy is flown in a helicopter to the area, along with other attendees. Mike, Sylvia and Brian cycle to the cabin on the cool and grey day. Also attending are members of past Stoney Creek resident families: the Fullers (1945 to unknown), the Woledges (post-1945 to pre-1949), the Krafts (1953 to 1954) and the Coggins (1959 to 1965).

Dorothy is overwhelmed with emotion. She remembers the days with Ed and when her two older sons were little boys. However, she dispenses with the tears and gives a speech. She talks about the remoteness of the cabin, drawing water for baths and other things that made the life of a backcountry family unique.

Frank Coggins, who had one of the longest warden stays at Stoney, says while he lived there, a grizzly liked to use the door jamb as a scratching post. Colleen, Frank's wife, was only 16 years old when she moved to the cabin. Like Dorothy, she knew little about using a wood stove to cook. In fact, she didn't know how to cook at all.

***

There has been a moratorium on development in communities within national parks. As well, anyone living in Banff has to be employed in Banff. In 2000, *The Panel on the Ecological Integrity's* work is released. It discovers that Parks Canada isn't doing enough to protect parks. The panel makes 127 recommendations and federal Heritage Minister Sheila Copps, the minister responsible for national parks, uses the findings to create an action plan. The strategy is to restore and ensure national park ecological integrity is "the centrepiece of every decision we make for the future of Canada's national parks."

Out of the action plan comes a new Canada National Parks Act in February 2001. It's not something Dorothy pays close attention to, but since Banff is a Parks town, she hears the news. She's glad wilderness regions in the Banff area have been declared and conservation is a priority. The chatter around the table while she's serving coffee at the Banff Seniors' Centre or helping out with its Monday lunch program always turns back to family. Dorothy tries to make it to her grandchildren's birthdays and no matter what the theme is, she'll be participating. At one Perren party, the Hawaiian shirts and leis have Dorothy hula dancing with the kids. She is not just young at heart.

Don't you dare call Dorothy a senior! Absolutely not. She volunteers around town with a number of seniors' organizations and sings in the Banff Senior Citizens Choir but she's not elderly. At 82, she is fitter than most 42 year olds. She's ageless.

There's a 24-year age difference between Dorothy and Cheryl Craver. Yet, they feel no gap. The two became friends a few years ago when Dorothy was 69 and Cheryl was 45 but they have a longer history than that.

In the 1980s, Cheryl worked summers at the Johnston Canyon resort's front desk. She had heard stories about a woman from England who pushed her babies in a pram for miles to have apple pie with the resort's owner. Cheryl put a face and a name to the story when she met Dorothy.

After Cheryl moved to Banff for good in 1989, she saw Dorothy and Ed out at functions and parties. Cheryl was also a volunteer and played the piano at the hospital where Dorothy was singing. Someone suggested they team up.

They did. While Ed was alive, Dorothy and Cheryl were mainly acquaintances who made people sing, tap their toes and clap their hands. One day, Cheryl, who lived near the Carletons' Rainbow House, noticed Dorothy was walking alone. Ed had died.

Cheryl invited Dorothy over for supper one evening and then it turned into a regular thing. They had more in common than they realized. Both are adopted, love the outdoors and have similar personalities. They're kindred spirits.

The friends talk about almost everything and anything under the sun. There are discussions about England and what is going on there now and what Dorothy had left behind. They talk about music and debate song lyrics. They talk about Dorothy's sons and the antics of their kids. They talk about Banff and the weather. The one thing they don't talk about is Ed. It has taken Dorothy a while to accept he's gone. Now that she has, she settles into a routine that's all her own. It's another chapter of her life and she's only at the beginning.

Hiking, Family and Milestone Birthdays (Just don't call Dorothy old.)

Another oral history project by Banff National Park takes Dorothy on a road trip in the summer of 2002. She's part of a team identifying the warden cabins and road camps of yesteryear. Parks is researching park use trends, as well as wildlife and human interaction. Twelve people are interviewed, including Dorothy and former Parks helicopter pilot Jim Davies. Jim tells a story about Dorothy.

Jim spent some time as a child at Saskatchewan River Crossing. His father Bert was a warden stationed there. A couple of years ago, Jim was back in the area, near Bow Lake, hunting for a cabin. He could not find it.

"We need Dorothy!" he said to his wife Sue.

Dorothy's House at the End of the Rainbow is her haven. It hasn't changed much since she moved in with Ed in the 1960s. The roses grow abundantly as do the elk pellets on the lawn. A company called Guenther's does most of Dorothy's yard work now. She always rewards the workers with her Rocky Roads squares.

Lake O'Hara is an annual fall hiking adventure for Dorothy and Cheryl. They take the bus up the Yoho National Park road to where the larches glow a burnished gold. It's an enchanting place for Dorothy's 85th birthday. The family stays at the Elizabeth Parker Hut, an Alpine Club of Canada cabin that has shared dormitory accommodation. Strangers sleep side-by-side on two wide bunk bed platforms. Dorothy is on the lower bunk and two German men keep her up all night with their snoring.

Brian and Terry bring up huge coolers filled with wine, beer and food. No one is going hungry or thirsty. The other hikers and climbers using the hut as a home base gnaw on granola bars while the Carletons feast on lamb chops.

Dorothy uses the outhouse like everyone else. The air high up at this elevation (2,040 m / 6,700 ft) is crisp in September. She won't be surprised to see snow on the ground in the morning. Back in the large and open living room, she sits close to the woodstove and begins to sing. It's not long before she is joined by other voices.

Num-Ti-Jah Lodge is hosting Dorothy and several others as part of a Heritage Fireside Series in 2005. Brian Bindon organizes the talks examining the "tales and energies of women" that have been essential to the warden service. The second session is cut into two parts: the early pioneers, like Dorothy, in Banff's district years, followed by a segment about the modern era. One of the moderators of the Apr. 2 event, titled *(not so) Silent Partners and Woman Wardens*, is Kathy Calvert, one of Parks' first women wardens. She asks Dorothy how she became involved in the mountain warden life. We all know the answer to that, as Dorothy likes to quip: "I thought I was coming to live on a gopher ranch."

Responding to the question about what she learned about herself in the backcountry, Dorothy says she became self-sufficient.

"It gave me self-esteem. At least I like to think it gave me so much confidence in myself."

Dorothy's friend Flo Spear dies in May 2006. She was about two months shy of her 101st birthday. For 27 years, Flo was the famous " mom" of the Ike Inn (now known as Castle Mountain Wilderness Hostel). Many people around the world have fond memories of Flo and her beautiful Chesapeake dogs.

At 88, Dorothy walks at a quick pace. It's the same with hiking. She and Cheryl go to the Ink Pots, tiny ponds made by underground springs, in the summer of 2007. The trail starts at the busy but beautiful Johnston Canyon, a spot both friends know well. The pair of older hikers actually pass some younger hikers on the slow and steady incline. It's not Dorothy's intention to get to the ink pots first. She knows this isn't a race and her only goal is to enjoy the day. At the ink pots meadow, Dorothy and Cheryl sit down for lunch. That's when one of the women they passed stops at their bench to talk to Dorothy.

"Just how old are you anyway?" she asks.

Dorothy giggles.

The Perrens take Dorothy on a few of their day hikes. They go to Rockbound Lake, near Castle Mountain and Dorothy's former home at Eisenhower Lodge. Rockbound is one of two lakes in the area that Ed used to help stock with fish.

Top left: Dorothy hiking Tower Lake. Photo: Peter Perren.

Top right: Dorothy and Cheryl hiking Lake O'Hara.
Photo: Cheryl Craver

Sunshine Meadows hike. Bottom (seated left to right): Moe Vroom (Bill Vroom's wife), Peter Perren's son Alex, Peter Perren, Dorothy, Peter's daughter Heidi Perren, Peter's wife Chris Perren. (Standing) Peter's daughter Meredith Perren.
Photo: Perren Family

Rockbound had cutthroat trout and Tower Lake was stocked with splake, a hybrid of lake trout. The splake didn't survive in Tower. The water was too shallow and froze.

At one point on the trail, Dorothy thinks she might not be able to make it to Rockbound. She's tired from the steep climbing. However, she rallies and completes the 15-km (9.3 m) round trip. She's going to need a hearty meal.

Friday nights is fish and chips for Dorothy and Cheryl at the Georgetown Inn in Canmore. It has a fireplace and a Tudor-style English pub could almost pass for a real British watering hole. Almost. Hanging on the wall are old photos from the warden service, including pictures from Cuthead College.

On Sunday afternoons, the friends often drive to Vermilion Lakes, a favourite spot of Dorothy's. She used to stroll along the path with Ed or her friend Em Chisholm. Em had two boys (one who became a warden) and she swapped anecdotes with Dorothy. They wondered if raising girls would be easier.

Vermilion Lakes is a popular location for photographers because of the spectacular view of Mount Rundle. The mountain looks like a giant rock cut in half. When the lake water isn't frozen, the crag is reflected in it. It's peaceful and Dorothy and Cheryl come out here with cappuccinos for a stroll or sometimes they just sit and drink in the landscape.

Dorothy always sees people she knows at Vermilion Lakes. As a warden's wife and a volunteer in the community, she has met many people through the years. Nevertheless, there are always new people coming to Banff, especially with the parks service.

Cheryl and Dorothy are driving to supper out at Johnston Canyon one night when they spot flashing lights up ahead. It's a Parks truck. A warden gets out and stops Cheryl's vehicle. Dorothy is worried someone or something is hurt.

"What's happened?" she asks the warden through the open window.

"We're looking for park passes," he says. "You need a pass if you're in the park. Like right now."

To Cheryl's dismay, her pass is expired. Thankfully, the warden lets them off the hook. Dorothy thinks that with over 60 years spent in the park, she shouldn't need a pass. But, the brief brush with the law has excited her.

"You know," she says to Cheryl when their vehicle's rolling again, "it's hard to believe there are 25 years between us because we have so much fun together. You do have fun, don't you?"

Of course, Cheryl does. It's hard not to when Dorothy is around. She's always smiling, always happy. She has her concerns about things but they never bring her down. Another friend, Sally Macdonald, feels the same way about Dorothy. They live up the alley from each other and Sally sees the "plucky little ray of sunshine" walking by her house almost daily.

Sally and Dorothy are introduced to each other at a Terry Fox Run around 2008. Then, they begin chatting when Dorothy heads to or from downtown. There is a large age gap but again, it's only a number and soon, the two are sharing cups of tea, stories and songs. Dorothy tells the young mother about her childhood in Reading, as well as the move to the backcountry.

"Are you still afraid of bears after all your years in the districts?" asks Sally, who has a healthy respect for the animals.

"No," says Dorothy. "But I wouldn't want to meet one while I was on the way to the loo!"

***

At any holiday or birthday celebration, Dorothy is surrounded by family. She has more family than ever as her grandchildren marry and then have children of their own. Dorothy likes having people over to the House at the End of the Rainbow, but she's also fine with drives into Calgary and High River.

On her 90th birthday, Dorothy celebrates her milestone in the British Columbia backcountry. It takes a while to get to Assiniboine Lodge in Mount Assiniboine Provincial Park B.C. From Banff, it's about an hour's drive southwest to the trailhead. Then, you hike for 27.5 km (17 mi) until you reach the large log cabin. It's a lot quicker to get to the lodge if you take a helicopter, as Dorothy does. What a hoot! She loves being in the air, swooping over the peaks and under the clouds.

Mike, Sylvia, Erik, Karen Messenger (Erik's girlfriend) and Patrick take the long way to the lodge. Dorothy flies in, along with Brian, Terry and Kevin.

When the helicopter lands, the manager, Sepp Renner,[100] lifts Dorothy from her seat and puts her on the ground. She takes in the scenery and spies Mount Assiniboine, the Matterhorn of the Rockies, sticking straight into the sky. She's never seen this particular mountain before and it's another new sight for her in the backcountry. She never stops seeking adventures.

The Carleton party is there for two nights. Dorothy is in a cabin near the lodge with Sylvia, who is keeping an eye on her. The rest of the family is at a Naiset hut (a dormitory-style log cabin built by the Alpine Club of Canada in the 1920s) about a kilometre (.6 mi) from the lodge. The first day everyone is out on separate excursions: Erik, Karen and Patrick scramble Sunburst Peak; Mike and Brian head out hiking (Brian has his fishing rod in tow); Terry and Kevin hike up to Wonder Pass; and Dorothy and Sylvia walk around the area. All of a sudden, there's a quick change in weather – from fine to furious. It starts hailing! There are soaking wet Carletons scurrying back to camp from all directions. When everyone meets, they find out that Dorothy and Sylvia had been trapped in the outhouse. They couldn't sprint to the lodge in between the hailstones. Kevin is soaked and has to change into his pyjamas – that's all he has that's dry.

At night, Brian is pelted by falling objects of a different kind. His nephew Patrick is sleeping above him on the bunk bed. Every time Patrick rolls over, he nudges something loose from his belt hanging on a railing. Needless to say, Brian doesn't get a restful sleep.

---

100. Sepp Renner is Sara Renner's father. Sara is a Canadian three-time Olympian and silver medallist in cross-country skiing.

Dorothy at Mount Assiniboine for her 90th birthday, September 2009.
Photo: Carleton Family

Mary Lou has stayed in Banff to organize a gathering so all Dorothy's friends can party with her. There's a celebration at 139 Rainbow in the afternoon everyone returns from the lodge. Mary Lou has almost everything prepared. Where's the beer? Brian, Terry and Kevin make a mad dash for cold brewskies.

Dorothy's 90th festivities stretch out over a couple of weeks — everyone wants to celebrate with her. People drop by the house and there are parties at the seniors' centre, the legion and other locations.

A highlight is the Warden Service 100th anniversary celebration, held in September in Banff. There's a huge tent set up and more than 400 people attend. Many old-timers are there, including the Hermanrudes, Smokey Guttman and his wife Vin, Peter Spear and John Laut. Dorothy knows John right away and he's amazed she recognizes him after all these years. He was just a kid in 1956. He tells Dorothy that he counts his two seasons in Banff with her and Ed as the best of his entire life.

At 90, Dorothy is given the baton and asked to be the director of the Banff Senior's Choir. She not afraid of tapping the stick on the music stand to get anyone's attention. You're there to sing, not chat.

Dorothy's volunteer work gets her noticed. In 2009, she's given a provincial government Seniors in Service Award for providing entertainment and support at the Banff Mineral Springs Hospital Auxiliary for 20 years and also assisting at the Banff Senior Centre. Dorothy, Mike, Sylvia and Terry go to Edmonton for a gala dinner at the Legislature of Alberta.

Dorothy receives her award from Marie Stelmach, wife of Alberta Premier Ed Stelmach. As usual, Dorothy breaks out into song when accepting her honour. She sings *When You're Smiling* and receives thunderous applause.

In 2010, Dorothy is on the spring cover of the Covenant Health newsletter, Our Compass - Compassionate Care Led by Catholic Values. Dorothy is featured as one of the 2,522 volunteers who serve at Alberta Covenant Health facilities. It talks about her singing songs from the Second World War to seniors at the continuing care unit (St. Martha's Place) at the Banff Mineral Springs Hospital. Even though they are part of "her" generation, Dorothy doesn't feel their age. Dorothy says singing is a tonic for sadness and it makes her feel good to make others feel good. She also likes to hand out her Rocky Roads squares to people in the hospital.

Celebrity sightings in Banff happen all the time. The 2011 Sports Illustrated Swimsuit Issue is being shot around town and Lake Louise. But Dorothy doesn't have to put on a bikini to get noticed. People flock to her. Cheryl and Sally have a term for it: Dorothy Jams. It's when Dorothy is walking down the street and a friend stops to talk to her and then another person stops, and another person stops and well, you get the idea. Tourists stop to chat, too.

At a Terry Fox event, Dorothy uses her clout to start a little later than the runners and walkers. Brian accompanies her and they do a short but slow stroll. By the time they reach the finish line, all the other participants are long gone. Nevertheless, the numerous volunteers remaining are cheering and clapping for Dorothy. She made it.

After a well-deserved sit down with some fruit and a cookie, it's time to go. Just as Dorothy is about to leave, a friend comes over to see her. After some pleasant conversation, the man says goodbye to Dorothy.

"Who is that lady?" a volunteer asks the man. "Why is she so special?"

"That's Dorothy Carleton. She's the Queen of Banff."

In the car, Brian repeats what he had heard.

"Did you hear that, Mum? You're the Queen of Banff."

"Oh no, I'm not," she says, with the hugest of smiles on her face.

Dorothy puts her royalty-slash-star status to work in 2011. She's taking people on Banff's first Jane's Walk, a free organized walking tour interwoven with history and stories. Jane Jacobs, an American-Canadian urban critic, inspired the international movement of meeting neighbours through storytelling. Dorothy is the perfect guide for Banff's walk as she's a piece of walking history herself.

Dorothy, along with Rob Crosby, whose family also has strong ties to the town through the Brewster company, Deer Lodge and his own sporting exploits, take just under two dozen people around town on an overcast day in early May. Stories emerge from Rob and Dorothy about what life was like when Banff was quieter. (But not too quiet.) There were always events and parties to attend. At the Louis Trono Gazebo, Dorothy can't help but sing where she had sung with Louis a long time ago. *When You're Smiling* gets everyone smiling.

The Jane's Walk was put on by the Banff Community Foundation. The Whyte Museum of the Canadian Rockies has another occasion for Dorothy to talk about the past: a museum exhibit is about women adventurers in the Rockies, and Dorothy fits right in with the theme. Except she thinks she doesn't.

The museum has chosen 10 women to showcase in the exhibit and the list has some spectacular people on it who have done some spectacular things. Some of them have been long gone, like Mary Schäffer, who explored the Banff area in the early 1900s. Others are still active and continuing to live their lives pursuing their goals. Nancy Hansen has climbed all of the Canadian Rocky Mountain 11,000-foot peaks (mountains over 11,000 ft or 3,352 m), making her the first woman to summit all 54. In 1992, Diny Harrison became an internationally certified mountain guide, a first for a woman in North America. She guides, instructs and consults today in the outdoor arena.

"I've done nothing compared to those women," says Dorothy. "Why does the museum want me?"

Whyte Museum curator and executive director Michale Lang tells her it's because her story is part of the wider story of women in Banff.

Without Dorothy's history, and other wardens' wives like her, a Parks voice would be lost. Dorothy is part of a generation of wives who worked, unpaid, alongside their husbands. They brought up children in cabins lit by lanterns and fed them with food made on a rustic wood stove, spent hours washing clothing with cold water from creeks, chopped wood and helped their husbands with their work, too. All the while, living with limited contact from family and friends.

At the opening of the exhibit on Jun. 19, 2011, Dorothy finds herself among peers and friends. She speaks to the crowd at the museum and tells them she couldn't have imagined a better life. She owes it all to Ed.

Shine On

Brian retires from Parks Canada in 2012. He has been with Parks for 33 years, 1979-2012. He's worked all over the area and like his father, enjoyed the work outdoors the most. The role of Parks Canada in Dorothy's life isn't as prominent as it had been when Ed was a warden. She does catch the occasional piece on the television news or over the radio. The Canadian Parks and Wilderness Society (CPAWS) is lashing out at the federal government after it cuts Parks' budget in 2012. The organization says Parks is going backwards when it comes to boundaries, development, research and safeguarding wildlife.

Indigenous people are finally given lifetime access to the Banff National Park. Before the agreement was made with Parks Canada, Ĩyãhé Nakoda members had to pay to access the park like everyone else — except they weren't like everyone else: the park is their ancestral homeland.

At 93, Dorothy's hitting another first. She's been recognized for *being an inspiration to Banff residents.* She's named as part of the Banff SHINE program, Developed by the Banff Community Foundation. SHINE stands for Share, Help, Inspire, Nurture and Enrich — things that Dorothy does every day. She's one of 11 shining examples of people doing good work in the town. Dorothy, in particular, *has a positive attitude and gives of her time without expectations.*

She has no thoughts of slowing down. Her sons warn her to take it easy. She's healthy, although she's had a couple of falls and broke her wrists in one accident and her hip in another. Constant knee pain, though, knocks some wind from her sails.

Dorothy is in pain and is given injections to help ease the pinching and burning in her knees. The needles don't do much to take away the hurt. It's time for surgery.

Brian drives Dorothy to Mike and Sylvia's home in Calgary. Dorothy can't climb the stairs to the bedroom so Mike makes up a cot for her in the living room. The next morning, they get up at 6 a.m. and leave for the hospital. Mikes drops her off and heads home. After the procedure, Dorothy phones her eldest son.

"I'm OK," she says, "but I really want to see a familiar face."

Mike and Sylvia visit Dorothy and find her tired but in fairly good spirits. The next day she's moving around with a walker, starting physio and very reluctant to take more pills. That's Dorothy. Nothing will keep her down. She's driven back to Banff by ambulance to a room at the Banff hospital.

She's still in the hospital as her birthday approaches. Thankfully, she gets a pass and is out to celebrate with a big crew. Her granddaughter Ingrid's family is there as well as Erik, Karen and Terry's family. Dorothy sings along to *Happy Birthday* and a few other favourites. She shows off her knee and the bandage. She's back on her feet in no time.

Dorothy with The Wardens, Ray Schmidt, Bradley Bischoff and Scott Ward, at the Banff Centre May 4, 2017.
Photo: Carleton Family

Dorothy goes back to Calgary but not to the hospital. She makes trips to Market Mall with Cheryl. Dorothy ends up with shopping bags full of goodies for her grandkids. She could spend all day shopping. Cheryl is usually the one who wants to go home first and ends up sitting in the dressing room while Dorothy whirls about trying things on.

The two spend three to four times a week with each other. Some people may think Dorothy is like a mother to Cheryl or that Cheryl is looking after an elderly person but it's not like that. They are friends. Truly.

Dorothy is the most senior person when it comes to the *Seniors versus Seniors* softball game at the Banff Elementary School. She hits the ball on the first swing, impressing some of the seniors in Grade 6. Rounders was among one her favourite sports while attending Alfred Sutton Central School. That was almost 90 years ago and Dorothy doesn't bat an eye when telling the kids she's 93 years old. Besides the baseball diamond, she's keeping up with them on social media: she's on YouTube!

A storytelling series launches in February 2013, launching Dorothy back into the limelight. Fireside Chats at the Whyte Museum gets the tales of mountain women and men straight from the source. Dorothy kicks off the program on Feb. 17 and her session is professionally recorded. She chats with Chic Scott, a Banff author and adventurer, at Abegweit House, the Crosby family's beautiful, historic home and part of the Whyte Museum. She tells the audience how she baked bread in the stove, fetched water from the creek and raised children in the backcountry. She's 93 and has the crowd laughing out loud with her tale about hitching her horse to the hornet's nest.

At the peak with the remains of the time capsule! Left to right: Erik Carleton, Mike, Sanne Van Der Ross, Karen Messenger and Sanne's dog Milo, 2014.
Photo: Carleton Family

After the hour-long chat, Dorothy stands up and leads the crowd like they're a choir, one that has been practising for months. Cheryl accompanies her on the piano and everyone sings *I've Got a Lovely Bunch of Coconuts.*

Dorothy's stories have caught the ear of singer and songwriter Scott Ward, who is also a warden (and was a pallbearer at Ed's funeral). He's part of a trio of musical Banff National Park wardens, along with Bradley Bischoff and Ray Schmidt. They're in a band called The Wardens. Scott sets Dorothy's life to music in a song called *War(den) Bride.*

Dorothy's grandson Erik takes her to see The Wardens play a concert at the St. Michael's Church Hall in Canmore. Erik watches his grandmother swaying to the beat, she knows the song is about her. At the end, The Wardens add a line of *Happy Trails* and Dorothy raises her arms up into the air. Everyone is standing and applauding and it's an emotional time for everyone in attendance.

The tune will always get Dorothy singing and swaying. She knows all the words by heart because it's her journey. The song begins with her transformation from war bride to warden bride and ends with her thriving in her mountain home.

Did you remember that there's a time capsule on top of Castle Mountain? Mike has never forgotten the treasure his father and Walter Perren cemented into the rock. He wonders if it has been battered into oblivion by the elements or if it remains part of the crag.

It's time to find it.

On Aug. 6, 2014, Mike and a crew of Carletons, along with Peter Perren and various friends, ascend the mountain. They're on the hunt for the Verwoerds' tribute to Dwight. D. Eisenhower and the mountain that once bore his name. Would the rocket-shaped piece of history still be at the peak?

Mike, Sylvia, Erik, Karen, Peter Perren, Romeo Bruni, Sanne Van Der Ross and her dog are going to see. They hike up Castle and begin their search. Mike has tried to find the capsule once before. He climbed to the summit with Brian and sons Erik and Patrick in 1994 but they descended empty-handed.

Not today.

Erik finds a hole beneath a cairn at the summit and is digging away. What's this?

It's the time capsule. However, it's empty.

Half of the mystery is solved though. Mike is happy to have found something on the summit as proof of Ed and Walter's mission. As well, to find something touched by Ed 57 years ago is special to him.

The hunt for the capsule makes the *Rocky Mountain Outlook* newspaper. In the article, Mike asks anyone to contact him if they have information on what was in the rocket or any ideas about how to get in touch with the Verwoerds. Replies range from how interesting the story is, to a few people saying "well done!" A couple of people have theories of why the capsule is empty. One suggestion is that the capsule was destroyed in protest over the name of the mountain. Mike thinks the rocket just weathered away over time. The half-of-a-time-capsule has a place of honour at Dorothy's 95th birthday.

A portrait of Dorothy as a young war bride brings Dorothy a thrill. The art is done by Canadian Bev Tosh, a painter who has been working on a project painting the stories of war brides. Bev's mother was a war bride (who left Saskatchewan with her New Zealand Air Force husband after the Second World War) and Bev wanted to capture her image and story. She has painted more than 150 subjects and collected their stories for the series War Brides.

The 121 cm by 30 cm (4 ft by 1 ft) oil on wood has a hint of colour in the grain that represents Dorothy's End of the Rainbow home. The work itself shows Dorothy in her wedding dress. She's glowing, surrounded by a soft yellow light, and her smile is the same smile she has today. Her blue eyes in the portrait jump out at you and sparkle as if to ask you if you want to go on an adventure … or at least join her in song.

The Town of Banff celebrates 25 years of incorporation the same year Dorothy is 96. Banff has gone through a revitalization and newer buildings and hotels dot the streets, however, commercial development hasn't grown exponentially.

(It has in Canmore, outside the national park.) But it's not the same as when Dorothy first arrived. There's bumper to bumper traffic, especially in the summer. The town can handle 20,000 vehicles a day and it often exceeds that limit. On Sunday, Aug. 3, 2015, 33,096 vehicles are on the streets of Banff. Over 3.9 million people visit Banff this year.

Banff National Park is more than a park. It hosts running races, film and book festivals, diverse cultural events, workshops and seminars at the Banff Centre for Arts and Creativity, a mountain farm market, hockey tournaments, downhill and Nordic ski races, golf and spa days, concerts, photography classes, conferences and so much more. Dorothy doesn't recognize many of the faces while she's strolling along Banff Avenue. However, she hasn't been doing much of that lately. She's been using a walker to get around. Nevertheless, she's back at the Whyte Museum's Back to Banff Days baking cookies in the old wood burning oven. It's been 27 years and she's not about to throw in the apron. Talking to the visitors about her life brings her delight as she shows children how to bake without electricity. She can even convince some of the tourists to sing a song with her.

Dorothy likes to get out in any kind of weather. It amazes her friend Sally that at 96, Dorothy rarely refuses an invite to lunch, tea or a concert. What energy! Dorothy seems to buzz with delight in the presence of others. She starts singing and dancing to any music or song request. In short, she's the life of the party. The English Rose has good cheer for all she meets and it truly amazes Sally. Many a tourist enjoys a Second World War song as Dorothy strolls down Banff Avenue. Sally says Dorothy remains a showgirl at heart.

Dorothy also remains living in her home alone. She manages OK. She's proud of her house, the beautiful green and lush yard and the full and layered roses that she still looks after carefully. Those pesky elk remain a problem, especially in the fall, and Dorothy counts how many gather on the lawn to eat her plants.

Dorothy dubs herself a "gadabout" and is happy when company comes, a family member or friend, with whom to have a cup of tea or a sip of sherry. Her spirit (no pun intended) is such that she's looking for the best no matter what the situation. As people age, some might be upset or bitter over what's happening to them. They could get frustrated over an illness or other things that creep into aging bones. Not Dorothy, although she has not escaped life unscathed. She had a full knee replacement in 2013 and a hip replacement before that. Otherwise, she's aging gracefully and takes every day as it comes.

The trick to living independently is not doing everything at once. To get the laundry from the main floor to the washer in the basement, Dorothy throws her clothing and linen down the stairs. To bring up the washing, she takes two pieces at a time. She cooks her own food because she isn't a fan of the meal service options in Banff. She has neighbours like Sally and Marion Oakes who check in on her. Her family also makes sure she is taking care of herself. Nevertheless, accidents happen.

One early January morning in 2015, Brian is shovelling his mother's driveway. Almost half a metre (19 in) of snow had fallen overnight and Brian is clearing it away.

Once he's done, he knocks on Dorothy's door.

No answer.

He knocks again.

No answer.

With rising panic, he gets the key to her home and runs in to find Dorothy crumpled on the floor. She's delirious and in pain. Brian calls 911 and the paramedics bring her to the Banff hospital.

Dorothy's first day at Cascade House, September 2015. She's with Terry (left), Mike's wife Sylvia and Terry's wife May Lou.
Photo: Carleton Family

Dorothy tells them she had fallen the morning before and couldn't get back up. The 96-year-old had been on the cold floor without water or anything to eat for 24 hours. Brian, Mike and Terry aren't prepared to see their strong and dynamic mother so pale and fragile. However, they know that Dorothy won't be the same, physically and mentally, again.

The House at the End of the Rainbow is rented out and Dorothy moves into Cascade House, a supportive living centre near downtown Banff. She is somewhat independent but there's communal eating and 12-hour care. Dorothy is on her own at night. Despite not being in her own home, Dorothy adapts to life at Cascade House. She enjoys community meals and pleasant staff. Nevertheless, she's missing her long walks into town.

There's a bridge over the Bow River that Dorothy used to take to and from downtown when she lived at the End of the Rainbow. The span was built around 1920, and with its river stone construction, it resembles something found in ancient Scotland. The globe lamp posts (not ancient) and Indigenous reliefs make the bridge an impressive entrance, or exit, to the Banff Springs Hotel or the House at the End of the Rainbow. From the bridge, you have a 360-degree view of craggy mountains, a chance to hear the gurgling of the river and take a deep breath of fresh air. Dorothy wants to walk it one more time and fortunately, Cheryl has a grand idea of how to make Dorothy's wish come true.

Cheryl picks up Dorothy in her vehicle and parks at Cascade Gardens, a few steps away from the bridge. Dorothy gets out and walks along the bridge until she gets to the other side. At the legion, just a couple of paces from the bridge, she sits down on one of the outdoor benches. She feels an immense sense of accomplishment and pride. Her reward is some sunshine.

At 97-years-old, Dorothy is told she needs to use a walker. She gets one and still goes for her daily jaunts downtown all by herself. She needs fresh air daily, once telling Mike that even the cold wind feels good on her cheeks.

A solo stroll causes a bit of a ruckus in Banff one busy summer day. Dorothy is slowly crossing a busy alleyway. She takes a tiny little step, looks up, pushes her walker ahead and then repeats the process.

It is taking her 10 minutes to go one metre. Vehicles are stuck – drivers can't turn in or out of the alley. There's a massive traffic jam. After that, she's told she needs to find a new route.

Cheryl turned Dorothy onto cappuccinos at Evelyn's Coffee Bar in Banff's core. Family and friends often accompany her to get her coffee and then have a seat on an outdoor bench to watch the people walk by. For a long time, Dorothy wouldn't use her walker as a chair. She says she was told by the nurses that it was a walker, not something to sit on. She acquiesces at last and Mike finds a board to put across the handlebars. It makes a fine table for her cappuccinos, while she sits on the walker and watches people go by. Someone always recognizes her and greets her with a gentle hug.

The Last War Brides Reunion

An English Carleton had found her way to Canada in 1981. Russ's daughter Christine moved to Regina, Saskatchewan with her husband Peter after he got a job with a transport company called Swift Current Freight Lines.

Dorothy and Ed saw the couple whenever they went to war bride reunions in Saskatoon and Regina. Those events were full of late night partying – singing and dancing. After Ed died, Sylvia took Dorothy to war bride events. Over the years, there are fewer and fewer war brides coming to the reunions. The women are getting older and trips are getting harder to do. Phyllis, a war bride who had returned to her home country, had passed away in 1995. Dorothy is bothered by the loss of her friends and peers. It's a sign of things to come.

At the end of June 2016, Dorothy is invited to an Alberta War Brides event. The association is marking the 70th anniversary of the War Brides' immigration to Canada. There's going to be a party in Edmonton. Dorothy says she'll be there.

Brian drives his mother to Calgary and Mike drives both her and Sylvia the three hours north to Edmonton. Besides caring for his elderly mum, Mike is also caring for his wife. Sylvia is getting confused lately and Mike is worried about both her and Dorothy. He spends a sleepless night at the hotel.

The big event is at the Edmonton Coast Plaza Hotel. Dorothy's granddaughter Ingrid is alongside her. The reunion is very formal and the Lieutenant-Governor of Alberta, Lois Mitchell, gives a speech and there are presentations and some stories. Along with Dorothy, there are 11 other war brides in attendance. Dorothy loves the attention and enjoys the buffet lunch. There's a cake cutting and much ado over picture taking. A new book, Alberta War Brides and Families: Sharing Memories, is being passed around and Dorothy relates to many of the stories of women who made their

Dorothy (standing, seventh from left) at the Alberta War Brides 70th Anniversay on Jun. 26, 2016 at the Chateau Louis Hotel Edmonton. "Thanks Mom" is written on the cake.
Photo: Carleton Family

way across the Atlantic to Canada. The reunion is a good time but there is one thing missing: singing. There aren't many songs ringing out and filling the venue with joyous energy.

Canada has a big birthday to celebrate in 2017 and Parks Canada and Banff National Park are helping to mark 150 years of Confederation. The federal government makes park admission free for everyone. (It's usually around 23 CAD for an adult day pass.) From coast to coast to coast, there are events commemorating the natural and historical significance of the year. It has also been close to 140 years since bison roamed in Banff. Now they're back.

As Parks Canada considers bison to be a keystone species, they should be a part of the modern wildlife ecology. The animals maintain meadows and grasslands and are culturally important to Indigenous people. Sixteen plains bison from Elk Island National Park, near Edmonton, are brought to an enclosed pasture in the Panther Valley, an area Ed once patrolled. The herd is part of a five-year pilot project that will eventually see the animals free-roaming in Banff.

Dorothy thinks bringing the bison back is a positive move. She believes Ed would have supported the endeavour. However, knowing how remote some areas of the park are, she thinks he would have been concerned about the bison staying inside the Banff boundaries.

Top: The Carleton "Family Photo" taken on Remembrance Day. Banff Legion, 2017. Photo: Carleton Family
Bottom left: Dorothy and Sylvia at BowCrest Care Centre in Calgary, January 2018. Photo: Carleton Family
Bottom right: Dorothy walking on the Bow River Bridge, August 2016. Photo: Cheryl Craver

There have been countless ecological projects and studies in the park over the years, including wildfire research, monitoring grizzly bears and wolves, bringing back native fish species and building wildlife corridors. Wardens are involved in many aspects of the work and are also the front-line men and women who interact with tourists every day. Dorothy has seen the remarkable changes over the past 67 years in the park.

After 68 years, the Ike Inn, now known as Castle Mountain Wilderness Hostel, is closing its doors for good. Dorothy is surprised at the news. She recalls all the fun she had there with Mrs. Spear. Nevertheless, time marches on and after a New Year's Eve party on Dec. 31, 2017, the hostel and land returns to the Siksikaitsitapi Confederacy. It's part of a lands claim agreement between Siksika and the Canadian government.

The new year also brings a major transition for Dorothy. She is saying goodbye to Banff, the place she has lived well over half of her life. It's not an easy decision but it's one the family has to make.

Dorothy's dealing with mobility issues, pain and dementia. She mixes up a few historical facts but always remembers family and close friends. Another issue is falls. Dorothy has fallen a couple of times at night at Cascade House and since it doesn't offer around-the-clock care, she isn't found until morning. One fall ends up putting her in the hospital for several days before going back home. She needs 24-hour support and she's adamant she won't go to St. Martha's Place.

St. Martha's has been a place where she has gladly volunteered serving coffee and singing to the residents. Nevertheless, the long-term care unit is not for her.

"St. Martha's is where people go to die," she has always said to her sons. "It's not a place for me."

There isn't another option for her in her mountain town. There's nothing in between the 12-hour assisted care and St. Martha's. The Carleton sons receive doctor's orders to move their mother to the hospital until a room in a long-term care centre in the city opens up for her. Dorothy will gladly visit the hospital, no problem, but she's not going to go in for a stay. Mike and Sylvia take Dorothy on a walk and walk into the hospital with her.

"You tricked me," she says.

Her words crush Mike and he counts it as one of the worst days of his life.

In January 2018, a transition nurse arranges for Dorothy to be moved to Calgary to the Bow-Crest Care Centre. Calgary is a completely foreign place to her. It's a sad reality that the Carleton family and other small-town families have to face. Dorothy and Banff are synonymous. You can't have one without the other. Without her daily fresh air tonic, who knows how long Dorothy can sustain herself. For almost 70 years, Dorothy's life has revolved around the seasons, people, animals and landscape of Banff. Now, at 98 years old, her roots are being chipped out of the Rocky Mountains and she's being sent away. It's not fair, but it's what has to happen.

When the ambulance arrives to take Dorothy to the city, she won't get in. It takes some convincing before she accepts her ride to Calgary. She begrudgingly leaves Banff and catches flashes of the snow-capped mountains out of the emergency vehicle's window.

The first time she saw these summits, she thought they were a giant impenetrable fortress created out of rough stone – not welcoming at all. Today, she can name every one of the peaks.

"Goodbye my old friends," she whispers to the mountains as the ambulance brings her closer and closer to skyscrapers, steel and an unknown world.

Parks Canada Royalty

At the long-term care home in Bowness, an area of Calgary, Dorothy's sons see her trying to make the best of the situation. She sings old songs with them and when someone plays the piano in the Bow-Crest Care Centre's atrium, she listens intently. She walks laps in the hallway with her walker while humming *You are My Sunshine*. She even gets some of the staff to sing with her.

Dorothy has always accepted life as it comes. It's the same now. She doesn't let things drag her down. Peter Perren has had many chats with Dorothy and he thinks her strength comes from gratitude. She came from nothing and was adopted and it's this thankfulness for her life that bolsters her now.

In February 2018, her sons tell her they're selling the House at the End of the Rainbow. She shakes her head at them.

"What are you doing that for?" she asks.

Dorothy has never talked to her family or her friend Cheryl about dying. Dorothy lives in the moment and looks forward to each new day. At Bow-Crest, she wants to be where the action is and doesn't like sitting in her shared room with her cranky roommate. She parks herself by the nursing station, greeting people and singing to them. Her family takes her on short outings around the city and Mike drops by every day, sometimes with a cappuccino from Angel's Café, a tiny coffee shop on a Calgary river pathway. When Terry visits, he bundles his mother up in her coat and Olympic toque so they can head out to enjoy nature. Brian also gets his mother walking with her walker and when she starts using a wheelchair, he pushes her around in it. A few stretches of the sidewalk are frost-heaved, cracked and bumpy and he tells Dorothy to hang onto her hat as she's jostled from side to side.

Visitors from Banff include Cheryl. Although Dorothy is 98, Cheryl never thinks of her as being an older person. They met on an equal footing and remain equals. People tell Cheryl that she's a good person for being so nice to Dorothy but it is a balanced friendship. They're "two peas in a pod."

Everyone thinks Dorothy will certainly make it to 99, 100 even. She wants that letter from the Queen. At the 2018 Mother's Day lunch at Mike and Sylvia's home, Dorothy looks tiny and frail sitting in the wheelchair but her personality is strong and vibrant. She's telling stories, cracking jokes and singing to her great-grandchildren. She's a force.

Despite doing well for several months, it's obvious to Cheryl in May that Dorothy is losing her spark. She's falling more and more into memories of her childhood in Reading and living in the Banff backcountry. When she's not talking, she's humming and singing snatches of songs like *Zip-a-Dee-Doo-Dah.* As well, she can't leave her room on her own and detests being cooped up inside.

The doctors tell Dorothy's sons that their mum isn't eating much. It's June when she enters a semi-palliative state, breathing but barely conscious. Mike spends time at Dorothy's bedside playing her songs on his phone. She responds to the U.K. singer Vera Lynn and mouths the words.

"We'll meet again, don't know where, don't know when, but I know we'll meet again some sunny day" goes the lyrics of Vera Lynn's popular Second World War recording of *We'll Meet Again.*

Mike wipes his tears away and gets up to find his wife. Sylvia often accompanies him when he calls in on his mother. However, Sylvia has Alzheimer's and won't sit for long. She usually wanders the facility while Mike is talking to Dorothy.

Sylvia is nowhere to be found.

"Have you seen my wife?" Mike asks the front receptionist.

"Yes," she says. "She walked out of here about half an hour ago."

It is a heart-wrenching, heart-racing and heart-stopping moment for Mike. He runs to his vehicle and starts searching for Sylvia. She could be anywhere at this point: on a major road, in a dark alley or on one of the myriad of pathways by the river.

He looks and looks but he can't find her. Where is she?

It's a low moment in Mike's life. His mother is dying and his wife is missing.

Finally, Mike calls the Calgary Police Service. Officers find Sylvia almost two kilometres (more than a mile) away from the care centre. She's fine.

Terry and Mary Lou come to spend time with Dorothy and then Brian and Patrick. They are the last family to see Dorothy alive, on Jun. 29. She tells them she's not in pain. She is getting butterflies, little injections of morphine, to keep her comfortable. The shots make her drowsy and she drifts off to sleep.

At 5:45 a.m. on Saturday, Jun. 30, Brian, staying at a hotel, receives sad news over the phone. Dorothy is gone. She passed away in her sleep. The Carletons' hearts are heavy but they know she lived a full and wonderful life.

In articles and stories celebrating her 98 years, Dorothy's referenced as "Parks Canada royalty." She has made a mark on the people she has met. Her neighbour Sally thinks of her when she's outside in the mountains. Dorothy enjoyed the simple things in life like friends and family. She also had that plucky English "keep calm and carry on" attitude that meant she never dwelled on the negative things. Long-time friend Olive Openshaw remembers her special friend, someone who can never be replaced.

A funeral is held for the family on Jul. 24, 2018, at St. Paul's Presbyterian Church. Cheryl plays the piano while Dorothy's loved ones sing *Happy Trails.* A Celebration of Life for friends is held on Friday, Sept. 7, 2018, at the Banff Park Lodge. There is a crowd of 400 people in attendance. The Wardens, Scott Ward, Brad Bischoff and Ray Schmidt, perform two songs at the end of the tribute to Dorothy, *High Country Nights* and *War(den) Bride*, Dorothy's song. Then, lodge staff pours over 300 shots of Bristol Cream sherry and there's a toast to Dorothy followed by The Wardens leading *Happy Trails.* The main verse is repeated, just as Dorothy used to sing it.

The family had also asked the lodge staff to make 29 dozen Rocky Roads with Dorothy's recipe. The treats are passed out after the ceremony. Many a friend share a memory or two over the squares. Mike, Terry and Brian are told how kind Dorothy was and how she was a bright light to all. People were inspired by her positive outlook, can-do attitude, energy and enthusiasm.

For those who grew up in town, Dorothy was a backbone of the community and along with Ed, the "essence" of Banff.

She even left a lasting impression overseas. Her great-nephew Mark Carleton, Russ and Phyllis's grandson, remembers meeting her in England when he was a young boy. He was enthralled with Aunt Dorothy's backcountry tales and is upset he'll never get to Canada to hear her stories in person.

Dorothy's sons are overwhelmed by the outpouring of love for their mum. Brian is proud of his mother. She was always there for anyone who needed her. Terry had called her every week from High River and the two talked for at least an hour at a time. He'll miss her voice and her energy. He'll miss his mum.

Dorothy stood behind her words. It was through her actions that Mike understood the value of caring for others. He carries that forward today in his own family of 14.

The day after the celebration, a tweet by Banff Elementary shows Dorothy is not forgotten. It posts a video of a choir of children singing *The Banff Song.*

So much to do, so much to see, our town of Banff is home to me.

"Dorothy Carleton would have been beaming to hear Gr 6s singing The Banff Song!" says the tweet.

During the first Christmas without Dorothy, 2018, Cheryl decorates a bench with evergreens and festive bows. This isn't any old wooden bench, it was specifically made for Dorothy. A few years ago, a Banff resident, Ken Waterhouse, set up the bench. It sits beside the street on the way to the House at the End of the Rainbow. It was there for Dorothy to rest when she was on her way home. Dorothy had appreciated the bench and Cheryl is sure she'd love the festive theme.

Dorothy's legacy branches out like one of Banff's aspen trees. She was full of positivity, happy energy, kindness and always ready with a cup of tea and a listening ear. Peter Perren says Banff was a better place because of her.

"She really lifted everyone's spirits. I felt very close to her right to the end. Thinking of her even now helps me cope with what can be very stressful days."

***

Banff is no longer a little mountain town. The streets are busy with traffic and the sidewalks full of tourists. People flock to see Banff National Park in all seasons, hitting the ski hills in winter and the hiking paths in summer. They travel up and down roads, through quiet forest paths and over white-water rivers to seek unimaginable views — views that will never disappoint. Sightseers look at the peaks and the waterways and see wildlife and see nature at its finest. Ed and Dorothy were once the caretakers of this incredible land. The privilege that had been passed down to them from Banff's forbearers, has been given to the future to carry. The Carletons' stories, like Wild Bill, are now part of Banff's mountain legends.

War(den) Bride
by Scott Ward
Dorothy Lyrics

War bride to warden bride, living in the countryside
Far removed from England's shore, nothing like she's lived before
In her dreams it's Stoney Creek. Bow Summit, Observation Peak
Deep in the backcountry, now a part of history
Dorothy
War is over a Canadian soldier brought her to this place
When shown her new home he could tell by the look upon her face
No power and no water, she could only frown
Thirty miles by horseback to the nearest one horse town
Haul in water, stack up wood. get that stove alight
Alpine glow on mountainside quickly turns to night
Bread bakes in the oven, chaps hang from a nail
Saddles stowed, blankets aired, horses thrown a bale
CHORUS
Bridge
She remembers the crossing of an ocean
Recalling the life she left behind
A life that's filled with love and devotion
Visions frozen deep in time
Winter came, seasons changed, she learned to survive
From city girl to mountain legend Dorothy did thrive
With confidence her skills they grew with each passing year
Came to love this wilderness, this wilderness frontier
Dorothy's gone, spirits strong, the legend will live on
Her smile, her grace, her cheery face honored in this song
Our thoughts go back to Stoney Creek, sixty years have passed
A one-room shack with a shed for tack, in a wilderness so vast
CHORUS

Ed and Dorothy sharing a laugh in the Buffalo Paddock kitchen. Photo: Carleton Family

ENDNOTES

Olive (Beasly) Openshaw

Summer 2018

As of the summer of 2018, Olive (Beasly) Openshaw was living at her home in England. She says she grew up "very fast" because her father died when she was 14. During the Second World War, Olive wanted to join the Women's Auxiliary Air Force (WAAF). However, she was too young. Olive was engaged to a Royal Airforce pilot when she was 17 but he died after being shot down in 1941. She met her husband Danny while he was a soldier stationed at Reading. Danny had signed up for service in 1939 and went through to the end. He saw action in Normandy, Germany, and finally Belgium. The couple married when Olive was 18. Danny had wanted them to have a child before he left for Normandy but it was not meant to be. They had their first born, Dannette, in 1945 when Olive was 21. Olive and Danny were married for 58 years.

Herbert Cerezke on the mountain pine beetle

Spring 2019

The Mount Eisenhower Field Station was closed in 1970 when the Calgary main office was shut down. The field station was handed over to the national parks. The current mountain pine beetle situation in Alberta was predicted to really expand this year with major infestations in the Jasper to Hinton area but after the prolonged and severely cold temperatures that we experienced in February 2019, I have heard from a University of Alberta study that 90 per cent of the overwintering mountain pine beetle population may have been killed. This would be good news for the province and industry but it's that remaining 10 per cent that will remain at endemic levels until the right conditions arise again for population expansion.

Our changing climate has no doubt helped to sustain and maintain this beetle as a new invasive enemy of Alberta's forests. The fight tactics deployed toward controlling the beetle have not really changed much since the 1950's; i.e., it still boils down to finding and removing infested trees before the mature beetles exit the tree to re-infest new trees. This is done by either clearcutting and processing the trees before the beetles emerge, or cutting and burning infested trees as they are found. What has changed over the years is a lot of technical applications of new information applied in aerial surveys, ground monitoring and sampling techniques at different stages of the life cycle, modelling of population dynamics and dispersal movements, deploying pheromone attractant baits, etc.

The research work done in the 50s and 60s at the field station was helpful in the fight against the beetle and it was definitely helpful in understanding the basic biology of the beetle and its complex relationships with its host pine trees and with blue stain fungi which the beetle carries with it. I think that the early studies helped in understanding all of the seasonal sequence of events between beetle and host dynamics and this information has certainly been incorporated into current beetle management strategies, in both B.C. and Alberta.

Inez (Mattson) Peyto
Winter 2019

Inez Peyto passed away on Dec. 12, 2019 aged 99. She was born a Mattson and her family moved to Exshaw, Alberta when she was six years old. Her father worked at the cement plant there. Inez came to Banff to work. She had a job through Colonel Moore and his wife, who owned several properties on Fox Street. Inez met her husband, Stan, through friends Jim and Marg Morrison. Stan was Walter Peyto's son and nephew to Bill. There were six kids in Walter's family.

Stan and Inez married in 1941. They enjoyed skating together at Mather's Rink on the Bow River in winter. The rink was in a beautiful setting with evergreens all around. It also had a board fence surrounding it and separate changing rooms for the boys and girls. Al Mather played such nice music for the skaters.

During the Second World War, Stan was stationed at several locations across Canada, including Vancouver Island. He worked as a mechanic who "kept the tanks going." Inez accompanied him until he was sent overseas.

George A. Morasch
Winter 2020

George A. Morasch has been invited to be a part of the Government of Canada's official delegation to the Netherlands to mark the 75th anniversary of the liberation of the Netherlands in May 2020.

Fern and George A. Morasch at the Calgary Highlanders Ball, Mar. 2, 2019. Photo: George A. Morasch

In May 2019, George, 96, attended a Calgary Highlanders Memorial Service for Lieutenant Colonel Donald George MacLauchlan. Lt.-Col. MacLauchlan remains were interred at the Field of Honour – Queen's Park Cemetery in Calgary, Alberta. Lt.-Col. MacLauchlan was born in Prince Edward Island in 1905, and died in Ontario in 1992.

On Apr. 4, 2018, George was awarded the rank of Knight of the French National Order of the Legion of Honour. It's the highest national order of France and given to those who helped liberate France during the Second World War.

George was 94 when he was part of the Government of Canada's delegation travelling to France to mark the 75th Anniversary of the Dieppe Raid (August 19, 1942). On Aug. 19, 2017, George placed a wreath on behalf of the Canadian soldiers at the Dieppe-Canada Monument at Square du Canada in Dieppe.

Acknowledgements

Mike, Terry and Brian are tremendously grateful for George A. Morasch's input to the book. Ed never really spoke about the war with his family. His sons knew about his war wound and Mike recalls hiking down the trail as a lad with his dad and occasionally hearing him enthusiastically singing that raucous anthem of the Calgary Highlanders *Glenwhorple*. Otherwise, the Carleton sons knew little about what their father, George and the Calgary Highlanders experienced. It is a blessing that George is able to tell much of the story – as both a Calgary Highlander and friend of Ed's. Mike, Terry and Brian are amazed at what their dad and the others experienced and endured. The Calgary Highlanders were certainly "A Battalion of Heroes."

Many thanks goes to the people, groups and organizations that took the time to give us (Mike, Terry and Brian) stories, memories, research and inspiration. With your answers to our long list of questions, you've helped shape a book about two incredible people.

Thanks to Audrey MacKay, Baillie Carleton, Bill Crabbe, Bruce McTrowe, Cheryl Craver, Chris and Peter Perren, David Colbeck, David Fleming, David Zieroth, Denis Payne, Didsbury Museum, Don Mickle, George and Fern Morasch, Halle Flygare, Herbert Cerezke, Inez Peyto, John Laut, Jim Murphy, Kevin Openshaw, Lorna Carleton, Mac and Cathy Elder, Maureen Carleton, Olive and Danny Openshaw, Park Warden Service Alumni Society, Perry Davis, Peter Spear, Roy Andersen, Sally MacDonald, Scott Ward, Smokey Guttman, Steve Mallins, The Calgary Highlanders Regimental Museum and Archives, The Whyte Museum of the Canadian Rockies and Valerie Setz.

In the basement of the old Banff house at 139 Rainbow (the End of the Rainbow), a number of family treasures were discovered when the house was sold in 2016. In particular, dad's diaries. Somehow, despite a very busy work schedule and family commitments, dad found the time to record, with almost military precision, the events and people of the day. Reading through the diaries triggers many wonderful memories, of unique mountain experiences, and the people, many of them the "characters" of the day, who worked for Parks and the Warden Service.

Mum also wrote several diaries, very personal and caring, revealing her emotions, her caring about others, and her love of favourite activities, like "getting out for a walk in the fresh air." The diaries, and also some letters that were saved, have been a great resource for the book.

PRIMARY SOURCES

Carleton, Baillie,
Carleton, Brian
Carleton, Dorothy
Carleton, Ed
Carleton, Lorna
Carleton, Maureen
Carleton, Mark
Carleton, Mike
Carleton, Terry
Carter, Louise
Cerezke, Herbert F.
Colbeck, David
Crabbe, Bill
Craver, Cheryl
Fleming, David
Flygare, Halle
Fowler, Alice
Green, Fred
Guttman, Smokey
Laut, John
Macdonald, Sally
McKay, Audrey (Carleton)
McTrowe, Bruce
Mickle, Don
Morasch, George A.
Murphy, Jim
Openshaw, Olive
Payne, Denis
Perren, Chris
Perren, Peter
Peyto, Inez
Setz, Valerie
Spear, Peter
Tingay, Marjorie
Ward, Scott
Zieroth, David

Secondary Sources

Alberta Champions. "Calgary Mayors" Retrieved Aug. 24, 2018 from http://albertachampions.org/calgary-mayors.

AlbertaonRecord.ca. "Archives Society of Alberta Mather (family)" Retrieved Feb. 17, 2019 from https://albertaonrecord.ca/mather-family.

AlbertaonRecord.ca. "Peyto, Walter H." Archives Society of Alberta. Retrieved Nov. 7, 2018 from https://albertaonrecord.ca/peyto-walter-h.

Alpine Club of Canada. "ACC Ambassadors Nancy Hansen" Retrieved May 15, 2019 fromhttp://bit.ly/2XASJIP.

Albertawilderness.ca. "Grey Wolf" Alberta Wilderness Association Retrieved Dec. 5, 2018 from http://bit.ly/2JzGNC3.

Alexander, Rob. "Exhibit features mountain women with moxy" *Crag & Canyon* (2011)

AmericanAlpineClub.org. "Alberta, Mt. Blane" Accidents, Alpina Americana. Retrieved Mar. 20, 2019 from http://publications.americanalpineclub.org/articles/13196200700/Alberta-Mt-Blane.

AmericanAlpineClub.org. "Rockies, Tower of Babel" Accidents, Alpina Americana. Retrieved Mar. 27, 2019 from
http://publications.americanalpineclub.org/articles/13196700704/Alberta-Rockies-Tower-of-Babel.

Amundson, Quinton and Paulina Liwski. "The legend of the Fighting Tenth" *The Calgary Journal* (Jul. 30, 2014) Retrieved on May 28, 2018 from http://bit.ly/2YJ88YR.

Anderson, Sergeant Thomas Gordon "Red. "Private Papers of T G Anderson" Esplanade Arts & Heritage Centre, City of Medicine Hat

Andrews, Verity. "Huntley & Palmers Special Collections featured item for August 2009" (Aug. 2009) University of Reading (2009) Retrieved June 11, 2018 from http://bit.ly/2G47vSq.

Arborfieldhistory.org.uk. "Memories - Bombs on Berkshire, 1940-45" Arborfield Local History Society Retrieved Aug. 11, 2018 from http://www.arborfieldhistory.org.uk/C20/memories_bombs.htm.

ArchivesAlberta.org. "Extreme Landscape: the tragedy and the triumph" Whyte Museum of the Canadian Rockies Archives and Library (Oct. 2001) Retrieved Jan. 1, 2019 from http://www.archivesalberta.org/extreme/whyte.htm.

Archives Society of Alberta. "Fonds whyte-1078 - Bruno Engler fonds" Retrieved Feb. 18, 2019 from https://albertaonrecord.ca/bruno-engler-fonds.

Archives Society of Alberta. "The First Battalion Calgary Highlanders 1939-1945 fonds" The Calgary Highlanders 1939-1945 Retrieved May 30, 2019 from https://albertaonrecord.ca/first-battalion-calgary-highlanders-1939-1945-fonds.

Ashfm.ca. "Mountaineering & Climbing Timeline" Alberta Sports History Library. Retrieved Feb. 15, 2019 from https://ashfm.ca/absportslibrary/mountaineering-climbing/timeline.

Avalanche.ca. "Avalanche Canada Historical Incidents" Retrieved Oct. 1 2018 from https://www.avalanche.ca/incidents.

Banff Elementary School. (Banff_El_School) Dorothy Carleton would have been beaming to hear Gr 6s singing The Banff Song! @MountainEdu @Banff_Town (Sept. 8, 2018, 2:54 p.m.) Retrieved June 28, 2019 from https://twitter.com/Banff_El_School/status/1038546132970876928.

Banfflakelouise.com. "Banff and Lake Louse History and Heritage" Retrieved Sept. 28, 2018 from https://www.banfflakelouise.com/banff-national-park/history-heritage.

Banfflegion.ca. "Colonel Moore Branch # 26 Branch History" Retrieved Jan. 23, 2019 from http://bit.ly/32h37ch.

George A. Morasch was in France to mark the 75th Anniversary of the Dieppe Raid on Aug. 19, 2017. He placed a wreath on behalf of the Canadian soldiers at the Dieppe-Canada Monument at Square du Canada in Dieppe.
Photo: George A. Morasch

Banff National Park. "Park wardens restore Windy cabin" The Mountain Guide Centennial Edition (1985) Retrieved Apr. 24, 2019 from http://parkscanadahistory.com/brochures/banff/mountain-guide-1985.pdf.

Baseball-reference.com. "1960 World Series Game 5, Pirates at Yankees, October 10" Baseball Reference Retrieved Mar. 18, 2019 from https://www.baseball-reference.com/boxes/NYA/NYA196010100.shtml.

Bater, Kim. "Jane's Walk in Banff" KimBater.com (May 5, 2011) Retrieved May 15, 2019 from http://bit.ly/2NI7ud0.

BBC. "1940: London blitzed by German bombers" On This Day Retrieved Jun. 11, 2018 from http://news.bbc.co.uk/onthisday/hi/dates/stories/september/7/newsid_3515000/3515708.stm.

BBC. "Announcing the death of King George VI" News (Jan. 31, 2012) Retrieved Jan. 21, 2019 from https://www.bbc.com/news/av/uk-16767149/announcing-the-death-of-king-george-vi.

BBC. "On This Day - 1954: Housewives celebrate end of rationing" Retrieved Aug. 24, 2018 from http://news.bbc.co.uk/onthisday/hi/dates/stories/july/4/newsid_3818000/3818563.stm.

BBC. "What was the Battle of Britain?" Newsround (Sept. 15, 2015) Retrieved May 30, 2018 from https://www.bbc.co.uk/newsround/34257841.

BBC Archive "The Transcript of Neville Chamberlain's Declaration of war" WWII: Outbreak Britain on the brink of World War II Retrieved June 8, 2018 from http://www.bbc.co.uk/archive/ww2outbreak/7957.shtml?page=txt.

BBC News. "D-Day landing veterans in last Hayling Island reunion" (Sept. 15, 2011) Retrieved Oct. 18, 2018 from https://www.bbc.com/news/uk-england-hampshire-14926347.

Bercuson, David J. "Battalion of Heroes: The Calgary Highlanders in World War II" Calgary Highlanders Regimental Funds Foundation (Jan. 1995) Pages 25, 46, 48, 49, 50, 52, 57, 63, 106, 119, 140, 141, 241, 243

Biais, Gabrielle. "Records of Parks Canada." Federal Archives Division, Minister of Supply and Services Canada (1985) Retrieved Apr. 1, 2019 from http://parkscanadahistory.com/publications/rg84.pdf. Page 20

Boileau, John. "John Osborn, VC". The Canadian Encyclopedia, (Jan. 18, 2018) Historica Canada. Retrieved June 12, 2018 from https://www.thecanadianencyclopedia.ca/en/article/john-robert-osborn.

Boswell, Randy. "When Marilyn Monroe came to Banff . . ." *Calgary Herald* (Sept. 28, 2010) Retrieved Dec. 4, 2018 from https://calgaryherald.com/news/local-news/when-marilyn-monroe-came-to-banff.

Bousfield, Arthur and Garry Toffoli. "Fifty Years the Queen: A Tribute to the Queen on her Golden Jubilee" Dundurn; First Edition (Sept. 1 2002) Page 192

Bourassa, Rollie. "One Family's War: The Wartime Letters of Clarence Bourassa, 1940-1944" by University of Regina Press (May 30, 2010) Page 27

Bowriverfuneralcom. "Condolences" Dorothy Carleton (2018) Retrieved Aug. 14, 2018 from https://www.bowriverfuneral.com/index.php?f=condol_view%2C612.

Bragg, Melvyn. "World War 2 history: memories from the day war broke out told to Melvyn Bragg" *The Telegraph* (Aug. 27, 2009) Retrieved June 8, 2018 from http://bit.ly/2XRs1zT.

British Library. "The Great Depression" Learning Timelines: Sources from History" Retrieved on June 4, 2018 from http://www.bl.uk/learning/timeline/item107595.html.

Britton, Phyllis. "Whither Thou Goest War Brides: an investigation and comparison of the experience of Canadian and American wartime marriages" Canadian War Brides. (Apr. 2003) Retrieved Sept. 10, 2018 from http://www.canadianwarbrides.com/documents/whither-thou-goest.pdf.
British-forces.com "British Civilian Life Civil Defence and Home Guard" Retrieved June 28, 2018 from http://wearcam.org/decon/cleansing_stations_civildefense.html.

Brown, Gordon. "The Capture of the Abbaye D'Ardenne by the Regina Rifles, 8 July 1944" Canadian Military History: Vol. 4 :Iss. 1, Article 10. (1995) Retrieved Sept. 18, 2019 from http://scholars.wlu.ca/cmh/vol4/iss1/10.

Brown, Graeme "Hercules Cycle and Motor Company celebrates 100 years" *Birmingham Post* (Jul. 30, 2013) Retrieved Jun. 7, 2018 from http://bit.ly/2S8OMtU.

Brown, Norman. "D-Day Memories" *Legion Canada's Military History Magazine* (May 1, 2004) Retrieved Jul. 15 2018 from https://legionmagazine.com/en/2004/05/d-day-memories.

Burns, Robert J. and Mike Schintz. "Guardians of the Wild: A History of the Warden Service of Canada's National Parks" University of Calgary Press (2000) Pages 230, 245, 258, 261, 367

Byrne, A. R. "Man and Landscape Change in the Banff National Park Area Before 1911" National Parks Series No. 1 (Apr. 1968) Retrieved Mar. 28, 2019 from http://parkscanadahistory.com/publications/nps/study-1.pdf. Page 146

Calgary Herald staff. "Alberta 150: The coal miner, the inventor and the suffragette" *Calgary Herald* (Jun. 14, 2017) Retrieved Jul. 21, 2018 from http://bit.ly/2LJuOo7.

Calgaryherald.remembering.ca. "Louis TRONO May 24, 2004" Retrieved Mar. 20, 2019 from http://calgaryherald.remembering.ca/obituary/louis-trono-2004-1065571399.

Calgaryherald.remembering.ca. "William Waterworth Obituary" Calgary Herald (Dec. 2009) Retrieved Jan. 23, 2019 from http://calgaryherald.remembering.ca/obituary/william-waterworth-1922-2009-1065708319.

Calvert, Kathy and Dale Portman. "Guardians of the Peaks: Mountain Rescue in the Canadian Rockies and Columbia Mountains" RMB Rocky Mountain Books (Oct. 30 2006) Pages 28, 37, 41, 42, 46, 56

Canadian Heritage Parks. "Canada State of the Parks 1997 Report" Minister of Public Works and Government Services Canada (1998) Retrieved May 9, 2019 from http://bit.ly/2JBgCLe.

Canadian Journal of Research. "THE TIMBER WOLF IN THE ROCKY MOUNTAIN NATIONAL PARKS OF CANADA Ian McTaggart Cowan" Abstract, 1947, Vol. 25d, No. 5: pp. 139-174 Retrieved Dec. 8, 2018 from http://bit.ly/2LdANSG.

Canadian Parks and Wilderness Society. "The State of Canada's Parks 2012 Report" (2012) Retrieved May 15, 2019 from http://cpaws.org/uploads/cpaws_parksreport_2012.pdf.

Canadian Battlefield Tours. "The Battle for Woensdrecht" Retrieved Aug. 20, 2018 from http://www.canadian-battlefieldtours.ca/the-battle-for-woensdrecht.

CanadaHistory.com. "Dieppe - August 1942" *Voyager* Aug. 2012 Newsletter Retrieved Jul. 5 2018 from http://www.canadahistory.com/sections/voyager/2012/August/Dieppe.html.

Canadian Soldiers. "Clair Tizon" Retrieved Jul. 21, 2018 from http://bit.ly/2lIHT6L.

Canadian Soldiers. "Wyneghem" Retrieved Sept. 2, 2019 from http://bit.ly/2mdmvXB.

Canadianwarbrides.com "Canadian War Brides FAQ" Retrieved Nov. 5, 2018 from http://www.canadianwar-brides.com/faq.asp.

Canadian War Museum. "Canada and the First World War, The War's Impact on Canada" (Jun. 20, 2008. Last update: Oct. 16, 2017) Retrieved May 28, 2018 from http://bit.ly/2JnrCgo.

Canadian War Museum. "Canada at D-Day 1944" Retrieved Jul. 26, 2018 from https://www.warmuseum.ca/cwm/exhibitions/chrono/1931d_day_e.shtml.

Canadian War Museum. "Canada and the South African War" Retrieved June 4, 2018 from https://www.war-museum.ca/cwm/exhibitions/boer/boerwarhistory_e.shtml

CaroleHarmon.ca. "Obituary – Aileen Harmon" Retrieved June 24, 2019 from http://www.caroleharmon.ca/Aileen/index.html.

Carrington, Damian. "Hedgehog numbers plummet by half in UK countryside since 2000" The Guardian (Feb. 7, 2018) Retrieved Oct. 1, 2018 from http://bit.ly/2L90OCJ.

CBC. "Canada – A People's History "Rise of the Fascists – Canada Goes to War" (2001) Retrieved May 29, 2018 from http://bit.ly/2md5jl0.

CBC.ca "Copps imposes moratorium on park development" CBC. (Posted: Feb 06, 2000, Last Updated: Nov. 13, 1998) Retrieved May 8, 2019 from http://bit.ly/2Jp7ieC.

CBC.ca. "Did you know we had to ration food during the war?" Retrieved Nov. 20, 2018 from https://www.cbc.ca/kidscbc2/the-feed/did-you-know-we-had-to- ration-food-during-the-war.

CBC Digital Archives. "Carnage on the beaches of Dieppe" (Aug. 20, 1942) Retrieved Aug. 23, 2018 from http://bit.ly/2NGlbt5.

CBC Digital Archives. "WWII soldiers return to Canada" Retrieved Aug. 23, 2018 from http://www.cbc.ca/archives/entry/wwii-soldiers-return-to-canada.

CBC Digital Archives. "Skier Karen Percy wins Canada's first medal at Calgary Games" (Feb. 18, 1988) Re-trieved Apr. 26, 2019 from https://www.cbc.ca/player/play/1754020520.

Cerezke, H.F. "History of forest entomology in Alberta" Proceedings of the 50th Annual Meeting of the Entomological Society of Alberta" Entomological Society of Alberta. (Sept. 2003) Retrieved Mar. 19, 2019 from http://www.entsocalberta.ca/procesa2002.pdf.

CFAC. "Broadcast of Calgary Highlanders Homecoming" (Nov. 25, 1945) Cassette tape.

Chen, Qi. "Who Won the Battle of Village Lake Louise? Park Planning, Tourism Development, and the Downhill Ski Industry in Banff National Park, 1964-1979 A thesis submitted in partial fulfillment of the requirements for the degree of Master of Arts in Recreation and Leisure Studies Faculty of Physical Education and Recreation" University of Alberta (2015) Page 8

Child, Chief Joseph Weasel. "Chief and Council Monthly Update" Aitsiniki Vol. 25 Issue 11 (March 2017) Retrieved Jan. 22, 2019 fromhttp://bit.ly/2LeukXB.

Childs, Martin. "Prunella Stack: Motivational leader of the Women's League of Health and Beauty" *Independent* (Feb. 28, 2011) Retrieved June 8, 2018 from http://bit.ly/2S6i64g.

Cleary, Helen. Victoria Cook, Phil Edwards and Bruce Robinson. "Fact File: Women's Auxiliary Air Force 1938 - 1945" *WW2 People's War BBC* (Jun. 2003 / Sept. 2005) Retrieved June 12, 2018 from https://bbc.in/2G3audZ.

Clouting, Laura. "8 Facts about Clothes Rationing in Britain during the Second World War" Imperial War Museum (Jul. 4, 2018) Retrieved Sept. 7, 2018 from http://bit.ly/2LQhiPw.

ClydeMaritime. "Letitia 1924 HMS - Armed Merchant Cruiser" (Oct. 20, 2011)Retrieved Sept. 10, 2018 from http://forums.clydemaritime.co.uk/viewtopic.php?t=14427.

CPAWS. "Human Impact" Retrieved May 9, 2019 from http://bit.ly/2XxMcP6.

Collection of Irish Songs Lyrics. It's a Long Way to Tipperary. Retrieved Sept. 7, 2018 from https://www.irishsongs.com/lyrics.php?Action=view&Song_id=172.

Colombo, Stephen J. *A Letter from Frank: An Unlikely Second World War Friendship*
Dundurn (Sept. 20 2011) Page 78

Commonwealth War Graves Commission. "Captain Theodor Marie Insinger" Casualties of the Dieppe Raid (Aug. 19, 2017) Retrieved Jul. 4, 2018 from http://bit.ly/2Jn2qXk.

Cook, Caroline. "The day the horrors of war came to Reading" *GetReading.co.uk* (Jun. 7, 2013) Retrieved on Jul. 5, 2018 from https://www.getreading.co.uk/whats-on/find-things-to-do/day-horrors-war-came-reading-4050176.

A portrait by Bev Tosh of Dorothy as a young war brid
Photo: Carleton Family

Cook, Tim. "Second World War Veterans" The Canadian Encyclopedia, (Sept. 29 2017) Historica Canada. Retrieved Sept. 5, 2018 from http://bit.ly/2xDYcUB.
Copp, Terry. "Taking Caen: Army, Part 95" *Legion: Canada's History Magazine* (Aug. 17, 2011) Retrieved Sept. 18 20, 2018 from http://bit.ly/2niszxQ.

Copp, Terry. "The Approach To Verrières Ridge: Army, Part 25" *Legion: Canada's History Magazine* (Mar. 1, 1999) Retrieved Aug. 20, 2018 from http://bit.ly/2S6KIKy.

Copp, Terry. "The Battle North of Antwerp" Part 37 *Legion Magazine* (September/October 2001) Retrieved Aug. 20, 2018 from http://bit.ly/2XUHHCj.

Cooper, Alex. "50 years in the making: the opening of the Trans-Canada" *Revelstoke Review* (Jul. 18, 2012) Retrieved Mar. 18, 2019 from http://bit.ly/2XRtWEB.

Costa, Elio and Gabriele Scardellato. "Lawrence Grassi: From Piedmont to the Rocky Mountains" University of Toronto Press, (May 27, 2015)

Crerar, Stewart. "Banff senior living life as an adventure" *The Valley, Crag & Canyon* (Jun. 2, 1999)

University of Calgary Libraries and Cultural Resources Digital Collection - The Banff Crag & Canyon
"4-Year-Old Found After All-Night Search, July 9 1958" University of Calgary Libraries and Cultural Resources Digital Collection. Retrieved Mar. 15, 2019 from http://bit.ly/2NJ9bHo.

"100 Years in the Warden Service advertisement" (Mar. 2005)

"3500 Ride Gondola Lift on Labor Day Weekend, Sept. 9, 1959" University of Calgary Libraries and Cultural Resources Digital Collection. Retrieved Mar. 15, 2019 from http://bit.ly/2XW6vdd.

"Action Needed Sept. 16, 1959 (editorial)" University of Calgary Libraries and Cultural Resources Digital Collection. Retrieved Feb. 28, 2019 from http://contentdm.ucalgary.ca/digital/collection/p22007coll2/id/5920

"August Dismal, Sept. 9, 1959" University of Calgary Libraries and Cultural Resources Digital Collection. Retrieved Mar. 15, 2019 from http://contentdm.ucalgary.ca/digital/collection/p22007coll2/id/5915/rec/17.

"Banff Gold Course Played by 'Bing,' July 8, 1959" University of Calgary Libraries and Cultural Resources Digital Collection. Retrieved Mar. 14, 2019 from http://bit.ly/32fP5aN.

"Body of Rundle Climber Found After Long Search, Aug. 13, 1954" University of Calgary Libraries and Cultural Resources Digital Collection. Retrieved Mar. 15, 2019 from http://bit.ly/2XZ8k98.
"Brilliant Aurora "Reserved" for Banff Wednesday, February 12, 1958" University of Calgary Libraries and Cultural Resources Digital Collection. Retrieved Feb. 28, 2019 from http://bit.ly/2LI9UG0.
"Ed Carleton Retires" (Jun. 14, 1978)

"Engler Charge by Irate Moose, Sept. 9, 1959" University of Calgary Libraries and Cultural Resources Digital Collection. Retrieved Mar. 15, 2019 from http://bit.ly/2XW6vdd.

"Four Fined for Feeding Bears Jul. 8, 1959" University of Calgary Libraries and Cultural Resources Digital Collection. Retrieved Mar. 14, 2019 fromhttp://bit.ly/32fP5aN.

"Gondola Life Featured on CBC News, Aug. 26, 1959" University of Calgary Libraries and Cultural Resources Digital Collection. Retrieved Mar. 15, 2019 from http://bit.ly/2S2Bteq.

"Grizzly Bear Mauls 3 Banff Residents, Jul. 8, 1959" University of Calgary Libraries and Cultural Resources Digital Collection. Retrieved Mar. 14, 2019 from http://bit.ly/32fP5aN.

"Legion Notes, Jun. 5 1953" University of Calgary Libraries and Cultural Resources Digital Collection. Retrieved Mar. 14, 2019 from http://bit.ly/2LJARcj.

"Letters to the Editor Sept. 23, 1959" University of Calgary Libraries and Cultural Resources Digital Collection. Retrieved Feb. 28, 2019 from http://contentdm.ucalgary.ca/digital/collection/p22007coll2/id/5922.

"Officers Installed by Banff Rebekahs, Jan. 30, 1953" University of Calgary Libraries and Cultural Resources Digital Collection. Retrieved Mar. 15, 2019 from http://bit.ly/2XzoaDr.

"Present 25-pin to Woodworth, Sept. 24, 1958" University of Calgary Libraries and Cultural Resources Digital Collection. Retrieved Mar. 15, 2019 from http://bit.ly/2Xxdr17.

"Pride of Banff Dorothy Carleton" (Dec. 29, 1999)

"Queen Elizabeth and Prince Philip See Banff, Jul. 15, 1959" University of Calgary Libraries and Cultural Resources Digital Collection. Retrieved Mar. 15, 2019 from http://bit.ly/32fPERX.

"Retirement ends 30 years of service" (May, 31, 1978)

"Race Results, Jun. 20, 1956" University of Calgary Libraries and Cultural Resources Digital Collection. Retrieved Mar. 14, 2019 from https://cdm22007.contentdm.oclc.org/digital/collection/p22007coll2/id/5113/rec/17.

"Royal Couple Here for Two Hours on Jul. 10, June 10, 1959" University of Calgary Libraries and Cultural Resources Digital Collection. Retrieved Mar. 14, 2019 from http://bit.ly/2Jz0WIq.

"Ski Development on Sulphur "Not Likely" September 30, 1959" University of Calgary Libraries and Cultural Resources Digital Collection. Retrieved Feb. 28, 2019 from http://bit.ly/2Jwtd2w.

"Stephanie Townsend Takes Ski Opener, Nov. 25, 1959" University of Calgary Libraries and Cultural Resources Digital Collection. Retrieved Feb. 28, 2019 from http://bit.ly/2YI0EFB.

"Too Commercialized" Says Visiting Victorian, Jun. 20, 1956" University of Calgary Libraries and Cultural Resources Digital Collection. Retrieved Mar. 14, 2019 from http://bit.ly/2S2prS6.

"Wardens Find Lost Fisherman, Sept. 9, 1955" University of Calgary Libraries and Cultural Resources Digital Collection. Retrieved Feb. 28, 2019 from http://bit.ly/2XXnr2Q.

"Wardens Hold Winter School at Cuthead, Feb. 25, 1955" University of Calgary Libraries and Cultural Resources Digital Collection. Retrieved Feb. 28, 2019 from http://bit.ly/2LLlwrR.

"'Would Like to stay Here' Says Viscount Montgomery, Jun. 6, 1956" University of Calgary Libraries and Cultural Resources Digital Collection. Retrieved Feb. 28, 2019 from http://bit.ly/2XRhAw9.

D-day Overlord. "Caen (Calvados) Normandy cities and towns in 1944" *D-Day and Battle of Normandy Encyclopedia* Retrieved Aug. 1, 2018 from http://bit.ly/30ndPMz.

Dean, Joanna, Darcy Ingram, and Christabelle Sethna. "Animal Metropolis: Histories Of Human-Animal Relations in Urban Canada" University of Calgary Press (Feb. 2017) Retrieved Mar. 14, 2019 from http://bit.ly/2JnygDt.

Department of National Defence and The Wartime Information Board. "Welcome to War Brides" Brochure (1944)

Derworiz, Colette. "Then and now: 25 years ago, Banff became a town" Calgary Herald (Updated: Mar. 7, 2015) Retrieved May 1, 2009 from https://calgaryherald.com/news/local-news/town-of-banff-turns-25.

Dettling, Peter. "The Will of the Land—Updated Edition" RMB Rocky Mountain Books; Revised ed. edition (Oct. 1 2012) Page 113

Dickin, Janice et al. "Influenza (Flu)". The Canadian Encyclopedia (Mar. 21 2019) Historica Canada. Retrieved May 23, 2018 from https://www.thecanadianencyclopedia.ca/en/article/influenza.

Peel's Prairie Provinces Collection, University of Alberta Libraries - *Didsbury Pioneer*
C.G.I.T. and Boys 'Groups Hold Church Service, Mar. 30, 1933, Page 1, Item Ar00103" Peel's Prairie Provinces Collection, University of Alberta Libraries. Retrieved Sept. 24, 2018 from http://bit.ly/2LbOX6U.

"Didsbury Welcomes Back Service Personnel, Jan. 3, 1946, Page 1, Item Ar00112" Peel's Prairie Provinces Collection, University of Alberta Libraries. Retrieved Sept. 24, 2018 from http://bit.ly/2Xz5DqR.

"Former Resident Dies in Hospital, Dec. 12, 1957, Page 1, Item Ar00116" Peel's Prairie Provinces Collection, University of Alberta Libraries. Retrieved Sept. 24, 2018 from http://bit.ly/2XRlAg9.

"Killed Attempting to Board Freight, Jun. 20, 1935, Page 8, Item Ar00809" Peel's Prairie Provinces Collection, University of Alberta Libraries. Retrieved Sept. 24, 2018 from http://bit.ly/2XyKgpn.

"Local and General, Apr. 28, 1938, Page 8, Item Ar00803" Peel's Prairie Provinces Collection, University of Alberta Libraries. Retrieved Sept. 24, 2018 from http://bit.ly/2NJWBYh.

"Local and General, Feb. 9, 1939, Page 6, Item Ar00606" Peel's Prairie Provinces Collection, University of Alberta Libraries. Retrieved Sept. 24, 2018 from http://bit.ly/2Y1R6bz.

"Local and General, Jul. 17, 1941, Page 8, Item Ar00803" Peel's Prairie Provinces Collection, University of Alberta Libraries. Retrieved Sept. 24, 2018 from http://bit.ly/2YEUOVo.

"Local and General, Mar. 30, 1944, Page 10, Item Ar01003" Peel's Prairie Provinces Collection, University of Alberta Libraries. Retrieved Sept. 24, 2018 from http://bit.ly/2G48Sk3.

"Local and General, Jan. 8, 1942, Page 8, Item Ar00803" Peel's Prairie Provinces Collection, University of Alberta Libraries. Retrieved Sept. 24, 2018 from http://bit.ly/2XwyUam.

"Local and General, Aug. 6, 1942, Page 8, Item Ar00803" Peel's Prairie Provinces Collection, University of Alberta Libraries. Retrieved Sept. 24, 2018 from http://bit.ly/2S8Ja2z.

"Local News, May 29, 1946, Page 8, Item Ar00803" Peel's Prairie Provinces Collection, University of Alberta Libraries. Retrieved Sept. 24, 2018 from http://bit.ly/30vXlSx.

"Local News, Aug. 14, 1946, Page 8, Item Ar00805" Peel's Prairie Provinces Collection, University of Alberta Libraries. Retrieved Sept. 24, 2018 from http://bit.ly/32rAKZ4.

"Local News, Apr. 7, 1948, Page 8, Item Ar00803" Peel's Prairie Provinces Collection, University of Alberta Libraries. Retrieved Sept. 24, 2018 from http://bit.ly/2LJ9JKt.

"Local News Item, May 19, 1948, Page 4, Item Ar00403" Peel's Prairie Provinces Collection, University of Alberta Libraries. Retrieved Sept. 24, 2018 from http://bit.ly/2XH102Z.

"Local News Item, Mar. 7, 1929, Page 5, Item Ar00508" Peel's Prairie Provinces Collection, University of Alberta Libraries. Retrieved Sept. 24, 2018 from http://bit.ly/2G7abPk.

"Local News Item, Aug. 23, 1945, Page 1, Item Ar00112" Peel's Prairie Provinces Collection, University of Alberta Libraries. Retrieved Sept. 24, 2018 from http://bit.ly/2YMo3pm.

"Local Items of Interest, Nov. 21, 1951, Page 8, Item Ar00806" Peel's Prairie Provinces Collection, University of Alberta Libraries. Retrieved Sept. 24, 2018 from http://bit.ly/2XBFooB.

"Mrs. O. D. Carleton Hostess to British Brides, Jan. 16, 1947, Page 1, Item Ar00104" Peel's Prairie Provinces Collection, University of Alberta Libraries. Retrieved Sept. 24, 2018 from http://bit.ly/32gpGhg.

"Payne-Freeman Co. Take Over Bulk Station at Olds, Apr. 30, 1947, Page 1, Item Ar00117" Peel's Prairie Provinces Collection, University of Alberta Libraries. Retrieved Sept. 24, 2018 from http://bit.ly/2XBuIpY.

DiManno, Corrie. "Seniors Swing Away" *Crag & Canyon* (Jun. 11, 2013) Retrieved May 21, 2019 from https://www.thecragandcanyon.ca/2013/06/11/seniors-swing-away/wcm/886ff9dc-4029-7406-cdb7-8656e76f0901

Dixon, Ann. "Silent Partners Wives of National Park Wardens" Dixon and Dixon Publishers; First edition (1985)

Dixon, Tyler. "Searching for Wild Bill's Cabin" Readers Digest Retrieved Oct. 24, 2018 from https://www.readersdigest.ca/travel/canada/searching-wild-bills-cabin.

Dree, Laurie Meijer. "Indian's Bygone Past" The Banff Indian Days, 1902-1945 University of Alberta (2008)

Eckert-Lyngstad, Nicole. "The Backcountry as Home: Park Wardens, Families, and Jasper National Park's District Cabin System, 1952-1972 A thesis submitted to the Faculty of Graduate Studies and Research in partial fulfillment of the requirements for the degree of Master of Arts in Anthropology" University of Alberta (Spring 2013) Page 63

Edmonton Journal. "Earl Porter Cummins Obituary" (Jul. 6, 2012)

Edmonton Journal. "Bikinis in Banff Buff Up Our Image" (Feb. 11, 2011)

Ellis, Cathy. "Backcountry Memories" The Valley, Crag & Canyon (Jun. 13, 2001)

English, John A. "The Canadian Army & Normandy Campaign" Stackpole Books (2009) Page 75

Everts, Christine. "Park Use Trends an Oral History Project" Banff National Park (2002) Page 28

Everts, Christine. "Park Use Trends an Oral History Project 2002" Banff National Park Page 8

Fairmont.com. "Fairmont Banff Springs Then and Now - Banff Springs History: Retrieved Sept. 28, 2018 from https://www.fairmont.com/banff-springs/promotions/fairmont-banff-springs-history

Famoushotels.org. "The Most Famous Hotels in the World William Cornelius Van Horne (1843-1915)" Retrieved Sept. 28, 2018 from https://famoushotels.org/news/william-cornelius-van-horne-1843-1915.

Farran, Major Roy. "The History of the Calgary Highlanders 1921-54" The Bryant Press Limited (1955).

Ferguson, Eva. "1988 Olympics transformed Calgary" Calgary Herald (Jan. 8, 2013) Retrieved April 26, 2019 from http://bit.ly/2nlqEIT.

Find My Past. "Race meets and murder: Berkshire in 1939" Retrieved June 4, 2018 from https://www.findmypast.co.uk/1939register/berkshire-in-1939.

Finkelstein, Maxwell W. et al. "Banff National Park". The Canadian Encyclopedia (Nov. 22, 2018) Historica Canada. Retrieved Sept. 28, 2018 from https://www.thecanadianencyclopedia.ca/en/article/banff-national-park.

Flexercise. "About Us" Retrieved June 8, 2018 from https://www.fl-exercise.com/.

Flying Dutchman. "The most terrifying sounds of World War II" (Apr. 5, 2011) YouTube. Retrieved Sept. 1, 2018 from http://bit.ly/2nTZQQs.

Foot, Richard. "D-Day and the Battle of Normandy" The Canadian Encyclopedia (Feb. 20, 2019) Historica Canada. Retrieved Aug. 2, 2018 from https://www.thecanadianencyclopedia.ca/en/article/normandy-invasion.

Forestry Commission. "A brief history of British woodlands" Published by the Royal Forestry Society, by kind permission of Forestry Commission England. 2015 Retrieved June 4, 2018 from http://bit.ly/2xJUFnD.

Fort, Hugh. "Remembering the 41 people who died on the day Reading was bombed, A German plane dropped four bombs on Reading town centre in 1943" GetReading.co.uk (Feb. 9, 2018) Retrieved Jul. 14, 2018 from http://bit.ly/2XVRYyi.

Fort, Linda. "Alfred Sutton Primary School celebrates opening of new buildings" GetReading.co.uk (Mar. 8, 2016) Retrieved Jul. 14, 2018 from http://bit.ly/2xG0tic.

Fowler, Brittany "Brits may roll their eyes at 'Keep Calm and Carry On' — but here's why they secretly love it" *Business Insider* (Jun. 23, 2015) Retrieved Aug. 2, 2018 from http://bit.ly/2NIXxfG.
Fusionfootage.com. "Two Men Feeding Bear Cubs At Lake Louise 1958-Vintage 8mm Film" Retrieved Feb. 28, 2019 from https://www.fusionfootage.com/video/20473080.
GETDOWN.ca "1970s Calgary: The Growth of Downtown" Your Calgary Downtown Blog (Jun. 22, 2018) Retrieved Apr. 19, 2019 from http://bit.ly/2JLhRI7.

Genealogytoday.com. "Canadian War Ration Books" Canadian Genealogy (2014) Retrieved Nov. 20, 2018 from http://www.genealogytoday.com/ca/canadian-ration-books.html.

Geni.com. "Geni War Brides" Retrieved Sept. 7, 2018 from https://www.geni.com/projects/War-Brides/27146.

Genius.com. "Pack Up Your Troubles In Your Old Kit Bag" Florrie Forde Retrieved Sept. 25, 2018 from https://genius.com/Florrie-forde-pack-up-your-troubles-in-your-old-kit-bag-lyrics.

Genius.com. "I've Got A Lovely Bunch Of Coconuts" Retrieved May 16, 2019 from http://bit.ly/2xE4jbv.

Genius.com. "We'll Meet Again" Retrieved Aug. 2, 2018 from https://genius.com/Vera-lynn-well-meet-again-lyrics.

Glenbow.org. "Glenbow Molson Breweries, Western Division fonds Series 26" Retrieved Jan. 24, 2019 from https://www.glenbow.org/collections/search/findingAids/archhtm/molson.cfm#molson26.

Goldman, Aaron L. "Press Freedom in Britain during World War II" University of Nevada, Las Vegas (Winter 1997) Retrieved Aug. 2, 2018 from http://bit.ly/2LLslJZ.

Gooch, Jane Lytton and Robert W. Sandford. "Mount Assiniboine: Images in Art" RMB Rocky Mountain Books; 1 edition (Dec. 3, 2007) Page 40

Goodall, Felicity. "Life during the blackout" *The Guardian* (Nov. 1, 2009) Retrieved Aug. 20, 2018 from https://www.theguardian.com/lifeandstyle/2009/nov/01/blackout-britain-wartime.

GOV.UK. "Past Prime Minsters" History Retrieve Jul. 21, 2018 from http://bit.ly/2LdAWFU.

Government of Alberta. "Albertans recognized for their service to seniors" Press release. (May 15, 2009)

Government of Canada. "Artist/Maker name "Harisch, William" Artists in Canada National Gallery of Canada (2008) Retrieved Mar. 16, 2019 from http://bit.ly/2XCEIiI.

Government of Canada. "Banff National Park Bison Reintroduction Project" Parks Canada Retrieved May 21, 2019 from https://www.canada.ca/en/parks-canada/news/2018/08/banff-national-park-bison-reintroduction-project.html.

Government of Canada. "Hourly Data Report for August 26, 1961" Retrieved Sept. 20, 2019 from http://bit.ly/2lL5Eeq.

Govier, Katherine. "History of the Fantasy How the enthusiasms of the day shape our notions of what Banff is" *Alberta Views* (Jul. 1, 2012) Retrieved Nov. 16, 2018 from https://albertaviews.ca/history-of-the-fantasy.

Grace's Guide. "The Hercules Cycle and Motor Co" Grace's Guide to British Industrial History Retrieved June 7, 2019 from https://www.gracesguide.co.uk/Hercules_Cycle_and_Motor_Co.

Granatstein, J.L. "Five battles that shaped Canada" *Legion: Canada's Military History Magazine* (Nov. 1, 2016) Retrieved Aug. 22, 2018 from https://legionmagazine.com/en/2016/11/five-battles-that-shaped-canada.

Graveland, Bill. "Rogers Pass avalanche marked 105 years after taking 58 lives" CBC (Mar. 6, 2015) Retrieved Nov. 6, 2018 from http://bit.ly/2NE9VgD.

Hamilton, Graeme. "The shady past of Parks Canada: Forced out, Indigenous people are forging a comeback - Among Indigenous leaders, there is more talk of a day when their people will return to the parks — not to amuse tourists, but to live and work" *National Post* (Aug. 25, 2017) Retrieved Jun. 13, 2018 from http://bit.ly/2L9billL.

Hampshire Cultural Trust. "Thornycroft of Basingstoke "Retrieved June 6, 2018 from http://bit.ly/2LJ0x96.

Hart, E. j. "Banff A History of the Park and Town" Summerthought Banff (2015), Page 190

Hart, E. J. "Jimmy Simpson: Legend of the Rockies" RMB Rocky Mountain Books (May 11 2009)
Head, Elan. "Heli-Ski Nation" *Skiesmag* (Mar. 31, 2014) Retrieved Mar. 22, 2019 from http://bit.ly/2Jnn1ux.
Herd, Alex. "Dieppe Raid" The Canadian Encyclopedia, (May 13, 2019) Historica Canada.
Retrieved Jul. 4, 2018 from https://www.thecanadianencyclopedia.ca/en/article/dieppe-raid.

Hermer, Joe. "Regulating Eden: The Nature of Order in North American Parks" University of Toronto Press, Scholarly Publishing Division (Nov. 2, 2002)

History.com Editors. "Benito Mussolini" A&E Television Networks (Oct. 29, 2009 Updated Aug. 21, 2018) Retrieved Jul. 21, 2018 from https://www.history.com/topics/world-war-ii/benito-mussolini.

History.com Editors. "History Eisenhower takes command" A&E Television Networks (Feb. 9, 2010 Updated Feb. 27, 2019) Retrieved Aug. 2, 2018 from https://www.history.com/this-day-in-history/eisenhower-takes-command.

History Learning Site. "Operation Spring" Retrieved Dec. 18, 2018 from http://bit.ly/32eKi9y.

History Matters. "Obey Your Air Raid Warden: Big Band as Public Service Announcement" Retrieved June 11, 2018 from http://historymatters.gmu.edu/d/5148/.

History of Canadian Broadcasting. "CFAC-AM" Retrieved Aug. 24, 2018 from http://bit.ly/2S6SbJr.

Historic UK. "World War 2 Timeline – 1944" Retrieved Aug. 17, 2018 from http://bit.ly/2S8ZaBU.

Hitx, Luzi. "A Glance at Switzerland's Skiing History" International Skiing History Association Retrieved Feb. 18, 2019 from https://skiinghistory.org/history/glance-switzerlands-skiing-history.

Hmsausonia.co.uk. "HMS Ausonia In Memory of HMS Ausonia and Her Crew Ascania" (Last updated May 15, 2019) Retrieved May 15, 2019 from http://hmsausonia.co.uk/history/cunard-a-class-ships/ascania.

Hodgins, Douglas W. and J. Douglas Cook. "Parks Canada National Parks Occasional Paper No. 10 The Banff-Bow Valley Study: A Retrospective Review" (2000)

Hope and Bear. "The Story of The Hope & Bear" Retrieved Sept. 5, 2018 from http://bit.ly/2XFJdcs.

Hostelling International. "2018 Annual Report" Hostelling International Canada Pacific Mountain Region (2018) Page 10

Hotsprings.ca "Banff Upper Hot Springs" Retrieved on Sept. 28, 2018 fromhttp://bit.ly/2xFqq1c.

Houtermanm, Hans and Jeroen Koppes. "Officers" 1st British Airborne Division Arnhem, September 1944 Retrieved May 2, 2019 from http://www.unithistories.com/officers/1AirbDiv_officersK.htm

HuntleyandPalmers.org.uk. "Collection Reading Biscuit Town, Biscuits" Retrieved June 4, 2018 from http://bit.ly/2xBnxP2.

HuntleyandPalmers.org.uk. "The Second World War" Retrieved June 11, 2018 from http://bit.ly/2G3kWCf.

International Lyrics Playground. "There'll always be an England" Retrieved June 1, 2018 from http://bit.ly/2XCTYfm.

IODE.ca. "IODE in Nova Scotia" Retrieved Sept. 11, 2018 from http://www.iode.ca/iode-in-nova-scotia.html.

Jarratt, Melynda. "War Brides: The Stories of the Women Who Left Everything Behind to Follow the Men They Loved" Dundurn (May 25, 2009)

Independent. "Couple Finishes Mountain Capsule" (Aug. 7, 1955), Retrieved Feb. 21, 2019 from https://www.newspapers.com/clip/841161/independent Page 10

Independent. "Ensign the flew above Capitol to Grace Peak" (Jul. 29, 1957) Retrieved Feb. 21, 2019 from https://www.newspapers.com/clip/841149/independent Page 7

Independent Press-Telegram. "Mt. Ike" (Sept. 22 1957) Retrieved Feb. 22, 2019 from http://bit.ly/2JnIeET.

Independent Press-Telegram. "They Photograph wildlife" (Jul. 3, 1955) Retrieved Feb. 22, 2019 from https://www.newspapers.com/clip/873900/verwoerds_1955_info/ A, Page 74.

Jasper Fitzhugh. "Parks rescue pioneer, legend dies" Archive Retrieved Apr. 16, 2019 from http://bit.ly/2L-9cJjX.

Johnson, Hubert. "Wilderness delights warden" *Calgary Herald* (1985)

Jones Sweetgrass, Jessica. "Lifetime park passes granted to Stoney Nakoda members" *Aboriginal Multi-Media Society Alberta* (2012) Retrieved May 15, 2019 from http://bit.ly/2GgIoft.

Johnson, Ben. "The King's Speech" Historic UK Retrieved June 11, 2018 from http://bit.ly/2XyJduB.

Johnson, Ben. "World War 2 Timeline – 1940" Historic UK. Retrieved May 29, 2018 from http://bit.ly/2JE1NYi.

Johnstoncanyon.com. "A Brief History of Johnston Canyon" Johnston Canyon Lodge and Bungalows Retrieved April 4, 2018 from http://www.johnstoncanyon.com/about-us-history.

JunoBeach.org. "Canada in the Second World War" Juno Beach Centre Retrieved Mar. 14, 2019 from https://www.junobeach.org/canada-in-wwii/articles/field-marshal-bernard-montgomery.

Kay, C. E., B. Patton, and C. A. White. "Historical Wildlife Observations in the Canadian Rockies: Implications for Ecological Integrity" *Canadian Field Naturalist* (2000) Retrieved Dec. 13, 2018 from http://bit.ly/32fVtih.

Keating, Bob. "Touted as world's largest avalanche-detection system, $3M Rogers Pass network faces first big snow test" CBC News (Dec. 1. 2019) Retrieved Dec. 4, 2019 from http://bit.ly/2Yf9awr.

Kernaghan, Lois and Richard Foot. "Halifax Explosion" The Canadian Encyclopedia (Dec. 6, 2018) Historica Canada. Retrieved on May 28, 2018 from https://www.thecanadianencyclopedia.ca/en/article/halifax-explosion.

Killan, Gerald. "Review of Hart, E. J. (Ted), J. B. Harkin: Father of Canada's National Parks" H-Canada, H-NetReviews (Mar. 2011) Retrieved Aug. 18, 2018 from http://bit.ly/32i45oE.

Lane, D.W. "Juno Beach - The Canadians On D-Day" Junobeach.info (Dec. 2002) Retrieved Jul. 26, 2018 from http://www.junobeach.info.

Laurenson, Art. "Eisenhower Forest Station (Camp Castle) History" Banff Warden Office (Nov. 2006) PDF. Pages 8, 21, 36, 38, 44.

Legacy.com. "Bernard Mason Obituary" Retrieved Apr. 4, 2019 from https://legcy.co/2JwMQY4.

Legion Magazine. "Back to Dieppe" (Nov. 1, 2002) Retrieved Nov. 1, 2018 from http://bit.ly/2LJoKfn.

Legion Magazine. "Clearing the Scheldt" (Oct. 31, 2018) Retrieved Nov. 1, 2018 from http://bit.ly/32dOhmJ.

Lethbridge Herald Newspaper Archives. Monday, October 26, 1953 - Page 5, Monday, June 13, 1960 - Page 5

Levido, Trish. "Dorothy Carleton - Oral History by Trish Levido" (Jun. 2012) CD

LibertyEllisFoundation.org. "Ellis Island Statue History" Statue of Liberty Retrieved Mar. 19, 2019 from https://www.libertyellisfoundation.org/statue-history.

Liedtke, Gregory. "Canadian Offensive Operations in Normandy Revisited" *Canadian Military Journal* (Jun. 20, 2007) Retrieved Sept. 28, 2018 from http://bit.ly/2xDdGIz.

Lloyd, Matthew. "Theatres in Reading, Berkshire" ArthurLloyd.co.uk Retrieved June 28, 2018 from http://www.arthurlloyd.co.uk/ReadingTheatres.htm.

Locke, Harvey. "The Last of the Buffalo –Return to the Wild" Canadian Bison – A Brief History Summerthought Publishing; 1st edition (Sept. 15, 2016)

Longmate, Norman. "Hitler's Rockets: The Story of the V2s" Skyhorse Publishing (Jul. 23, 2009)

Lothian W.F. "A History of Canada's National Parks Volume I Chapter 2 Expansion in the West (1900 to 1972) The Automobile Arrives" Parks Canada History PDF edition (Mar. 11, 2013) Retrieved Sept. 28, 2018 from http://parkscanadahistory.com/publications/history/lothian/eng/vol1/chap2.htm.

Lothian W.F. "A History of Canada's National Parks Volume III Chapter 6
Townsites and Subdivisions (1885-1973)" Parks Canada History PDF edition (Mar. 11, 2013) Retrieved Oct. 1, 2018 from http://parkscanadahistory.com/publications/history/lothian/eng/vol3/chap6.htm.
Lothian W.F. "A History of Canada's National Parks Volume IV Chapter 7 Preserving Canada's Wildlife" Parks Canada History PDF edition (Mar. 11, 2013) Retrieved Dec. 13, 2018 from http://bit.ly/2LbLGV8.

Lothian W.F. "A History of Canada's National Parks Volume IV Chapter 9 Guardians of the Wild First Forest Ranger" Parks Canada History PDF edition (Mar. 11, 2013) Retrieved Oct. 1, 2018 from http://parkscanadahistory.com/publications/history/lothian/eng/vol4/chap9.htm Accessed Oct. 1, 2018

Lothian W.F. "A History of Canada's National Parks Volume IV Chapter 10 Minerals and Timber" Parks Canada History PDF edition (Mar. 11, 20130 Retrieved Dec. 4, 2018 from http://bit.ly/2Xy5V0Z.

Luxton, Eleanor G. "Banff: Canada's First National Park" Summerthought, Limited; 2nd Edition (Apr. 1, 2008) Page 57

Lyster, Eswyn. "A Bloody Miracle" *Legion: Canada's History Magazine* (Aug. 1982, reprinted Jan. 13, 2014) Retrieved Sept. 18 20, 2018 from http://bit.ly/2mcGRjK.

MacEachern, Alan. "Ian McTaggart-Cowan in Banff & Jasper: Bringing Wildlife Science to the National Parks" Network in Canadian History & Environment (NICHE) (Apr. 29, 2016) Retrieved Apr. 29, 2019 from http://bit.ly/2xEIXea.

MacEachern, Alan. "M.B. Williams and the Early Years of Parks Canada" The University of Western Ontario History Department (2011) Retrieved Oct. 1, 2018 from https://ir.lib.uwo.ca/historypub/173.

MacLauchlan, Lt.-Col. D. G. "War Diary of the Calgary Highlanders" (July – August 1944) Textual Records RG 24, The Department of National Defence Fonds RG 24-C-3Volume 15020.

Markham-Starr, Susan. "Celebrating Women in the Parks: From Goddesses to Ministers of the Crown" Manuscript for presentations at Red Deer College, 1999; NASSH, 2000 Malaspina University-College, 2001; and Acadia University, 2001 Retrieved Aug. 5, 2018 from http://bit.ly/32jPYze.

Martel, Lynn. "Three Things I've Learned: Dorothy Carleton" Inside Volume 2:Crowfoot Media (2018) Retrieved Aug. 6, 2018 from http://bit.ly/2G42KZ7.

Mapledurham House. "History" Retrieved June 7, 2018 from http://www.mapledurham.co.uk/maplehurham-house.

Martel, Lynn. "Whyte resurrects oral tradition with Fireside Chats" Crag & Canyon (Feb. 2013)

March, William. "Battle of Britain" The Canadian Encyclopedia (Feb. 26, 2016) Historica Canada. Retrieved on May 30, 2018 from https://www.thecanadianencyclopedia.ca/en/article/battle-britain.

Mason, Amanda. "What is the Women's Land Army?" Imperial War Museum (Jan. 30, 2018) Retrieved June 11, 2018 from https://www.iwm.org.uk/history/what-was-the-womens-land-army.

McCoy, Craig R. "Horror on the mountain 11 boys, 1 ice ax, and unforeseen heroism" *Philadelphia Inquirer* (Jul. 12, 2017) Retrieved Feb. 5, 2019 from http://bit.ly/2YJzuhp.

McEwan, Maureen. "Historic high-mountain Abbot Pass Hut closed due to erosion" *Crag & Canyon* (Aug. 22, 2018) Retrieved Oct. 15, 2018 from http://bit.ly/2XyErx2.

Mestern, Pat. "Beatty Bros." Mestern.net (March 19, 2004) Retrieved Feb. 13, 2019 from http://bit.ly/2XBvhjt.

Midgley, Neil. "Why Churchill thought attacking Italy could win him World War Two" *The Telegraph* Retrieved Jul. 21, 2018 from http://bit.ly/2S6n94y.

Canadian Press. "Death Due to Poor Leadership " *Medicine Hat News* Newspaper Archives (Friday, Aug. 12, 1955) Page 1

Minard, Jenny. "Sumer Is Icumen In at Abbey ruins" BBC Berkshire Retrieved June 1, 2018 from https://bbc.in/2LdE6tg.

Missadventure.ca. "Y2K in Banff National Park" (Dec. 31, 1999) Blog. Retrieved Jan. 11, 2019 from https://missadventurerca.wordpress.com/2014/12/31/y2k-in-banff-national-park.

Mosby, Ian. "Food on the Home Front during the Second World War" Wartime Canada Retrieved Nov. 20, 2018 from http://wartimecanada.ca/essay/eating/food-home-front-during-second-world-war.

Mr. White. "First V-1 'Doodlebug' bomb attack on London" Forces War Records (Jun. 13. 2017) Retrieved Aug. 3, 2018 from http://bit.ly/2NYjMyn.

Mustangpowder.com.. "Diny Harrison – Lead Guide" Mustang Powder Retrieved May 15, 2019 from https://www.mustangpowder.com/mustang-powder-staff/diny-harrison-lead-guide.

NancyGreene.com. "Nancy Greene Ski League" Retrieved Apr. 1, 2019 from http://bit.ly/2HSLlF4.

National Defence. "Recommendation for Award for MacLauchlan, Donald George" (Sept. 1944) Retrieved June 25, 2019 from http://www.cmp-cpm.forces.gc.ca/dhh-dhp/gal/cao-aco/doc/D2_LOV-MAH_079.pdf

Nelson, Chris. "After the war - The Military Museums displays colourful history of Calgary's soldiers, sailors and flyers" *Calgary Herald* (Jun. 27, 2014) Retrieved Aug. 3, 2018 from http://bit.ly/2S6Nobe.
Nelson, J. G. and R. C. Scace. "The Canadian National Parks: today and tomorrow. Proceedings of a Conference Organized by The National and Provincial Parks Association of Canada and the University of Calgary, Calgary, Alberta" (October 9th-15th, 1968) 2 vols. Studies in Land Use History and Landscape Change - National Park Series No. 3. Calgary: University of Calgary (1968) (Vol. 1, Vol. 2) Pages 42, 867, 1004

Newfoundland and Labrador. "Government Backgrounder Historic Chronology of National Parks" News release Retrieved Apr. 25, 2019 from https://www.releases.gov.nl.ca/releases/2005/exec/0122n02back4.htm.

Newspaperarchive.com. Winnipeg Free Press Newspaper Archives (Tuesday, Aug. 10, 1954) Page 1 Retrieved Jan. 11, 2019 from https://newspaperarchive.com/winnipeg-free-press-aug-10-1954-p-1.

Newworldencyclopedia.com. "Banff National Park" New World Encyclopedia (May 11, 2016) Retrieved Spet. 4, 2018 from http://www.newworldencyclopedia.org/entry/Banff_National_Park.

Nguyen, Hoang. "Britain's Great Depression" Washington State University (Spring 2016) Retrieved June 4, 2018 from https://history.libraries.wsu.edu/spring2016/2016/01/19/research-assignment-number-1.

Num-ti-jah.com. "Num-Ti-Jah Lodge Our Legendary Beginnings" Retrieved Nov. 16, 2018 from https://www.num-ti-jah.com/history.

Oglestone, Bard and Carol Robideau. "Lake Louise Reunion '84" Booklet (1984)

O'Keefe, David. "Vindicating 'Ham' Roberts" *Maclean's* (Aug. 17, 2017) Retrieved Jul. 4, 2018 from https://www.macleans.ca/dieppe-75-years-later.

Olympic.org. "Innsbrick 1964" Retrieved Mar. 27, 2019 from https://www.olympic.org/innsbruck-1964.

Our Compass. "Warm Heart, Busy Feet – Award-winning volunteer stays active and connected to her community" Covenant Health (Spring 2010)

Patton, Brian. "Tales from the Canadian Rockies" McClelland & Stewart (Reprint edition Feb. 27 1993) Pages 218, 279

Parkinson, Ange. "Hostel celebrates history – Castle Mountain Hostel reaches its half-century mark" *Crag & Canyon* (Oct. 27, 1999)

Parkinson, Justin. "Is the art of shorthand dying?" BBC News Magazine (Jan. 16, 2016) Retrieved June 5, 2018 from http://www.bbc.com/news/magazine-34603886.

Parks Canada. "Banff Bison 101" Banff National Park (June 6, 2017) Retrieved Dec. 13, 2018 from https://www.pc.gc.ca/en/pn-np/ab/banff/info/gestion-management/bison/info.

Parks Canada. "BATTALION NUMBERS" Canada's Historic Places Retrieved May 29, 2018 from http://www.historicplaces.ca/en/rep-reg/place-lieu.aspx?id=5724.

Parks Canada. "Elk in Banff National Parks" Banff National Park (Apr. 13, 2017) Retrieved Feb. 28, 2019 from https://www.pc.gc.ca/en/pn-np/ab/banff/decouvrir-discover/faune-wildlife/wapiti.

Parks Canada. "Elk management" Banff National Park Government of Canada (Jun. 1, 2017) Retrieved May 5, 2019 fromhttp://bit.ly/2XBDowy.

Parks Canada. "Enemy Aliens, Prisoners of War: Canada's First World War Internment Operations, 1914-1920" Banff Retrieved Sept. 28, 2018 from http://bit.ly/2LctmeO.

Parks Canada. "First Priority Progress Report on Implementation of the Recommendations of the Panel on the Ecological Integrity of Canada's National Parks" Minister of Public Works and Government Services Canada (2001) Retrieved May 9, 2019 from http://publications.gc.ca/collections/Collection/R62-336-2001E.pdf

Parks Canada. "History of fish stocking" Banff National Park (Date modified Mar. 31, 2017) Retrieved Oct. 26, 2018 from https://www.pc.gc.ca/en/pn-np/ab/banff/info/gestion-management/enviro/aqua/ensemencement-stocking.

Parks Canada. "Origin of Place Names" Kootenay National Park (Dec. 12, 2018) Retrieved Apr. 1, 2019 from https://www.pc.gc.ca/en/pn-np/bc/kootenay/culture/endroits-places.

Parks Canada. "History" Mountain Safety (Apr. 1, 2017) Retrieved Jun. 11, 2018 from http://bit.ly/2xD0eo3.

Parks Canada. "National Park Warden Service Who We Are What Do We Do How To Join" (1986) Retrieved Oct. 1, 2018 from http://parkscanadahistory.com/brochures/park-warden-e-1986.pdf.

Parks Canada. "Post War Immigration National Event – Halifax, Nova Scotia" Directory of Federal Heritage Designations Retrieved Aug. 6, 2018 from http://bit.ly/2S828GH.
Parks Canada. "The Burning Question" FD Productions and Parks Canada (2012)

Parks Canada. "The Parks Canada mandate and charter" Parks Canada Agency (Dec. 18, 2108) Retrieved Aug. 6, 2018 from https://www.pc.gc.ca/en/agence-agency/mandat-mandate.

Parks Canada. "Wildlife corridors – a 'moving' story" Retrieved May 21, 2019 from http://bit.ly/2YOKhas.

ParksCanadahistory.com. "Leaders of Parks Canada" (Last Updated Jan. 23, 2017) Retrieved Oct. 1, 2018 from http://parkscanadahistory.com/centennial/leaders-full.htm.

Parkwardenalumni.com. "Ya Ha Tinda Centennial 1917 – 2017" National Park Warden Alumni Society Retrieved Nov. 1, 2018 from https://parkwardenalumni.com/2016/11/12/ya-ha-tinda-centennial-1917-2017.

Patillo, Roger W. "The Canadian Rockies: Pioneers, Legends and True Tales" Trafford Publishing (Oct. 24 2005) Pages 106, 387

Patton, Brian. *Tales from the Canadian Rockies* McClelland & Stewart; Reprint edition (Feb. 27 1993) Pages xvi, 278

Payne, Rosabelle Margaret. "Fact File: Growing up in wartime in Tilehurst, Reading" WW2 People's War BBC (Nov. 28, 2003) Retrieved Aug. 1, 2018 from https://bbc.in/32gZkf3.

Pier21.ca. "Betty M. Ryckman" Canadian Museum of Immigration at Pier 21 Retrieved Aug. 11, 2018 from https://pier21.ca/stories/english-war-bride-betty-m-ryckman.

Penner, Andrew. "Perfect powder: Heli-skiing a lift to high-mountain adventure" *Calgary Herald* (Updated: Mar. 11, 2017) Retrieved Mar. 22, 2019 from http://bit.ly/2LLwZro.

Perrenblackett.com. "Our Team" Perren Blackett Law Retrieved May 6, 2019 from https://perrenblackett.com/team.

Perryman, Francesca. "See photos of Reading's Olympia Ballroom throughout the ages" GetReading.co.uk (Feb. 17, 2017) Retrieved on June 12, 2018 from http://bit.ly/2L9ff9T.

Peyto, David. "Bill Peyto" Peyto Lake Books Retrieved Nov. 1, 2018 from http://bit.ly/2xBxpIy.

Province of Alberta. "Inquest" Banff (Jul. 15, 1955) Retrieved Feb. 6, 2019 from http://bit.ly/2JrB8Og.

Province of Alberta. "Inquest" Banff (Aug. 10, 1955.) Retrieved Feb. 5, 2019 from http://bit.ly/2YKwa5N.

Raska, Jan. "Major Waves of Immigration through Pier 21: War Brides and Their Children" Canadian Museum of Immigration. Retrieved Sept. 11, 2018 from http://bit.ly/2S3n4yx.

Rawding, Brian G. "To close with and destroy: The experience of Canloan officers in the North West European Campaign, 1944-1945(World War II)" Theses and Dissertations (Comprehensive). 31. Wilfrid Laurier University (1998)

Rayburn, Alan. "Naming Canada: Stories about Canadian Place Names" University of Toronto Press, Scholarly Publishing Division; 1 edition (Mar. 15 2001) Page 88

Reading Evening Post newspaper (Dec. 2003)

Reading Museum. "Five Fascinating Facts about Reading's River Thames" (Sept. 29, 2017) Retrieved June 7, 2018 from https://www.readingmuseum.org.uk/blog/five-fascinating-facts-about-reading%E2%80%99s-river-thames.

Reading Museum. "Trenches in Palmer Park, Reading" History Retrieved June 12, 2018 from http://bit.ly/2NI10Lc.

Reading Museum. "Why did Jane Austen go to school in Reading?" (Oct. 19, 2017) Retrieved June 1, 2018 from https://www.readingmuseum.org.uk/blog/why-did-jane-austen-go-school-reading.

Revolvy.com. "Mount Lefroy" Revolvy Retrieved Oct. 15, 2019 from http://bit.ly/2Jpx2ru.

Rocky Mountain Outlook / RMOUTLOOK.com

"A slice of Canadian history – the remittance men" (Dec. 15, 2016) Retrieved on Nov. 16, 2018 from https://www.rmoutlook.com/article/a-slice-of-canadian-history-the-remittance-men-20161215.

Brian on the swing at Mount Eisenhower Lodge.
Photo: Carleton Family

"Artist pays tribute to war brides" (Jan. 15, 2015) retrieved May 23, 2019 from http://bit.ly/2JoP5Of.

"Banff Mansion to expand" (Nov 7, 2013) Retrieved Mar. 27, 2019 http://bit.ly/2XBAW47.

"Clues found in search for lost treasure on Castle Mountain" (Aug. 21, 2014) Retrieved Feb. 21, 2019 https://www.rmoutlook.com/article/clues-found-in-search-for-lost-treasure-on-castle-mountain-20140821.

Robinson, Bruce. "World War Two: Summary Outline of Key Events" BBC (Mar. 30, 2011) Retrieved Jul. 21, 2018 from http://www.bbc.co.uk/history/worldwars/wwtwo/ww2_summary_01.shtml.

Robinson, Zac And Stephen Slemon. "The Shining Mountains" Wired (2015) Retrieved Oct. 15, 2018 from https://www.artsrn.ualberta.ca/sslemon/slemon/ALP_51_Wired.pdf.

"Roby Crosby Passes in Banff" (Aug 24, 2017) Retrieved May 15, 2019 from http://bit.ly/2XDHTXt.

Rooney, David R. "Former Warden Ed Carleton mourned by many" *Crag & Canyon* (Aug. 17, 1994)

Rose Coloured Glasses Stories from Fraser Valley War Brides. "Across the pond and on a train." Retrieved Sept. 10, 2018 from http://app.ufv.ca/fvhistory/studentsites/wwII/warbrides/acrossthepondandonthetrain.html.

Ross, David. "Mapledurham House" *Britain Express* Retrieved June 4, 2018 from http://bit.ly/2L93Rel.

Sanche, Anna-Lynn. "Alberta War Brides and Families: Sharing Memories" Published by the Alberta War Babies, (2016)

Scott, Chic. "Powder Pioneers: Ski Stories from the Canadian Rockies and Columbia Mountain's Rocky Mountain Books (Sept. 1 2005) Pages 96, 97, 126
Scott, Chick. "High Times: The Adventures of Jim Davies" *Highline Magazine* (Sept. 24, 2015) Retrieved May 9, 2019 from http://highlineonline.ca/high-times-the-adventures-of-jim-davies.
Schwinghamer, Steve. "Historic Pier 21" Canadian Museum of Immigration at Pier 21 Retrieved Sept. 10, 2018 from https://pier21.ca/research/pier21/historic-pier-21.

Second World War History. "World War 2 Events by Country – Britain" SecondWorldWarHistory.com Retrieved June 12, 2018 from https://www.secondworldwarhistory.com/events-by-country.php?nations=britain.
Shea, Kevin. "Spotlight Soviet Union 1972 – 1976" Official Site of the Hockey Hall of Fame (May 14, 2015) Retrieved Apr. 16, 2019 from https://www.hhof.com/htmlSpotlight/spot_oneononeTmSovUnion7276.shtml.

Sheffield, R. Scott. "Indigenous Peoples and the World Wars" The Canadian Encyclopedia (Oct. 31. 2018) Historica Canada. Retrieved Sept. 5, 2018 http://bit.ly/2xOpeZL.

Skibanff.com. "Discover the history behind Sunshine Village" Retrieved Nov. 2, 2018 from http://bit.ly/2JB-vJnW.

Ski Banff advertisement. *Skiing Magazine*. Vol. 29, No. 5 (Jan 1977) Page 118M

SkiLouise.com "The Lake Louise Ski Area Unspoiled, Unparalleled, Unforgettable" Media kit (2009/10) Retrieved Mar. 6, 2019 from http://www.skilouise.com/images/news-and-info/media-kit/MediaKitLakeLouise2009_10.pdf.

Smith, Winston. "Stories I Tell" (2012) Retrieved Mar. 20, 2019 from http://bit.ly/2xHkdSk.

Southampton City News. "War Brides Relive Dugout Memories in Southampton" Press Release (May 13, 1986)

Spaar, Ilona. "Swiss Guides Shaping Mountain Culture in Western Canada" The Consulate General of Switzerland Vancouver (2010) Retrieved Nov. 5, 2018 from http://bit.ly/2JAjzLY.

Spry, Irene M.. "Palliser Expedition" The Canadian Encyclopedia, Historica Canada. (Mar. 4, 2015) Retrieved Feb. 22, 2019 from https://www.thecanadianencyclopedia.ca/en/article/palliser-expedition.

St. Mary's Parish. "History" Retrieved Mar. 1, 2019 from http://www.stmarysparishbanff.ca/history.

Stephens, Chris S. "Blackout your windows" A Wartime Scrapbook: The Teachers' Pack Pont (2004)

Sterling, Christopher H. "Churchill Afloat – Liners and the Man Finest Hour 121" International Churchill Society (Winter 2003-04) Retrieved May 14, 2019 from http://bit.ly/2LKnf0I.

St. Ann's And Hungerhill Allotments "Dig for Victory" Nottingham during World War Two Retrieved June 11, 2018 from http://bit.ly/2xEc7u4.

Striking Women. "The inter-war years 1918 – 1939" Women and Work Retrieved June 4, 2018 from http://www.striking-women.org/module/women-and-work/inter-war-years-1918-1939.

Swanson, Tera. "The Ultimate Timeline of Ski History in Banff National Park" Crowfoot Media. Retrieved Mar. 6, 2019 from https://crowfootmedia.com/2015/12/09/ski-banff-ultimate-timeline.

Taylor, C. J. "Banff in the 1960s: Divergent Views of the National Park Ideal" A Century of Parks Canada 1911 – 2011 U of C Press (2011) Retrieved Mar. 28, 2019 from http://bit.ly/2NKjhYx. Page 134

Terraine, John. "White Heat – the new warfare 1914-18" Pen & Sword (Jul. 1 1992)

Terry, Anne. "Cove West Heath Picture - a Memory of Cove" Francis Frith (Nov. 15, 2007) Retrieved May 31, 2018 from https://www.francisfrith.com/cove/cove-west-heath-picture_memory-26411.

Theanchor.ca. "War Bride Stories Live On" *The Chestermere Anchor* (Oct. 23, 2013) Retrieved Sept. 21, 2018 from https://www.theanchor.ca/2013/war-bride-stories-live-on.

The Calgary Highlanders. "Albert Canal" Calgaryhighlanders.com Retrieved Aug. 22, 2018 from http://bit.ly/2YFg51m.

The Calgary Highlanders. "Battle of the Scheldt: October - November 1944" Calgaryhighlanders.com Retrieved Aug. 20, 2018 from http://www.calgaryhighlanders.com/history/highlanders/1939-45/scheldt.htm.

The Calgary Highlanders. "Calgary Highlanders Battle Drill" Calgaryhighlanders.com Retrieved June 12, 2018 from http://www.calgaryhighlanders.com/history/highlanders/1939-45/battledrill.htm.

The Calgary Highlanders. "Calgary Highlanders Overview" The Calgary Highlanders in the Victory Campaign July 1944 - May 1945 Calgaryhighlanders.com Retrieved Aug. 17, 2018 from http://bit.ly/32hcVTK.

The Calgary Highlanders. "Calgary Highlanders Regimental Songs" Calgaryhighlanders.com Retrieved May 29, 2018 from http://www.calgaryhighlanders.com/prosemusic/songs.htm.

The Calgary Highlanders. "Clair Tison" Calgaryhighlanders.com Retrieved Aug. 17, 2018 from http://www.calgaryhighlanders.com/history/highlanders/1939-45/clairtison.htm.

The City of Calgary. "Calgary Celebrating 100 Years of Parks – From the Ground Up" (2010) Page 30

The Governor General of Canada. "The Viscount Alexander" Retrieved Feb. 25, 2019 from http://bit.ly/2LM8M48.

The Memory Project. "Veteran Stories: Amos "Wilkie" Wilkins Army" Second World War Retrieved Jul. 5, 2018 from http://www.thememoryproject.com/stories/1134:amos-wilkie-wilkins.

The Memory Project. "Veteran Stories: Kay Ruddick (née Douglass)" Retrieved Sept. 24, 2018 from http://www.thememoryproject.com/stories/2050:kay-ruddick-douglass.

The Rotarian. Vol 169 No. 1 (Jul. 1996) Page 10

The Town of Banff. "2015 Traffic Data" Banff.ca Retrieved May 21, 2019 from http://bit.ly/2Jyejsy.

The Town of Banff. "Learn About Banff" Retrieved May 1, 2019 from http://banff.ca/index.aspx?NID=252.

The Town of Banff. "The Bow River Bridge" Banff.ca Retrieved May 21, 2019 http://bit.ly/2S97AsP.

The Town of Banff. "The Government of Canada and the Government of Alberta Town of Banff Incorporation Agreement Consolidated with Amendments up to and including May 21, 1998" Retrieved Apr. 30, 2019 from http://banff.ca/documentcenter/view/154.

The Wardens. "About" Wardensmusic.com Retrieved May 17, 2019 from http://thewardensmusic.com/about.php.

Thursday Day Films. "Michael Bond" Sites of Significance, Reading Museum (2013) Retrieved Jul. 7, 2018 from http://www.thursdayfilms.com/portfolio/michael-bond-sites-of-significance,-reading-museum.aspx.

Tosh, Bev. "War Brides: Introduction" Warbrides.com Retrieved May 4, 2019 from https://warbrides.com.

Tourism Alberta. "Alberta Tourism Market Monitor" (2015) Retrieved May 21, 2019 from http://bit.ly/2XzZAar.

Traces of War. "Laloge, Emile Jean" Retrieved Nov. 1, 2018 from http://bit.ly/2QcPJiO.

Transcanadahighway.com. "History of the Trans-Canada from Lake Louise to the National Park Gates" Alberta's TCH Retrieved Aug. 7, 2018 from http://bit.ly/2G59x4E

Trent University Archives. "National and Provincial Parks Association of Canada fonds" Trent University Archives Retrieved Apr. 1, 2019 from https://www.archeion.ca/national-and-provincial-parks-association-of-canada-fonds.

Twila. "Interview preview with the wardens" Folkontheroad.ca (Feb. 6, 2017) Retrieved May 4, 2019 from http://bit.ly/2XRFFTr.

Tyzack, Anna. "Michael Bond: How Paddington Bear went from darkest Peru to London's Olympic Games" *The Telegraph* (Jun. 28, 2017) Retrieved Jul. 7, 2018 from http://bit.ly/2LLQWhC.

University of Exeter. "Bombing, States and Peoples in Western Europe 1940-1945 - The Bombing of Britain 1940 – 1945." Retrieved Sept. 20, 2018 from http://bit.ly/2XzGOe7.

University of Victoria Digital Records. "Ian McTaggart Cowan field notes (1943): Rocky Mountains" University of Victoria Retrieved Mar. 1, 2019 from http://bit.ly/2S6sM2G.
University of Victoria Digital Records. "Ian McTaggart Cowan field notes (1944-1945): Rocky Mountains" University of Victoria Retrieved Mar. 1, 2019 from http://bit.ly/2L9ihLj.

Upper Hutt Leader. "Princess Margaret's Canadian Tour" Upper Hutt City Library Volume XV, Number 33. (Aug. 28, 1958) Retrieved Feb. 25, 2019 from http://bit.ly/2XxKixW.

Vernon, Michael. "Morasch, George A. Corporal George Morasch (Calgary Highlanders) and his wife Fern" YouTube (May 15, 2016) Retrieved Aug. 2, 2018 from https://www.youtube.com/watch?v=2eEYHpa6atY.

Veterans Affairs Canada. "Abbaye d'Ardenne" (Feb. 14, 2019) Retrieved Aug. 1, 2018 from
http://www.veterans.gc.ca/eng/remembrance/memorials/overseas/second-world-war/france/ardenne.

Veterans Affairs Canada. "Back to "Civvy" Street: Post-War Veteran Re-Establishment" Retrieved Aug. 23, 2018 from http://www.veterans.gc.ca/eng/remembrance/history/historical-sheets/civvy.

Veterans Affairs Canada. "Canada's Role in the Second World War" (May 16, 2019) Retrieved May 28, 2018 from http://www.veterans.gc.ca/eng/remembrance/history/second-world-war.

Veterans Affairs Canada. "Canada - Italy 1943 – 1945" Minister of Supply and Services Canada (1993) Retrieved Jul. 21, 2018 from http://bit.ly/2XGKU4w.

Veterans Affairs Canada. "Canadians in Hong Kong" Minister of Veterans Affairs (2005) Retrieved on July 18, 2018 from http://www.veterans.gc.ca/eng/remembrance/history/second-world-war/canadians-hong-kong .

Veterans Affairs Canada. "Canadian National Vimy Memorial" Retrieved May 2, 2019 from https://www.veterans.gc.ca/eng/remembrance/memorials/overseas/first-world-war/france/vimy.

Veterans Affairs Canada. "Canadian War Brides" Retrieved Aug. 17, 2018 from http://bit.ly/2G4qyvL.

Veteran Affairs Canada. "Chronology of the Second World War" Retrieved Aug. 22, 2018 from http://www.veterans.gc.ca/eng/remembrance/history/historical-sheets/wwchronol.

Veteran Affairs Canada. "Epilogue" Retrieved Aug. 22, 2018 from http://www.veterans.gc.ca/eng/remembrance/history/second-world-war/canada-and-the-second-world-war/epilogue.

Veterans Affairs Canada. "Normandy 1944 D-Day" Minister of Supply and Services Canada (1994) Retrieved Aug. 1, 2018 from http://www.veterans.gc.ca/eng/remembrance/history/second-world-war/normandy-1944#dday

Veterans Affairs Canada. "The 1942 Dieppe Raid" Department of National Defence (2005) Retrieved Jul. 4, 2018 from https://www.veterans.gc.ca/pdf/history/secondwar/dieppe_rememseries_e.pdf.

Veterans Affairs Canada. "The Calgary Highlanders" (Feb. 2, 2019) Retrieved May 28, 2018 from http://www.veterans.gc.ca/eng/remembrance/history/second-world-war/dieppe-raid/calgary_highlanders.

Veterans Affairs Canada. "The Canadian Wives Bureau in London." Retrieved Sept. 5, 2018 from http://www.veterans.gc.ca/eng/remembrance/history/second-world-war/canadian-war-brides.

Veterans Affairs Canada. "The Korean War" Canada Remembers the Korean War Historical Sheet Retrieved Feb. 25, 2019 from https://www.veterans.gc.ca/eng/remembrance/history/korean-war/koreawar_fact.

Virtualmuseum.ca. "Canadian Remembers: War on Land – Battle Drill" Virtual Museum of Canada (2002) Retrieved June 12, 2018 from http://bit.ly/30nXI1b.

Virtualmuseum.ca. "Didsbury and District Historical Society Didsbury, Alberta Community Memories" Echoes of the Past Virtual Museum of Canada Retrieved Sept. 24, 2018 from http://bit.ly/2XTFzL4.

Walker, Nick. "Throwback Thursday: Castle Mountain's controversial name" Canadian Geographic (Feb. 18, 2016) Retrieved Jan. 22, 2019 from http://bit.ly/2YGVjyp.

Wally Byam Caravan Club International. "WBCCI History" Retrieved Feb. 25, 2019 from http://bit.ly/2YHZjhT.

Waiser, Bill. "Park Prisoners" Canada's History (Aug. 16, 2013) Retrieved Sept. 28, 2018 from https://www.canadashistory.ca/explore/historic-sites/park-prisoners.
WartimeCanada.ca. PDFs include information on coming back to Canada, getting jobs and going back to school. Retrieved Sept. 2, 2018 from http://bit.ly/2Y2dj9q.

Ward, Meghan J. "Annie Staple: The Guardian of the Gates" Crowfoot Media (2017) Retrieved Mar. 27, 2019 from https://crowfootmedia.com/2017/06/27/the-guardian-of-the-gates.

White, Brad. "Development Of Avalanche Safety And Control Programs In The Canadian Rocky Mountain National Parks An Historical Perspective" International Snow Science Workshop, Banff National Park Warden Service Penticton, B.C. (2002) Retrieved Jan. 22, 2019 from http://bit.ly/30matth.

White, Cliff. "Wildland Fires in Banff National Park 1880 – 1980" Minister of Supply and Services Canada (1985) Retrieved Sept. 28, 2018 from http://parkscanadahistory.com/series/op/banff-wildland-fires.pdf.

Whitfield, Dave and Cathy Ellis. "Parks Royalty Passes Away" *The Bow Valley Crag & Canyon* (Jul 11, 2018)

Whyte Museum. "Fireside Chat with Dorothy Carleton" Whyte Museum of the Canadian Rockies (Updated Oct. 5, 2018) Retrieved Aug. 9, 2018 from http://bit.ly/2XU4jCR.

WhyteMuseum.blogspot.com. "Bill Peyto Rocky Mountain Guide and Outfitter" Official Blog of the Whyte Museum of the Canadian Rockies (May 21, 2011) Retrieved Nov. 1, 2018 from http://bit.ly/2S5Itah.

WhyteMuseum.blogspot.com. "Bill Waterworth - Second World War" Official Blog of the Whyte Museum of the Canadian Rockies (May 21, 2011) Retrieved Jan. 23, 2019 from http://bit.ly/2Xz0rDm.

Williams, Cheryl. "The Banff Winter Olympics: Sport, tourism, and Banff National Park A thesis submitted to the Faculty of Graduate Studies and Research in partial fulfillment of the requirements for the degree of Master of Arts in Recreation and Leisure Studies Physical Education and Recreation" University of Alberta (Fall 2011)

Williams, Jeffery. "Far from Home: A Memoir of a Twentieth-century Soldier" University of Calgary Press, Calgary (2003) Page 129

Windsorscottish.ca. "Operation Daddy" Canada's Scottish War Brides" History: Scots in Canada. Retrieved Sept. 11, 2018 from http://www.windsorscottish.ca/hist-sic-opdaddy.php.

Zickefoose, Sherri. "Man who killed Banff cabbie for less than $130 in 1990 gets full parole" *Calgary Herald* (Jul. 12 2012) Retrieved May 14, 2019 from http://bit.ly/2LbwF5A.

Zoological Society of London. "ZSL London Zoo during World War Two, Artefact of the month" (Sept. 1, 2013) Retrieved May 23, 2019 from http://bit.ly/2LcAuYC.

Zuehlke, Mark. "Terrible Victory: First Canadian Army and the Scheldt Estuary Campaign: September 13 - November 6, 1944" Douglas & McIntyre; First Trade Paper Edition edition (July 1 2009) Page 140

Zuehlke, Mark. "The 2015 Ross Ellis Memorial Lecture "A Perfectly Engineered Killing Ground: Calgary Highlanders and the Walcheren Causeway Battle" Journal of Military and Strategic Studies VOLUME 16, ISSUE 3 (2015) Pages 69, 72

Zuehlke, Mark. "The Italian Campaign " The Canadian Encyclopedia (Jul. 11, 20170 Historica Canada. Retrieved Jun. 21, 2018 from https://www.thecanadianencyclopedia.ca/en/article/italian-campaign.

Zurowski, Monica. "It was 30 years ago today, Calgary's Olympic Games opened: Facts and figures" *Calgary Herald* (Updated: Feb. 27, 2018) Retrieved Apr. 26, 2019 from http://bit.ly/2xC1w2v.

Ed and Dorothy's monument at the Mountain View Cemetery Field of Honour. Their grandson Kevin Carleton carved the stone. The emblems are for the Royal Canadian Legion and the Calgary Highlanders.
Photo: Carleton Family

Left to right: Terry, Dorothy, Ed, Brian and Mike Carleton, Buffalo Paddock.
Photo: Carleton Family

ourfamilylines.ca

Manufactured by Amazon.ca
Bolton, ON